TELL ME WHY

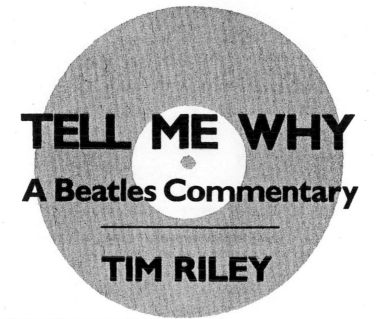

TELL ME WHY

A Beatles Commentary

TIM RILEY

DA CAPO PRESS

Owing to limitations of space, acknowledgments of permissions to reprint
previously published material will be found on page 452.

Cataloging-in-Publication data for this book is available from the Library
of Congress.

First Da Capo Press edition 2002
This Da Capo paperback edition of *Tell Me Why* is an updated republication
of the English-language edition first published in 1988 by Alfred A. Knopf.
It is reprinted by arrangement with the author.
ISBN-10: 0-306-81120-0   ISBN-13: 978-0-306-81120-3

Published by Da Capo Press
A Member of the Perseus Books Group
http://www.dacapopress.com

Da Capo Press books are available at special discounts for bulk purchases in
the U.S. by corporations, institutions, and other organizations. For more
information, please contact the Special Markets Department at the Perseus
Books Group, 11 Cambridge Center, Cambridge, MA 02142, or call (800)
255-1514 or (617) 252-5298, or e-mail j.mccrary@perseusbooks.com.

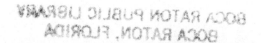

FOR MICKEY

Writing about music is like dancing about architecture. **—ELVIS COSTELLO**

Roll over Beethoven, dig to these rhythm and blues. . . . **—CHUCK BERRY**

CONTENTS

SELECTED PARLOPHONE/ APPLE DISCOGRAPHY

THE BEATLES SIGNED with the Parlophone label, a subsidiary of Electrical and Mechanical Industries (EMI) in Britain, after producer George Martin heard their audition in August 1962. Until 1968, when they formed their own label, Apple, EMI distributed their records in Britain, and Capitol Records distributed in America. After Apple was formed, Capitol retained distribution rights to Beatles records in America, even though the records bore the Apple label.

The American versions of Beatles records were assembled by Capitol, and until the release of *Sgt. Pepper* in 1967, they bore little resemblance to their Parlophone counterparts. (The British EP, an extended-playing single averaging four songs, was also disregarded by Capitol.) "Bit of a drag, isn't it?" McCartney once remarked to a BBC interviewer about the arrangement. Most American Capitol albums contain ten songs: Parlophone's average fourteen. This meant that the extra songs on British albums that the Americans didn't get would be transferred onto synthetically arranged collections in order to produce more product from the same amount of material. Capitol's *Yesterday and Today* and *Hey Jude* albums are the grossest examples—they have no Parlophone counterparts whatsoever. It was profiteering at its most aesthetically corrupt.

The discrepancy between British and American releases makes for some confusing perceptions. Because the Beatles were sensitive to the way an album was laid out, the Parlophone releases remain the truest display of what they wanted to publish. The American issue of *Rubber Soul*, for example, although it features the same portrait on the cover, omits three of the songs included on Parlophone's version and contains two songs that appeared on the Parlophone version of *Help!* For some American fans, it is still hard to imagine a *Rubber Soul* that begins with "Drive My Car," as the Beatles intended it to.

With the release of the entire Beatles catalogue on compact disc by EMI and Capitol beginning in February 1987, the Parlophone editions—titles, song sequences, and even liner notes—are restored to their original design; as soon as the singles become available in this form (nonalbum tracks like "She Loves You," "I Want to Hold Your Hand," and "Hey Jude"), the reissue campaign will be complete. These Parlophone formats are still the best reflections of the Beatles' intentions, and offer a better picture of their development in turning the record album into a new art form.

What follows is a selected discography that omits unnecessary repetitions (such as singles and EPs that draw their material from albums) and represents the most logical rundown of the focus of this book. For a complete and detailed discography, consult Castleman and Podrazik's notorious *All Together Now* (Ballantine, 1975).

Release dates refer to the British issues. Names of lead singers are in parentheses. All songs are by Lennon-McCartney except those in which composer credits, in brackets, follow the name of the lead singer. Songs not written by the Beatles are asterisked. According to John Lennon in the final *Playboy* interviews, as a general rule the lead singer of any given song is the chief creative force behind the song. Knowing that Mc-

Cartney is the lead singer on "All My Loving," for example, clues us in to the fact that he was the song's auteur, if not the sole author.

Bootleg albums are not included in this discography, although they can be useful in interpreting the commercial releases (see Charles Reinhart's *You Can't Do That*). In general, the Parlophone/Apple releases in Britain are the closest thing to the published Beatles catalogue; the bootlegs should be thought of as rough drafts and outtakes not meant for public release.

The Beatles catalogue also has the dubious distinction of being the most varied in the world markets. Different versions and stereo mixes of songs were released in different parts of the world, consigning collectors to a lifetime's worth of pleasure—and stupefaction—in retaining all resulting editions. For this text, the main source for stereo mixes has been the Mobile Sound Lab's original master recording pressings, except where noted. Since all the British singles were originally published in mono (single-channel) mixes, certain American stereo mixes (such as the one for "Strawberry Fields Forever") have been substituted to help delineate instrumentation.

Love Me Do (Paul)/P.S. I Love You (Paul)
(Parlophone R 4949) *Released: October 5, 1962*

Please Please Me (John)/Ask Me Why (John)
(Parlophone R 4983) *Released: January 11, 1963*

PLEASE PLEASE ME (Parlophone PCS 3042)
Released: March 22, 1963

I Saw Her Standing There
(Paul)
Misery (John)
Anna (Go to Him)* (John)
[Alexander]
Chains* (George) [Goffin-King]
Boys* (Ringo) [Dixon-Farrell]
Ask Me Why (John)
Please Please Me (John)

Love Me Do (Paul)
P.S. I Love You (Paul)
Baby It's You* (John) [David-
Bacharach-Williams]
Do You Want to Know a Secret
(George)
A Taste of Honey* (Paul)
[Marlow-Scott]
There's a Place (John and Paul)
Twist and Shout* (John)
[Russell-Medley]

From Me to You (John and Paul)/Thank You Girl (John and Paul) (Parlophone R 5015) *Released: April 12, 1963*

She Loves You (John and Paul)/I'll Get You (John and Paul) (Parlophone R 5055) *Released: August 23, 1963*

WITH THE BEATLES (Parlophone PCS 3045)
Released: November 22, 1963

It Won't Be Long (John)
All I've Got to Do (John)
All My Loving (Paul)
Don't Bother Me (George)
[Harrison]
Little Child (John)
Till There Was You* (Paul)
[Willson]
Please Mr. Postman* (John)
[Holland-Bateman-Gordy]

Roll Over Beethoven* (George)
[Berry]
Hold Me Tight (Paul)
You've Really Got a Hold on
Me* (John) [Robinson]
I Wanna Be Your Man (Ringo)
Devil in Her Heart* (George)
[Drapkin]
Not a Second Time (John)
Money* (John) [Gordy-
Bradford]

I Want to Hold Your Hand (John and Paul)/
This Boy (John, Paul, George) (Parlophone R 5084)
Released: November 29, 1963

*Long Tall Sally** (Paul) [Penniman]/I Call Your Name (John)/
Slow Down* (John) [Williams]/Matchbox* (Ringo) [Perkins]
(Parlophone GEP 8913) EP, *Released: June 19, 1964*

A HARD DAY'S NIGHT (Parlophone PCS 3058)
Released: July 10, 1964

A Hard Day's Night (John and
Paul)
I Should Have Known Better
(John)
If I Fell (John and Paul)
I'm Happy Just to Dance with
You (George)
And I Love Her (Paul)
Tell Me Why (John)
Can't Buy Me Love (Paul)

Any Time at All (John)
I'll Cry Instead (John)
Things We Said Today (Paul)
When I Get Home (John)
You Can't Do That (John)
I'll Be Back (John and Paul)

I Feel Fine (John)/*She's a Woman* (Paul)
(Parlophone R 5200) *Released: November 27, 1964*

BEATLES FOR SALE (Parlophone PCS 3062)
Released: December 4, 1964

No Reply (John)
I'm a Loser (John)
Baby's in Black (John and Paul)
Rock and Roll Music* (John)
[Berry]
I'll Follow the Sun (Paul)
Mr. Moonlight* (John)
[Johnson]
Kansas City/Hey, Hey, Hey,
Hey!* (Paul) [Leiber-Stoller/
Penniman]

Eight Days a Week (John)
Words of Love* (John and
Paul) [Holly]
Honey Don't* (Ringo) [Perkins]
Every Little Thing (John and
Paul)
I Don't Want to Spoil the Party
(John)
What You're Doing (Paul)
Everybody's Trying to Be My
Baby* (George) [Perkins]

Ticket to Ride (John)/Yes It Is (John)
(Parlophone R 5265) *Released: April 9, 1965*

Help! (John)/I'm Down (Paul) (Parlophone R 5303)
Released: July 23, 1965

HELP! (Parlophone PCS 3071) *Released: August 6, 1965*

Help! (John)
The Night Before (Paul)
You've Got to Hide Your Love
Away (John)
I Need You (George) [Harrison]
Another Girl (Paul)
You're Going to Lose That Girl
(John)
Ticket To Ride (John)

Act Naturally* (Ringo) [Russell-
Morrison]
It's Only Love (John)
You Like Me Too Much
(George) [Harrison]
Tell Me What You See (Paul)
I've Just Seen a Face (Paul)
Yesterday (Paul)
Dizzy Miss Lizzie* (John)
[Williams]

(Lennon's smoldering version of "Bad Boy," by Larry Williams, is recorded during sessions for side two of *Help!* and

appears on Capitol's *Beatles VI,* but it doesn't show up in Britain until Parlophone releases *A Collection of Beatle Oldies* [Parlophone PCS 7016] at the end of 1966.)

RUBBER SOUL (Parlophone PCS 3075)
Released: December 3, 1965

Drive My Car (Paul)
Norwegian Wood (This Bird
  Has Flown) (John)
You Won't See Me (Paul)
Nowhere Man (John)
Think for Yourself (George)
  [Harrison]
The Word (John and Paul)
Michelle (Paul)

What Goes On (Ringo)
Girl (John)
I'm Looking Through You
  (Paul)
In My Life (John)
Wait (John and Paul)
If I Needed Someone (George)
  [Harrison]
Run for Your Life (John)

Day Tripper (John)/*We Can Work It Out* (Paul and John)
(Parlophone R 5389) *Released: December 3, 1965*

Paperback Writer (Paul)/Rain (John)
(Parlophone R 5452) *Released: June 10, 1966*

REVOLVER (Parlophone PCS 7009) *Released: August 5, 1966*

Taxman (George) [Harrison]
Eleanor Rigby (Paul)
I'm Only Sleeping (John)
Love You To (George) [Harrison]

Here, There and Everywhere
  (Paul)
Yellow Submarine (Ringo)
She Said She Said (John)

Good Day Sunshine (Paul)
And Your Bird Can Sing
  (John)
For No One (Paul)
Doctor Robert (John)

I Want to Tell You (George)
  [Harrison]
Got to Get You into My Life
  (Paul)
Tomorrow Never Knows (John)

Penny Lane (Paul)/*Strawberry Fields Forever* (John)
(Parlophone R 5570) *Released: February 17, 1967*

SGT. PEPPER'S LONELY HEARTS CLUB BAND
(Parlophone PCS 7027) *Released: June 1, 1967*

Sgt. Pepper's Lonely Hearts
  Club Band (Paul)
With a Little Help from My
  Friends (Ringo)
Lucy in the Sky with Diamonds
  (John)
Getting Better (Paul)
Fixing a Hole (Paul)
She's Leaving Home (Paul)
Being for the Benefit of Mr.
  Kitel (John)

Within You Without You
  (George) [Harrison]
When I'm Sixty-four (Paul)
Lovely Rita (Paul)
Good Morning, Good Morning
  (John)
Sgt. Pepper's Lonely Hearts
  Club Band (Reprise) (all)
A Day in the Life (John and
  Paul)

All You Need Is Love (John)/Baby, You're a Rich Man (John)
(Parlophone R 5620) *Released: July 7, 1967*

Hello Goodbye (Paul)/I Am the Walrus (John)
(Parlophone R 5655) *Released: November 24, 1967*

MAGICAL MYSTERY TOUR (Parlophone SMMT ½) 2 EP's
Released: December 8, 1967

Magical Mystery Tour (Paul)
Your Mother Should Know (Paul)
I Am the Walrus (John)

The Fool on the Hill (Paul)
Flying (instrumental) [all]
Blue Jay Way (George) [Harrison]

YELLOW SUBMARINE (Apple PCS 7070)
Released: January 17, 1969
[new tracks recorded mid-June 1967† and early 1968#]

Yellow Submarine (Ringo)
Only A Northern Song# (George) [Harrison]
All Together Now† (Paul)
Hey Bulldog# (John)
It's All Too Much# (George) [Harrison]
All You Need Is Love† (John)

George Martin Orchestra:
Pepperland
Medley: Sea of Time/Sea of Holes
Sea of Monsters
March of the Meanies
Pepperland Laid Waste
Yellow Submarine in Pepperland

Lady Madonna (Paul)/The Inner Light (George) [Harrison] (Parlophone R 5675) *Released: March 15, 1968*

Hey Jude (Paul)/Revolution (John) (Apple R 5722) *Released: August 30, 1968*

THE BEATLES ("White Album") (Apple PCS 7067/8)
Released: November 22, 1968

Back in the U.S.S.R. (Paul)
Dear Prudence (John)
Glass Onion (John)
Ob-La-Di, Ob-La-Da
  (Paul)
Wild Honey Pie (Paul)
The Continuing Story of
  Bungalow Bill (John)
While My Guitar Gently Weeps
  (George) [Harrison]
Happiness Is a Warm Gun
  (John)

Birthday (Paul)
Yer Blues (John)
Mother Nature's Son (Paul)
Everybody's Got Something To
  Hide, Except Me and My
  Monkey (John)
Sexy Sadie (John)
Helter Skelter (Paul)
Long Long Long (George)
  [Harrison]

Martha My Dear (Paul)
I'm So Tired (John)
Blackbird (Paul)
Piggies (George) [Harrison]
Rocky Raccoon (Paul)
Don't Pass Me By (Ringo)
  [Starkey]
Why Don't We Do It in the
  Road? (Paul)
I Will (Paul)
Julia (John)

Revolution No. 1 (John)
Honey Pie (Paul)
Savoy Truffle (George)
  [Harrison]
Cry Baby Cry (John)
Revolution No. 9 (John)
Good Night (Ringo)

LET IT BE (Apple PXS I) Released: May 8, 1970
[recorded January 1969, except # in January 1970]

Two of Us (Paul and John)
Dig a Pony (John)
Across the Universe (John)
I Me Mine# (George) [Harrison]
Dig It (John)

Let It Be (Paul)
Maggie Mae* (John and Paul)
  [trad.—arr. Lennon,
  McCartney, Harrison,
  Starkey]

I've Got a Feeling (Paul and
John)
One After 909 (John)
The Long and Winding Road
(Paul)

For You Blue (George)
[Harrison]
Get Back (Paul)

Get Back (Paul)/Don't Let Me Down (John)
(Apple R 5777) *Released: April 11, 1969*

The Ballad of John and Yoko (John)/Old Brown Shoe
(George) [Harrison] (Apple R 5786)
Released: May 30, 1969

Let It Be (Paul)/You Know My Name (Look Up the Number)
[all] (Apple R 5833) *Released: March 6, 1970*

ABBEY ROAD (Apple PCS 7088)
Released: September 26, 1969

Come Together (John)
Something (George) [Harrison]
Maxwell's Silver Hammer
(Paul)
Oh! Darling (Paul)
Octopus's Garden (Ringo)
[Starkey]
I Want You (She's So Heavy)
(John)

Here Comes the Sun (George)
[Harrison]
Because (John)
You Never Give Me Your
Money (Paul)
Sun King (John)
Mean Mr. Mustard (John)
Polythene Pam (John)
She Came in Through the
Bathroom Window (Paul)
Golden Slumbers/Carry That
Weight/The End (Paul)
Her Majesty (Paul)

Selected Solo Recordings

RINGO STARR

Sentimental Journey (1970)
Beaucoups of Blues (1970)
"It Don't Come Easy"/"Early 1970" (1971)
"Back Off Boogaloo"/"Blindman" (1972)
Ringo (1973)
Goodnight Vienna (1974)
Blast from Your Past (Greatest Hits) (1975)
Ringo's Rotogravure (1976)
Ringo the 4th (1977)
Bad Boy (1978)
Stop and Smell the Roses (1981)

GEORGE HARRISON

All Things Must Pass (1970)
The Concert for Bangladesh (1971)
Living in the Material World (1973)
Dark Horse (1974)
Extra Texture—Read All About It (1975)
Thirty-Three & ⅓ (1976)
George Harrison (1979)
Somewhere in England (1981)
Gone Troppo (1982)
Cloud Nine (1987)

PAUL McCARTNEY

(WITH AND WITHOUT WINGS):
McCartney (1970)
"Another Day"/"Oh Woman, Oh Why" (1971)

Ram (1971)
Wild Life (1971)
"Give Ireland Back to the Irish"/
"Give Ireland Back to the Irish" (version) (1972)
"Mary Had a Little Lamb"/"Little Woman Love" (1972)
"Hi, Hi, Hi"/"C Moon" (1972)
Red Rose Speedway (1973)
"Live and Let Die"/"I Lie Around" (1973)
Band on the Run (1973)
"Junior's Farm"/"Sally G" (1974)
Venus and Mars (1975)
Wings at the Speed of Sound (1976)
Wings over America (1977)
"Mull of Kintyre"/"Girls' School" (1977)
London Town (1978)
"Goodnight Tonight"/"Daytime Nighttime Suffering" (1979)
Back to the Egg (1979)
McCartney II (1980)
Concert for the People of Kampuchea (1981)
Tug of War (1982)
"Wonderful Christmas Time"/
"Rudolph the Red-Nosed Reggae" (1982)
Pipes of Peace (1984)
Give My Regards to Broad Street (1984)
Press to Play (1986)

JOHN LENNON
(WITH AND WITHOUT THE PLASTIC ONO BAND)
Unfinished Music No. 1: Two Virgins (1968)
Unfinished Music No. 2: Life With the Lions (1969)
Wedding Album (1969)
"Give Peace a Chance"/"Remember Love" [Ono] (1969)
"Cold Turkey"/"Don't Worry Kyoko (Mummy's Only
Looking for her Hand in the Snow)" [Ono] (1969)
The Plastic Ono Band—Live Peace in Toronto (1969)

"Instant Karma (We All Shine On)"/
"Who Has Seen the Wind?" [Ono] (1970)
Plastic Ono Band (1970)
"Power to the People"/"Open Your Box" (1971)
Imagine (1971)
"Happy Xmas (War Is Over)" [Lennon-Ono]
"Listen the Snow Is Falling" [Ono] (1971–U.S.; 1972–U.K.)
Some Time in New York City (1972)
Mind Games (1973)
Walls and Bridges (1974)
Rock 'n' Roll (1975)
Shaved Fish (1975)
Double Fantasy (1980)
Milk and Honey (1983)
John Lennon: Live in New York City (1986)
Menlove Avenue (1986)

TELL ME WHY

Lots of people asked us what we enjoy best, concert, television, or recording. We like doing stage shows, cos, you know, it's great to hear an audience enjoying themselves. But the thing we like best is going into the recording studio to make new records. . . . What we like to hear most is one of our songs taking shape in the recording studio, one of the ones that John and I have written, and then listening to the tapes afterwards to see how it all worked out. . . .

PAUL McCARTNEY,
in the 1963 Fan Club Christmas Message

The records are the point. Not the Beatles as individuals!

JOHN LENNON,
in *Playboy,* 1980

INTRODUCTION

"Give Me Love" by Rosie and the Originals. An amazing record. It's one of the greatest strange records, it's all just out of beat and everybody misses it—they knocked off the B side in ten minutes.
                        —*John Lennon to Jonathan Cott, 1968*

ROSIE AND THE ORIGINALS released their only 45-rpm single in early 1960. "Angel Baby," the A side, reached number five in America, but it never even saw the light of day on the British charts. The song is dismissible, a one-hit wonder from singer Rosie Hamlin that didn't deserve a follow-up. But the B side is something else entirely. For one thing, one of the Originals is hogging the mike, and Rosie is nowhere to be heard—a mystery that the label doesn't explain. The record is much as Lennon describes: after a revved-up guitar intro, the drums vanish and leave everyone else playing straight off the top of their heads. The listener eavesdrops on a sloppy rhythm-and-blues concoction, with jealous lyrics sung to unrehearsed riffing—it's so sloppy, so incoherently diffuse, that it's more laughable than it is danceable. To say "Give Me Love" sounds spontaneous doesn't begin to suggest its strangeness; the musicians themselves don't seem to know where the next downbeat is going to land. The listener has trouble making sense of the music—but then again, so do the musicians. Far from backing up Rosie's willful debut, it sounds as though someone left the tape machine running during an early-morning musical reverie—sounds that were completely random became crystallized on tape. It exposed the would-be Originals as crudely inspired amateurs, who weren't even able to sustain their façade as a group from one side of a 45 to the other.

To the young John Lennon, this was what pop music was all about. That he prized this oddity says a great deal about what he listened for: he put the *feel* of a record above everything else, and treasured the magic and humor of ordinary situations where most heard unkempt discord. To John, Paul, George, Ringo, and their Merseyside peers, the singles like these which they begged off the Cunard Yanks at the Liverpool docks meant much more than they could really express. They would practice their guitars to these records, mimic their favorite singers, go nuts over their favorite moments, and crack up at inside jokes they shared. In the beginning, they weren't much different from millions of other teenagers in the late fifties: they invested a lot in their fantasies. It was youths like the Beatles all over the world who helped invent the outrageous dimensions that Little Richard, Jerry Lee Lewis, Buddy Holly, Chuck Berry, and Elvis Presley—the undisputed King—inhabited.

Pop completed their young world in ways that television and movies couldn't—it made them feel connected up to something that confirmed their adolescent impulses and gave voice to their most private emotional secrets. Because the Beatles were avid participants in the pop life, they learned a lot from it, not only about themselves and their own capabilities but about the medium they would go on to transform. "You Know My Name (Look Up the Number)," which began after the *Sgt. Pepper* sessions and got stuck on the back of "Let It Be" ten years after Rosie and the Originals made their mark on Lennon, is somewhat more developed than "Give Me Love" but no less absurd. The droll opening duet, sung conspicuously low, gives way to a snazzy nightclub cha-cha. Lennon's emcee welcomes us to club "Slaggers" and introduces McCartney's unctuous lounge-act alter ego, "Dennis O'Dell," who oozes lovesick sentimentality through a glib vibrato ("You *know* you know my name . . ."). Then Lennon interrupts McCartney's prodding announcer with a spectacled granny scolding, surrounded by penny whistles. After a verse of cacophonous counting, a precocious piano solo gets grumbled and scatted over by everybody, and the mock variety show ends with one last bark of Lennon's gibberish. ("What's the New Mary Jane," the A side that Lennon prepared for "You Know My Name" in late 1969, was rejected for sounding even more inchoate.)

Like "Give Me Love," "You Know My Name" captures the unstudied spark of a first or second take—the mistakes are left in, and the casual tone is an essential part of its hit-or-miss appeal. The Beatles are making this music as a lark, more for themselves than for the microphones and the listeners beyond. This aura of a shared secret informs even the Beatles' most accomplished recordings, like "She Loves You" and "I Want to Hold Your Hand"; there's something extra at work in these tracks that transports the musicians as they play. Even when in complete command of the music, they're intoxicated with the sounds they're making.

None of the Beatles was formally trained, but this fondness for mystery and offbeat humor in rock 'n' roll counts as the best education they ever could have given themselves. Listening to records like "Give Me Love" hundreds of times, they soon developed an uncanny sense of what makes music tick, both as material and as recorded sound. It taught them about the aspects of pop they would go on to revitalize, both the 45-rpm single (the form they grew up on) and the full-length album (the form they redefined). Their aspirations for the pop album spring directly from this affection for obscure B sides; and as they progressed, the longer form blossomed into an artistic statement—the idea of the long-playing album grew to be larger than the idea of each individual song. As Rolling Stone Keith Richards would later put it: "Both the Beatles and us had been through buying albums that were filled with ten tracks of rubbish. We said, 'No, we want to make each track good. Work almost as hard on it as you would work on a single. . . . .' " (*The Rolling Stone Interviews*, Volume II, Ben Fong-Torres, ed., pp. 235–6) The unaffected feel of any given Beatles track shows just how well they understood what it takes to pull this feat off: their songs became increasingly self-conscious, but their playing always shunned affectation; they were never more cerebral than they were visceral.

So MUCH HAS ALREADY been written about the Beatles, so many biographies, memoirs by friends, and scattered critical tracts, that another volume requires justification. Their story is so big, means so many different things to so many different people, that it would be impossible for one book to tell it all. And yet so far, the story has been one-sided. Their music always put it best; and in the end, that counts for more anyway. But it is as *music* that their catalogue still begs for commentary: the two major biographies (Hunter Davies's *The Beatles: The Authorized Biography* and Philip Norman's *Shout!*) concentrate on their lives and do not attempt to analyze their music. *Twilight of the Gods* by Wilfrid Mellers and *A Musical Evolution* by Terence O'Grady are both attempts at strict analysis, but written in such arcane academic terms that even when their interpretations provoke, they tend to miss the point entirely. Mellers insists that the final E-major chord of "A Day in the Life" has something to do with heaven; O'Grady mistakenly bases his "evolutionary" account on the distorted American Capitol editions. Both these scholars may know a great deal about the history of the Western classical tradition, but they tend to isolate the Beatles from the history of rock 'n' roll, the popular form they grew up with; strict musicology falls far short of explaining how well the Beatles communicated with their audience and why their records are as important as any artistic legacy of our age.

The Beatles deserve to be addressed on their own terms. What's missing from most Beatles criticism is a sense of how they best expressed themselves: through instrumental and vocal interplay, both in riveting singles and on their carefully constructed albums. They saw themselves first and foremost as recording artists, and their records still demonstrate all that pop can be. In order to understand what it was the Beatles had to say to the world, and why their message was so powerful and convincing, their work, both words and music, deserves more attention than their marriages. How are such strong emotional effects achieved? Why is a given vocal delivery so penetrating? How does a guitar solo inflect a verse, a refrain, a transition? And most of all, what does it all mean?

Their ubiquity tends to steal attention from their significance—the fact that they have been covered by everyone from Siouxsie and the Banshees ("Dear Prudence") to Robert Goulet testifies to their pervasive influence, even though songs like "Happiness is a Warm Gun" and "Hey Jude" are still widely misunderstood. Their musical merit is rarely questioned. Highbrows like Leonard Bernstein, Ned Rorem, and Joan Peyser have long since offered their stamp of approval, as if that mattered. But their Parlophone catalogue deserves a thorough exegesis. To hear "A Day in the Life" as background Muzak in an elevator is to hear just how much we have come to take their work for granted. Since Michael Jackson's purchase of the Lennon and McCartney publishing rights (Northern Songs), "Help!" and "Revolution" have been prostituted as television jingles for cars and sneakers.

Returning to the original Beatles catalogue not only rewards close listenings, it sheds light on the styles they inspired and the reactions that followed. They're best heard on their own records, playing their own songs with their own arrangements. This text is meant to accompany close listenings for a detailed look at a very intricate art.

Rock 'n' roll began with Sam Phillips and the young Elvis Presley in 1954 at the Memphis studios of Sun Records, Phillips's independent label. With his first record, "That's All Right (Mama)," an old Arthur Crudup blues sped up to intensify the singer's resentment, Presley effectively turned black rhythms and a caustic, taunting delivery into a style that whites could readily identify with—the black-influenced beat was forbidden, but the singer was incredible before race came into the discussion. When he signed with RCA in late 1955 and released "Don't Be Cruel," "Teddy Bear," and "Jailhouse Rock," Presley crossed over to number one on what had once been three irreconcilable charts: pop, country, and rhythm and blues. When Presley wasn't being dirty ("Heartbreak Hotel") or threatening ("Hound Dog"), he could turn on the sentimentality ("I Want You, I Need You, I Love You") and transform the rhythms he had released as anger into harmless, rollicking fun ("Blue Moon of Kentucky"). The power of the music lay in its directness: rhythm and harmony were boiled down to basic essentials and used to convey primal human passions—impatience, pride, sexual yearning, simple pleasures, confusing doubts, and sheer hilarity. The recording medium rock 'n' roll was invented in proved to be the perfect outlet for these passions, and when linked with radio, it inspired a mass connection among teenagers everywhere who were quickly smitten by the new sound—in part because Elvis enacted the sexuality they had been taught to repress, but also because he put more into his music than had previously seemed possible, an eccentric resolve that simply compelled attention. It is no small measure of Presley's greatness that we speak of songs like "I Can't Help Falling in Love with You" and "Love Me Tender" as Presley's, even though he never wrote a note of music in his life.

The Beatles are a pivotal part of rock's story not just because their music can still dazzle but because their arrival as rock 'n' rollers with an endless stream of original material challenged what anyone had imagined pop could become. They weren't the first or the only ones to dare toward such encompassing celebrity-hood. The foundations had been laid for them by Sinatra, Presley, and a handful of others, and they shared the sixties stage primarily with the Rolling Stones and Bob Dylan. But as a microcosm of the rock experience, nothing equals the Beatles catalogue: it integrates the best of what came before and signals the array of styles that would soon follow. They may not be responsible for everything, but nearly everything that comes after would be impossible without them. Strictly speaking, the Mothers of Invention's *Freak Out* has claims as the first "concept" album, but *Sgt. Pepper* was the record that made that idea convincing to most ears. Their influence touches every extreme: "She Said She Said" certainly inspired Lou Reed, and "Birthday" perfected the kind of infectious guitar riff that a hundred derivative bands like Cheap Trick used as excuses for careers.

The Beatles and their generation were the first to go through puberty with rock 'n' roll on the radio. The chief concern of rock 'n' roll is youth, and it distinguishes itself from jazz in this way. That other great American art form, rock 'n' roll's essential predecessor, celebrates musical creativity itself, stressing improvisation (more often de-emphasizing lyrics) as a means toward self-expression. (Both styles derive their titles from black slang words for sex.) In early rock 'n' roll, the main concern is puberty itself, the search to assimilate experience into a cohesive self-identity. What the Beatles heard in the rock 'n' roll they fell in love with was the potential not just for variety but for summing up a long tradition of popular styles. Their artistry grew from their eclectic love for the entire spectrum that stretched from ragtime to Broadway, from a desire to synthesize the best of the rock 'n' roll they had grown up with with the larger heritage of pop they saw as its backdrop. Explicitly, these roots go as far back as ragtime or Victorian dance halls; implicitly, the wedding of country swing to rhythm and blues (white to black) can be traced back to the rhythms of African folk cultures and the vignettes of English storytelling.

Greil Marcus's excellent essay on Elvis Presley in *Mystery Train* articulates Presley's role in giving rock 'n' roll its mass appeal:

Echoing through all of rock 'n' roll is the simple demand for peace of mind and a good time . . . Satisfaction is not all there is to it, but it is where it all begins. Finally, the music must provoke as well as delight, disturb as well as comfort, create as well as sustain. If it doesn't, it lies, and there is only so much comfort you can take in a lie before it all falls apart. (p. 162)

To this we can add the idea of liberation: the boundaries that Presley seemed to break in his singing become metaphors for ways of thinking about life. The most aggressive rock 'n' roll is a testing of limits, a combustive enactment of the frontier spirit. With a combination of determination and good luck, anything is possible, the sound seems to be telling us. We hear it in all the great rock recordings from "Hound Dog" and "I Want to Hold Your Hand" right up through Bruce Springsteen's "Hungry Heart." Good rock 'n' roll is simple but not dull—it must bear repeated listenings. It relies on impact, saying a lot in a short period of time, and it innovates as well as conforms to conventional patterns. Ideally, rock 'n' roll plays with our expectations, making each experience of a given song different.

In 1963, the sound of British youths singing the distinctly American style must have been jarring. Only seven years earlier, adults had reeled at the sight of Elvis belting out blatantly black rhythms on the Ed Sullivan show as their children gaped in wonder. Now here was another level of detachment, and hence another level of potential, with the Beatles copying their American idols at the same time they gave the form a new lease on life—their ironic detachment from the music's roots suddenly made it all sound new again. Inanities like "Be-Bop-A-Lula" and "Tutti Frutti" had reached across the Atlantic and gripped Britain. If rock 'n' roll could do that, anything might happen. And the Beatles' early cover versions of their favorite rock standards didn't just hint at the possibilities; they laid the groundwork for the surprises that kept coming. Their obsession with rock 'n' roll was infectious, and quickly inescapable, surrounding the audience and zeroing in on its wants, needs, desires, and fetishes.

W HEN THEY SPOKE about their heroes in interviews, the Beatles revealed impeccable taste: they named themselves after Buddy Holly's band, the Crickets (John changed the "ee" to "ea" to make the pun on "beat" explicit) and they idolized Chuck Berry, Carl Perkins, Jerry Lee Lewis, Fats Domino, and the Everly Brothers to the extreme. They caught the British tours of Eddie Cochran, Gene Vincent, and Little Richard at every possible opportunity. John flipped at the audacity of someone dubbing himself "Dr. Feelgood"; he loved the manic intensity of Larry Williams's delivery and the soulful vocalism of Arthur Alexander. Paul cited Little Richard, Peggy Lee, the Platters; George mentioned girl groups like the Shirelles and doo-wop favorites like the Chiffons; Ringo wanted to move to Texas because "that's where Lightnin' Hopkins came from." And they all emphasized Elvis.

Elvis embodied the rock 'n' roll myth. Myths combine fact and fiction, feeding off both the images they project— real and fictive—and the imaginative space their records inhabit. "Johnny B. Goode," the 1958 Chuck Berry hit, is loosely based on Elvis Presley's story: the country boy who finds fame in Hollywood from the railroad rhythms he plays on his guitar. The idiosyncrasies of Presley's real life lend themselves to such treatment: he was a mother's boy, polite to a fault, and had a twin brother who died at birth. (Johnny's name even suggests what Lennon's mother may have told him as a boy— "be good.")

> *He used to carry his guitar in a gunnysack*
> *Go sit beneath the tree by the railroad tracks*
> *Old engineer would see him sittin' in the shade*
> *Strummin' with the rhythm that the drivers made*

When people passed him by they would stop and say,
"Oh my, but that country boy can play!"

The heart of the music is its rhythm—it still makes more
sense when you dance to it—but to young Johnny, the train's
motion seems to mean a lot more than just a beat to strum
to. It symbolizes his turning from a boy into a man in the big
world, leaving poverty behind for the big time and separating
from his mother. When Elvis returned from his Army stint in
1960, Berry wrote a sequel, "Bye Bye Johnny," about how
Johnny builds a mansion by the railroad tracks where he can
settle with his new wife and his mother. By then, Elvis Presley's mother had died near Graceland, the mansion he had
built.

The Beatles cavorted their way through "Johnny B.
Goode" on BBC radio broadcasts, and the Rolling Stones were
still sneering "Bye Bye Johnny" as late as their 1972 tour. But
Elvis wound up living out the dark side of success, the kind
that feeds on bottomless desires: according to Elaine Dundy
in *Elvis and Gladys*, he never overcame his mother's death.
Bruce Springsteen would write the final song of the B. Goode
legend, "Johnny Bye Bye," about Elvis's funeral in Memphis
("They found him slumped up against the drain/A whole lotta
trouble runnin' through his veins . . . ").

To British youths, the Americanisms that loomed inside rock's aura must have been that much more grand and
desirable. After all, in 1963 the world looked down on British
pop—the Beatles themselves couldn't stand it—and the sun
that was finally setting on the British Empire had brought a
sense of resignation. Britain had in a generation lost its position as a world power. In spite of an often pragmatic approach to the end of the Empire, a feeling of defeat was in
the air.

The Beatles knew they were better than that national
self-image, just like a lot of postwar babies did—the stories

of hardship and war they were told took root in ways the parents never expected. The British had sacrificed almost everything in order to save Europe from the threat of Hitler; now their kids arose to claim what they concluded was theirs: the luxury of freedom, the opportunity for success, and the requisite dividends of pleasure. Born during Germany's Liverpool air raids and conditioned to life as young men in a sleazy district of Hamburg, the Beatles followed Britain's new-wave sensibility—the angry young men—as rebels with a single cause: to have fun. Their intelligent frivolity targeted the core of the music, the hope that undergirds even Elvis's most bitter putdowns (Leiber and Stoller's "Hound Dog"), the place in the sound that promises more from life than is commonly assumed; the idea that beyond paying dues and disciplining talent, the only thing that stands between a person and a happier life is the act of questioning, demanding satisfaction and acting out dreams of something better.

What they gained from their relatively provincial upbringing was something worth living for: not to settle for the security their parents had fought for but to take advantage of what the new world had to offer; not to betray the values of the past but to see how far they could be taken when given half a chance. It involved a wholly different kind of risk—a more personal kind of outlook, both at the world outside and at the dread within.

Paul's mother, Mary, died of breast cancer when Paul was fourteen, and John's mother, Julia, was struck by a bus just before John turned eighteen—losses that each of them would draw on in their work. Moreover, Julia had turned John over to her sister Mimi soon after his birth, and at age five he was kidnapped by his seafaring father, Fred. When Julia tracked them down several days later in Blackpool, young John was asked choose between living with his mother and his father in a traumatic scene: after first choosing his father, he ran back into Julia's arms, and she returned him to his home with Aunt Mimi. The fact that Lennon also lost a surrogate father figure, Aunt Mimi's husband, George, as well as a best friend and early band member, Stu Sutcliffe, all in the space of seven adolescent years, made his resentment even deeper. At the very least, both John and Paul must have felt as though the world owed them something. Their parents' generation had made sacrifices for certain liberties; the Beatles were determined to use those freedoms as much as they could to make life as meaningful as they intuited all along. Their enormous ambition was only part of it; the richness they felt from their own experience—and heard in Presley's singing—demanded something more. The bomb scars that they posed in front of for Dezo Hoffman in 1962 were ruinous, but they knew the optimism of the baby boom generation better than the carnage that was its cost.

THE BEATLES MYTH resembles Presley's in important ways: supposedly, they sprang from nowhere as overnight sensations, working-class northerners who stormed the British ruling class of pop in London, four happy-go-lucky moptops to whom life meant fun and then some. But like Berry's version of the Presley legend, much of the Beatles myth is drawn from conclusions not based on fact: only Ringo's Dingle neighborhood upbringing can be called poor; the other Beatles were solidly middle-class grammar-school types, more privileged than underprivileged. To Americans, it may have seemed as though they enjoyed overnight success, but a glance at their schedules (in Mark Lewisohn's exhaustive *The Beatles Live!*) in Hamburg and British dance halls between 1957 and their first Parlophone recording session in 1962 argues against it.

The most misleading part of their myth is the idea that Liverpool is "nowhere," for nowhere else in Britain—and probably the world—was beat music as alive as it was in the Merseyside scene when the Beatles cut their chops. Over three hundred bands worked the area, over thirty of them engaged several nights a week at the popular clubs like the Cavern for both lunchtime and evening slots. The musical community fed on a furious energy: bands scouted other bands, keen for the best unnoticed B sides of American popular records that the Yankee sailors would bring them from across the Atlantic on the Cunard shipping lines. Along with a mutual respect for quality, there was a competitive edge between groups that challenged them all to greater heights. Opening acts would stump their headliners with a newfound beat thriller that no one had even heard before, and headliners would be forced to try to outdo what came before them. There were many other groups that could hold their own in this arena (the Searchers, Derry and the Seniors, the Big Three), but the Beatles had the peculiar advantages of Brian Epstein's fancy and the luck of a Parlophone contract. It's no accident that they came from the active musical life of Liverpool, but they quickly outdid all their peers with a talent and ambition that left the others behind. After all, they wanted to be bigger than Elvis.

Like the other Merseyside bands at the time, the Beatles subscribed to the ethic of copying the American sounds they loved as closely as possible, faithful to all the licks, fills, guitar solos, and vocal treatments from their favorite Stateside records. The old dictum that artists' early work is first recognized by their influences could not be truer than with the Beatles, and the paradox is that the more they polished their imitations of songs, the closer they came to an individual sound. The more John sang Richie Barret's "Some Other Guy," the more he invested his own jealous longing into it; the more Paul sang Little Richard's "Lucille," the more he flavored it with his giddy brand of camp. George couldn't help sounding like George even when he mimicked Eddie Fontaine's "Nothin' Shakin' (but the Leaves on the Trees)." What they learned from the records they copied was not merely how to sound like someone else but how to play and sing, how to put a song forward. "Don't copy the swimming teacher, learn how to swim!" is how John later put it.

They all cited Lonnie Donegan's "Rock Island Line," a skiffle treatment of Huddie ("Leadbelly") Ledbetter's blues song, as one of the most influential records of their youth. A fluke hit in Britain in 1956, it caught their ear not only because it was catchy, rhythmic, and somewhat raw but because they could master it immediately. With other hits, they crammed all the sounds they heard into the two-guitar, bass, and drums format, reworking sax solos, string arrangements, and high female vocals along the way. They omitted the string ornaments from the girl-group songs they covered in part because of studio costs, but more because they wanted to project the entire imaginative illusion by themselves. Had Decca Records signed them on the merits of their audition tape (now widely available, and astonishing), they would have been treated like any other pop group—given material to play, told how to sound, and recorded and mixed by a professional "slick" pop producer.

But since George Martin wasn't really a pop producer (he was best known for his comedy records) and was won over by their original songs, the Beatles debuted with an enthusiasm won by their determination to be true to an ideal they cherished, not a sound targeted for a presumed listenership. Martin trusted their sense of their potential audience, instead of trying to define it for them, as producers usually do. This was a radical posture: in remaining faithful to the sounds they loved, they redefined pop in their own terms and sparked their career-long journey toward self-definition. They became recording artists soon after bucking the surefire-hit system, but they mastered their craft from the inside out—not by having studio technique applied to their music for effect but by allowing their material to incorporate more sophisticated effects as needed. The difference is everything.

TO BE BIGGER THAN Elvis, the Beatles had to propose bigger challenges, put across even more provocative ideas. From the outset, they embodied the notion that an individual can realize his own identity in a community, even when it consists of four utterly different—even contradictory—parts. Their view of the world, as seen through their records, affirms a sense of perspective no matter what they happen to be singing about: whether it's a broken heart or some shattered illusion, the individual slant is always framed in a group context. When they covered the Isley Brothers' 1959 debut, "Shout," they rotated singers: after Paul and John kick things off, George takes it down ("a little bit softer now"), Ringo brings it back up ("a little bit louder now"), Paul re-enters with call-and-response "hey"s, and Lennon goes out howling "I'm foockin' shoutin' now!" In their own work, their exchanges illuminate each other's personalities even more: the conflict in "We Can Work It Out" sounds as nonthreatening as a simple misunderstanding to Paul (who sings "We can work it out"), more like an argument to Lennon (who answers "There's no time for fussing and fighting . . . "). Paul's strongest heartache songs ("Yesterday" and "For No One") are contrasted with the bottomless sorrow and longing in John's "Julia" or "Don't Let Me Down"—different emotional climates surrounding the same subject matter. And to get such radically opposing views on similar topics from the same band fulfilled any audience's demand for simple variety at the same time that it enlarged their impact.

LENNON AND McCARTNEY are an unusually polarized songwriting team, even though they were both madly in love with rock 'n' roll when they began playing together. The difference was, they both loved it for entirely different reasons. Paul McCartney's upbringing was decidedly more working-class than John Lennon's, even though John's more middle-class family life was probably more traumatic. Paul's father, Jim, was a cotton salesman who worked his way up in a respectable manner and played in a big band on the side as a hobby. Mary had to work full-time as a midwife in order to make ends meet for their two children. By comparison, John's

Aunt Mimi stayed home and kept house while her husband, George, worked at the local dairy. Mimi could even afford to have a gardener come in twice a week. Lennon, who was given the gentlemanly middle name "Winston" after Prime Minister Churchill, grew up with a servant—the McCartneys would never have dreamed of such a luxury. This working-class ethic was instilled in Paul at a very young age, and it represents a major difference in the way he and John approached their music: John, always more concerned with expressing himself, came to see his music as an art, while Paul became a consummate craftsman; he saw pop music more as a trade.

The songs each chose to sing lead on for their early BBC radio spots clue their separate traits: John identified with the broken family in Chuck Berry's "Memphis, Tennessee," the rampant consonants of Berry's wordy "Too Much Monkey Business," and the tenderness that turns to frustration in Phil Spector's "To Know Her Is To Love Her." Paul loved the fun side of Chan Romero's "Hippy Hippy Shake," the Hollywood sentimentality of "The Honeymoon Song," and the high melodrama of "Bésame Mucho." As Greil Marcus writes, "Lennon's writing always admitted struggle; McCartney's always denied it." To say that McCartney aims to please is not really going too far—to this day he loves to entertain, and he's in his element when he's upbeat, celebrative, and downright whimsical. In the 1963 Christmas Message he told his fans, "We'll try to do everything we can to please you with the type of songs we write and record next year. . . ." Paul McCartney is a comfortable person: looking both inside himself and at the world around him, he waxes positive—life suits him. His personality plays itself out musically with lyrical melodies dressed in clever harmonic frameworks (the two-key layout of "Here, There and Everywhere," the major-minor tension of "Eleanor Rigby"). And his appetite for kitsch is at least as large as his hero Elvis Presley's.

Lennon had more in common with Presley's rebellious

posture—the side that provoked questions, confronted assumptions, and challenged authority. When he looked at himself and the world around him, he felt unsettled, dissatisfied; life wore on him. The creative process for Lennon was a working out of this discomfort—he got a lot off his chest in song. He was, as McCartney himself has said, a more autobiographical writer than his partner. Events in his life directly influenced the songs he wrote: with McCartney, the same is not as often true. "Norwegian Wood" is about an affair Lennon had; "Michelle" has nothing to do with McCartney's own love life. Lennon's musical personality is obsessed with rhythm, and his lyrics most often rise above Paul's. Paul was primarily a melodic thinker, both in the lyricism of his vocal lines and in the sweep of his bass playing; his gift lies in linear phrases, while Lennon's jagged beats disrupt songs horizontally. McCartney's texts are usually witty, charming, narrative, or sentimental. Lennon's are more extreme: acerbic, confessional, or maddeningly obtuse.

A knowledge of the music Lennon and McCartney had in their ears by 1962 explains the sources of some of their licks, but the bands who carried on to record after Beatlemania hit prove that the Beatles weren't the only four Liverpudlians who knew and cherished their girl-group 45s. What matters more is how they digested what came before and turned it into something they could call their own: you can hear Elvis's corn in Paul's rendition of "Till There Was You," and Little Willie John's howling jealousy when Lennon sings "Leave My Kitten Alone" (from the *Beatles for Sale* sessions), but you can't explain either Paul or John by pointing to their exemplars. In the best sense, they define one another.

Lennon and McCartney immersed themselves in songwriting, to the point where they threw away between fifty and a hundred tunes before they wrote "Love Me Do" (some of these, like "One After 909," "I'll Follow the Sun," "What Goes On," and "When I'm Sixty-four" were revived later on). When they dueted on Carl Perkins's "Sure to Fall," they learned as much from its style as from its construction; the small silences in their cover of the Everly Brothers' hit "So How Come (No One Loves Me)" taught them the value of such tricks. Among their performing heroes, many wrote their own songs (Buddy Holly, Carl Perkins, Little Richard, Smokey Robinson, Chuck Berry, Roy Orbison), and the Beatles were always covering or copping ideas from pop's great tunesmiths (Leiber and Stoller, Goffin and King, Shuman and Pomus, and Motown's Berry Gordy).

Their individual tendencies dictate the form a song takes. McCartney prefers dramatic settings, complete with characters: "Eleanor Rigby" and "She's Leaving Home" are like pop-song short stories. The two-key harmonic framework of "Penny Lane" articulates its double narrative structure. Lennon is more interested in projecting moral visions with mythical figures like "Nowhere Man" or "I Am the Walrus," and he addresses his audience more directly. As collaborators (and competitors—the distinction is often subtle), they constantly influenced one another and were well aware of their differences. It is not completely a joke that Lennon enjoyed referring to "Why Don't We Do It in the Road?" as McCartney's best song.

As collaborators, their idiosyncrasies appear explicitly in dialogues like "We Can Work It Out," a song about a lovers' quarrel that turns out to be an argument in itself, and "A Day in the Life," where two separate ideas are stitched together into one musical setting. But the same dynamic also produces opposing visions like the "Penny Lane"/"Strawberry Fields Forever" single: here each song springs from the same desire to depict a personal vision of childhood. McCartney's is charming, of "ordinary" lunacy at the corner barbershop. Lennon's song uses an image of homelessness (the title refers to an orphanage near where he grew up) and poses despairing questions about abandonment. McCartney could never have penned the disturbing "Happiness Is a Warm Gun," just as

Lennon would never have bothered with "Maxwell's Silver Hammer."

Because they often contradicted themselves in interviews, we can't know in detail who contributed what to many songs. Hunter Davies describes them writing "With a Little Help from My Friends," bouncing ideas off of each other for Ringo's *Sgt. Pepper* spotlight. But the specifics of what else we know make their partnership seem utilitarian; they would use one another when and if they wanted to. Lennon rewrote "Drive My Car," which McCartney brought in as "Baby, You Can Wear My Diamond Ring"; Paul introduced the first draft of "Hey Jude" as gibberish and John dubbed it finished; John discarded several descriptive verses for "In My Life," but Paul claims to have written the melody; and Paul suggested the lopsided drum hook for Lennon's "Ticket to Ride."

As musicians, their personalities complement each other, enlarging the scope of what would otherwise be individual statements. Paul's lyrical harmony and melodic bass playing shade Lennon's intensity in "Don't Let Me Down." Lennon's background harmony to the last verses of "Hey Jude" lends it a warmth and spirit that no other singer could provide. If they didn't always work together when writing—they composed more and more separately as the years passed, even though the publishing citations still credit them jointly—they were almost always generous toward each other in performance.

THE PERSONAL RELATIONSHIPS these four men shared were also an ever-changing mixture of different balances, but John Lennon was clearly the one they acknowledged as their leader from the start. To begin with, Lennon had more of a vision of what the Beatles were about and what they could be; he spoke of it more in interviews and he lived it out more in his life. (It was John who invited Paul to join the Quarrymen, as much out of respect as fear of competition.) If, as Greil Marcus suggests, "it was the Beatles who opened

up the turf the Stones took as their own—there was no pos-
sibility of a Left until the Beatles created a Center," the same
can be said to be true of the different creative spaces Lennon
and McCartney inhabited. McCartney can be called the
group's center, the middle of the road; Lennon stands for the
fringes that are rock 'n' roll's true holy ground. Paul went
along with Brian Epstein's stylized suits and deep bows; John
always wanted to skip the formalities. Paul covered the standard classic ballads as a matter of course; John made certain
their early records finished to the sound of him wailing "Twist
and Shout," "Money," and "Dizzy Miss Lizzie." The exceptions prove the rule: John's "Good Night" is as smarmy as
anything McCartney ever wrote, and "Helter Skelter" is Paul's
heavy-metal scorcher. But Paul's cover of "Long Tall Sally"
is rollicking where John's "Money" is utterly vicious; Lennon's love ballad "Julia" is oedipal, and follows Paul's "I Will"
on the "White Album" the way "Dear Prudence" follows
"Back in the U.S.S.R."—from the ridiculous to the sublime.
In the final analysis, Lennon's struggle with life more often
outweighs McCartney's contentedness.

There is an undeniable sympathy between them as singers that makes their best duets something different still. Paul's
romanticism curbs John's angst ("If I Fell"), and Lennon
shoots McCartney's puerile excesses through with humor
("Yellow Submarine"), one making up for what the other may
lack. They are a team as naturally suited to one another as
Astaire and Rogers, Rodgers and Hart or Hammerstein, Hep-
burn and Tracy. They magnify this power not just because
they are two but because their combined chemistry is so much
more than one plus one.

This is true of the band as well: their group identity far
outweighs their separate talents. The interplay between
McCartney's bass and George's guitar during the guitar solo
of "Something" is one of the best things about the song itself—Paul comes close to stealing the show.

Ringo Starr is still an underrated drummer. To begin

with, he keeps flawless time—never giving in to the tendency to rush or slow down—an essential element of driving rock 'n' roll. He doesn't dominate his set the way the Who's Keith Moon did, nor does his relatively earthy musicality compete with that of a jazzer-turned-rocker like Charlie Watts of the Rolling Stones. But his role in the band is impossible to discount. Each track has its own drum sound, its own specific patterns, and he gives each song a special feel by adjusting his rhythms to suit the musical tone. His partnership with Paul's increasingly active bass playing is still a lesson in how variously the bottom can support the top in rock. Beginning with "Boys," Ringo is given a song to sing on nearly every album, and supported with musical affection; by the time he delivers "Yellow Submarine," his presence is central.

George Harrison's work will always suffer from the comparison he invites to Lennon and McCartney; such brilliant company inevitably makes his efforts sound weaker. Like silent partners John Entwistle in the Who or Bill Wyman in the Stones, he counts as an essential ingredient of the band's character more than a striking standout. His strong moments are notable by any other standards, songs like "Taxman," "While My Guitar Gently Weeps," and "Here Comes the Sun" have earned their place in rock history, even if his excursions into Indian sitar-based exoticism are now largely dismissable. He's best thought of as a lead guitarist, the one who turned in the effervescent solo on "And Your Bird Can Sing" and the brief and breathless interruption in "Got to Get You into My Life." Like Ringo's, his musical competency supported, rather than competed with, his elder peers.

On record, the Beatles play up their personalities, enjoying their implications as well as their contradictions. The visual presence they commanded onstage accentuated this: John's Rickenbacker, George's Gretsch, and Paul's Hofner each had a distinctive design to it; they were more than phallic, they were logical extensions of their owners' musical wit. Their stage presence was haloed by an illusory arc that stretched from the neck of Lennon's Rickenbacker on the right, over Ringo's drums, to the tuning pegs of Paul's bass, which he played left-handed while sharing a microphone with George. Their long hair made them arty and outrageous, and as their looks changed over the years, they projected the idea that the way one appears affects the way one perceives oneself.

As an ensemble, their interplay is a constantly shifting exchange of combinations. The simple two-guitar, bass, and drums setup allows for a number of different combinations: at the simplest level, Paul's bass provides the harmonic foundations and teams with Ringo's drumming to form the rhythm section. On top of this, John's rhythm guitar flanks George's lead. These elementary patterns lead to more intricate configurations: a song can pit lead guitar against the drums ("I Feel Fine") or let the bass play lead almost exclusively ("Rain").

The two songwriters carry the lead vocal parts, and are supported by pairing the remaining lead singers behind (Paul and George back up John, John and George back up Paul). In "Long Tall Sally," Paul leads the band; in "Roll Over Beethoven," George lets them carry him; in "Money," John pits himself against the others, turning the act of performance into a competition of will, endurance, and emotional thrust. A singer can impose his emotional presence on the way the band actually sounds: John's authority on "Bad Boy" conjures up a completely different imaginative space than Paul does on his equally masterful "Kansas City."

THE BEATLES ARE our first recording artists, and they remain our best. The growing significance of pop music in the sixties paralleled advances in recording technology, which suited their own creative inclinations to stop touring and concentrate on studio work. The expanding technical possibilities influenced their music to a greater degree than pop had ever been subject to before. Phil Spector's work with the Ronettes, Ike and Tina Turner, the Crystals, and the Righteous Brothers are paragons of how studio technique can turn the simple essence of pop into grand, dramatic surges of sound. But Spector was more an auteur than he was a full-fledged artist—his catalogue bears his signature but not his soul. The Beatles' work came to be conceived with the studio in mind—all the production values a mixing board had to offer were used to serve the ideas conveyed in their music. A Beatles record is more than just a collection of songs; it's a performance for tape. The recording industry still measures itself against ingenious achievements like *Sgt. Pepper* (recorded on two four-track recorders), even though digital circuitry is now far beyond the eight-track machines that were used to tape their last album, *Abbey Road*.

George Martin, a classically trained oboist, produced almost all of the Beatles' material for the recording medium. His technically experienced ears lent a disciplined sensibility to Lennon and McCartney's ideas. The classical touches bear Martin's fingerprints (the string quartet on "Yesterday," the baroque keyboard solo in "In My Life"), and when Lennon wanted two different versions of "Strawberry Fields Forever" spliced together to capture the best of both, even though they were in different keys and tempi, it was Martin who figured out how to do it. His creative presence is notably absent on *Let It Be*, the only Beatles record he didn't oversee. Phil Spector produced "Let It Be," "The Long and Winding Road," and "Across the Universe" for that record with strings and female chorus. It's obvious from the resulting clash of sentiment and schmaltz that Spector doesn't speak the Beatles' language as well as Martin does. Martin's care for detail and nuance are why other artists' recordings of Beatles songs are usually less satisfying than their original counterparts. Each element of the production on Beatles records is so carefully placed that it becomes part of the song itself. As time went on, the Beatles weren't so much songwriters as they were *record* writers; the studio became a lab where musical ideas were exchanged, reworked, and restructured for tape.

The merits of a recorded performance compared with those of a performance in the live arena are often disputed in rock 'n' roll. While Bruce Springsteen might contend that rock's most noble values are played out in concert, where artist and audience engage in shared imagery at the same time in the same place, the airwaves are where the music lives in day-to-day life; and since day-to-day life is pop's subject, its medium is its most important message. The very idea that highly individual messages can be shared on a mass scale is enough to make Rosie and her Originals seem almost oracular.

The Beatles' understanding of how the recording medium could be used was intuitive and unfeigned. In "Strawberry Fields Forever," sounds roam from place to place; the voice is filtered to warp the sense of space (at times it sounds as if Lennon were singing underwater); and even some of the instruments are unrecognizable because of what surrounds them. For a song that grapples with the disturbing questions of alienation and self-identity, the setting alone conveys much of the text's confused tone.

The studio effects don't need to be fancy, though: for the final verse of "I've Got a Feeling," Phil Spector simply separates the lead voices into separate stereo channels, dividing the duet into two distinct parts, type-casting Lennon and McCartney's swan song by putting it through separate speakers. The way the rhythm instruments are distinguished from the lead vocals on earlier albums enhances the texture: each instrument etches a clear line in the web of sound. These early mixes (vocals opposite instruments) sound simplistic today, but they grew into such lopsided treats as "Yer Blues," with the drums all the way over to the left, and "Maxwell's Silver Hammer," with its overwrought labyrinth design.

WITH THE WEALTH of material the band produced, it's surprising to remember that their recording career lasted only seven years. A lifetime in pop is very short, and seven years has come to signify about one generation: seven years after the Beatles' dissolution, in 1977, punk and new wave came to the fore; roughly seven years after that, in 1984, a new crop of underground hopefuls—the Replacements, Hüsker Dü, the Minutemen—came into maturity. The Beatles' seven years of recording (1962–69) were loaded with creativity, and when their work is seen as a self-contained world, there is a progressive direction implicit in the best of it. The seeds of their later period can be heard in the early stages, and as early as *Help!* their world is self-reflective. "You're Gonna Lose That Girl" is basically a rewrite—the unsung threat—of "She Loves You."

The idea of turning the long-playing record into an artistic statement came about largely because of the Beatles' own career. John Rockwell points out how records like Frank Sinatra's *Only the Lonely* have an underlying theme that makes their songs part of a whole, but the concept album as we know it came into its own with *Sgt. Pepper* and has never been the same since. To say that a record has an "inner logic" (to use Robert Christgau's term) suggests something more than a common theme. It has to do with the rhythm of an album side, the way songs relate to one another, and the way a listener becomes engaged with the imaginative landscape of sound. In the same way that great movie actors relax and forget their self-consciousness in front of the cameras, the Beatles' ease in front of the microphones lets us hear them feel the music as they play it—the way Ringo plows right into "Birthday," for instance, or the tight grip that John keeps on his rhythm guitar in "I'm Happy Just to Dance with You." Their relationship with the material can be heard in the way a song is played through time, either gaining momentum toward the finish (as in "Twist and Shout") or ebbing and flowing of its own accord ("If I Needed Someone").

The Beatles treated the album as a journey from one place to another. They built cornerstones into their records by positioning the songs in relation to one another: beginnings and endings of sides can sum up, contradict, qualify, or cast a shadow over the songs they introduce or follow. Each Beatles album has its own nooks and crannies, its individual contours, speckled with personal moments listeners can latch on to and call their own—a favorite guitar solo, a treasured vocal ad-lib, any number of lyrical indecipherables. Their "inner logic" is best understood by hearing the songs out of their normal sequence, as on the collection LPs that followed their breakup. After "Something," the ear wants to hear "Maxwell's Silver Hammer"; after "Back in the U.S.S.R.," "Dear Prudence."

They took great care in assembling their records—they had a keen sense of how the order of songs gives shapes to the experience of an album. On most of their LPs, placing the songs in any other sequence would lessen their impact, detract from the entirety they form. This is true not only on their "concept" albums but on the earlier designs that led up to them. The way "Twist and Shout" finishes off their debut LP provides direction as well as a rousing finale; *Revolver* wouldn't have the same flavor if it didn't start with Harrison's bitter "Taxman." This sense of arranging the material evolves into works like *Sgt. Pepper,* which had a self-conscious beginning, middle, and end. Side two of *Abbey Road* has a a collage effect—the individual songs are less central than the way they relate to one another as parts of an integrated mosaic. Again, the exceptions prove the rule: "Dizzy Miss Lizzie" sags after "Yesterday" on the *Help!* album; "Run for Your Life," the last song on *Rubber Soul,* blemishes that album by undermining its ambiguities.

Once immersed in their catalogue, it's hard to separate any single song from its context. Their rendition of Barrett Strong's hit "Money" is simply more powerful when heard after listening to the rest of *With the Beatles,* the album it closes. "Hey Jude," 1968's summer single, would have changed its character considerably on the "White Album"—

as a single, it stands out more than if it had been surrounded by that album's abundance. 1967's "Penny Lane"/"Strawberry Fields Forever" single may be the most striking use of aural montage in the medium. Understanding their entire output enhances the enjoyment of any particular song.

THE ENTIRE BEATLES catalogue witnesses a growth—both musical and personal—that extends from the unleashed enthusiasm of *Please Please Me* to the resigned farewell of *Abbey Road*'s "The End." Their early sound peaks with *A Hard Day's Night*, progresses uneasily through *Beatles for Sale* and *Help!*, ripens and blooms on *Rubber Soul* and *Revolver*. By 1966, after barely four years of recording, *Revolver* stands as the pinnacle of all they can do: there are no weak tracks, and most of what follows deserves to be measured against it. The rest of the catalogue maps their dissolving partnerships: *Sgt. Pepper*, the most famous, is also the most overrated; *Magical Mystery Tour* and *Yellow Submarine* are embarrassments; the "White Album" is a patchwork interwoven by great playing; *Let It Be* is an overhauled modesty. *Abbey Road*, although a success, doesn't quite extend or improve upon what *Revolver* attained.

The Beatles weren't always conscious of this larger picture, but its implications are broad: they came of age through their music as their audience came of age. The innocence heard in "I Saw Her Standing There" and "There's a Place" quickly gives way to the qualified commitment of "If I Fell," the sadness that pervades "And I Love Her." Their singing, playing, and album conceptions followed their artistic temperaments, so that at each step of the way, their identities as musicians and writers were served by their natural abilities and their comparatively unschooled studio technique.

By digesting rock 'n' roll during adolescence and recreating it in their own image as they progressed, the Beatles helped the form come of age and gain the capacity to express more adult themes: isolation, despair, alienation, loss, and the positive correlatives of peace, communication, self-worth, vision, and hope. The term "rock 'n' roll" was abbreviated to "rock." Rock 'n' roll still expresses adolescent concerns (which still pack a wad of excitement when Bruce Springsteen closes a show with Eddie Cochran's "Summertime Blues"). "Rock" refers to the larger spectrum of adult experience and embraces everything from the mature work of Bob Dylan, the Rolling Stones, the Who, and others to punk and new wave, with talents like Elvis Costello and the Talking Heads continuing to explore the genre. The Beatles symbolize this growth toward maturity, even if the weight of the journey is shared by others. Their early work charges adolescent themes with a greater urgency, and their maturation more than delivered on their early promise.

THE BEATLES COMBINED the physicality of Elvis with a British zeal for verbal flair. The point of a good pop lyric is not to be haughty or arcane but to communicate by twisting assumed meanings, using images out of context or emphasizing things in a new way. The Beatles had an uncanny flair for cleverness without being artful or supercilious—their word painting conjures up varied associations with the simplest of references. Sometimes it's not the performance that is most riveting; it's the singularity of ideas that strikes the imagination. At other times, the emotional energy of a vocal performance seems to carry the band along behind, transcending any hidden references in the words. The poignancy of generational conflict in "She's Leaving Home" makes up for its sentimental setting; and the two lines that Paul repeats in "Why Don't We Do It in the Road?" are shot through with some masterful vocal gymnastics.

Making intelligent lyrics and arrangements accessible to a popular audience is a formidable challenge. Although the Beatles' lyrics are made up of clichés and colloquialisms, we always sense a strong voice behind their words, a personality that draws on pop's language as a means of expression, not just lines used to fill up spaces in the sound—the sentiment generates the lyrics instead of clichés being forced to fit. Whether it's "I am the walrus" or "yeah, yeah, yeah," they constantly reanimate their language. Simple verbal phrases are made to carry an emotional weight beyond their capacity, and when combined with music, they signify much more than what is implied on the surface. These commonalities are treated so that the familiar seems fresh, the ordinary seems special, and the secular somehow becomes holy. The transformation of idioms can be ironic: the slang phrase "turn you on" of the drug culture becomes a humanitarian plea for enlightenment in "A Day in the Life"; in "Let It Be," Paul sings as much to his companions as he does to his audience.

The attitude of the lover toward his beloved in early songs is constantly shifting—Lennon can be spiteful and pretentious as easily as he can be vulnerable and paranoid. Women seem to taunt him as much as they symbolize satisfaction: "If I Fell" takes a simple second-time-around scenario and wrings a song of real consequence from its emotional implications. The transition toward selfhood is found all through their catalogue, from a deceptively simple heartbreak song like "Yesterday" on *Help!* (which came to mean much more to an entire generation that lost its innocence to the sixties revolution) to "You Never Give Me Your Money" on *Abbey Road*, which laments the inevitable responsibilities of fame. "Help!" itself was once thought of as simply the title song for a mock James Bond movie, but it has survived as a young man's desperate cry for intimacy. The pessimism in "Happiness Is a Warm Gun" sounds that much darker when weighed against the unflinching exuberance of "I Want to Hold Your Hand."

Later, as they begin to address the larger concerns of adulthood, their masks and innuendos change. Paul's financial terminology on side two of *Abbey Road* stems directly from the legal confrontations the Beatles were then facing with their publishers. Lennon's identity crisis at the height of his fame spawned a number of self-referential confessionals about his innermost personality ("Help!," "Strawberry Fields Forever," "She Said She Said") and alternative realms of the imagination that reached beyond the conscious world ("To-morrow Never Knows," "Lucy in the Sky with Diamonds"). The layered levels of inference in a song as full of imagery as "I Am the Walrus" or even "Hey Bulldog" have the welling sense of the uncontrollable; the storyteller sounds barely in control of his story, never mind his subject. Lennon had to write "A Day in the Life" before he could return to basics with songs like "Revolution," "I Want You (She's So Heavy)," and "Don't Let Me Down."

The effect of time on people's lives is treated both ro-mantically (as in "It Won't Be Long" and "Things We Said Today") and humorously ("When I'm Sixty-four," "Ob-La-Di, Ob-La-Da"). The sophomoric images of nature found in "And I Love Her" mature into the sublime restraint of "Dear Prudence." "All My Loving" is ripe with irony; the joy of the performance belies the sentiment of the text. "Drive My Car" has even more sophisticated ironic wit. This wealth of mate-rial goes way beyond diversity, and it takes many forms—it can pop up as a respectful parody like "Honey Pie" (which can still stand on its own) or it can lie in the grooves between such different songs as "The Word," an uptempo community song by Lennon, and McCartney's "Michelle," with its un-abashed cabaret setting. The Beatles hated overintellectuali-zation of their songs ("Glass Onion") almost as much as they hated not being taken seriously ("I'll Get You," "I'm So Tired," and "Sexy Sadie").

As their music develops, the basic primal passions of rock 'n' roll are carried forward and enlarged. When rock 'n' roll first appeared, it challenged some basic assumptions. Presley's conjunction of black and white was radical enough for some; but along with this, rock 'n' roll raised the whole issue of freedom (again). The Beatles played out the concept of "the beat can set you free" and emphasized the freedom even more than the beat. Their beat was enormous (as Marcus points out), but the possibilities of what it could do became even bigger. What kinds of freedom could rock 'n' roll address? Initially, of course, it was sexual freedom—Elvis Presley's image was both racial and physical. But the Beatles didn't so much sharpen rock's sexual and cultural arrows as they did infuse the style with an even greater musical intelligence. If Elvis Presley symbolized everything that rock 'n' roll could stand for, the Beatles took it all apart and put it back together in ways that made the music sound infinitely resourceful, adaptable, rich. They didn't reinvent rock 'n' roll itself so much as how one could look at it, transforming it into a style both bold enough to provoke and seasoned enough to sustain itself—they played up possibilities that didn't seem feasible on the surface. Without being explicit, their work inspired their audience far more dramatically than protest songs and peace-love-and-brotherhood propaganda would have ("The Word" and "All You Need Is Love" are the only songs that flirt with flower power). Lennon's rendition of "Twist and Shout," with all its lust, has kernels of spiritual longing. The way he sings "Money" on the next album makes the physical-spiritual tug of war more apparent: the spirit of his singing tells us that he sees right through the materialist doctrine he's supposedly endorsing.

Eventually, the beat conveys more complex notions of freedom—and what lies beyond. The *Revolver* album confronts mortality and seeks transcendental and romantic avenues toward peace of mind. The incessant rhythm track of "Tomorrow Never Knows" is merely bedding for tape loops and a backwards guitar solo—instead of riding the beat like a wave, it's like they're inside the wave itself. The beat of "Rain" is mesmerizing; the layered patterns of "Happiness Is a Warm Gun" make the stomach turn; and the variety of rhythmic sequences in "I Want You" gives the simple text a potent framework. "She Said She Said" condenses three stages of life into less than four minutes by letting the beat tell half the story. As complex as their rhythmic ideas can get, they never lose sight of where it all springs from: the backbeat. The finale to *Abbey Road* has as its centerpiece a simple guitar jam, as fundamental as anything from *Please Please Me.* Their love of simple rock 'n' roll was always a springboard for messages of higher implication, and their achievements encompass not only new musical styles but new ways of looking at the world.

The Beatles never seemed to question whether rock 'n' roll could speak to all these concerns; they simply acted as if it could. Along the way, they transformed the style nonchalantly, whipping off dazzling record after dazzling record, transforming the very idea of the rock album each time out, making technical and artistic feats sound not only easy but fun. By the time they bade their audience farewell with "Her Majesty," they had developed new vocabularies for pop, whether it's the way an album begins and ends or the flashes of brilliance in between that their singles embody. The journey from unknown upstarts to consummate artists is a story best told by the music.

BEFORE SETTING FOOT in a recording studio, the Beatles paid their dues like any other band. They started playing wherever they could—at church dances, picnics, and the small clubs that would let them open for bigger acts. When Allan Williams decided to manage them, bookings were scarce. They simply weren't very good yet, and none of them had the means to devote the time to a career—it meant giving up jobs and school. But when Williams got them a long-term contract to play the Reeperbahn in Hamburg, they leapt at the chance. It was steady income, and it meant they could devote their lives to music. To see an early picture of the band in front of the Arnhem War Cemetery on their first trip to Hamburg in 1960—with the tragic figure of Stu Sutcliffe in place of a mysteriously absent John Lennon—is to have a strange retrospective sense of prophecy. The tomb they are posed upon reads: THEIR NAME LIVETH FOR EVER MORE.

FROM THE GARAGE
TO THE DANCE FLOOR

Love Me Do (Paul)/P.S. I Love You (Paul)
Released: October 5, 1962

Please Please Me (John)/Ask Me Why (John)
Released: November 26, 1962

PLEASE PLEASE ME *Released: March 22, 1963*

THE RECORDING WORLD is full of sharks, crooks, and people on the run (like Elvis Presley's manager, Colonel Tom Parker), but Brian Epstein was a genuine shopkeeper. A former window dresser for his father's furniture store, he was running his own record business around the corner from the Cavern when he signed on as the Beatles' manager in December 1961. His idea of making the Beatles marketable was to clean up their stage act: he put them in collarless jackets, made them put out their cigarettes, insisted that Lennon stop cursing onstage, and taught them to do ridiculous hanging bows after every number. As Lennon later put it:

> We were just a band that made it very, very big, that's all. Our best work was never recorded . . . because we were per- formers—in spite of what Mick says about us—in Liverpool, Hamburg and other dance halls. What we generated was fan- tastic, when we played straight rock, and there was nobody

could touch us in Britain. As soon as we made it we made it
but the edges were knocked off . . . you know Brian put us all
in suits and all that and we made it very, very big. But we sold
out, you know. The music was dead before we even went on
the theater tour of Britain. We were shit already, because we
had to reduce an hour or two hours' playing, which we were
glad about in a way, to twenty minutes, and we would go on
and repeat the same twenty minutes every night.
(*Lennon Remembers*, pp. 45–46)

Although Lennon is at his most bitter in this 1970 interview, his remarks about their transformation toward market-
ability (in Epstein's eyes, at least) are revealing. Some of what
they compromised must have been regrettable, but aside from
the "Hamburg Star Club" tapes of December 1962 (which is
actually late in the period Lennon is referring to), we can't
know just how regrettable.

Trimming their live shows inevitably influenced their
music. To begin with, their condensed sets distinguished them
from the blues circuit in London, which was just beginning
to nurture such talents as the Rolling Stones, the early Yard-
birds (with their alumni of outstanding guitarists, Eric Clapton, Jimmy Page, and Jeff Beck), and the Who. These bands
were obsessed with American blues—the black sounds and
heroes that had influenced Elvis Presley—and worked long,
impassioned guitar solos around dramatic vocalism. The
Stones' early repertoire included songs by Slim Harpo and
Muddy Waters (they even named themselves after Waters's
"Rolling Stone"): the Who played an emphatic rendition of
James Brown's "Shout and Shimmy" that made them sound
much blacker than the Beatles' equivalent (the Isley Brothers'
"Shout!" and "Twist and Shout!"). The Beatles were taking
the road that led to pop, although a much more sophisticated
kind than even they imagined at the time.

Their musical preferences were made clear by appearances on radio shows like the BBC's "Saturday Club" and

"Here We Go," where their selection displayed a much broader range of taste and versatility than their London counterparts. Lennon sang Chuck Berry's "Carol," the Presley version of "I'm Gonna Sit Right Down And Cry (Over You)," and Arthur Alexander's "A Shot of Rhythm and Blues"; McCartney did the syrupy "Beautiful Dreamer," the Coasters' "Searchin'," and Ray Charles' "Hallelujah, I Love Her So"; George sang Buddy Holly's "Crying, Waiting, Hoping" and Eddie Fontaine's "Nothin' Shakin' (but the Leaves on the Trees)." John and Paul duetted on Goffin and King's "Don't Ever Change" and the Everly Brothers' "So How Come (No One Loves Me)," and all three romped through the refrains of the Coasters' "Three Cool Cats" (Leiber and Stoller) with George taking the verses. The Beatles weren't interested in playing the blues—their repertoire emphasized *hits*. And as their popularity grew, their live show began to feature original material more and more and got concise to the point of rudeness: they teased their audiences with ferocious forty minute sets (at the outside)—their screaming fans were always left screaming for more. This meant that some improvisation had to be sacrificed.

They were, in effect—for better and not, as Lennon implies, for worse—a recording band from the minute Epstein began tailoring their Cavern Club act. Instead of embellishing things here and there, as is the custom in front of an audience, each time Harrison took a guitar solo he began to play the same set of notes he had played the night before. The harmonies, solos, drum fills, intros, and cutoffs began to fit a predetermined set of gestures that quickly became habits. And they kept up all the bowing. To watch clips of them singing "Twist and Shout" during this period is to see an example of what Lennon called "dead": there are virtually no deviations from the standard arrangement in literally hundreds of concerts. As performers, this made for a dull, nonthinking kind of music making, and it was after several years of this musically (although not energetically) inert live show that they retired from the stage to concentrate on recording.

But the repetitive polish of their stage shows had unintentional and extraordinary consequences. The art they arrived at relies more on subtleties of writing and recording than on live stage shows. Elvis Presley before them had leapt straight from being a performing dynamo to Hollywood, and even though his blues singing far outstripped his acting, his recordings, although still hits, took a back seat. (Later in his career, free from the bondage of his movie contracts, Elvis returned to the live arena with zeal.) If rock 'n' roll up to that point was still derided as a fad whose bubble might burst as quickly as the hula hoop's had, the Beatles consolidated its staying power not only with their songwriting and playing skills but with their commitment to recording. The medium that best suited their act was just waiting for salvation: the long-playing record.

Love Me Do (Paul)/P.S. I Love You (Paul)
Released: October 5, 1962

G E O R G E   M A R T I N   R E M E M B E R S hearing several original songs, including "Ask Me Why" and an early, slow rendition of "Please Please Me," before they decided on "Love Me Do" for their first Parlophone single. It was not an auspicious debut for a pop group: no one listening to it in the last months of 1962 would have believed the career awaiting these young men. Yet with almost no promotion from Parlophone, the single reached number 17 on the *New Musical Express* charts in December 1962, a year after the Decca label had turned them down. (Brian Epstein bought thousands of copies of the single for his own shop to help tilt the chart position—a maneuver called "padding" that is still practiced.) This limited success was respectable enough to continue recording, although the record was weaker, both commercially and critically, than what would immediately follow. "I was by now

absolutely convinced that I had a hit group on my hands,"
Martin says in his memoirs, "though I knew that I hadn't got
it with the first record, feeling the quality of the song wasn't
really up to it."

Lennon's harmonica (he called it his harp) opens the
tune, but not with the same enthusiasm that would soon color
"I Should Have Known Better." John and Paul's vocal harmony is patterned after the Everly Brothers, minus the refinement. The dash of Beatles magic comes as they reach the
end of the verse and bounce together on the strung-out
"pleeeeeeease . . ." answered by Paul's solo " . . . love me
do." The spirit in the harmony and the expectant silence that
follows heightens the sense of anticipation, a different take on
the same Everlys effect before the "ooh-la-la"s in "Wake Up
Little Suzie." For a moment at the end, when Paul ad-libs
during the fade-out, the spirit cuts loose again. But the song
has a skiffle or washboard beat that only hints at rock's aggressiveness—it's not meant to cut loose. The general effect is
tame: the urgency is more charming than impassioned.

The B side, "P.S. I Love You," is a crooner by Paul, the
early model for "And I Love Her" and "Yesterday." The hook
lies in the harmonic turn at the end of the verse, on "P.S., I
love *you*" (it climbs back up from the flatted six chord on the
words "you, you, you"). ("Paul was even more intense about
fancy pop chords and corny pop tunes than he was about
Little Richard," write Christgau and Piccarella.) In a subtle
way, this simple turn creates a tone of sincerity, and it's more
of a song because of it. He darts out of his candor with his
off-the-cuff scat near the end ("You know I want you to"),
dancing around the always-be-true intentions. What might
have been a simple declaration of faith is juiced up with a
touch of humor, enlarging its emotional range.

AN EMBARRASSING ATMOSPHERE hung over the Beat-
les' first recording session. George Martin had his doubts about
Pete Best, the drummer who had played with them for the

audition, so he hired a professional drummer, Andy White, to play for their first studio session. This was common practice; and since the Beatles were Martin's first pop group, employing studio musicians for sessions was a typical move, if not the rule. In the meantime, the Beatles had replaced Best with Ringo Starr, late of Rory Storm and the Hurricanes, and an old friend from Hamburg—they had even played a recording session there together. For the long-awaited first taping session, Ringo, the newcomer, had to watch another drummer play his parts as he stood by with a tambourine. But Ringo did sit in for at least one take—the one without the tambourine on it. And this turned out to be the version of "Love Me Do" that was released as their first single. (Andy White plays drums on "P.S. I Love You.")

Martin provides the best description of Ringo's talents in his *All You Need Is Ears* (p. 127):

. . . I did quickly realize that Ringo was an excellent drummer for what was required. He's not a "technical" drummer. Men like Buddy Rich and Gene Krupa would run rings round him. But he's a good solid rock drummer with a super steady beat, and he knows how to get the right sound out of his drums. Above all, he does have an individual sound. You can tell Ringo's drums from anyone else's, and that character was a definite asset to the Beatles' early recordings.

For all the critical abuse Ringo has taken as the least talented of the four, this is high praise from the only man in London to take on the group from Liverpool. One of the key strengths of the Beatles' sound—early or late—is their symbiotic blend, the warm ensemble playing that communicates so much meaning as well as the joy of playing together. There is a natural give-and-take between the four players that is special in any style of music, and the wealth of shared experience in their sound never gets in the way of each member's individuality. That Ringo joined the band at this juncture in their career—as they made the leap to recording—is no co-incidence.

Pete Best had been their drummer since 1960, paying dues with them in Hamburg and traveling throughout England, sticking with the band through disappointment after disappointment during recording auditions. His mother, Mona Best, had been a former booking agent of sorts for the band and sponsored them regularly at her Liverpool club, the Casbah. Best owned the essential drum kit, had good looks and a loyal following of fans and a mother who helped them get gigs. He was a sullen-faced type, always pictured with a dour grimace—his good looks were overshadowed by the antics of the rest of the band, his stoical posture an unlikely contrast to Lennon's maniacal outbursts. In most pictures, he looks as though he doesn't even enjoy playing. On the Decca audition taped the first day of January 1962, released as a bootleg entitled "The Deccagone Sessions," Best's presence is unobtrusive, undistinctive.

But when the Parlophone contract came about, the commitment to making recordings immediately overrode whatever else Best had going for him. The others had been wanting to sack him for some time, and they chose this moment to do it. (Some say they were jealous of Best's Liverpool popularity.) To replace him they chose Ringo, a clumsier-looking fellow with an enormous nose. His local standing was already doomed: George Harrison suffered a black eye from the fist of a Best fan at the outburst of protest surrounding his removal. But for the Beatles, recording had become a higher priority than good looks, the studio was suddenly more important than Best's mother's club.

Ringo's dopey smile was preferable to Pete's static gaze, and his drumming fit in snugly with the ensemble sound they had developed without him. His character leveled the band's presence: the head that rocked from side to side behind the set was as oddly interesting as McCartney's left-handed bass, and the unimpressed droop that was Ringo's natural facial expression offset Lennon's acerbity in a way no words ever could. When Martin says "he knew how to get the right sound out of his drums," he means in part that Ringo wanted to serve the songs rather than show off. As a songwriter's drummer, Ringo was the type of musician who could follow instructions as he complemented the overall sound. His commitment to the music was always bigger than his ego. Ringo's "audition" for Martin as they selected material and recorded the first single was convincing—when they entered the studios on November 26, 1962, to record their next single, Martin's confidence in Ringo was secure. He realized that they shared his impressions of Best's talents, and he didn't bother to hire an alternate percussionist.

WITHOUT ALWAYS BEING conscious of how their sources influenced them, pop history had an enormous effect on the Beatles' approach. Besides preparing them for the rigors of world touring, the dues that they paid in Hamburg and throughout the dance halls of Britain before the Parlophone contract sealed their determination to be original songsters. By the end of 1962 their live set included a large selection of songs from the popular catalogue, tunes they had grown up to and learned to play their instruments by—material that had inspired them to make music in the first place. It's easy to hear the Beatles' covers as nostalgic now, even though most of the songs were less than seven years old at the time. But Greil Marcus points out how they thought of the great rock 'n' roll hits they were playing as alive and well, a tradition as well as a way of thinking, a history as well as something living in their immediate present.

In the Merseyside music scene, there were two definite attitudes prevalent among the bands playing beat music. There were the purists—the faithful—and the aspirants, or slickers—the ones willing to compromise in order to get a hit record. The Beatles were purists, who in the process of trying to sound close to the originals they covered developed a group approach. The more they performed Carl Perkins's "Lend Me Your Comb," the more they turned it into a *Beatles* song first and foremost. They were seeking out an ideal sound, and the closer they got to that ideal, the more self-revealing their ensemble became. The truth is, they were essentially better than their heroes to begin with—except for Presley, whose songs they played but dared not record.

More than anything else, their broad array of other people's material maps their development as a band. As they matured, they found secret places hidden in these familiar songs that hadn't even occurred to the original performers: the urgency that was implicit all along in "Please Mr. Postman" and "You've Really Got a Hold on Me," or the way the ultra-cool "cheat-cheat" sounds more cutting when sung by males on "Baby It's You."

By performing their favorite pop songs over a long period of time as a band, they grew as a unit, as four players who responded to one another's personalities, ambitions, and high standards. As the defiant kicks that nearly obliterate "Bésame Mucho" on the Hamburg Star Club tapes demonstrate, their ensemble has more to it than just four people playing at the same time—there's a unity of attack that lets them second-guess just where those kicks are going to land. The exhilaration in the send-off to "Please Please Me" doesn't happen automatically with musicians: it takes time, and a common infatuation with a sound they all carry around in their heads.

Finally, performing all these classics fertilized Lennon and McCartney's songwriting talents. Meredith Willson's "Till There Was You" may have been unbearably simpy for Lennon (we hear him jeering McCartney's soupy delivery on *Live! At the Star Club in Hamburg, Germany*), but it pointed the way toward ballads like "P.S. I Love You" as McCartney the apprentice began to turn craftsman. Lennon's interest in songs about envy and disappointment like Richie Barrett's "Some Other Guy" (co-written with Leiber and Stoller) leads to his own treatment of similar themes ("No Reply" and "You Can't

Do That"). Incorporating their good taste with their creative muses meant that the Beatles could begin their career with a richer perspective on what they wanted to say and how they wanted to put it across. By the time they showed up for their next recording session, they were certain that their new up-beat version of "Please Please Me" compared with anything they had played by anybody else.

FOR THEIR SECOND single, George Martin was anxious to do better than number 17 on the charts. He selected a song by Mitch Murray called "How Do You Do," which he insisted the Beatles put down on tape before he would hear of any more arguments for their own material. The demo that survives epitomizes the way the London pop machinery would have packaged the Beatles—smooth, unthreatening, almost charmless. The duet that John and Paul turned in actually might have charted—at first, Martin was pleased. But afterwards, they convinced him to listen to a new arrangement of "Please Please Me," which they had sped up. Because they had gumption enough to believe in their own material—and more importantly, because Martin gave it an honest chance—what they arrived with on "Please Please Me" overwhelmed Murray's mainstream tactics by not sounding anywhere near as studied.

Knowing that most of their American heroes (Buddy Holly, Chuck Berry, Little Richard, Carl Perkins, Smokey Robinson, Roy Orbison, Arthur Alexander) were themselves self-sufficient—performers as well as writers—gave Lennon and McCartney's homespun ambition ample precedent in their minds. Sticking up for their own material seemed logical, even crucial. The fact that they had just been forced to play a song they didn't really like gave "Please Please Me" a competitive edge: they cut "How Do You Do" as well as any group might, but "Please Please Me" has more spark to it, even though it is not as "well-written." Their high spirits more than compensated for the lack of the applied ornaments a conventional producer might have used to tame them musically the way Epstein cultivated their look. Martin heard the difference and came away from the second session bowled over. "Please Please Me" became their first number one single.

Please Please Me (John)/Ask Me Why (John)
Released: November 26, 1962

THE AGGRESSIVE THRUST of "Please Please Me" makes it instantly more exciting than "Love Me Do"—the lyrics are more suggestive, and Lennon's singing is more spirited, sexier. Christgau and Piccarella call it "the first real oral sex pop song," although it probably wasn't heard that way at the time. The polite word "please" takes on a different hue than elsewhere ("plee-ee-ease . . . love me do" in "Love Me Do" and "Oh please say to me you'll let me be your man" in the third verse of "I Want to Hold Your Hand"); the tension in the title is in the shift of meaning between a pleasantry and a wishful fantasy. In the drawn-out "plee-ee-ease" of "Love Me Do" the lilting harmonies yearn politely—in "Please Please Me" it's dirty and polite all at the same time.

John and Paul's verse duet gains on the Everly formula: Paul stays on the initial high note as John pulls away beneath him ("Last night I said these words to my girl"), putting the Everlys' "Cathy's Clown" lilt to a brighter beat. The rasp in Lennon's voice on the repeated "come on"s is far from innocent—he wants this woman to do more than just hold his hand. As they hit the second "please," Paul and John leap away from the pleasantry of the first, soaring up to convey a real adolescent sexual frustration. Even the sound of the band has more rough edges than the thunking bass of "Love Me Do." Where the first single is genuinely coy, the second makes a "polite" demand on the female, and Lennon deliberately tries to stir up a reaction.

.   .   .

''A s k M e W h y ,'' the B side, has the lyricism of "P.S. I
Love You," but it's buoyed with a greater sense of humor:
the background vocals' "woo-woo-woo"s that follow "you,"
and Lennon's own "I-I-I-I"s before "should never, never,
never be blue-oo," which ends the phrase with a tripped leap
to falsetto (the same vowel reiteration that moves "I Should
Have Known Better" on the word "mine" near the end of the
bridge). It's a two-dimensional love song, but Lennon milks
it for all it's worth. The affection they have for all these pop
snippets of wordplay make the song more of a treat—the way
Lennon basks in the song's corniness is half of its pleasure.

T h e s e f i r s t t w o singles have variety and spirit—but not
quite artistry. There's a formal acuity just beneath the enthusiasm that hasn't come into its own yet, even though we
hear it differently in retrospect. Paul's sincere ballad will
become standard, as will John's wordplay, lust, and self-
mockery. But with just these four songs, their opposing
tendencies are not as clear as they soon will be. The most
imposing thing about these relatively simple songs is how
quickly they are improved upon, how adventurous they are
not in comparison with most of the first album. The most
pretentious thing about them is that they are all originals—
which is brasher than any other debut group dared to be in
1962. It meant they were staking claims to be as audacious as
the rock 'n' roll heroes that had inspired them.

PLEASE PLEASE ME *Released: March 22, 1963*

Where "Love Me Do" still sounds somewhat imitative, *Please
Please Me,* the debut album they recorded in twelve hours, is
something more than innovative. It mixes the youthful spirit
of the best rock 'n' roll that came before with the promise of
the greatness that would follow: from the romantic lyricism
to the uncompromising rockers, the infectious early Beatles

sound is captured as the raw, determined ebullience it must have felt like at the Cavern. Even the cover photo is dashing: four deliriously happy youths stand peering from the balcony of "what seems to be a block of Council flats," writes Philip Norman—it was actually EMI headquarters in London. "No one seen in the Top Twenty since Tommy Steele had made so overt a declaration of being working class," Norman writes in *Shout!* More important, though, was their long hair: despite their suits, they greeted their audience—musically and visually—on their own terms.

The local legend still stands: to experience the Beatles live, you had to hear them inside the sweaty Cavern—there was simply nothing else like it. Martin's original idea was to record them onstage at the basement club to capture the group's sound as it was familiar to audiences there. This "concept"—capturing a live set—gives the record as much of a structure to work with as the mythical Lonely Hearts Club Band does for *Sgt. Pepper*: the record grows in spirits from Paul's jocular opening to the encore of "Twist and Shout." The microphones capture every stray note, every out-of-tune harmony, and the Beatles make these flaws work for them: they're intent on *saying* something, determined to have fun in the process; and studio polish would not only get in the way—it would waste precious time. *Please Please Me* remains the quintessential garage band record. They're the kind of musicians that are perfectly suited to their medium: the camaraderie in their casual approach excludes no one within earshot. And the frayed technical edges give the sound the willfulness of adolescence. The listener is effortlessly drawn into the unspoken bond of imperfection.

THE JOURNEY BEGINS with McCartney's celebrated count-off—"One, two, three, faw!"—and the anticipation in his voice instantly signals that something big is about to happen. There is a simple, almost unconscious naiveté to his gusto, but it has become a classic call to rock, and it continues to resonate in the ripples of the history it helped to shape. Aside from the palpable thrill in his voice, the count-off shows just how important the beat is to everything that follows.

"I Saw Her Standing There" is as openly expectant as any seventeen-year-old might look on a dance floor. Paul's voice is assured, and the steady beat and pulsing handclaps strut out an impetuous cockiness known only to the young. The pauses that break up the playfully suggestive lines intensify the things that are left unsaid—the gaps in "Well she was just . . . seventeen / you know . . . what I mean" punctuate the implications. The conclusion fills in the blanks: "So how could I dance with another . . . OH! When I saw her standing there." The exclamatory "Oh!," which attempts to verbalize the unsung anticipation, is reinforced by a musical exclamation, a flatted-six chord; the pent-up energy the pauses have been pointing toward are suddenly unleashed at the same time that the fresh harmony takes the standard blues changes to new heights. The combined effect transforms the implied innocence into sexual bravado.

The second verse propels the singer into a too-cute-for-comfort lyric, as though he's seduced by both the girl and the music they're dancing to: "Well she looked at me/and I—I could see/that before too long I'd fall in love with her . . ." The bridge lets the gush roll: "Well my heart went boom/When I crossed that room/And I held her hand in miiiii-eeene!" The energy in this passage finds such ecstatic release on the word "mine" that the singers can't contain themselves—the leap to falsetto is a natural outburst of the bridge's momentum. It's not just the girl, it's the whole idea of young love that's contained in that surge of feeling.

For the singer, the world turns on asking this seventeen-year-old to dance and holding her hand. The immediacy of the recording mirrors this immediacy of feeling: the Beatles themselves are seduced by this music; they too believe in its magic as they perform their first great original piece of rock 'n' roll. The exhilaration of the sound betrays their passion for the music and the thrill they feel playing it together—from Ringo's drum fills into each bridge to the euphoric screams that send off the guitar solo, the track reeks of excitement. The song, the performance, and the recording all put across the simple but penetrating rush of adolescent desire. And even the rush is expectant, anticipatory—it's the first track of their first album, side one, song one of their album career.

"LENNON AND MCCARTNEY seem always to have distrusted songs whose deliberate aim was to move people, the slow violin-filled sagas of sentimentality," David Laing writes in *The Sound of Our Time* (pp. 122-23). "Before almost any of their songs moves, it delights," he writes, describing the "creation-elation" element to their sound, "the consciousness of themselves as performers, delighting themselves and us." This principle gives Beatles songs "a dimension which most pop songs lack," he says, and he cites as his prime example "Misery," the cut that follows "I Saw Her Standing There."

"Misery" contradicts its own title: it parodies the type of song it embodies. John hardly sounds sad: and even when he does, in the middle eight bars, the descending piano octaves that echo his melody are too saccharine to believe—they could be aural tears falling like rain. He makes his pitch for pity in the dramatic opening moments of the song, as if on his knees to the audience, pleading—"The world is treating me bad, *misery.*" John sings it with an impish glint in his eye—he doesn't buy it any more than he wants us to, it's just a romp. (If Paul had sung this song, we would be treated to something quite sincere, and John would be holding back guffaws in the background.)

The wink-wink hilarity of the repeated "misery"s at the end draw the joke out even further, as Lennon's simpy groan grows to the mockery of the "la la la"s—Christgau and Piccarella point out the "Little Darlin' " referent—he's sending up the very idea of a song that would call itself "Misery." The paranoiac slant of the line like "Send her back to me/*Cos everyone can see*" shows the sort of self-conscious uneasiness that will show up again in songs like "You Can't Do That" and "I'm a Loser." And the macho overtones of a line like "She'll remember and she'll miss her only one/Lonely one" are typically overconfident: she's supposed to return to him, not the other way around. It's the same aggressive posture that will rear its head in "Run for Your Life." He sings it as a lark, but he can't help spilling his true self in the process.

The differences between Lennon and McCartney emerge quickly on this record: either of them singing the other's songs would completely alter the implication of the words. Paul on the dance floor could be anybody; John invests too much of himself for us to detach who he is from what he's singing about—we can't hear the first-person voice as anyone other than Lennon. Their vocal styles influence the way we hear what they're saying to at least as great an extent as Bob Dylan's delivery qualifies the words he constantly reinterprets. Their voices and personalities complement each other in both obvious and subtle ways. (The intricacy of their blend also accounts for the intensity of the breakup.) For McCartney, "Misery" might have been an exercise in martyrdom, convincing but facile. But by playing the fool Lennon turns this cheeky romp into a depiction of how many teenagers cope with their troubles: by laughing them off. There's already much more to it than that, with Lennon's insecurity and machismo inflecting every turn. And undergirding all this is a slight but unmistakable strain of tenderness, a quality that will pervade even his toughest songs.

THE COVER (nonoriginal) material a group records sets down the way it looks at rock 'n' roll and how it views itself in rock's continuum. The best cover songs expand upon what their original material puts forth and sheds new light on how an artist or a band wants to project itself. Al Green's "Take Me to the River" makes the new wave ontology of the Talking

Heads' second album (*More Songs About Buildings and Food*) sound more rooted. Since the Beatles' debut singles were all originals, their first three cover songs, which follow "Misery" ("Anna," "Chains," and "Boys"), refer to both the heroes and the history they aspire to be a part of as songwriters and pop stars. On this album, only "A Taste of Honey" would have been recognizable to anyone who didn't follow the charts. All these songs were independent-label top twenty hits in America, but only Dixon and Farrell's "Boys" was a number one, in 1960, and then only as the B side to the Shirelles' "Will You Love Me Tomorrow" (by Goffin and King). The Beatles emphasized hits when they played live, but when it came to choosing songs for their albums, they relied on their gut sense of what songs worked best for their personalities.

Lennon belts out the bridge to Arthur Alexander's "Anna" with a desperate loneliness. Ringo's lanky, off-balance drum pattern frames the song with a lazy, sluggish motion, giving it the resigned tone of a lover who has given up trying, and the flat singing in the background vocals has a roughness that is this record's signature: we meet the Beatles just as they begin to have a sense of professionalism, and they drop their guard without knowing it—the lack of self-consciousness is as expressive as their playing. John's repeated cry of "What am I, what am I supposed to do?!!"—the pitch at the end of the bridge—suits his character perfectly: he can't understand why all these girls leave him, and singing is his only recourse. His acoustic guitar is an intimate presence among the electric guitars that surround it (a texture he will return to later to better effect).

The next two covers introduce George and Ringo: "Chains," a Goffin-King song, opens with Lennon's harp and provides a good stage for three-part harmony, with Harrison on lead and carrying the middle eight bars himself. George's awkward intonation is expressive, but he doesn't measure up to Lennon's and McCartney's performances just before—a shadow that will plague him for the rest of his life. Ringo's vocal debut in "Boys" may be lacking in quality, but it's loaded with personality. The Shirelles' original version is slinky and seductive, but Ringo's disbelief at how he makes his girl feel makes "Boys" sound as though it were written with him in mind. The "bop-bop-shoo-op"s in the background and the whoops for joy all seem to stem from his goofy grin. At one point, Ringo shouts "All right, George!," cajoling him into his guitar solo, passing him the spotlight as casually as if it were a football.

The album moves from celebration ("I Saw Her Standing There") to parody ("Misery") with two originals, followed by three covers: from Lennon's straight ballad delivery of "Anna" to the medium-tempo "Chains," building to the rocker of "Boys." Spotlighting George and Ringo rounds out a complete picture of the band before the record needs turning over, and the impressions their voices create play against one another well—we can imagine these four people working together in a group.

The two original tunes that follow are sturdy enough to stand next to the covers without apology. For songwriters, this kind of assurance is rarely arrived at so soon (if it happens at all)—Lennon is only twenty-two, McCartney just twenty—but by the end of side one they have already established a new standard in rock 'n' roll, in terms of both style and substance. Things would never be the same if only because so much had already changed.

The first of these two, "Ask Me Why" (the B side to the second single), is amorous wordplay. They draw out "you" by echoing the "woo-woo-woo-woo" the same way the harmony lingers on the minor chords before settling back down into the major key that is home at the end of each line. This song takes on a sly inside joke when heard in the context of the album: "I can't conceive . . . of any more . . . MISERY!" evokes the earlier song, and the effect is disarming—it's sung with relish rather than despair, itself an echo of "Misery" 's parodic tone.

"Please Please Me," the second single, closes the side, ignoring the conventional practice of putting the hit up front and fleshing the album out with weaker material.

MCCARTNEY'S PERSONALITY opens side two, nestling the first single squarely in the middle of the album. "Love Me Do" is not a strict solo, but his personality pervades its upbeat approach: his ad-libs see the song out. "P.S. I Love You" places McCartney's own love ballad before his cover, "A Taste of Honey," its youthful earnestness deferring to the established standard.

Lennon breaks the sentimentality on the Bacharach-David-Williams "Baby It's You," skipping up to the second part of the verse with a suave "uh-oh"—the kind of American soul convention so doted on by the Rolling Stones. The low guitar doubled with celeste in this song's solo offers the most period-sounding Muzak on the entire record (the original it's drawn from has an even tackier organ), but it lies awkwardly next to Lennon's soulfully mannered delivery, which reaches a fine pitch at the end of each verse. Both of Lennon's covers on this album are about broken affairs. In "Anna" he reluctantly sets his girlfriend free: in "Baby It's You," the love is unrequited, and he's left behind, trapped by his own convictions. (Shirley Alston, the Shirelles' lead singer, sounds eerily like Yoko Ono on their 1962 hit.)

"Do You Want to Know a Secret" is among the better-crafted early songs, and it's given to George. The hook is in the downward chunk-a-chunk motion of the guitar, echoed in the backup vocals on "doo-wa-doo." But the high point harmonically lies in the middle section ("I've known the secret for a week or two") where it veers off into the subdominant. This simple twist is an early flexing of what will become deft harmonic muscle—their songs often change keys, but it always sounds natural. (The short introduction where George pleads "You'll never know how much I really love you / You'll never know how much I really care" starts off in E minor and passes through G major to prepare for E major, the key of the verse; the bridge is in A major.)

The stop-time opening to "A Taste of Honey" resembles "Do You Want to Know a Secret" and "Misery," but now it's Paul who is singing, and he's absolutely serious. During the bridge, his voice is double-tracked with a reverb that enhances the professionalism of the sound, and his high notes are flawless. The only personal touch to what is essentially a standard reading is the last chord: it ends in major instead of the minor tonality of the rest of the song (a Picardy third).

"There's a Place" places deft songs like "Ask Me Why" and "Do You Want to Know a Secret" into the teeny-bopper context they ultimately deserve. This first-person narrative is about what goes on inside a teenager's head aside from just girls—and it's a much better song than its American cousin, Brian Wilson's "In My Room." In Christgau and Piccarella's discussion, they compare Lennon's song with Wilson's, concluding that Lennon's is more confident:

> Lennon has better places to go but his room, and better ways to get there than Brian Wilson . . . In its avowal of self-sufficiency—of the singer's ability to transcend the isolation he dreads (not to mention time itself) by retreating dreamlike into that part of the Beatle being he calls home—this early song typifies his urge to say a great deal (though not everything) within the conventions of the rock and roll love song. . . .
> (*The Ballad of John and Yoko*, pp. 249–250)

In addition to the lyrical breakthrough, the Lennon-and-McCartney vocal blend doubles the effect of any comparable Beach Boys effort. Although John and Paul can be worlds apart (as this album demonstrates), when they harmonize the common brilliance they achieve is breathtaking. The two share a space of musical effervescence that only they know how to reach for, and they hit it with uncommon grace. If the Beatles had never recorded anything more than this, they would have secured themselves a place in pop history.

Guitars play an upbeat into a harp solo by John, but here the harp cries out like never before. It sits stubbornly on an uneasy note, the kind of pitch it can't rest on for long; and when it does move, its resolution never sounds final. The lead guitar plays the harp line an octave below it but out of sync, the harp always lagging behind rhythmically. The two lines sound both together and askew from each other, and the effect is that of an uneasy, confused teenager.

The song kicks into high gear after the word "blue," when the quirky triplet of "And it's my mind" is punctuated by the drumming, sending the verse to new heights. On the second line of this stanza ("And there's no time"), the words are sung in triplets atop a regular backbeat. The consistently imbalanced patterns (guitar against harp, vocals against the beat) give the song its yearning but uncertain tone.

During the bridge, on the words "Don't you know that it's so?" the voices leap up in unison, and the song reaches its pitch. It's as if the singer is urgent for something—some peace, some relief—but he's not articulate enough to express it yet, so he lets the music say it for him. The spirit of the sound has more expressive currency than the lyrics. The final section repeats "There's a place," with John, Paul, and George in harmony, Ringo filling in the spaces between exhortations, and the harp recalling its opening melody in abbreviated form. Since it's in major and the end fades out, the effect is liberating: the singer achieves some kind of peace for the moment, if only through the charm of the music. But the rhythmic tension of the song suggests an uneasiness below the surface that remains unresolved. The singer knows that pleasant thoughts alone won't sustain him: and even though he has a girl in mind, the song is more about the peace he seeks within himself, not through any outside experience. For now, he has figured out a way to pick himself up out of his slump by reveling in music. No resolution is given to the combatting sentiments—hope versus vexation—but their clash is real, and projected with verve. It put the Beatles in touch with the basic emotional stirrings of teenagers everywhere.

THE ONLY WAY to top this (and other groups might not have even tried) was to play an all-out rocker and blow the roof off the place. Martin's request for a last tune prompted a quick huddle, and they chose "Twist and Shout," a 1962 Isley Brothers hit they used to close with at the Cavern.

> All we did really was to reproduce the Cavern performance in the relative calm of the studio. I say "comparative," because there was one number which always caused a furor in the Cavern—"Twist and Shout." John absolutely screamed it. God alone knows what he did to his larnyx each time he performed it, because he made it sound rather like tearing flesh. That *had* to be right on the first take, because I knew perfectly well that if we had to do it a second time it would never be as good. (Martin, p. 131)

The first and last songs on the album, "I Saw Her Standing There" and "Twist and Shout," are its bookends: both revolve around the idea of falling in love on the dance floor. But where Paul gets the dance floor jumping, Lennon makes the earth move. It's as raunchy as anything the Beatles ever recorded, and it stands up beautifully to records with raunchier reputations (like the Stones' "Satisfaction"). Where the opening tune suggests an adolescent sexuality, "Twist and Shout" conveys a loss of innocence; where Paul's singing is charged but charming, Lennon's delivery is nothing short of lustful.

Throughout rock, and throughout the history of music—from Bach's French Suites to Ravel's *La Valse*—the image of the dance in music has been linked to the act of sex. In "I Saw Her Standing There," it is not fully played out, but here it is, either as a metaphor for or as a prelude to lovemaking, and it puts across what Lennon would later talk of as the meaning behind all of rock 'n' roll:

> I know Fats Domino was makin' records in '48, and there was lots of stuff called rhythm 'n' blues you could've called rock 'n' roll, but it was hard to get in England. Rock 'n' roll only came into our consciousness when white people did it. I think it was a euphemism for fucking—the actual expression meaning being in bed and rocking and rolling. So this bit about "when did rock start?" really means "when did the honkies start noticing it?" i.e., "when did we know it was something strong and powerful and beautiful?" So it doesn't matter when; it's what it did to us that matters—that it changed our lives when we heard it. . . . (*Playboy*, p. 70)

The band sounds warmer by this point—the album is almost finished, they have been playing all day—and the ensemble rocks with a meaningful pulsation. (Since there's no audience in the studio, they push themselves even harder to bring the song to life.) The way Lennon takes the beat and squeezes it, cramming four "come on"s on top of the drum break as if he's just under the wire—too many words and not enough time—gives a physical tug to the music that would draw even the meekest out to the (metaphorical) dance floor. It's the kind of sound that makes rock music the sexiest music of all—it makes you want to *move*.

After two verses, the singers—John with Paul and George in support—back off to play their guitars for a verse, as if resting for the final round. When the voices come back in, the personalities we've heard throughout the record stack up one by one for the rave-up, building the chord with mounting excitement. At the top of the ladder, they spill over the edge with hysterical screams, the musical dam breaks, and before we know it they're into the last verse. It's the musical equivalent of an orgasm, and it counts among the most exciting moments in all their music. The final verse is pure glee—

they're riding a wave: Ringo kicks the "Shake it, shake it, shake it, baby" refrain that Lennon tacks on at the end to give one last rush of adrenaline before the final rave-up to the cutoff. There is a faint "hey!" after the song—and the album—finishes. The day is over, and they've finished on a high, spontaneous burst of energy.

"Twist and Shout" sums up the album like something that needs no encore—there's nothing more to say. Once the record is familiar, the song becomes a kind of center of gravity: all the other songs point toward it; it gives the entire sequence direction. The moment it captures lifts the Beatles' status beyond that of a pop act to that of performers who have something urgently important to say to the world. It's not that they're telling teenagers to dance or have sex: they're simply enjoying life so much that they can't contain themselves—they want the beat to seduce the whole world into having fun. After "Baby It's You" and "Anna," Lennon's feisty delivery ("You know you got me goin' now/Just like you knew you would") has more than one passion driving it along; the concluding celebratory piece isn't naive. As a whole, the record proclaims adolescent experience to be at least as significant as adult experience, with "Twist and Shout" as a redemptive anthem to good times, as though playing together and getting a dance floor hopping were the most rewarding antidote to the angst of being a teenager.

In its hysterical scope, "Twist and Shout" adds to its obvious sexual overtones an unmistakable yen for something more—the insecure yearning of "There's a Place" coupled with the let-it-loose gullibility of "I Saw Her Standing There"; the spiritual hunger that Lennon sets loose is as determined as it is uncontrollable. As a starting point, the album it closes sets an intimidating standard that the Beatles would now have to live up to. As an enactment of rock's implications and the thrills it can achieve, it has few peers.

"I WANNA BE FREE!!!"

From Me to You (John and Paul)/Thank You Girl
(John and Paul) *Released: April 12, 1963*

She Loves You (John and Paul)/I'll Get You
(John and Paul) *Released: August 23, 1963*

WITH THE BEATLES *Released: November 22, 1963*

I Want to Hold Your Hand (John and Paul)/This Boy
(John, Paul, George) *Released: November 29, 1963*

PLEASE PLEASE ME was released in Britain in March 1963
and quickly rose to a thirty-week reign at number one from
May into November. Before their next recording session in
July, they toured as a supporting act with Roy Orbison and
Helen Shapiro, performed on "Top of the Pops," and appeared frequently on Brian Matthews's "Saturday Club" on
BBC radio. By the fall, the British press had latched on to
them as the perfect respite to the Profumo scandals that
rocked Harold Macmillan's cabinet.

Please Please Me was still at the top of the charts in November, the month the Beatles appeared at the Royal Variety
Performance as national heroes—it stepped down to number
two to make way for *With the Beatles* in December. Before
the year was out they got their own radio shows: "Pop Go
the Beatles," and a series of specials, "From Us to You," for
which they reworked their next single as the theme.

There's a proverb in Liverpool that says the only way a person can survive there is to have a sense of humor. The Beatles were essentially the same type of characters that Liverpool's comics are renowned for—unembarrassed skeptics who delighted in puncturing social decorum. One of George Martin's key credentials for Lennon was that he had worked with the flighty comic Peter Sellers, originator of the radio "Goon Show" with Spike Milligan.

But their sense of humor was also protective—the only sane response to the growing adulation their records began provoking. Their success was so swift and encompassing that snappy retorts became a useful dodge to questions like "What are you going to do when the bubble bursts?" (Lennon's answer: "Sit back and count my money.") To them, a political scandal like the Profumo Affair was a good laugh, all but predictable coming from the political duplicity it exposed. In the studio, they were eclectic packrats, assimilating what they digested from their favorite pop records into a fresh sound; in interviews, they were constant pranksters, casually tossing darts of sarcasm at the establishment. Their music was irresistible, but as personalities they were so offhandedly funny that they were hard not to like even when they were being rude to their hosts. "Brian's nose is peeling, folks," John blurted out as BBC's Brian Matthews was introducing him.

From Me to You (John and Paul)/Thank You Girl
(John and Paul) *Released: April 12, 1963*

NONSENSE WORDS IN pop are often filler for something that needs fleshing out, but with the Beatles these devices are rarely gratuitous, even this early on: word snippets and trivial asides are played up, the smallest details bring life to the whole. The "Da-da-da, da-da-dun-dun, dah" at the top of "From Me to You" is a melodic teaser, sung rather than played on guitar to voice the nameless feelings that live inside every teenager. It draws the listener in even before words are sung,

tripping Ringo's brief tom-tom fill into the final seconds before the verse. By bookending the song with the same melodic
tease played on harmonica and guitar, they show just how
much care each moment is given—every advantage is taken
to make one minute and forty-nine seconds swell with life.
"From Me to You" amounts to a formal arrival: the high
spirits in Lennon and McCartney's voices are suddenly translated into song. (It was written during their tour with Helen
Shapiro in February 1963, and it spent six weeks at number
one alongside the album it didn't even appear on.)

John and Paul's vocal duo gives everything else contour.
The joyous leap from unison to harmony in the second line
("If there's anything *I can do*") points to a larger sense of
control: they know just where a harmony is needed and just
where it would clutter an otherwise unfettered melody. The
verse lines combine unison and harmony ("If there's anything
that you want") and alternate in the bridge ("I've got arms
_____ that long _____ to hold you" sung in unison, "*and
keep you by my side*" harmonized). When they inflect the end
of the bridge with a new color (augmenting the chord on
"satis*fied*"), it propels the falsetto "ooh!" and Ringo's pert fill
naturally—the ad-libs are written right into the transition.
At the end of the second bridge, George adds triplet guitar
chords behind the same phrase—in those fleeting moments,
the sound is even more rapturous than the high "you"s at the
end of "Please Please Me." (Their ad-libbed screams spring
from the same musical instinct: there are times when their
whoops seem so perfectly timed, so *right*, that it's hard to
imagine the song without them.) The tight writing unleashes
energy rather than strapping it in.

"Thank You Girl" also varies the unison and harmony
singing, and reverses the verse-bridge verbal games of "From
Me to You": on the A side, the bridge holds out words, romanticizing the promises of the verses ("I've got arms _____
that long _____ to hold you"). On the B side, the bridge
irons out the lyricism of the verses into stepwise motion

(Thank _____ you _____ girl _____ for _____ lo_____-
ving _____ me _____ . . .”). The verse places held notes (“I
_____ could tell the world _____ a thing or two _____
about our love”) on top of alternating chords, which makes
the shift to vocal duet on the following line that much more
appealing. The intricacy of the harmony on the words “And
_____ eternally _____ I’ll always be _____ in love with
you” grows out of the unison line that precedes it, stemming
from it and taking it further—Paul’s upper harmony is already implicit in the line it follows. This alternation is compressed in the refrain: “And all I’ve gotta” in unison is
punctuated by “do” in perfect harmony, answered by the title
line, “Thank you girl,” first in unison, then repeated in harmony. The vocal ingenuity is bolstered by the harp and tom-
tom intro (repeated in the middle) and Ringo’s start-and-stop
snare fills at the end of each refrain.

It’s a dashing setting to such a wide-eyed lyric, and like
“From Me to You,” what its words lack is made up for musically. The small silences that punctuate “Love Me Do” and
“Ask Me Why” are fleshed out with new tricks—the way John
and Paul’s duets dynamize already sturdy melodies, the way
verses and bridges work off one another. Their spontaneous
playing surrounds this formal leap as though it’s all coming
to them off the cuff. Even though the ending is arranged—
returning to the three “oh”s from the intro—Ringo injects
more excitement with each successive drum flurry.

Given the constraints of the pop format—three or four
chords at most, no song yet over three minutes long—the invention that begins creeping into these early singles is remarkable. By varying every element at their disposal, from
the vocal arrangements to the drum breaks that charge up
endings, they cram worlds of inventiveness into simple vessels
of pop songs. The inventiveness goes hand in hand with their
unabashed love for pop’s confections; what they savored in
their favorite pop records, they used in new ways—the play-

ful nonsense words, like the "a-tack a-tack a-tack" that Chuck Berry sets loose in "Almost Grown"; the breathtaking high "ooh"s; the thrill of a simple but sturdy hook. The simplicity of "From Me to You" and "Thank You Girl" floats above a richness of nuance that makes every instant count.

BY THE SUMMER of 1963, the Beatles were national celebrities, and anxious to move on from the everyday life that was Liverpool. Their ambition, after all, was in part a reaction to the provincial self-image they had grown up with there, and a desire to shake free from it like Elvis did. But if the Beatles were to be bigger than Elvis, they would soon have to face the dilemma of wider popularity: by reaching for a larger audience, they risked losing the close give-and-take they shared with the Cavern crowd and local fans who had made them successful in the first place. After George let it slip that he liked "jelly babies" (jelly beans) during a radio interview, they were affectionately pelted with them everywhere they played. Birthday presents began pouring in, and the mail to their Liverpool fan club was already expanding beyond what could be handled locally. This groundswell of adoration would gain a momentum of its own—first Britain, then Europe, then America—until the Beatles became captives of their own popularity, forced to isolate themselves from their audience. But with their records monopolizing the number one spot, a responsibility to their growing audience crept in, and the even greater success that loomed was too enticing for them to remain at home. Before the choice was made for them with "She Loves You," they moved to London, eager for the acceptance that all of England—and eventually the world—seemed to be offering them.

She Loves You (John and Paul)/I'll Get You (John and Paul)/*Released: August 23, 1963*

O F A L L T H E early singles, no other combines their mastery
of pop styling with the rapture it incited from their audience—Beatlemania—as manically as "She Loves You." Everything here can be traced to earlier material (the beat, the
hooks, the formal ingenuity), but nothing that came before
hints at this kind of power. The brazen performance is coupled with the originality of the narrative twist: the singer still
sings in the first person, but he's singing about someone else's
love affair—a friend stepping in to carry a message and give
advice. The lyric no longer relies on the music.

The recording has become a symbol: historians dote on
it as the hallmark of an era obsessed with youth—"Yeah,
yeah, yeah" are the nonsense words the Beatles immortalized,
"a truth known only to young gods and the biggest giggle in
the world simultaneously," write Christgau and Piccarella.
Dave Marsh goes so far as to say that "She Loves You" was
"as good as it got because it was as good as it *needed* to get."
Part of its magic is its status as a single: it exists outside the
context of an album, surrounded by other songs. At two minutes and eighteen seconds, it packs twice the number of ideas
in even less space than usual, and blasts the future of rock
wide open. The original version is such a riveting performance that succeeding generations of rockers pay it the highest
praise by simply leaving it alone—"She Loves You" is among
the least covered Beatles songs, as much out of respect as awe.
(John refers back to it in the fade-out to "All You Need is
Love" and at the ends of verses on *Abbey Road*'s "Polythene
Pam.")

As the Beatles gain more assurance with song forms, they
begin toying with different ways of grabbing a listener's attention; their introductions become less a setting up of what
will follow than a physical yank into what's already happening. Ringo's tom-tom fill that is "She Loves You" 's first sound

doesn't establish the beat so much as it tumbles down into it—there isn't a firm downbeat until the final "yeah" at the end of the fall, and the effect is like jumping onto a moving train. The song itself is about an interrupted love affair; the singer is bringing his friend the hope of reconciliation as if he can't contain himself any longer. The Beatles embrace their listeners in the same rush of anticipation that the unsuspecting lover feels when he hears his friend's breathless encouragement.

The opening is a truncated version of the refrain, and it too is less an introduction than an unprepared exclamation. The drums alternate between the low tom-toms and the accented snare, making the vocal cries the center of attention. The harmonies unfold step by step until the final (tonic) landing point, where the added sixth (Harrison's idea) makes the tonearm quiver. On this last "yeah," Ringo turns out to his loosely closed high-hat, letting the cymbals ring against each other more than usual, and George sneaks in a salty little guitar lick beneath the vocals, riding out the pleasure that's released to the breaking point. When the first verse begins, it's like a whole new world opening—the music defines ecstasy.

The verse melody climbs right up the scale ("You think you've lost your love"), unwinds from unison into harmony ("Well I saw her"), and closes with the playful bounce John and Paul take on the words "yesterday-ee-ay," and "say-ee-ay." Everything points toward the hook—the good news—of "She loves you," which is kicked with a syncopated stroke from the whole band before they finish singing the word "you." The lead guitar anticipates the "yeah, yeah, yeah" of the refrain after the line "and you know that can't be bad"; and the half-diminished chord on the following line ("She loves you . . . and you know you should be glad") gleans both fear and pleasure: there is some anxiety at the prospect of getting back together. The second and third time this passage is sung, however, they add a disarmingly quick high "ooh" to

set up the refrain as intimidation gives way to expectancy.
Saving the refrain until after the second verse, they increase
the anticipation for it—the ear wants to hear it again. When
it finally rolls around, everything plummets straight into it.

With the words "She loves you, yeah, yeah, yeah" the
opening texture returns: Ringo heads for his tom-toms and
kicks the third "yeah" with delayed triplet raps on his snare,
pulling the motion back just where it wants to leap forward.
At the end of the fall, the concluding "with a <u>love</u> <u>like</u> <u>that</u>"
emphasizes the momentum that has built up by stripping it
down, leaving an irresistibly small silence in the middle of all
the hoopla (just after "<u>love</u> <u>like</u> <u>that</u>"). The musical gesture is
as sharp as it is persuasive—the singer is winning his friend
over with sheer enthusiasm.

The third verse sneaks lyrics of subtle wisdom into the
scenario, breaking from standard pop clichés:

> *You know it's up to you. I think it's only fair*
> Pride can hurt you too, *so apologize to her*
> *Because she loves you!*

It's the kind of advice only a very good friend can offer, and
even though the singer may desire this woman as much as his
friend does, his words aren't as jealous as they are sympathetic. (This love triangle may have been inspired by Lennon,
but it's not as rash as "I'll Get You" or "You Can't Do That.")
The refrain after this verse has a pause after the words "you
know you should . . ."—the harmonies are drawn out, giving
some relief from the track's wired feel as well as supplying a
dramatic pause from which to spring. They linger on those
words so teasingly that the final refrain virtually erupts from
its coyness (". . . be glad!"). The "yeah, yeah, yeah"s take
the ending home as the vocals outlast the final guitar chord,
still shimmering on that added sixth.

A song that penetrates with this much punch isn't luck,

it's a gift. Intelligent listeners like Bob Dylan (recalling the early Beatles in 1971) heard this at the time:

> We were driving through Colorado [and] we had the radio on and eight of the Top Ten songs were Beatles songs. In Colorado! "I Want to Hold Your Hand," all those early ones.
>
> They were doing things nobody was doing. Their chords were outrageous, just outrageous, and their harmonies made it all valid. . . . But I kept it to myself that I really dug them. Everybody else thought they were for the teenyboppers, that they were gonna pass right away. But it was obvious to me that they had staying power. I knew they were pointing the direction where music had to go . . . in my head, the Beatles were *it*. In Colorado, I started thinking but it was so far out I couldn't deal with it—eight in the Top Ten.
>
> It seemed to me a definite line was being drawn. This was something that never happened before. (in Anthony Scaduto, *Bob Dylan*, pp. 203–4)

"She Loves You" entered Britain's consciousness that summer of 1963 like no pop song ever had, and set Beatlemania ablaze. In America, it didn't enjoy success until after "I Want to Hold Your Hand" broke through in early 1964. But with this kind of euphoria bursting forth from the radio each day, it's no wonder a generation was turned on. "She Loves You" transforms the Beatles from upstart pop enthusiasts to pop sensations in their own right.

THE GENTLE SWAY of melody that swings the verse of "I'll Get You" (the B side of "She Loves You") is broken by the determined refrain, a simple repetition of the title. But the sound is vigorously innocent, and along with "Thank You Girl" "I'll Get You" counts among the best neglected songs the Beatles ever recorded. Astride the meteoric potency of "She Loves You," it compromises none of its aggressiveness to achieve a real sweetness; its lure is gently seductive ("Imagine

I'm in love with you"), and pressing only when the singers' passion overtakes them on the swelling line "It's not like me to pretend/But I'll get you, I'll get you in the end." Innocence is overcome by desire. The "oh yeah"s of the introduction give way to the deliberate stutter of "many, manymanytimes before" (the "ore" becoming "oh" to rhyme with "know") and "never, nevernevernever blue." The all too predictable bridge breaks into harmony:

> *Well there's gon-na be a time*
> *When I'm gonna change your mind*
> *So you might as well resign yourself to me, oh yeah. . . .*

They take such pride in finding the word "resign," that they can be forgiven the mistakenly sung words, the simplistic attitude, and the repeated first verse. The beautiful truth that lies in the harmonic blend of their voices says that they believe in what they're singing ("oh yeah")—and since the song is not really a threat but a self–pep talk, that's all that really matters.

WITH THE BEATLES *Released: November 22, 1963*

The Beatles' second album starts out like the first, only with more sparks flying. Greil Marcus describes its American counterpart, *Meet the Beatles*, as "joyous, threatening, absurd, arrogant, determined, innocent and tough" to which "It Won't Be Long" alone adds bad puns, razor wit, and a recklessly taut form. It immediately enriches the simple romance of *Please Please Me:* "It Won't Be Long" is about urgency in a relationship—the urgency to begin again something that has been interrupted, to be reunited after a separation.

By beginning with four originals from three different writers, *With the Beatles* secures their stance as songwriters. Backed with the cover-original alternating layout of side two, it dramatizes how they begin to outdo their models, as well as claim new musical territory. Because their creativity is so abundant, the sound of them doing Chuck Berry's "Roll Over Beethoven" next to Paul's "Hold Me Tight" affects the way we hear both: they're showing where their approach came from as it develops. There's as much irony in "All I've Got to Do" 's angst-filled pledges and "All My Loving" 's goodbye smile as there is in the way "Till There Was You" sits next to "Please Mr. Postman," or the way John's aggressive reading of Smokey Robinson's "You've Really Got a Hold on Me" is followed by Ringo's inimitable nonchalance in "I Wanna Be Your Man." Moods and ideas ring out in magnetic opposition, strengthening both the band and the album.

LIKE *PLEASE PLEASE ME*, the record uses an original and a raucous cover as bookends as it takes things to a higher level—Lennon's "It Won't Be Long" portends more than falling in love on the dance floor, and it makes that announcement grandly with the ingenious way the beat lassos the listener into the vocal arrangement. A pun is worked out along the way: "It won't *be long*" becomes "till I *belong* to you" as the refrain heads for the verse. There isn't another upbeat original here that delivers the same expectant thrill: Paul's "Hold Me Tight" has an steady charge but not the same authority, even including its refrain's own antiphonal buildup. "It Won't Be Long" outdoes "I Saw Her Standing There" formally without sacrificing any of the earlier song's impulsiveness, and it whets the appetite for something bigger than garage-band ambition. Until they reach the two covers that close side one ("Till There Was You" and "Please Mr. Postman"), the new stature is manifest in original terms.

Lennon barks out the record's opening words alone, and the background vocals leap in immediately, tossing "yeah"s back and forth with his lead. The "yeah"s are less exuberant than they are in "She Loves You"—they're pent up and anxious—and the antiphony conveys the distance between lovers as well as the tug between frustration and satisfaction that the singer feels within. The opening sequence is also the refrain, which sandwiches a major response in between two minor outcries and moves to the major verse on the concluding line with a major chord ("till *I*") that passes through minor ("be*long* to you"). The refrain's cries find comfort in the verses, which move from self-pity ("sitting all on my own") to the happiness of what lies ahead ("Every day we'll be happy I know").

During the final refrain, Paul jumps up in the middle of his background singing for a final charged "yeah" (the fifth of seven), filling up the expectancy with a whoop of unleashed delight. To close, the band actually slows things down, tacking on a stop-time break for Lennon's lead (on the last "till I belong . . . to you") before spreading into a vocal harmony on the last word. But the melodramatic ritard can't summarize the drama compacted in the refrain's combatting emotions, where hope rallies with anxiety.

"It Won't Be Long" is confidently overdesirous ("Now I know that you won't leave me no more"). In "All I've Got to Do" it's as if by declaring his devotion Lennon wants to plow under any hint of insecurity by just singing. The beat moves from quick to medium tempo, from the sturdy promise of love to the jerky, accented angst of love itself. His brooding intensity gives him away: he doesn't sound confident, as his lyrics would have us believe—he sounds positively scared.

Paul's harmony that joins John's lead on the title phrase has an eerie quality, the kind of self-consciousness that teenagers live with from day to day. John plays with the phraseology in this song the way he plays verbal games in others, running consonant-laden words together to answer lines with their own phonetical inverse:

when I _____ *I wanna kiss you yeah*
All I gotta do _____

Ringo's jerky drum patterns and the tart high-hat accents that fill up the dead spaces after verses make everything sound jittery. As the sound swells into the bridge ("And the same goes for *me*"), Lennon gains on his fear and suppresses it with the concluding lines, sung in block harmony ("You just gotta call on me"), which he repeats as if to convince himself. But when he sings about wanting to kiss this woman in the second verse, he's got next to no nerve about it.

The track's most remarkable moment comes during the second bridge, when Lennon plays with the lead vocal line on the words "I'll be there, yes I will." He comes unhinged on the first word, skidding all over the beat before landing back in the groove in the nick of time. It's a compressed musical symbol of what the song is about: regaining a suave demeanor as his innards fall apart. His performance of that one line, that one *word*, combined with the cool held notes of the verse, makes the song something much more than it would be in the hands of a lesser singer. His uncanny rhythmic delivery is rife with layered emotions.

One of Lennon's chief strengths as a writer is in expressing this uneasy balance of sentiments. Like "Any Time at All," the range of feelings "All I've Got to Do" turns over is extraordinarily controlled, even though it expresses the most complex self-doubt: the threat of rejection is coupled with the fear of gaining a love he doesn't feel worthy of, of wanting an intimacy he might not let himself enjoy. It has such an idiomatic tinge to it, it is so wholly Lennon, that it is among the least covered songs in their repertoire.

L ISTENING TO THE IRONY of "All My Loving" with the perspective of Paul's later solo work suggests he wasn't in control of the clash between the rollicking music and the fare-thee-well lyrics—it works better as a happy goodbye song than a cheery denial of reality, the kind of pep talk John gives himself in "There's a Place" and the bridge to "No Reply." Above a confidently walking bass, a constantly ringing guitar defines the texture, and the band rolls along with such daft happiness it helps Paul sound less and less upset about the impending separation. The minor refrain, where Paul sings "Darling, I'll be true," sounds more devotional than resigned, and the silences that follow each verse are packed with delight, not sorrow. Even George's guitar solo greets Paul's loss unaffectedly. As Lennon chimes in for the harmony on the last verse, the sound actually gets happier, more at ease. Paul doesn't deny the pain so much as win over his lover—and his audience—with a beaming resolve.

"All My Loving" follows "All I've Got to Do" in a revealing way: John is suffering behind a contented mask; Paul is rallying toward a happy attitude even though he's saying goodbye to his true love. Lennon can sound whiny, whereas McCartney seldom stoops to self-pity. The first three songs on this side begin with voice alone, and the same approach works differently for each lead singer. Lennon's two numbers project an emotional urgency; he's not just alone, he's self-ensnarled, unable to escape from himself. Paul sounds liberated, free not just from heartache but from insecurity of any kind. In toying with the same possibilities, they wind up sounding even more different than if they had stuck to their own idiosyncrasies.

WOULD WE APPRECIATE George Harrison's songs if they weren't featured on Beatles records? "Taxman" has a place all its own as the entrance to the world of *Revolver,* and even "Within You Without You" is a harmless way to get side two of *Sgt. Pepper* going—it's the perfect foil for the camp of "When I'm Sixty-four," which follows. But "Don't Bother Me" is a weak songwriting debut, especially since George sounds so much better on something Lennon would write for him on the next album ("I'm Happy Just to Dance with You").

George has been taking in what Lennon and McCartney have been pouring out: "Don't Bother Me" has a variety of texture; good use is made of the stop-time breaks before each verse; and there is a brooding, almost malevolent quality in the singing that suits the lyric (the modal harmonic design sets dorian verses off an aeolian bridge). He sounds like the perennial misunderstood teenager, his voiced pinched in desperation ("Because I *know* she'll always be . . .") without being compelling; and his guitar solo just sits there—it's dry, nearly lifeless. In between two such good dance numbers it can hardly miss as a good beat song; no one will leave the dance floor just because the tune fails critically. It actually shows off the life of this ensemble that they find a groove in this tune despite its flaws. As always, they play with an uncanny sense of rhythmic timing, its tensions and releases; and George winds up being carried by the others.

LENNON'S HARP breaks open the last original on this side with complete abandon: the pleasure comes as much from the harp itself as from the Lennon personality it projects. "Little Child" is happy blues, with a slightly altered bridge, and the first throwaway dance number here. The vocal harmonies ("I'm so sad and *lonely*") bring out the kitsch in Lennon, who does it all with his unmistakable glint—the slide on "lonely" sounds like something Paul thought up, and they sing it with panache. During John's harp solo it sounds as though he and Ringo make eye contact and goad the thrust of the beat together. Lennon becomes more successful at this kind of camp by the next album, where in "Tell Me Why" he combines just the right amount of swing with a more seasoned lyric about jilted deception.

WHERE "ALL I'VE GOT TO DO" walked the fine line between ballad and medium-tempo dance, Paul's cover of Meredith Willson's "Till There Was You" (from the Broadway musical *The Music Man)* is the first out-and-out ballad here. Among the many standard vehicles Paul sang in Hamburg and on their radio appearances (Roy Orbison's "Dream

Baby," "The Honeymoon Song" from the 1959 film *Honeymoon*, and other cream-puff titles), "Till There Was You" may have been chosen above the others because of the flamenco-style guitar solo George worked up for it. Otherwise, it follows Peggy Lee's sensuous arrangement but not her breathy delivery. Paul's singing is flawlessly polished; he doesn't set up any challenges and doesn't deliver much more than heart-on-the-sleeve sentimentality. His original efforts in this vein ("And I Love Her") will soon surpass this performance.

Part of the Beatles' broad appeal is due to the way they place this kind of kitsch on an album that ends with the scandalous "Money," the same way "A Taste of Honey" doesn't suggest the sound or fury of "Twist and Shout." It superimposes the larger pop tradition the Beatles embraced on the rock 'n' roll heritage. Because they include this kind of vocal showcase, it makes them sound less at odds with the formal lineage of composers like Richard Rodgers and Cole Porter than many of their contemporaries do. The Rolling Stones would never have recorded such saccharine material—some of their followers even balked at their cover of "Under the Boardwalk." Dylan's sentimental side, when successful, is usually ironic or verbose. That the Beatles see songs like "Bésame Mucho" and "That's All Right (Mama)" as feeding the same musical currents points up their eclecticism; that they perform "Till There Was You" as lovingly as "Please Mr. Postman," which follows, makes that pop vision credible.

THE FIRST THREE songs on this side open with solo vocal pleadings; "Please Mr. Postman" reverses the same trick—the background vocals yell "Wait!" to a crisp high-hat break before Lennon answers. The opening "Wait!"'s are sung as though the Beatles were caught in midair—as in Dezo Hoffman's famous leap photos—not so much in harmony as in desperation. As George and Paul sing the refrain, Lennon dances all around them with rhythmic lyricism ("Pleeeze, pleeeze, Mr. Po-wo-wostman"). By the time he arrives at the first verse the track isn't just warmed up; it's almost boiling over. The beat is tremendous, pounding out the flip side of Lennon's pumped-up enthusiasm on "It Won't Be Long": *not* hearing from the woman he's separated from, and dying with lovesick agony when he sees the postman leaving. Christgau and Piccarella write that "when the Beatles outdo their exemplars, John is usually why" (p. 247). The original Marvelettes recording, which Motown's Berry Gordy helped arrange for them, is subdued, almost relaxed in comparison. The Beatles sound delirious, pent up and manic all at the same time; there's no room to breathe in this sound—it's an aural equivalent of what it means to feel strung out. In the second refrain, where Lennon sings along with the backup vocals instead of scatting off of them, it's where he dabbles slightly from the others that he generates the most excitement. The repetitions into the fadeout unloосh him foi two solo breaks; on the second ("Deliver the let-tah, the sooner the bett— you gotta waitaminute!"), he gets too carried away to even finish: the first part of that line is enunciated with tickling fancy, the ending is madly out of breath. Like all great rock 'n' roll, it sounds perilously close to falling apart at any minute. This is the most reckless and completely irresistible playing yet on the record, and the most flammable rock 'n' roll they've given us since "She Loves You."

SIDE TWO ALTERNATES covers with original material, unlike the slew of originals that opened side one, and the common ardor poured into every track makes it swing from heartfelt indebtedness to informed originality. Like their "Please Mr. Postman," each performance of somebody else's song competes with the freshness of their own, and it all sounds as though it springs from the same bottomless well of inspiration.

. . .

GEORGE'S STRENGTH early on lies in his simple honesty with his audience; he never tries to hide his utter willfulness; his competence is outstripped by his earnestness. The opening guitar lick to "Roll Over Beethoven" is the standard set of figurations used to open this tune by countless bands, but George sounds thoroughly rehearsed—he's comparing himself with others, even though his listeners may not be. It's not until the band enters that he settles back into the groove and lets it work for him. This sense of camaraderie can be heard in his singing: he's not trying to sound like Chuck Berry as much as he is intent on just getting the words out. Since the text is a fast-moving string of one-liners that roll easily off his tongue, he does fine. Chuck Berry's rock 'n' roll imagery perfectly suits George—we can just picture him writing a letter to his local deejay. His kid-brother act explains the misunderstood tone of "Don't Bother Me."

Musically, the track detonates. The motion settles down to a cool rumble in the middle section ("Well if you're feeling like it . . .") and opens up again for the guitar solo, which George delivers with the utmost humility. He knows how to tickle the meter: when he hits a rhythmic pattern and repeats it over the bar, he understands exactly what Berry had in mind—the guitar mocking the rest of the band, defying the gravity of the backbeat. Even where he apes Berry's fluidity more than masters it, his deadpan determination is simply glorious.

The final line ("Dig to these rhythm and blues") is sung with the same out-of-tune good intentions, and the final guitar chord that's patched on at the end doesn't sound as unnatural as it somehow should (it's obviously been added after the original live take). The timing of this final chord is perfect, and the ring of that last stroke is like makeup for the rest of the song's inaccuracies. It's not exactly cheating, but it doesn't make full use of the pitch the band has built to by the end, either.

For all of George's matter-of-factness, the Beatles' version of "Roll Over Beethoven" has strong undercurrents: it's a significant statement about how this music transformed—and continues to transform—people's lives. The simple fact that ordinary English youths were driven to play this style raised its stature with its home audience. Lennon might have turned Berry's good-humored elitist snub into a rebellious jab at musical snobbery, but George's simple determination makes their love for rock 'n' roll something different, something more appealing: it pronounces how accessible this music was to youth like George, who had no musical training; that this music is as important to its audience as any other form is to any other audience. Recording songs like "Roll Over Beethoven" makes the idea of rock 'n' roll—the community of youth and the joyous commercialism it exonorates—a living presence on Beatle records.

Like "She Loves You" and "I Want to Hold Your Hand," McCartney's "Hold Me Tight" uses the tag end of a later portion of the song as its introduction, throwing the ear as to what harmony is actually solid ground. The confusion sorts itself out by the middle of the verse, and succeeding listenings reorient the listener to the trick—it's another sly entrance into what could have been just another midtempo rocker. The variation in what would otherwise be the basic Paul treatment is in the way the backup harmonies precede the solo voice instead of the other way around (as in "From Me to You"). Paul sings it straight; he doesn't try to redeem the standard formula of the song with any ad-libs (like he does at the top of the third verse to "I Saw Her Standing There"). The performance is a clean and polished rocker in the same the way that "Till There Was You" is a clean and polished ballad, and although the slow-to-stop ending sets up the next song's medium tempo, it doesn't do justice to the witty opening.

. . .

SMOKEY ROBINSON SINGS his "You've Really Got a Hold on Me" with a light touch—the beat swings gently—and gives way to feeling most when he steps outside his sweet vulnerability to vary the melody (the way he sings "Baaaaby! Baby!" on the second refrain). The outbursts gain immediacy from the controlling context. The Beatles tart it up by having Ringo's bass drum drag the conviviality of the vocals—where the Miracles sound elegant, Lennon sounds ruthless. He takes the song's tug personally, finding bitterness, frustration, and resentment alongside its warmth, repentance, and longing. You can hear it in the way the "hold me"s are linked by Lennon's irrepressible "please" and "squeeze" responses, or the way he makes each successive "tighter" more urgent, compressing greater feeling into each repeat before dropping back down for the verses. The politesse it took for a black man to make this hunger for love acceptable gets drowned in Lennonesque revenge.

''I WANNA BE YOUR MAN'' was written for the Rolling Stones (*Ready, Steady, Go*)—John and Paul whipped it off in a brief studio huddle that floored Mick Jagger and Keith Richards (and inspired them to write more songs of their own)—but Ringo brings such a personal touch that it sounds as if it could have been written with him in mind. Its chief hook is the way the harmonies tilt downward on the last "I wanna be your *man.*" The harmonic progression has been tilting downwards all along, and this quick final vocal tilt buffers the drift of the whole refrain. When set against the drumbeat, pounding out the raw rhythm after the guitars have dropped out, it has a sneering yank to it. The screams of delight that send it home during the fadeout approach the euphoria of "Postman" but don't quite make the leap into hysteria.

THE TOM-TOM INTRO at the start of "Devil in Her Heart" is quicker than the one into "You've Really Got a Hold on Me," and George throws himself into his "No, no, no"s, but this cover of the Donays' 1962 original doesn't have the intensity of John's bow to Smokey Robinson. The arrangement casts George arguing with the background vocalists—they sing the title line with such clipped enunciation, it's like they're scolding him. Harrison gets the last word ("No, she's an angel sent to me") but loses the debate.

LIKE "ANY TIME AT ALL," Lennon's "Not a Second Time" is at odds with its own setting. His decisive lecture is resolute, but his singing is confused and hurt. He has trouble just getting started: piano and guitar vamp between major and minor chords, before the line "I see no use in wondering whyyyyyIiii criiiiiied, for yoouuuu." It's one of the longest melismas—traveling held vowel passages—Lennon ever wrote for himself, and it hovers over several emotions. The uneasy balance between trepidation and determination is sung desperately, making the wish for reconciliation implicit in the overstatement of the refusal:

> You're giving me the same old line
> I'm wondering why
> You hurt me then,
> You're back again,
> No, no, no, not a second time.

The piano solo recalls the Muzak of "Baby It's You" from the first album, dating the sound, and it couldn't be more out of place: it's balming where it should sting, complacent when it should be resentful. This song doesn't achieve the emotional urgency of "If I Fell," which extends similar emotions in a love triangle. In that song, the singer is both soft and vengeful, ready to fall in love again if only to get back at the woman who has jilted him. Here, Lennon's desire can't sneak through his defenses.

.   .   .

IT'S NO ACCIDENT that the cover songs Lennon chooses to sing on this record are about heartache, conflicted desire, frustration at forces beyond his control, and finally, freedom. His own songs are about resentment, double-crossings, and uneasy assurances cast in more personal terms, instead of the universality Paul often attains. Lennon can never mask his true nature, whether it comes out in his singing or in his playing, and the choice of "Money" to close the album lets him cut loose in the way he still knows best: in a rock 'n' roll song that first revealed its possibilities to him. It doesn't matter that the piano intro seems tame by today's standards—at the end the mix is so gloriously cluttered and full of motion that "Money" overshadows every other cover song they ever recorded. He takes an already great song and makes it greater, personalizes its social implications by turning a defiant howl from within into an outrageous public act.

The tension between the sell-out message of the text and the never-say-die tenacity of the performance gives the track its sarcastic tinge and makes "Twist and Shout" sound relatively meek. The Barrett Strong original isn't nearly as suggestive—and coming from a black man, not half as ironic. The spiritual-material tug-of-war here is right out in the open: there is much more to life than the quest for money, Lennon's spirited chicanery tells us, and to miss that point is to miss what all the fuss over rock 'n' roll is about. The artistry at work is in the way he makes these cynical words sound hopeful, his vulnerability sound powerful. The most important thing he learned from his hero Elvis Presley was the value of individuality at all costs, as Marsh would say, without essential compromise. "Twist and Shout" challenged adults to let Lennon go out with their daughter; "Money" pits Lennon's rage at what he sees as the gap between conventional platitudes and what life *really* has to offer. It's the first political statement he ever makes: if "Twist and Shout" was the musical equivalent of an orgasm, "Money" is the rock 'n' roll equivalent of giving society the finger.

When Lennon cuts loose during one of the final choruses and screams "Whoa! yeah, I wanna be free!!!" he sings it with such intensity that it's as much a demand as it is a threat. It's one of the broadest declamations ever made by a rock 'n' roller, as unmistakably final as Elvis singing "Blue Suede Shoes" or even "Hound Dog." Lennon's presence embodies all the virtues of great rock 'n' roll as he testifies that its strengths—hilarity, self-determination, celebration in the face of despair, the courage to rise above conventional standards—can alter forever the way a person looks at life, as well as lives it out. He does more than take this music seriously; he lives inside of it, accepts its terms completely.

The Beatles can sound spanking clean compared to the animal in Elvis, the greasy-haired earthiness of Chuck Berry, and especially the outlandish peacockery of Little Richard. But their precision is far from careful, and it gets overridden by the brutality of their attack: they discover an unmistakable power from the sheer strength of their convictions. In *Feel Like Going Home*, Peter Guralnick claims they "never really did anything to see that their influences were recognized," while the Stones "paid their respects from the first" (p. 28). But Lennon and McCartney were not the blues archivists Jagger and Richards were—never wanted to be, never claimed to be. When the Beatles placed original statements like "Not a Second Time" and "All I've Got to Do" next to covers like "Roll Over Beethoven" and "You've Really Got a Hold On Me," they do more than "pay their respects." Their original material affects the personality of their covers the same way their covers inflect their originals. Building upon what they had learned from such heroes, they re-enact their infatuation with rock's past in the present while making airs toward its future. The Beatles took what came before and made it real for an entire culture, not just the cultists. Lennon paid his respects to people like Strong in "Money" by conceiving rock 'n' roll as something more than just a career, a way of making money, which is how Elvis wound up conceiving it. For the

Beatles—and through them, their audience—rock 'n' roll became a way of confronting the world.

That's why this album reveals so much more about Lennon than about McCartney: of the eight originals, four are essentially Lennon songs, and Paul sings only two of the others. Paul's cover, "Till There Was You," may have more polish, but it still bears a close resemblance to "A Taste of Honey" as a dismissible crooner. Lennon's numbers revolve around the constricting forces at work in a relationship or in living one's life.

The record's weaknesses ("Little Child," "Don't Bother Me," and "Hold Me Tight") are as telling as its strengths, halfway between the aspirations of *Please Please Me* and the polish of *A Hard Day's Night:* all the musical virtues are there (variety of textures, mood, content, singers, and styles) but without the artistic flair that will mark what follows. And this is the last time that a cover song will say it all for Lennon. His next classic moment comes with "Rock and Roll Music," the Chuck Berry cover on *Beatles for Sale;* but by then his original work is beyond what these standards have to offer him, and he never again gleans "Money" 's ethical hooliganism from another person's song.

I Want to Hold Your Hand (John and Paul)/This Boy
(John, Paul, George) *Released: November 29, 1963*

AMERICANS REMEMBER "I Want to Hold Your Hand" as among the first things they heard from the Beatles. Vee Jay, a small independent label in Chicago, had released both the "Please Please Me" single and the album with little radio support and unremarkable commercial returns. But Capitol Records, a major American company, supported it with a $50,000 promotion campaign when it began releasing Beatles records in early 1964, to coincide with the band's Ed Sullivan debut. This song was their first major stateside single, and when

Americans bought their first Capitol Beatles album, *Meet the Beatles*, this was the first track they heard on side one. In Britain, however, it was released only as a single that came out the week after Parlophone's *With the Beatles*. (It was recorded during the same sessions as that album, and they performed it as early as August 1963). Like "She Loves You," it stands better alone than if it had been surrounded by the songs on that album. Its exuberance is rivaled only by that pre-album counterpart—the two singles encase the second album with boundless energy and musical wit.

"I Want to Hold Your Hand" brings the pop structures they had been toying with around to a full expression of their possibilities, much like "She Loves You" does: hooks, textural contrasts, harmonic variation, and physical dynamism crammed into the two-and-a-half-minute format with a touch of genius. The introduction alone is a simple two-chord progression drawn out with a welling anticipation (the same music later sung to the words "I can't hide, I can't hide") it sets the mood as it should, but the arousal it contains in just four bars is more than most songs ever attain. Just before the vocals land in the home key of the verse, a repeated chord is drawn out until it might burst, creating anticipation everywhere and excitement in everything. Only then do they start singing.

The first two words act as an assertive upbeat; Lennon sings them with a declamatory punch, and the song is off. The first two clipped lines are completed by one longer one:

Oh yeah
I'll
Tell you something
I think you'll un-der-stand—
When I
Say that something
I want to hold your hand _____

I want to hold your hand ———
I want to hold your hand.

The harmonic setting plays fourths off one another, first tonic to dominant, then relative minor to *its* implied dominant. The concluding couplet repeats the title line twice in a standard IV–V–I–vi progression that brings the harmony back to the home key.

But it's the smattering of details that really breathes life into the song: the handclaps after the short lines echoed in the rhythm guitar after the long line; the chromatic bass movement that steers everyone toward the minor harmony (setting up the line "I think you'll understand"); and the final vocal leap of an entire octave the first time they sing the title. The harmonized landing point of "hand" is supported by drum fills gliding beneath the vocalists. (The third time the line is sung, bringing the harmony back around for the second verse, Lennon sings it alone.) This is plainly a classical rise and fall of the most archetypical design: everything in the arrangement and performance is meant to highlight a certain moment (the octave leap up to the word "hand") either by pointing to it or falling from it. And the sound that the band achieves in the process defies analysis: it's not just happy, it's enchanted; they enact the inspired pleasure in the music as they play it out.

After the second verse, there is a sudden hush: the electricity fades out almost completely, and a calmer, acoustic sound intrudes—guitars become less rhythmic than atmospheric, and the vocals harmonize throughout, growing from close thirds to the open fourths of "I can't hide, I can't hide." The change in texture conveys the shift in mood from the outgoing verse to the relative introspection of "And when I touch you I feel happy inside." At the end of the second line, the gut impulse of glee rises at each repetition of "I can't hide" (the same way that the introduction did without the words), as if the lover simply can't contain himself. The verse and bridge fit together symbiotically, one excited, the other reflective.

As the song winds to a close, the title line is sung four times instead of the usual three, with an extra harmonic twist: on the third of these, the band swiftly pounds out a new chord before the fourth and final plea wraps things up. (The chord is major and corresponds to the implied dominant harmony in the verse on the word "under*stand.*" In addition to adding an extra surge of energy to the final measures, they touch all the harmonic bases of the song before sending it home.) As if any more ingenuity were needed, triplet quarter-note kicks are added beneath the final word, "hand," buffering the momentum of the entire track. Imagine it ending any other way and you'll hear something duller, less compelling, and less vital to all that has gone before—the simple act of halting the motion draws attention to just how charged it was to begin with. It completes what was kicked off by the opening rhythmic jerks the same way that the "Yeah, you" at the start of the last verse echoed the "Oh yeah, I'll" at the top of the song. For all this music's frenzy, its structural reinforcements couldn't be tighter.

"I Want to Hold Your Hand" is often used to show the difference between what the Beatles had on their minds (holding a woman's hand) and what the Stones had on theirs (spending the night with her), and the larger difference between pop and the blues, between acceptability and defiance. It's a comparison that is too pat, ignorant of the musical goals each group aspired to. The Stones were purists posing as hoods; the Beatles were openly more varied in their taste— but that doesn't make them the good guys to the Stones' rude boys. In its innocence, "I Want to Hold Your Hand" has what can be called "charm," but the performance is certainly something more: where the lyrics tickle, the sound explodes. The spirit of the playing plows under any lyrical prissiness, the way it does in "Thank You Girl" and "From Me to You," only more. The inarticulateness of the singer in "There's a

Place" propelled him to musical heights; the lyrics in this song get tarted up by the energy of the performance. Listen to the way Harrison bends his lead note just before the initial vocal entrance, or the way McCartney makes that brilliant vocal leap upward every time he sings the title line—these moments imbue the lyrics with more substance than the words alone imply. Its joy is charged in large part by what the Beatles find themselves saying *through* this music, which may well have been more than they originally intended. Marsh puts it this way: "[They] counsel[ed] acceptance of love as the greatest glory humanity can know. . . . Yes to love, yes to joy, yes to the transforming power of what they did, from the very beginning" (*The Compleat Beatles*, p. 67).

On their first album, they wanted to crack the whole world up with their beat—"Twist and Shout" extended dancing as a metaphor for sex into sex as a metaphor for fun. In "I Want to Hold Your Hand," their levity gets more implicative; the image of the loved one becomes an image of intimacy. The love relationship extends beyond one specific lover to the idea of love itself and an affirmation of all it can offer.

ON THE REVERSE side, "This Boy" goes beyond the coquettish "Do You Want to Know a Secret" and contains the promise of such breakthroughs as "And I Love Her" and "Yes It Is." "Just my attempt at writing one of those three-part-harmony Smokey Robinson songs. Nothing in the lyrics, just a sound and harmony," Lennon told *Playboy*. With its fantasies of revenge and its unrequited yearnings, Lennon may have copied Robinson's approach but not his emotional turf. A finely honed vocal trio built around a conventional I–vi–ii–V progression serves as the soundtrack for a jilted-for-another heartbreak scenario, a traditional doo-wop formula invested with Lennon's vengeful melodramatic touch.

The acoustic guitar intro plays in duple what the band soon fills out in $^{12}/_8$ time, introducing the plain vanilla chord sequence of the verse with a rhythmic tease. The vocal harmonies have a poignant moving note in the very opening line, altering the major seventh of the tonic to the root of the relative minor—it makes the title phrase sound tired, regretful, and genuinely compassionate. The restrained vocal trio of the verses erupt into John's solo outburst in the bridge, effectively contrasting song sections off one another once again.

As Lennon comes to the fore, supported by the backup "ah"s, there's little doubt that he intends to take things to the brink. He's singing straight from his gut, and the contrast of the trio's sentimentality with his raw outburst is gorgeous, building right to the stop-time of the bridge that leaves him wailing alone, as only he can, on the word "cry." The way he then slips right back into the vocal trio points up their control: the tension between cooing harmony and naked vocal audacity is built right in, and they understand its potency.

ALL OF THE MATERIAL examined up to this point was conceived and recorded before 1964, the year the Beatles "conquered" America, a point not lost on Marsh:

> The Beatles had not only arrived, they had arrived complete. They would not get better in the six years left to them, because there simply wasn't much better to get. What they did, instead, and to their everlasting credit, was become more sophisticated, take the same idea and never shy away from its complexities. But *better?* You don't improve on "I Want to Hold Your Hand" . . . you just elaborate. *(Compleat Beatles,* p. 66)

When Americans caught Beatlemania, these records held up the most intriguing reflection of their indigenous musical culture that they had ever heard. Surrounding the Beatles' view of rock's best moments ("Twist and Shout," "Roll Over Beethoven," "Money") with original material that extended and sometimes competed with that legacy in terms of urgency and power, they taught Americans how much there was to hear in one of their own folk musics—not only by exposing messages that had so far been implicit but by showing where such attitudes might be taken, and what value existed all along in shared enthusiasm on a mass scale. This low, common style, so derided for its vulgarity by the anti-Elvis establishment, was suddenly not only alive again but in better musical health. Elvis Presley's mystique was physical and racial—the poor white boy who gets rich singing black rhythms—and his records survive as vocal dynamos of technique and emotional presence. The Beatles greeted America with humility and irreverence, magnifying Elvis's mercurial impact with musical ingenuity. The torch was being passed.

BEYOND ADOLESCENCE

Long Tall Sally (Paul)/I Call Your Name (John)/
Slow Down (John)/Matchbox (Ringo)
Released: June 19, 1964

A HARD DAY'S NIGHT *Released: July 10, 1964*

THE BEATLES BEGAN 1964 with a flurry of international
activity. During a three-week appearance at the Olympia
Theatre in Paris as a supporting act for headliners Trini Lo-
pez and Sylvie Vartan (January 14 through February 5), they
composed most of the songs for their upcoming film debut, *A
Hard Day's Night*. By the end of the run they were the favorites on the bill, humbling the other stars with their crowds
as Beatlemania took root in France. On January 17, George
Martin was visiting them in their rooms at the Hôtel George
V to hear this new material when they received the news that
"I Want to Hold Your Hand" had gone gold in America.
There is a picture of them celebrating with Brian Epstein
sporting a pot atop his head. On January 29, they recorded the
vocals in German for "She Loves You" and "I Want to Hold Your
Hand" in the Pathé-Marconi studio, in addition to laying down
"Can't Buy Me Love," their next single, and their first effort for *A
Hard Day's Night*'s soundtrack.

Just two days after returning from Paris, they flew to
New York for the first time, where they were greeted by
three thousand fans and a hundred journalists. They floored
everybody at the airport press conference with their savvy

comebacks, but the attention seemed excessive to the extreme—seeing the crowd as they taxied toward the gate, the Beatles were certain that the greeting was meant for the President. American Beatlemania made the twist look like a rumor. During their two-week visit (February 7–22), they made their legendary live appearance on "The Ed Sullivan Show," but their stateside "arrival" was largely promotional: two concerts in Carnegie Hall and one in Washington, D.C., before a working holiday in Miami, where they taped more footage for another Sullivan program. But by then it didn't seem like work. "What do you think of America?" a journalist asked Ringo. "I think you've all gone mad," he replied.

Returning to London, they reentered the studios in late February for *A Hard Day's Night* sessions, which also produced "You Can't Do That," the B side for the "Can't Buy Me Love" single. The vocals for "You Can't Do That" were also taped onto the instrumental track that had been laid down in Paris the previous month. (Since "Can't Buy Me Love" and "You Can't Do That" are included on *A Hard Day's Night*, they will be discussed as part of that album.) Also during the final week of February, they recorded the four songs for their extended-play single *Long Tall Sally*, which was released on June 19 (the four-song British EP had no equivalent on Capitol). On March 2, they began six weeks of filming and recording for their first feature-length film as the American charts caught up with earlier British releases: on March 31, the top five singles on *Billboard's* Hot 100 were "Can't Buy Me Love," "Twist and Shout," "She Loves You," "I Want to Hold Your Hand," and "Please Please Me."

Long Tall Sally (Paul)/I Call Your Name (John)/
Slow Down (John)/Matchbox (Ringo)
Released: June 19, 1964

The Beatles first met Little Richard in 1962 when he performed at the New Brighton Tower in Liverpool, and Brian

Epstein arranged another concert for him at the Empire Theatre on October 28, 1962, with the Beatles as part of the supporting bill. Richard, the most overt influence on McCartney's belting style, still claims that at some point during his contact with the Beatles he gave Paul a screaming lesson. The bundle of outrageous American sexual and racial innuendos he embodied didn't seem to faze McCartney, who was more awed by the possessed wildness that sprang from Richard's vocal cords.

Richard's "Long Tall Sally" is McCartney's first statement as a rocker that there are other ways to go crazy than Lennon's spiritual hunger and moral indignation. Unlike Little Richard's brazen homosexual camp, Paul's commanding, out-of-breath mania makes him sound indomitable and acceptable all at once, lampooning his goody-goody sheen by smudging it. His sheer physical dynamism on this recording turns it into an out-of-control romp, an unhinged tour-de-force. After "Long Tall Sally," John no longer corners the market on riveting mayhem.

Insiders understood Little Richard's 1956 hit as code language for transvestism. The joy of "Tutti Frutti" and "Good Golly Miss Molly" ("Sure like to ball!") was what Little Richard got away with—his bouffant hairdo and audacious stage persona were simply too far out to be believed. When Paul screams "Long Tall Sally," the first song he ever did onstage, he acts as though Little Richard's drag queen persona is beside the point. He mows right over lyrics like "He said he had the mis'ry/But he got a lot of fun/Oh baby" and "Long Tall Sally's built pretty sweet/She's got everything that Uncle John needs/Oh baby"—the operative words for Paul are "have some fun tonight." He tarts the latter line up with exuberance and lets the rest implode—impact pulverizes meaning. Along with "Twist and Shout," "Money," and "I'm Down," it's a rock 'n' roll stance that rivals that of any of their heroes.

From the opening moments, Paul snubs pretense and flips out—his vocalism compresses the enthusiasm of the entire band into rip-snorting yelps, refusing to recognize the conventional limits on excitement. He's not interested in explaining his hysteria; and if you have to ask what all the excitement is about, you'll never understand the immediacy—there's no space for subtlety when all the stops are pulled out. The lyrics are all but unintelligible, as they should be: with the band pressure-cooking the beat all around him, his singing is all urgency and power. Together they demolish everything in their path.

The ferocity of their attack sounds like a fuse is burning quickly: pleasure mounts with each verse, and Paul's delivery frames two of George's finer guitar solos—it helps to get a wailing lead-in, but George's rhythmic timing has never been better, and they back him up with a beat that is both warm and cutting. On the vocal break after the solo ("Well long tall Sally's built . . . pretty sweet she got . . . everything that Uncle John needs oh baby"), Paul packs as much tension into the silences as he does into the words themselves. On the live version of this song off the *Hollywood Bowl* LP, this is the line he rips to shreds. The second guitar solo starts with an ensemble climb to the chord change—more combustion—before George cuts loose again.

The home stretch is one last lap of dementia: Paul sings "Have some fun tonight/Everything's all right" like it's all he's ever wanted to do in his life, searing the pleasure with his outlandish pace, careening around the last turn ("yeah, yeah, yeah"). George plays a new rhythmic figure, pushing him along from behind, and Ringo heads for his tom-toms. Without the cymbal timbre, everything condenses; the sound veers even closer to some tumultuous abyss. Just when it all seems ready to rupture, they rear back into the cutoff, sputtering and smoking like the end of a reckless car ride—near misses, rampant turns, and unpredictable spins—choked off by something besides lack of nerve. (The last live guitar chord is untouched, not the patched-on finale of "Roll Over Beethoven.") Clocked at under two minutes, the mess of sound they leave behind gives tenuous shape and order to feelings that otherwise would reap chaos. Little Richard's perversities get scorched by anarchic hilarity.

> That was my song. When there was no Beatles and no group. I just had it around. It was my effort as a kind of blues originally, and then I wrote the middle eight just to stick it in the album when it came out years later. The first part had been written before Hamburg even. It was one of my *first* attempts at a song. . . . (Lennon in *Playboy*, p. 180)

THE FIRST SOUND of "I Call Your Name" is a new guitar, but the shifting rhythmic patterns set the unsteady tone. George's Rickenbacker twelve-string has a big, ringing sound, a swarming electric tonic that became very influential (the instrument mesmerized Byrds founder Roger McGuinn when he saw *A Hard Day's Night*). It leads the band in and commands the ensemble interplay, the way Lennon's playing will in "You Can't Do That," a cousin to this song's jealous temper.

The clipped economy of the troubled verses is followed by melismas at the ends of stanzas ("for bein' unfair _____"), and the confessional middle eight has the most interesting turn of harmony as short lines are stretched from "Don't you know I can't take it" through the elongation of "I'm not gonna may-ee-ay-yake it," to the harmonic twist on the held note on "I'm not that kind of *man* _____." (The added harmony for this line is C major, the neapolitan of the dominant, B major, pivoting on the held tonic note E as a common tone between E major and C major.) George shifts into double time in this passage (playing twice as fast); the others keep the exact same time patterns behind him. The two rhythms couple uncertainty with restlessness; the band holds back as George tries to move forward.

Lennon remembered spicing up the guitar solo with "ska"—a style of reggae that emphasizes offbeats, and discards downbeats altogether: "I should have invested in reggae because I never thought the Americans would get on. The

Beatles made an attempt at ska—the middle—the solo on 'I Call Your Name' was ska—deliberate and conscious," he told Andy Peebles, in 1980 (*The Lennon Tapes*, p. 92). The transition between the reggae solo and the second bridge is overlapped: Lennon tugs the beat back into place early with the same linking words ("Don't you know I can't take it"); the others fall into sync a measure later.

Lennon's hyperemotionalism here is leveled by reality. The bridge emphasizes his vulnerability—the separation he can't take, the paranoia he fears giving in to, the kind of man he isn't—and leads to the one outlet of passion left open to him: the title line is the only declaration that isn't qualified by a negativism or a question of blame. "I never weep at night/I call your name" reels from self-consciousness—he doesn't cry about getting jilted, he sings. The fade-out rounds off the shifting meter by adding an extra kick ahead of the downbeat (which Ringo misses the first time around), and for the first time Paul steps forward to fiddle about on his bass just as the sound begins to die away—a fade-out device that will become a trait.

''SLOW DOWN,'' John's first Larry Williams cover, is a hoot—his vocal delivery is quixotic, hilariously straight, the same iconoclastic presence that makes "Money" danceable, only with more playfulness. On the original recording, Williams's band plays like gangbusters, jamming through an entire verse together before Williams lets go with his hustling delivery, clanky piano figures filling out the high end like bits of drunken poetry. Williams with his cool, condescending pose and forceful raillery, was just the kind of rocker Lennon patterned himself after. The elegant cat howl after the second verse is a Williams specialty, mixing arrogance with humor, but he doesn't impose the same command as Lennon, who nudges the same qualities toward both supremacy and self-mockery.

As with most of their covers, the Beatles stick to the original arrangement almost exactly and overwhelm the musical similarities with personality. They replace Williams's sax solo with a guitar, the tempo is slowed, and the overall feel is cleaner; but it's in the ad-lib vocal breaks that Lennon veers away from his role model even when he sings the same phrases. He brands his very purpose into his outcries, seizing naked moments with an even tighter grip than their author's. The way he sails in on top of the guitar solo with a long "weeelll" brings the last verse in with the kind of raucous grace Williams never dreamed of. Saving Williams's underwater "blblblblbl!!" lip flapping for a single break (Williams does it twice), Lennon is at his most intense—his humor is never simply funny. Even when he's laughing at himself, he takes his material utterly seriously.

RINGO'S FIRST Carl Perkins song, "Matchbox," follows like a shaggy-dog punchline—he turns the original down-and-out song into a what-the-hell aside. It's the most self-revealing song he's done yet, as if Perkins had written it especially for a Ringo revival. "Well, I'll be your little dog/Till your big dog comes" is the honest modesty Ringo always wore on his face. "What's a scruff like me doing with this lot?" he asked Hunter Davies. His utter bafflement at his own fame is what made him a legend.

A HARD DAY'S NIGHT *Released: July 10, 1964*

For all the flower-power naiveté, the sixties had a self-conscious streak. The Beatles loved to show their audience how they worked: *A Hard Day's Night* is a semifictional day in the life, calculated for laughs by screenwriter Alun Owen; *Let It Be* is nonfictional and uncalculated, edited as a "documentary" by Michael Lindsay-Hogg. Each film tries to defrock the myth that is their subject—(Who are these Beatles? How do they work together?), although a certain amount of suspended disbelief is required in each case. That the first introduces them to their worldwide audience and the latter (in effect) says farewell only makes the rehearsal-to-performance movement that both work around the more telling. A *Hard Day's Night* captures them at the peak of their powers; *Let It Be* plays off past glories.

The "And I Love Her" sequence in the first film shows the Beatles rehearsing for a live television broadcast from the vantage point of the television director, who looks down at the stage through video monitors from his control room above. Inside the heart of the studio, amidst different levels and channels of technology in that now primitive-looking TV director's booth, Richard Lester's direction points up just how self-conscious the Beatles' music is by this point, the relationship between their appearance and what goes into it. The sequence shows how electronic messages are being sent out into the world and how well the Beatles suit their medium. Before they play in front of a live studio audience they cut up together, mock their agent, put on the press, put down fashion experts, baffle the Victorian-costumed extras, ridicule their elders, cavort on an empty soccer field, flirt with women—in short, enact the music's flair and impulsiveness— before hopping on stage to deliver a set of such power and excitement that they themselves find renewal in playing it.

This record begins to show how the Beatles' music and the recording medium were meant for each other. George's double-tracked guitar solo on "Can't Buy Me Love" talks to itself across the left and right channels; he answers his own melodic question with an echoing response, countering Paul's rampant affability with stereo dialogue. The album's opening chord is unresolved—without a third, it's neither major or minor—and it sets off a string of harmonic turns. The major-minor nexus of "A Hard Day's Night" is put to use in almost every track: the major-verse-with-minor-bridge layout of "I Should Have Known Better," "I'm Happy Just to Dance with You," and "I'll Cry Instead" is reversed in "Can't Buy Me

Love," "Any Time at All," and "Things We Said Today," making the alternating major-minor ambiguity of "I'll Be Back" an overriding musical motif. "When I Get Home" skirts around musical keys so deftly that its angular final cadence points to the condensed key treatments of "Doctor Robert" and "Martha My Dear."

The distance between appearance and reality widens: the assured surface of "Any Time at All" belies its final complexity—it snags the listener with overtones of devotion before delivering annoyance, musical irony, and an overall tremulousness. In "If I Fell," Lennon sings to himself, his prospective lover, and his ex-lover all at the same time; "And I Love Her" is bittersweet, devotion underlined with sorrow; "I'll Be Back" promises as much as it hedges. But the spiritual energy that lifted *Please Please Me* out of the ordinary remains uncompromised. "I Should Have Known Better" is the kind of instant and sustained pleasure with no strings attached that inspires follow-ups like "Eight Days a Week"; and "I'm Happy Just to Dance With You" returns to the dance floor of innocence. Nuance and a growing musical formalism are laced with humor, sentimentality, and a bolder vulnerability, laid out sequentially to highlight the contrasts. *A Hard Day's Night* blends the Beatles' ardent vitality with restraint, and in doing so it gives their first all-original album claims toward being their most perfect record.

THE TITLE SONG to the Beatles' first movie was recorded on April 16, 1964, after much of the filming had been completed. "Whew, that's a hard day's night," Ringo quipped after a long day of shooting, and the phrase was adopted as the title. Lennon and McCartney then went off to come up with the song.

The clash of a chord that rips open the silence (a G7 with added ninth and suspended fourth) makes the opening to the record a stunning jolt of crash and ripples. There's so much space as George lets the sound ring that its suspended intervals harbor expectancy and promise for the enriched musical dialect of what follows. The distinctive tone is the new twelve-string guitar first heard on "I Call Your Name," and the song may have been written with just that instrument in mind. The same sound sees the song out with a repeating arpeggio, outlining the same notes from the opening chord as it spins into the fade-out. In the context of the film, it's easy to imagine how such a vibrant lick was written during the shooting.

The collaboration binds the almost single-note verses by Lennon in major with the bridge sung by McCartney in minor. Lennon sings assertively: the held vowels on the words "hard _____ day's _____ night _____" offset the drawn-out consonants of "workinnnn' _____" and "sleepinnnn' _____ ." The "like a dog" and "like a log" tags roll naturally off the energy that's wrung from the held notes they follow. With a short break into harmony ("But when I get home to you/I find the things that you do . . ."), Lennon eases back into the final line with bluesy inflections ("You know I feel all-right").

Like Lennon's, McCartney's portion is also double-tracked, and it's atypically aggressive: where Lennon leans back into his phrases, dipping into the beginning of each word, McCartney presses forward. The cowbell is brought up for a change in texture, and Paul starts with held notes and rolls into wordier second lines:

When I'm home _____
Everything seems to be right
When I'm home _____
Feeling you holding me tight . . . tight, yeah

The first time John re-enters for his verse, the transition from Paul's voice to his is smooth, not pronounced. The second time, Lennon sings a small "hmm" underneath Paul as he finishes, and this dovetailing changes the character of the exact same transition—it adds direction as it pronounces the personalities in collaboration. In a typical patriarchal setup, the singer's responsible toil in the real world is rewarded by his woman's comfort at the end of the day. But behind the considerable drive, some revealing vocal moments (the "hmm" before the final verse, the blue notes of "feel all right") imply not just sensuality but softness. As macho and dominating as Lennon's posture was, his delivery could never fully conceal what he later called "the little boy inside the man."

JOHN'S HARP BREAKS the silence into which George's guitar has drifted, with a fuller sound than on "Love Me Do" or "From Me to You"—"I Should Have Known Better" has a real swing to it, and Lennon plays it as a robust amorous fanfare.

The song is a marvel of economy, an ingenious manipulation of several very simple elements seamlessly joined: the initial held vowel ("I") grows and spills into words ("shoulda known better") with an easy momentum, despite all those consonants, before coming to rest one note higher than where it started out ("with a girl like *you*"). The second part of the phrase is repeated with different words and rounded out by repeating the last fragment of the melody: "And I do/Hey, hey, hey/And I do." The harp sneaks in just before the lyrics end to link things back up to the beginning. This transition makes as much musical sense as the one going into the bridge does with a line of logic (both lyrical and musical) that begs for elaboration: "Can't you see" flows smoothly into "That when I tell you that I love you . . ." (as a C-major chord tilts downward to B major, the dominant of the bridge's E minor). The interplay between John's harp and George's guitar during the solos imitates the verbal games; the harp reverses the word patterns: it starts with plenty of motion and finishes by holding out chords for the guitar to play off of.

The bridge ("That when I tell you that I love you . . .") is decorated by strummed chords from George's lead, establishing another layer of rhythmic texture, like the bridge of "I Call Your Name." Here George plays half time (instead of double time) against the unaltered rhythmic pattern in the rest of the band, suspending chords as the others play through them. Lennon's falsetto climb on "mi-hi-hi-hine" lifts him to the most stirring register in his range. He leaps to that high note half laughing, half crying (just after "And when I ask you to be mine," the only moment of hesitation), preparing it with the vowel reiteration that is the song's lyrical hook. His falsetto is always telling emotional secrets.

"IF I FELL" rests on as big an equivocation musically as its lyric does emotionally: the trepidation of that first word ("If") is sung above an uncertain E-flat-minor chord, the perilous half step above the song's D-major key. Christgau and Piccarella write that "the yearning for tenderness and the yearning for revenge become almost inextricable" as John's get-even tactics mix with Paul's gently reassuring vocal blend to realize the song's layered emotions. Love suddenly means more than "just holding hands."

At the end of 1963, music critic William Mann of the London *Times* wrote an essay on the theoretical attributes of Lennon and McCartney's compositional technique. He dubs the cadences at the end of "Not a Second Time" "aeolian," a quote that is still batted about with derision, even though what he says is true. (Lennon always held that the term "aeolian cadence" sounded like some strange exotic bird.) But Mann also writes that "one gets the impression that they think simultaneously of harmony and melody, so firmly are the major tonic sevenths and ninths built into their tunes . . ." (*The Beatles Forever*, p. 23). The duet that John and Paul sing in "If I Fell" is the best example of what Mann is referring to: the melody itself seems written as harmonized—both lines are so lyrical it's hard to say just which one is the "melody." The intertwining harmonies are so strong that they seem to carry the entire song along behind them. Melody and meaning govern the musical setting.

Paul's upper harmony enters with the verse, and is constant, as strong an imaginative presence as John's lead. Their voices align geometrically as they travel in the same direction ("If I give my "), part toward opposite paths in contrary motion ("heart"—where Paul falls and John rises—"to you"— where Paul rises and John falls), and wind up in unison for the final linking line ("I must be sure"). Breaking up lines with these harmony patterns only increases the temperamental dividends of McCartney singing atop Lennon: John sounds hurt, uneasy but still hopeful; Paul is romantic, yearning, and full of promise. Their vocal blend conveys the emotional quandary.

As they turn the corner into the bridge, it's on the key line "Don't hurt my pride like *her*," and the bridge admits vulnerability: "Cos I couldn't stand the pain." The rising line they sing to these words captures the essence of romantic pain, and is followed almost immediately by a tinge of regret, as the major chord flips into minor on the words "and *I*." Lennon does a neat glide down between the words "new" and "love," and Paul makes a delicious error when he cracks on the word "vain" at the end of the second bridge. In the middle of such a delicate arrangement, the mistake is priceless.

Lennon wants to strike a bargain with his new lover: he'll fall in love with her if she'll promise to be true, and if at the same time he can get back at the femme fatale who broke his heart—he seeks reinvolvement in order to gain revenge. What surer way for a love to "be in vain" than to base it on impractical pledges and retaliation instead of true affection? Lennon's dilemma is so honestly wrought that the contradiction doesn't matter—the minor chord (an altered subdominant) on the final title phrase summons past regrets (from "and *I*") as much as it aches for newfound comfort. The music empathizes how we hear Lennon's sense of consequence surrounding a new involvement—we share both his hope and his fear.

This love triangle exposes the emotional landscape that earlier Lennon songs inhabited: the brooding melismas that qualify the hopeful lyrics of "All I've Got to Do," the sympathetic anger of "Not a Second Time," and the humble infatuation that grows into unswerving determination in "I'll Get You." It's a key early heartache song, shedding light on his early romantic dilemmas the way "Julia" oedipalizes his view of women as a whole, filling out the mystery of "Norwegian Wood" and "Girl"; the way the solo "Woman" reconciles the domineering conceit in "You Can't Do That" and "Run For Your Life."

JOHN WROTE "I'm Happy Just to Dance with You" for George, and it interrupts the two ballads on this side. The thrust of Lennon's Rickenbacker demonstrates his exceptional rhythmic sense—his guitar playing virtually carries the rest of the band. Dancing-as-sex is downplayed, even though "If somebody tries to take my place/Let's pretend we just can't see his face" is a cool Lennon possessive, and the concluding title line of each verse is touched with timidity (the augmented chord on "just to *dance* with you"). Tom-tom accents (on the first and fourth eighth of each bar) give the major verses extra punch, and John and Paul add backup harmonies in the minor bridge. The way they fly off the end of their last "Oh!" eases the transition back to the verse. It goes out with that same soaring effect.

OF ALL THE McCartney songs with oedipal overtones (biographer Chris Salewicz cites "Yesterday," "Lady Madonna," and "Let It Be"), "And I Love Her" is the most genuinely stirring. With one stroke, he gains the status of standard balladeer composer that he strived toward as early as "P.S. I Love You." The haunting melody is dressed up with tasteful acoustic guitar playing, a subtle percussive line, and a deft key change for George's classical guitar solo to keep the ear interested in what would otherwise be a repetition of a simple musical idea. For the final chord, the minor tonality inverts to major (a better use of a trick from "A Taste of Honey").

The tension between the lyrics and the melody bears some similarity to the irony of "All My Loving"—the melody alone doesn't suggest such positive words. Paul sings it with melancholy against George's high guitar arpeggios that hover over the last verse. If these moon-in-June lyrics had been set in more ordinary fashion, the song would be dismissible. But considered by itself, this tune is among the best Paul will ever write, imbuing the cliché lyrics with a plaintive undertow. The tug between the two gives the song substance: the music underscores his loyalty with an unutterable sorrow.

THE TUMBLE OF drums into "Tell Me Why" breaks the romantic mood with a booming resonance, as if we're hearing them play in a large open ballroom. The Beach Boys covered this song on the *Beach Boys' Party!* album, sending up their own block vocal harmonies in response to the Beatles' tribute to their style. It's another tortured Lennon tune, but this one doesn't rock; it swings—the backbeat has a syncopated snazz that keeps it moving ever forward.

Like "If I Fell," emotions are pitted against each other— this time the act of singing is revengeful, the type of get-even pleasure Lennon tries to wash down his dread with. Listen to the way the giddy leap to falsetto is written right into the end of the line "And why you lie _____ to me _____." The joy in the singing is supplanted by the way Lennon twists up the melody, bending notes all over the place to juice the betrayal for all it's worth. He finds comfort in numbers as he exchanges lines with his backup singers:

LENNON: *Well I gave you everything I had*
ALL: *But you left me sittin' on my own*
LENNON: *Did you have to treat me oh so bad?*
ALL: *All I do is hang my head and moan!*

The bass line walks downward resolutely in the refrain, propelling the straight $4/4$ meter into a declamatory pulse, the

beat of the jilted. The regularity of the bass alone is one reason why the yanking kicks (after "lie to me") jerk so hard: the
syncopations tug at the beat with real physicality.

Lennon rips off a rolling rhythmic guitar flourish that
sends the song into its coda (one more verse with refrain):

LENNON (alone): *Well I beggin' on my bended knees*
                    If you'll only listen to my pleas
(in falsetto): *If there's anything I can do*
(down again): *Cos I really can't stand it I'm so in love with*
                    you. . . .

Plainly parodic but also strangely affecting, he pulls out
all the melodramatic stops without cloying. To hear it is to
laugh out loud, especially at lines as thick as "If you don't
[come back] I really can't go on/Holding back these tears in
my eyes." But he doesn't sing it with the farcical tinge of
"Misery," and even though the rolling guitar and the double-
stick drum solo that follow those lines sound like a show-
biz cliché, a forced encore, Lennon flings himself into the
two-dimensional lyrics and comes up convincing. Perhaps it's
Lennon having a laugh on himself, paying irreverence to
the broken-heart-song heritage. "They needed another upbeat song and I just knocked it off," Lennon told *Playboy*,
p. 204-205. "It was like a black New York girl-group song."
Whatever the slant, the real Lennon speaks through it—per-
severing but self-deprecating somewhere beneath the surface,
revenge folding into high spirits. The ending works the kicks
out logically, wrapping things up with fine pop styling, and
the final chord shuns extra notes, resolving all the fancy jazz
chords that lead up to it with a simple, unaltered tonic—
turmoil coaxing consonance.

AT ONE POINT in the film, scheduled and restricted like
some dog act before their taping, the Beatles escape from their

manager and director by stumbling outdoors via a fire escape. As they prance about a big open football field, Richard Lester films them leaping, bouncing, hopping, running into one another, running into nothing, twisting, falling, and cracking up in the freest kind of free-for-all. They were doing more than just burning up energy; they were releasing a carefree joy for life in visual terms—doing for the camera what they normally did for the microphone.

"Can't Buy Me Love" is the soundtrack for this giddiness, and it has the same bubbly thrill as the film's manic physicality. It's McCartney's loose response to Lennon's performance of "Money," but it doesn't really reach for those heights—it's a bouncy pop song, not a diatribe against hypocrisy. As a rearrangement of a standard blues, it points toward "I'm Down" and "She's a Woman," inflecting the same progression with a minor refrain, fleshing things out with detail: short piercing guitar chords on the right channel during the refrain (short-long, short long) add punch on the minor harmony, the bookend effect of a tom-tom drum in both the intro and the final refrain; Paul's lead vocal is double-tracked (there are no vocal harmonies); and the double-tracked guitar solo allows George to echo his own playing for one brief moment (the interplay between the center and the right channel, where the two separate guitar leads are mixed). It's the most intricate production of a song yet, with voice in the middle, lead guitar on the right (only on refrains), and acoustic guitar, bass, and drums on the left. Paul's unbridled buoyancy is exactly etched into stereo.

THESE SOUNDTRACK SONGS, composed on a rented piano in Paris, clean things up without selling out—accents are sharper, kicks hit harder, and lyrics carry more import. If the film showed the four moptops trapped by success but free to say and do as they pleased among themselves, these soundtrack songs do the same thing in musical terms. Epstein may have dressed them up in matching suits and uniform bows, but the angles their songs take and the music that pumps them up were provocative and humorous, loaded with more than three-minute songs were meant to carry. By crafting such considerable material for their score, they turned their out-of-place movie roles into something their fans couldn't resist and the older generation couldn't ignore. Like Bob Dylan in *Don't Look Back* (filmed a year later), they make the straight world's preoccupations look ridiculous, and the score puts this across without sounding uppity or smug. The *Hard Day's Night* songs overshadow *With the Beatles* technically while drawing on *Please Please Me*'s raucous thrills, catching the Beatles in the act of maturing.

LIKE SIDE ONE, side two begins with an explosive punctuation: Lennon's solo vocal entrance to "Any Time at All" is tripped by Ringo's upbeat drum accent just before John begins—it sounds as if the record might have skipped. The band is left and center in the mix with a single-note piano part on the right channel. Lennon's double-tracked lead links stanzas together: as he approaches the end of a line, one voice drops out in order to pick up the next line—the voice left behind catches up in the middle of the line already underway (the same overlapping that loops around itself in "Julia"). He's singing to his lover, but he's also singing to himself:

> *If you need somebody to love*
> *Just look into my eyes*
> *I'll be there to make you feel* right
>
> *If you're feelin' sorry and sad*
> *I'd really sympathize*
> *Don't you be sad, just call me tonight . . .*

The solo, shared between guitar (left) and piano (right), is also a dialogue: the guitar starts high and ends low; the piano begins low and ends up high. They play in contrary motion in the beginning (the guitar moving downward and the piano moving upward), join forces in the middle to play quarter-note triplets, and the piano summarizes the exchange by closing with the guitar figure that echoes each refrain (after Lennon sings "I'll be there . . .").

The melody struggles with one of the more awkward phrases Lennon has yet written. The one-line (title) refrain has trouble starting up; it takes a firm kick from the guitar and drums before any kind of groove is really established. Once set in motion, the same line is repeated, then repeated again as though at a loss for words, before a huge, consonant-filled line is inserted ("Yeah any time at all/Allyougottado iscall/And I'll be there") to cap the refrain. With the grace of songs like "I Should Have Known Better" on the other side, it's jarring that such a phrase gets this kind of forced attention, but it shows just how much Lennon wants to squeeze into the pop format. An unusual idea, one that doesn't suit the conventions, is made to seem plausible, almost suitable. A comforting sentiment ("any time at all") is seasoned with jerky, uneven rhythmic kicks, and then sung in anguish. The second, higher "any time at all" sounds as if he could be singing the words "please don't go" for all the despair he puts into it. It's the opposite of Paul celebrating a separation: instead of kicking his heels for joy, John sounds fearful that this woman *won't* call. The reassurances are directed inward as much as outward.

(The ending has a guitar chord edited onto it, but the patch is more successful than on "Roll Over Beethoven." This guitar seems to ring from out of the distance, and slowly comes to the forefront of the mix only on its second pulse. If it weren't for this guitar, the song would have ended as it began, with one of Ringo's adamant drum slams.)

"I'LL CRY INSTEAD" was written for the movie, but Richard Lester later rejected it for the football field routine.

"I wrote that for *A Hard Day's Night*," Lennon told *Playboy* (p. 205) in 1980, "but Dick Lester didn't even want it. He resurrected 'Can't Buy Me Love' for the sequence instead." The country acoustic feel couches the vengeful exaggerations in levity ("I'm gonna break their hearts all round the world")—it's cartoon revenge compared with "If I Fell." Paul's bass breaks on the third line of each stanza (behind "show you what your lovin' man can do") are precursors to those that Lennon will give him in "Rain" and "I'm Only Sleeping."

THE BALLADIC "Things We Said Today" separates four John songs with another love song from Paul. Both of McCartney's bittersweet ballads on this record are in minor, tempering the cheerful persona that normally excels in major positivisms (even for goodbye songs) like "P.S. I Love You" and "All My Loving." (This typically British underside will evolve into "Eleanor Rigby" and "For No One.") "Things We Said Today" is wistful and nostalgic, and it's one of the first from either Paul or John that takes on the issue of time in an explicit manner, even though it just skims the surface of the issue. Lennon's temporalities can be ominous ("Not a Second Time," "In My Life," "She Said She Said," "A Day in the Life"); McCartney's concern with time is less pronounced in "Yesterday" and more humorous in "When I'm Sixty-four."

The assertive acoustic guitar intro sets up an atmosphere of impending departure ("You say you will love me/If I have to go"), and the middle eight bars go batty with head-over-heels delirium. The melody is the sound of romantic longing: it has the roll-on flow of a constancy that is approaching change, as well as the swells of hope that greet the inevitable ("Someday when you're dreaming . . .")—Paul's voice is complemented beautifully during those moments. But the middle section, all rumble-tumble in major, stirs up the enchanting lift of love itself, not renouncing the impending sadness but resting beside it with a completely different tone:

Me I'm just a lucky guy
Love to hear you say that love is love
And though we may be blind
Love is here to stay and that's enough

Musically, the bridge kicks optimism in where the verse plaintively accepts separation. With his eyes on the distant future—

Someday when we're dreaming
Deep in love, not a lot to say
Then we will remember
Things we said today

—he can't help but revel in the present infatuation with love he feels as he sings. Goodbye heartache is assuaged with bottomless affection.

THE "WHOA I_____"'s at the start of the next song— "When I Get Home"—have a roaring pull to them, like a horse bucking beneath the rider. The vocal harmony on the refrain sounds deliciously out of sorts, as though they've imbibed, and the cantankerous delivery carries right over into the playing. Even Lennon's sharp rhythm guitar strokes are like barbs in the wire; he's leading the band with more than just his guts. Lennon's singing is so good, so full of enthusiasm for what he's doing, that it doesn't really matter what the words are (and they're fairly forgettable)—his fervency gains strength from a simple passion.

As in "I Should Have Known Better," the surface sentiment masks the musical intricacies: the lyric strings wordy lines against melismas and short phrases against held notes; the bridge mixes up the same patterns. The final cadence takes all the key flirtations and settles all bets: the repetition of "when I get home" at the end leads not into A minor as it has almost every other time but into C major, linking up both verse (C) and refrain (A) key areas in one simple gesture. It lays the groundwork for the treats that keep coming: "You're Going to Lose That Girl" is a two-key song, as are "Good Day Sunshine" and "Penny Lane." Starting with a relatively simplistic play with the different ways chords can relate to each other, the Beatles quickly learn the expressive value of such ploys.

"YOU CAN'T DO THAT" puts George's twelve-string up front again for a classic rocker, heir to the force that was with "I'll Get You." It may not have the same anger, but it has the same self-righteous smell, and Lennon ornaments it here with a fine guitar lick and sneering background vocals. Where "I'll Get You" had some sympathy (the seductive melody on "I think about you night and day"), this song is all aggressive—he's practically bawling his girlfriend out, you can almost hear him wag his finger on the hook ("because I *told you before*"). Ringo reacts to that line with a syncopated entrance, jerking the band back in rather than easing them around the curve.

"Everybody's gree-een cos I'm the one who won your love," is a subtle paranoid Lennonism—the green connotes envy—and it leads straight into "But if they'd see-een you talkin' that way . . ." Ringo interrupts that line to rub John's nose in the ultimate humiliation: "They'd laugh in my face!" When Lennon sings "I can't help my feelings/I go out of my mind" in the succeeding verse, his own personal nature spills effortlessly into song. His manic possessiveness is easily thrown into fits of jealousy.

John's guitar solo equals and then outdoes his insistent flippancy on "I'm Happy Just to Dance with You"—the block chords he starts off with are soon twisted into screaming rhythmic figures. The solo relies on emotional force, not the soaring melodic virtuosity that usually passes for brilliance. As a singer Lennon leads by tugging, tossing, and teasing the beat, and he does the same thing with his guitar—setting up premises just to smash them. The ending to this outburst thwarts expectations. The song doesn't come to the crashing finish one might suspect from this angry lecture; after the guitar utters its final recitation of the opening lick, the music slows to a complete stop on the last three notes. Instead of exploding, it simply runs out of steam.

ON THE FIRST two albums, the songs that finished off side two assumed special importance: the covers they chose reached beyond what had been said before in ways their original material still groped for. They shelved their songwriting ambitions and put their hearts into their performances. "I'll Be Back" is their first original closer, making the idea of the song more important than any end-of-the-album blowouts.

Lennon's romantic insecurities from "If I Fell" and "I'll Cry Instead" spread out incrementally in "I'll Be Back." With atypical timidity, John is asking for another chance after backing out, and his discomfort seeps into the music: after the introduction in major, John and Paul's duet enters in minor, wringing emotional ambiguity from dashed expectations; the "oh _____, oh" passages at the end of each stanza trip the meter, dropping two beats on the way toward the next verse. At the start of the bridge, John's solo "I _____" holds the humility and desire of the entire song in one outburst of feeling. The act of singing becomes apologetic, even though it hints at resentment ("You/Could find better things to do/Than to break my heart again") and never betrays his carping self-consciousness ("This time/I will try to show that I'm/Not trying to pretend"). Both verse and bridge waddle along so dodgingly between major and minor that at the end, instead of giving the listener a firm decision on the matter, the song simply fades out alternating between the two; any hope of resolution is left dangling in the air. Lennon has never before been this honest about being this indecisive.

The song links together the harmonic *motif* of the entire record: the verse (major)/bridge (minor) layout of the title track and the tinge of regret in "If I Fell" ("And *I* would be sad . . .") gets extended into an emotional symbol of ambiguity. Only "I'll Cry Instead" and "You Can't Do That" avoid the tensions implicit in pitting major against minor, and only "I Should Have Known Better," "I'm Happy Just to Dance with You," and "Can't Buy Me Love" are simplistic looks at love. The other film songs and the whole of side two take less resolute stances—they're either qualified pleasures, disrupted affairs, or regretful confessions. If this album ends more soberly than the heights of "Twist and Shout" or "Money," it's because the approach to what they're singing about is no longer two-dimensional: love is more than just "holding hands," and true love ("And I Love Her") confounds formula fantasies. A high-rolling barnbuster wouldn't undermine these sentiments, but it wouldn't emphasize them, either, which is why "I'll Be Back" is so well placed. (These songs have also grown to mean more in time: the possessiveness in "You Can't Do That" used to be the way men pledged their devotion.)

The gap between the commercial songs for the movie and the less conventional treatments on side two gives the album a duality (even though "I'll Cry Instead" was intended for the film): surefire recipes and tastefully practiced solos for the "soundtrack" sit astride more experimental impulses on side two (the jerky starting gate of "Any Time at All," the harmonic tricks of "When I Get Home," the irregular meters of "I'll Be Back")—a gap that will widen on *Help!* The freshness of the live performance and the intricacy of the recorded product will mesh in varying degrees for the next several records: *Rubber Soul* is often pointed to as the transition point, but *A Hard Day's Night* shows just as much spontaneity mixed with calculation. The idea of the album is beginning to take shape as a forum for ideas, different slants on what pop can address, and how variety can be arranged to best effect.

TIRED OF TOURING

I Feel Fine (John)/*She's a Woman* (Paul)
Released: November 27, 1964

BEATLES FOR SALE *Released: December 4, 1964*

THE FOUR WEARY faces on the cover of *Beatles for Sale* articulate the record's undertone of fatigue. Instead of the handsome profiles of *With the Beatles* or the playful expressions on *A Hard Day's Night*, the soft focus of Robert Freeman's lens casts somber shades on the Beatles' already tired expressions. After completing production work on *A Hard Day's Night* and winding up sessions for its soundtrack album, the Beatles played several British dates before taking three-week vacations with their wives and girlfriends in May 1964. They were to work steadily from the end of May until the new year. In June, Jimmy Nicol replaced an ill Ringo on drums for a tour of Denmark, the Netherlands, Hong Kong, Australia, and New Zealand. Twelve thousand fans greeted them as they returned to England on July 2, in time for the premiere of *A Hard Day's Night* at Piccadilly Circus on July 6. The album came out four days later.

July included appearances on the BBC's "Top Gear" and "Juke Box Jury," tapings, and several live shows and concluded with four performances at Johanneshovs Isstadion in Stockholm, Sweden. In August they hosted their own "From Us to You" on the BBC Light Programme, grabbed studio time as they could, and performed a few more live dates. On

August 18, 1964, they returned to America for a month-long tour, erratically criss-crossing the country to log fifteen thousand miles. When they returned to Britain in late September, they had only two weeks to complete sessions for *Beatles for Sale* in order for the album to be ready for the Christmas market. They then embarked on a month-long tour of England.

The "I Feel Fine"/"She's a Woman" single was released on November 27; the album came out on December 4. After a relatively light schedule in early December, they performed for three straight weeks, two shows per day (with only Sundays off), at the Hammersmith Odeon Theatre in London, billed as *Another Beatles Christmas Show*. The strain of their schedule finally began to catch up with them.

Still, the slip in quality doesn't compare with the disastrous second half of 1967, a period so below par that only "Hey Jude" could make up for it. Their work in late 1964 *is* uneven, especially compared with 1963's. But it does dramatize their connection with the white sources of rock 'n' roll's roots, and, although critically unpopular, it reveals a completely different—and essential—side of their musical personality.

I Feel Fine (John)/*She's a Woman* (Paul)
Released: November 27, 1964

"I FEEL FINE" was written in the studio, and Lennon always prided himself on producing the first feedback ever recorded:

> That's me completely. Including the electric guitar lick *and* the record with the first feedback anywhere. I defy anybody to find a record—unless it's some old blues record in 1922—that uses feedback that way. I mean, everybody played with feedback on stage, and the Jimi Hendrix stuff was going on long before. In fact, the punk stuff now is the Beatles. Before Hendrix, be-

fore the Who, before anybody. The first feedback on any record. (*Playboy*, p. 184)

The opening electric storm generates its own antidote—
a plucked note from Paul's bass sets off the lead guitar's reverberations, and when George breaks free into the melodic riff
that drives the whole song, it makes the beginning of "You
Can't Do That" sound tame. Everything that joins the central
guitar lick sounds like a natural extension of the energy it
generates. But as hook-bound as the guitar is (its rhythms are
melodic, its melody rhythmic), Ringo carries this groove even
more than George (eighth notes on two, tom-tom pop on
four)—his Latin undercurrent keeps everybody swinging.
(The guitar lick and some of the drum patterns are lifted
straight from breaks in Bobby Parker's "Watch Your Step," a
1961 single that picked up where Ray Charles's 1959 "What'd
I Say" left off, according to Lennon's ear.)

Like "Eight Days a Week," this is a feel good song meant
for the car radio, where subtleties are subsumed by pleasure.
The melody is a throwaway, a chip off the blues, and the
recording relies on John, Paul, George, and Ringo's playing
to make the kinesthetic connection—and they do. John's brisk
onslaught in the verses ("Baby's good to me/You know she's
happy as can be/You know. . .") are smoothed out by vocal
harmonies in the bridge ("I'm _____ so _____ glad _____").
As the band responds together to the excitement in the original guitar lick, the sound burgeons into a high tidal beat that
comes out of the speakers in waves—a Phil Spector wash stripped
of pretensions.

The drum fill that follows George's spirited and scrappy
guitar solo is a quantum leap from anything Ringo has done
before—he sounds enraptured by the beat, and not quite sure
where he's going to land. "When I'd do a fill I always felt I
went into a blackout. I didn't know what I'd do," he told
Max Weinberg in *The Big Beat* (p. 182). After several radiant
moments of syncopated second-guessing, he spins back into

his Latin patterns and the band is off again. Except for the guitar interruption, a repeat of the introduction, the attack is relentless. (This drumming sets the stage for the timing marvels in "Ticket to Ride" and the constant variations in "Drive My Car.") It all goes by so fast that Lennon's humming as the guitar fades out sounds like satisfied exhaustion—a nice kind of tired.

PAUL'S "SHE'S A WOMAN" approaches rhythm and blues more with a pop sweetness than with a dirty mind. The clipped guitar yelps that set it off tease the ear in a simpler way than the fade-in to "I Want to Tell You" will—only after the band enters do George's carefully yanked chords sink into the offbeat of the ensemble. Paul sings at the very top of his register, a high but not quite belting happy blues, and everything around him is arranged, from the piano that echoes his melody to George's solo, where he confines himself to the simplest of linked licks. Because good times and an easy way with a song are the heart of R&B, too much control can choke. If Ringo didn't open up to his cymbals on the middle four-bar break (instead of the usual eight-bar bridge) behind the words "She's the woman who understands/She's the woman who loves her man," the track would be almost too tightly strung.

BEATLES FOR SALE *Released: December 4, 1964*

Artistic slumps are revealing—they measure endurance, even if you're at the top. If *Magical Mystery Tour* demonstrates the limits of rock psychedelia, the country excursion of *Beatles for Sale* says something about how the Beatles view rock's antecedents. It would take until *Help!*—"Yesterday" 's string quartet—for them to begin conceiving sounds that they could never reproduce on stage; but "I'm a Loser" is the start of a self-revealing journey for Lennon that includes "Help!," "I'm

Only Sleeping," and "Baby You're a Rich Man" and concludes with "Don't Let Me Down" and "Instant Karma," a
string of work that charts his personal responses to fame.
McCartney's presence on the album is lesser, with only two
solo originals ("I'll Follow the Sun" and "Look What You're
Doing"—"Baby's in Black," "Eight Days a Week," and
"Every Little Thing" are duets), but in the final analysis, his
dash through "Kansas City" outdoes Lennon's unironic "Rock
and Roll Music." And even the flattest moments—"Baby's in
Black," "Mr. Moonlight," some of "Honey Don't," and
George's ill-placed Perkins fiasco—detract from what surrounds them only in context; the great moments don't suffer
as much as they should, which makes them even stronger (side
starters "No Reply" and "Eight Days a Week").

Lennon sings the opening words of the record ("No Reply") with a spite ("This happened once before/When I came
to your door") that suddenly melts into a knowing sneer
(" no reply oo lo io"); the verses are split between brooding mistrust and neurotic cries. Lennon's most tightly wound
story about getting dumped is also his first without any electric guitars, and the acoustic starkness jabs bluntly at his
words. A piano joins Ringo's heavy blows to his crash cymbal
(right) to make the pain in Lennon's voice palpable: the syncopated lines that interrupt the feigned aloofness of the verses
(the loaded "I saw the *light*," "I nearly *died*") are repeated
to set up the betrayals that spark his seething jealousy
(" 'Cause you walked hand in hand/With another man . . .
in my place").

In the bridge ("If I were you"), John delivers a pep talk
in double time, as though he could wash down the aftertaste
of betrayal just by singing about it. The question of whom
he's speaking to here—his lover or himself—shakes up his self-
confidence even more. McCartney's high harmony, along with
the handclaps and the piano, helps make it sound as though
he's regaining his self-confidence ("If I were you/I'd realize
that I/Love you more/than any other guy")—they reach for

the new harmonic territory with zeal. (The verse kicks land on A minor and E minor—"I nearly died" and "No reply"; the bridge visits A major by the way of E major.) Out of desperation, he goes so far as to offer forgiveness. But the sympathy that belies his earned cynicism returns to the final verses with resignation. Ringo anticipates the final two "No reply" cries (returning to C major) with one last piercing blow, dashing all hopes of a second chance.

Where "You Can't Do That" was accusatory simply to let off steam, "No Reply" is genuinely pained: the former song accused; the latter swallows deceit. It's the most disheartened opening to an album yet.

"I'M A LOSER" is a swollen contradiction: half country, half rock 'n' roll, with a narrative to match—half storytelling, half aggressive release. The stop-time intro recalls "Misery" without the mischief, the opening moments are direct and confessional: "I'm a loser/And I'm not what I appear to be." Among Lennon's songs, "I'm a Loser" is the first to admit anything but satisfaction at being a Beatle.

To Lennon, love is a matter of winning and losing ("I should have known she would win in the end"); and with lines like "Is it for her or myself that I cry?" he redeems the "tears . . . falling like rain" cliché of the second verse—he's singing more tellingly about himself than about any love that he's lost. His wailing harp solo is answered by George's best Carl Perkins guitar imitation before the third verse zeroes in on what's really troubling him—pride: "And so it's true pride comes before a fall/I'm telling you so that you won't lose all." He leads by reluctantly admitting that the cliché he hates is true; he follows through with a warning.

Only later, after "Help!" and "I'm So Tired," does "I'm a Loser" clearly resonate as Lennon's first song about the dispiriting façade of fame. Real fears about identity are couched in metaphors of romance: the love relationship is so clearly a code for his internal struggle that it marks how ingeniously he reimagined pop's conventions. "I'm a Loser" is an early self-portrait.

''BABY'S IN BLACK'' rounds off the unhappy subjects of the first three songs and very nearly parodies them. Its word-play ("Baby's in black and I'm feeling blue") doesn't revive its inferior lyric ("though it's only a *whim*"?), and it remains unclear why they included it. Other songs recorded during these sessions—notably Lennon's streak through "Leave My Kitten Alone"—didn't make it onto the album. Although "Baby's in Black" received an elegant cover from Elvis Costello and T-Bone Burnett in 1984, it sits uneasily next to the catharsis it follows.

THE EARLY BEATLES' inspiration for covers was an irre-sistible draw toward a given idea or performance—on "Money" and "Long Tall Sally," they sound as though they can't help but play with all their might. They did covers out of sheer affection for a sound and an urgent desire to get inside the imaginative space their heroes had shown them, allowing the cultural and racial contradictions to sort them-selves out along the way.

In "Rock and Roll Music," Lennon sounds worn, less in-volved with what surrounds him; he's not filled with rage or revenge ("Money"), not lustful or teasing ("Twist and Shout"). He runs this Chuck Berry classic pro forma, without the in-tensity or the edge that made the other two such rousing fi-nales. Because it's his only cover on this record, and his earlier covers said so much more, it seems to symbolize his frustra-tion with the form—we still hear his love for rock 'n' roll, but it revels in good humor more than it mocks assumptions.

That doesn't mean the track is banal—far from it. Len-non's voice builds to a beautiful pitch at the end of his verses, throwing the whole band into higher gear for each refrain. By the last verse, the momentum explodes into the downward glissando on the piano and the subsequent Johnny Johnson triplets way up high on the final chorus. But compared with the way he threw himself into "Please Mr. Postman" or "You've Really Got a Hold on Me," he sounds haggard, less captivated by the music's possibilities. Following the shaken confidence of "No Reply" and the layered interferences of "I'm a Loser," his delivery is almost flat. These grand old rock 'n' rollers don't say it all for him anymore: he's beginning to say things better for himself.

McCARTNEY'S LYRICISM is in full bloom in "I'll Follow the Sun"—his deceptive harmonies draw the listener into the gentle mood unaware that it masks a conceited cheat beneath the surface. With such a gorgeous key layout going for him, no wonder he didn't work on the lyrics. (The verse moves backward through dominant and subdominant seventh chords to tonic.) "I'll Follow the Sun" is not a love song; it's the precursor to such vain self-glorifications as Mac Davis's "Baby Don't Get Hooked on Me"—the singer is more interested in escaping than in saying goodbye, skipping the rain to stay in the sun. It's not a mutual separation: "One day you'll know/ I was the one" presumes much more than it sympathizes. This is why the harmonic cleverness is so apt: it tricks our ears the way Paul's singing betrays the lyrics' intentions.

LENNON'S FULL-THROTTLE vocal attack at the top of "Mr. Moonlight" smashes Paul's feigned sincerity with one of the most peculiarly engaging covers they ever set down. Their rendition of this 1962 B side by Dr. Feelgood and the Interns shows just how fanatic they were about obscurities, and how much everyone else took for granted by ignoring such oddities. Just as in Larry Williams's "Slow Down" John's true convictions cut through even the funniest moments; here his parody actually sounds plausible.

The singing is unbearably straight on the harmony sections, which allows Lennon to break loose with real gut energy on his solo lines ("And the night you don't come my way/

I pray and pray more each day. . ."). You can hear why Lennon had to record it: it lets him wear his heart on his sleeve in a way he never could have written for himself. The melodic limitations would never have appealed to someone like Paul; Lennon's melodies actually resemble this one-note kind ("A Hard Day's Night" or "I Should Have Known Better"). The comic touches are exaggerated: Ringo's tom-tom blows, which punch holes in the middle of verses; the organ's tasteless, velveteen solo. By taking the whole thing so seriously, they actually make it hysterical; even the arranged vocal fadeout, rising with each repeat, is one last musical guffaw.

LEIBER AND STOLLER'S "Kansas City" is a vehicle for Paul's singing. When he veers into Little Richard's "Hey, Hey, Hey, Hey!" McCartney seizes the moment with a deliciously raspy send-off; and as the background vocals join in for the response choruses with handclaps, the whole mix jumps with energy, from the steady beat Ringo drapes beneath to the high falsetto "whoo"s Paul adds to the top. It's cleaner than "Long Tall Sally," cleaner than even "Rock and Roll Music"; it charms the beat rather than desecrates it—and who said rock 'n' roll couldn't have charm? The high spirits of Paul's rock 'n' roll are always honest: he never puts on airs. Balancing out Lennon's soul-searching with a nearly unflappable cheerfulness, he winds up making John sound sane by comparison.

NOTHING ELSE ON this record compares with the pop electricity at the top of side two—"Eight Days a Week." Within its strictly confined conventions, Lennon writes a romantic but not too cheeky radio song, perfect for AM top forty's two-inch speakers. At the same time, he innovates: a fade-*in* to a song (like Chuck Berry's "Downbound Train"); acoustic guitars up front with electric guitars pushing from *behind;* a mixture of styles—not quite pure country, but certainly not driving rock 'n' roll. Greil Marcus cites this song as being among the ones that kept "virtually every promise rock 'n' roll over made" (the others being "There's a Place," "Every Little Thing," and "Money"), where, within a "classically simple rock structure," the Beatles sound "ready to blow up in the listener's face at any moment." In "Eight Days a Week," though, they sound less likely to blow up than to burst into uncontrollable laughter. Its freshness is impelled by its roots; the spirit is indebted as well as immediate.

The components of the song don't add up the way the actual performance does: the handclaps on the right channel, the variations in the vocal harmonies that build with successive verses, and even the irresistible hook of "Hold me, love me," repeated to sequential harmonies—all these devices have been used before. What they haven't been coupled with, however, is a beat that they actually seem to sit back in—the Beatles are good enough by now to let the medium tempo carry them instead of pushing it. The effect is lulling, almost hypnotizing—like the Byrds' sound, which it influenced—if it weren't for the vocals forcing attention at every step of the way. The little turns that both Paul and John inject are enough to bring surges of excitement to the sound. And during the middle eight, when they pause briefly after the melisma on "lo-o-ove you," the anticipation before Ringo picks up the beat swerves between teasing and tantalizing. The way Ringo then half fills out the space, stopping short instead of filling out both beats, suspends the expectation-release gesture in midair. His control is masterful, and the feeling he injects is understated sprightfulness.

That "Eight Days a Week" starts side two of the same album that began with the sharp pain of "No Reply" shows that the Beatles certainly aren't going out of their way to be the four happy-go-lucky moptops the press—and, to be fair, their audience—wanted them to be. But the expansion of both ends of their range, from angst-filled heartache to what Marcus calls "the pleasure principle," point toward a complexity that will soon make a single like "Penny Lane"/"Strawberry Fields Forever" possible. The variety inherent in each song is increasingly apparent on each record, as moods play off one another in deliberate contradiction. There is just as much pain in Lennon's moan in "Eight Days a Week" as there is delight in the charged bridge to "No Reply": the contradictions exist before an album is ever laid out.

THE ONLY BUDDY HOLLY song the Beatles released, "Words of Love," is the closest they ever got to an Everly Brothers cover (which they left for Simon and Garfunkel). As usual, the differences in arrangement between Holly's original and the Beatles' rendition are slight. George sounds more assured than Holly, or in purist terms, less hillbilly: the sound he gets from his electric guitar is more wiry than the original, but the playing is more refined.

But where Holly harmonizes with himself, John and Paul turn in a bona fide duet. Holly strings the lyrics out and caresses the endings of words gingerly, slyly hinting at sexuality. He sounds vaguely harmless, the boy next door delivering a pleasant melody with an exaggerated, aching tenderness. Paul smooths his tone above John's, whose earthy baritone sounds almost heavy with breath. Listen to the sensuality they draw out at the ends of phrases ("Darling I love you"); where Holly's vocals are crooked, the Beatles' are romantically curved. In their only cover of the band that inspired their name (the Crickets), they elevate what Holly sang as inspired corn.

LONG BEFORE RINGO ever realized his dreams might come true, he wrote to the Houston chamber of commerce in search of employment. As he told Max Weinberg:

> Liverpool's a port and it's probably the biggest country and western town in England. With all the guys coming off the

ships, they'd bring with them all these country and western records. But I was into the blues. I wanted to emigrate to America because of Lightning Hopkins. (Weinberg, p. 184)

He never has recorded the blues; but "Honey Don't," from the B side of the 1956 Carl Perkins hit that Presley would make famous, "Blue Suede Shoes," is already Ringo's second Perkins cover, following "Matchbox" with the same key ingredients. Perkins's style is Ringo's strong suit: he's humble, self-effacing and rollicking, and makes few demands on his audience. Rockabilly's magic lies more in its streak of character (its droll bemusement, its deadpan jollity) than in what it says. The medium tempo doesn't have the same edge as straight-ahead rock; it requires a laid-back approach to make the dry humor stick. Perkins's original delivery is that of a man with no class except for the simple dignity with which he carries himself. He's got more grit than natural charm, and the joke works because he knows what he's after. Ringo doesn't have the grit, but he'd loaded with luckless charm. The Beatles make it work because of Ringo, not in spite of him, and it adds even earthier pleasures to what John and Paul did with Buddy Holly.

''EVERY LITTLE THING,'' the next track, takes the middle road to Lennon's psychodramas: it's not twisted up, but it's not exactly a joy ride, either. The singer is a man in love but not quite sure of himself, on the verge of paranoia but not quite peeking over the edge. The title phrase ("Every little thing she does/She does for me") could be euphoric, spilling with rapture at the prospect of being loved (as in "I Want to Hold Your Hand" or "She Loves You"); but it's not—the mood is contained, and Lennon sings with a deliberate assertiveness, not abandon.

The verse caps two short phrases off with a longer one sung in triplets, melodically hesitant beneath the self-assurance of the text ("Yes, I know I'm a lucky guy"). A descending piano line touches up the last phrase of the irregular verse, and the refrain opens up a little rhythmically from the rest of the song. The timpani blows that accent the refrain are more original than George's guitar solo, which picks up on the earlier triplets; but there are no smudges in the production, and everything hums along nicely. As Paul joins for the upper part on the refrain, the odd harmonies give a tickle of interest—parallel fourths followed by parallel triads. They're somewhat ungrammatical in musical terms, the kind of harmonies only the Beatles could make work for them (like the "I can't hide" fourths in "I Want to Hold Your Hand.") The final touch is the irresistible melodic fragment they repeat during the fade-out ("Every little thing _____"), which is so instantly catching it might have been the catalyst for the entire song. As the guitar line links itself up beneath the voices, the melodic and rhythmic motifs weave together for a dialogue into the fade-out. It's the kind of brilliant closing gesture that makes the whole song seem memorable, even if that's the only thing left ringing in one's ears.

THE EMOTIONAL restraint of "Every Little Thing" comes undone in "I Don't Want to Spoil the Party": indecision turns to self-pity, and the punishment of being left alone threatens whatever reconciliation may be at hand. Lennon's lead vocal is double-tracked except in the bridge, where McCartney's upper harmony and the change in rhythmic texture lift the otherwise staple country number to a more buoyant level. The bridge resembles the middle section of "No Reply" in its search for hope and asserts the singer's own sense of purpose against the loss that he's confronting by emphasizing his devotion ("Though tonight she's made me sad/I _____ still _____ love _____ her"). The Carl Perkins–style guitar work throughout makes its inspiration clear.

WHEN A RHYTHM alone captures the listener's interest, it's a good bet that a talented artist is at work. Steve Gadd's suggestive drum patterns at the top of Paul Simon's "Fifty Ways to Leave Your Lover" hook the listener promptly; Steely Dan's first hit, "Do It Again," opens with the unadorned rhythms that backdrop the entire track; the Talking Heads use the same bait on "Warning Sign" (from *More Songs About Buildings and Food*). The opening drum break of "What You're Doing" compresses all the rhythmic tension of the song into a crisp, tart introduction—the trap is already set before the musical snag is even hinted at. The guitar riff that follows is modest—there's none of the infectiously charged dynamism that makes "I Feel Fine" irrepressible.

The modesty gives way to an unusual annoyance, especially coming from Paul. The verses all start out with a punch; single words are spit out angrily by all before Paul alone finishes the phrase. (The backup vocalists make an uncorrected mistake during the first round of the third verse, singing "you" where Paul sings "please" and "I'm" where he sings "you.") At the end of the bridge, Paul trails off the word "me _____" before the band re-enters with the same kind of punch for an upbeat back into the verse. The guitar solo is backed by razzmatazz piano for lack of anything better to do with it. The ending mirrors the beginning exactly with a return to the guitar riff, which drops out to drums alone. Then, quite unexpectedly, Paul turns in a brief but important bass solo and brings the whole band back in, piano and all, for the fade-out.

Both as song and performance "What You're Doing" dodges risks, but it does contain more than its share of pop ingenuity. Adding a piano for just the guitar solo and the final fade-out suggests the love of detail they would later develop more fully. (A live performance of this kind of song would feature a piano the entire way through, not just for eight bars.) The Beatles' conception of what the studio allowed them to do in altering textures and changing musical colors for different sections of songs is emerging as a stylistic trait, not just a gimmick. When they begin to conceive of expressive textures in terms of studio manipulation, they overturn the conventional notion that a pop record is a replication of a live performance. By the time they reach *Revolver*, the live performance is almost beside the point.

SONG PLACEMENT ON records is an expressive—not to mention political—group act. The only Harrison song to start an album will be "Taxman" at the top of *Revolver*. And the only George piece to close an album is his sober recitation of "Everybody's Trying to Be My Baby," which limps to the same finish line that "Twist and Shout" and "Money" streaked through. With "Roll Over Beethoven," George didn't have much choice but to be fast and energetic; on "Everybody's Trying to Be My Baby," he settles back into the beat with comfort and a modest glint in his eye. The Carl Perkins original, from the same record that contained "Honey Don't" (1958's *Teen Beat*), is similar in style to that song: pure rockabilly, the wildness of the singer is contained only by the boundaries of song. George belts out the opening lines inside a huge reverb, taking the same liberty with the pauses that Perkins does, and the guitars (one on each channel) are also boomier, more resonant, and more authoritative than their hillbilly exemplars. His solos are all true to the licks he learned straight off the Perkins original, and he tacks an extra kick onto the finale for a send-off, echoing his own cutoff the way he echoes Perkins's style.

Judged against "Twist and Shout" and "Money" as a showstopper, this song doesn't make up in excitement for what it lacks in creativity; both other finales are hard-hitting rockers where this is laid-back rockabilly. But by placing it at the end of the album, it invites the comparison, because those other finales said so much more.

Beatles for Sale doesn't have such an ending, in part because their conception of the record was pinched. After an exhausting American tour, their studio schedule was subject to the Christmas market deadlines. But "Everybody's Trying to Be My Baby" has its own significance in terms of the record it closes, even if can't make the same claims. From the opening cut, this album is the Beatles' most country flavored, spiced with true rock 'n' roll ("Kansas City," "Rock and Roll Music"), pop sidetracks ("Eight Days a Week," "Baby's in Black," and "What You're Doing"), a ballad, and a romp ("Mr. Moonlight"). Country and country-related roots are at this record's core, which is why electric guitars are de-emphasized throughout. It doesn't have the same impact of the albums that precede it (except for "Eight Days a Week," perhaps, or "Kansas City") but it does have a historical integrity. With the exception of Chuck Berry's "Rock and Roll Music," and Little Richard's "Hey, Hey, Hey, Hey!" performed in medley style with "Kansas City," as Richard did it, all of the allegiances the Beatles pay here are to *white* rockers. Leiber and Stoller wrote "Kansas City"; Carl Perkins's and Buddy Holly's styles dominate side two, both explicitly and implicitly. And more specifically, these last two were white rockers who specialized in country-inflected tributaries of pure rock 'n' roll: rockabilly, country swing, and plain old country (the Beatles covered Perkins's "Sure to Fall," his prettiest country ballad, on BBC radio).

As participants in the history of rock, the Beatles could hardly be better students of its past. By this point they've touched all the bases: from the manic Little Richard of "Long Tall Sally" to the Gene Vincent rocking crooner duality they admired; from the girl-group strains of "Boys" to the relentless drive of "Rock and Roll Music." This album injects the country element into their vision of rock 'n' roll as pop, and it plays right into their original material: "No Reply" and especially "I'm a Loser" are the sound of John the rocker attempting country (his charged-up bridges give him away); "I'll Follow the Sun" may be a standard ballad, but it doesn't have the high classical tone of "All My Loving"—like "I Don't Want to Spoil the Party," it has a front-porch singability to it, a lack of sophistication compared with "Things We Said Today." Most importantly, the Beatles added these rural inflections without compromising their stance as rockers.

PARANOIA AND INSOUCIANCE

Ticket to Ride (John)/Yes It Is (John)
Released: April 9, 1965

Help! (John)/I'm Down (Paul)
Released: July 23, 1965

HELP! *Released: August 6, 1965*

THE BEATLES' SECOND movie and its soundtrack compare poorly with their screen debut: *Help!* isn't the screwball success *A Hard Day's Night* is, even though a bigger budget and a longer production schedule allowed the Beatles a vacation in the Bahamas as they filmed. Lennon said they felt like "guest stars" in their own feature, and Richard Lester's flashy direction—zipping cutaways and zany asides—doesn't revive the forced laughs in the script. Shooting took place between February and May 1965, with recording sessions and more radio appearances sandwiched in between location work in Austria, Britain, and Nassau. By summer they were touring Europe: *Help!* premiered in London in July, and the album was released in August, the same month they toured America again, beginning with their unprecedented Shea Stadium concert in front of fifty-six thousand fans.

Like *Beatles for Sale, Help!* doesn't add up to the kind of fuller statements that *Please Please Me, With the Beatles,* and *A Hard Day's Night* are. Individual moments (the title song, "You've Got to Hide Your Love Away," "You're Going

to Lose That Girl," "Ticket to Ride," "Yesterday") outweigh
the effect of the record as a whole. The two singles that precede *Help!* are used to open and close side one's film songs;
but since the B sides to these singles do not appear anywhere
else in the Parlophone catalogue, they will be discussed first.
(It is a curious reversal of procedure that Capitol includes
Lennon's rip-snorting rendition of Larry Williams's "Bad Boy"
from these same sessions on the American *Beatles VI* LP; in
England the song appears only on Parlophone's *A Collection
of Beatle Oldies*, released in December 1966, and the British
version of *Rarities*.)

Ticket to Ride (John)/Yes It Is (John)
Released: April 9, 1965

"YES IT IS" resembles "This Boy"—block harmonies for
the verses and Lennon singing lead during the middle section.
Both "This Boy" and "Yes It Is" are in $^{12}/_8$ time, but there is
a sense of growth between the two: in the second the harmonies are more seasoned, the delayed duple against the triplet rhythms pull with more resignation (each time "Yes it is"
is sung in the verse), and the harmonic language is more intricate (the bridge hinges on the minor dominant to get to the
subdominant, and climaxes on the supertonic).

The second verse economizes the images of the first with
the same emotional thrust:

> *Scarlet were the clothes she wore*
> *Everybody knows, I'm sure*
> *I would remember all the things we planned*
> *Understand, it's true, yes it is . . .*

"Scarlet" (instead of red) implies betrayal; "everybody"
knowing is paranoid; and the final couplet links regretful
memory with a plea for understanding. As in "If I Fell," Lennon wants this new woman to love him even though he can't

shake the old flame from his heart, and the bridge explains
why:

I could be happy with you by my side
If I could forget her
But it's my pride, *yes it is, yes it is*
Oh yes it is, yeah . . .

"But it's my pride" is hastily, almost incomprehensibly sung—
he's savvy enough to know that it's his pride that gets in the
way of leaving the past behind, but weak enough still to be
overwhelmed. The authority Lennon commands as a singer
grows to a surge of feeling for the line "But it's my pride, yes
it is," making the last "*Oh* yes it is" an emphatic self-indictment
as well as an effective transition—listen to the way his last
"yeah" buffers the anxiety it follows to quiet the return of the
verse.

The varied meanings of the title phrase and the wordplay
in the final verse ("For red is the color that will make me blue/
In spite of you") don't get in the way of the sentiment—these
turns show them off as practicing tunesmiths, tinkering with
the possibilities of a lyric instead of tailoring clichés to fit. It
may not have the same poignancy of the duet in "If I Fell,"
but the use of imagery is resourceful and flexible. "Yes It Is"
blends sentiment with wit to make the angered confusion in
"This Boy" more explicit. (Both happen to sit aside electric A
sides, "I Want to Hold Your Hand" and "Ticket to Ride.")

Help! (John)/I'm Down (Paul)
Released: July 23, 1965

"I'M DOWN," PAUL'S first straightforward original
rocker since "I Saw Her Standing There," is a rock 'n' roll
classic as surely as his version of Little Richard's "Long Tall
Sally" is, even if some critics hold that Paul's original bears a
striking resemblance to that juggernaut of insanity. The fact

is, "I'm Down" is better suited to Paul than "Long Tall Sally" is, because it isn't hampered by the camp racial ironies he tackles in interpreting the Little Richard original. For all the gusto he wrings from "Sally," there's more Paul in "I'm Down," and more Beatles. It embodies the short phrase that novelist Mary Jo Parker uses to describe the essence of rock 'n' roll: "fun songs about sad stuff." If the first song was a tribute, a pitch toward Richard's mad, eccentric flair for the music, "I'm Down" is the claiming of that irresistible spirit twisted with Beatles rhetoric. Along with "Twist and Shout," "Money," and "She Loves You," "I'm Down" lights right through the Beatles' pop stardom and makes them rock 'n' roll legends.

As the singer, Paul plays the blue-balled protagonist—the pain in his voice stems from his unrequited passion. His lover won't give in, and he is beside himself—frustrated, crazed, inexorably *down*. But within this context, Paul turns the music into a celebratory frenzy, not a lament, but a raised clenched fist, twisting disappointment into a raging storm of self-assertion. If dancing on your problems is what rock 'n' roll is all about (as Pete Townshend says), then "I'm Down" follows in the tradition of songs like "That's All Right (Mama)" and "Blue Suede Shoes."

It resembles "Long Tall Sally" most during Paul's opening: one mad voice screaming at the top of its lungs. The band punctuates his singing fiercely, and the ensemble is tight to the point of bursting—Ringo's snare drum alone has a snap that literally stings. There's a power in the sound of these four men playing these three chords that has nothing to do with volume. As they swing into the refrain, the background vocals give away the tone: the shape of their phrase is parodic—"I'm *really* down." (There is a fourth, slightly concealed voice singing the bass line, holding out the roots of each chord on the word "down.")

After a full round of "I'm down"s, the band stops and the backup singers chide the vocalist with his own tormented question. The call-and-response figure is turned inside out, with the backups chiding "How can you laugh" and Paul responding "when you know I'm down?" Almost inadvertently, it gives the song balance: the verses all begin with this poor soul, and the refrains all end with his same naked cries, mocked by the supporting singers. Where Little Richard had a flair for code words and hairstyles, McCartney adds a knack for the dramatic.

George's guitar solo is his most confidently unhinged yet—it doesn't even have to be brought in by a scream. By the time Paul starts hollering behind him, George is already well off his head. Those repeated notes near the end—the ones he bends and prances on—sting as much as Ringo's snare. Paul twists the third and final vocal solo out of shape the same way he does on "Long Tall Sally," and his fury charges the band to even greater heights. As in "Money," they churn the whole mess into an unstoppable gait, daring the needle to jump the grooves. But the motion is both violent and giddily hysterical—it's as though they synthesized the determined grit of "Money" with the buoyancy of "Eight Days a Week."

Lennon's organ solo subsumes Paul's most irrepressible scream—"When you know I'm WAA!!!" In the film of their 1965 Shea Stadium concert, John's manic keyboard playing (elbow glissandos, howls of laughter) is like a comment on the absurdity of their own half-hour set. Surrounded by fifty-six thousand screaming fans who had trouble hearing the music much less seeing the group, the Beatles seem simultaneously nonplused and unfazed at what their popularity inspires: they perform as enigmas, not as musicians. The band's hysteria on this song mirrors their fans' deafening adulation, and this image of Lennon bashing his way through his friend's rocker, wet with sweat and too turned on to care, is the perfect visual track to this B-side manifesto.

Paul's ad-lib vocal climax before the fade-out makes even the initial outbursts sound civilized. When he sings "Well baby, *baby*, BABY!!!!" in growing annoyance at the taunting chirps of John and George's backup, he aims to blow the whole song's fuse. (These gut reactions to the excitement of the sound grow into the heraldic scat refrain of "Hey Jude" and the melodic delights of his early solo albums *McCartney* and *Ram*.) Meanwhile, the band veers breathlessly close to the edge of hysteria, and it's to Ringo's credit that things don't fall apart. The hardest assignment for any drummer is to let the others cut loose to the extreme while providing a steady beat for them to fall back on. Lesser bands would easily come unglued with a groove so addled and punctured; Ringo maintains a sure but unconfining backbeat for the madness, the strongest glue of all.

HELP! *Released: August 6, 1965*

Help! is better than *Beatles for Sale* if only because it points more forward than backward—*Rubber Soul* couldn't exist without it. Side one's songs are all of a common type, either pop single or ballad, and although the invention within forms is great, the second side doesn't advance these formats the way it does on *A Hard Day's Night*. Although any of the remaining songs conceivably could have been used in the film, they sit in awkward relation to their counterparts—the two distinct sides make it sound like a link in a larger chain. The disparity is much more apparent than it was on *A Hard Day's Night*, and overall these songs compare poorly with that score's—"Another Girl" is not as strong as "Can't Buy Me Love," and while "You've Got to Hide Your Love Away" *is* strong, it's not as complex as "If I Fell"; "I'm Happy Just to Dance with You" is better than "I Need You." But side two is half-baked: it begins with a Ringo prank and ends with a Lennon screamer but sags in between. "Tell Me What You See" is a naive version of "I'm Looking Through You"; "Yesterday" has probably given more people the wrong idea about this band than any other track in their career—its popularity is as much a curse as it is a virtue. "I've Just Seen a Face" is charmingly harmless, and "You Like Me Too Much" is a snoozer, but "It's Only Love" is still as offhandedly great as Ringo's cowpoke impression. The result is that the Beatles sound less interested in filling out an album conceived for them as a tie-in with film profits. In fact, from this point in their career on they make albums not for the conventional audiences of films and concerts, but solely for the as yet unrecognized audience of rock vinyl junkies.

> When *Help!* came out, I was actually crying out for help. Most people think it's just a fast rock 'n' roll song. I didn't realize it at the time; I just wrote the song because I was commissioned to write it for the movie. But later, I knew I was really crying out for help. So it was my fat Elvis period. You see the movie: He—I—is very fat, very insecure, and he's completely lost himself. And I am singing about when I was so much younger and all the rest, looking back at how easy it was. Now I may be very positive—yes, yes—but I also go through deep depressions where I would like to jump out the window, you know. It becomes easier to deal with as I get older; I don't know whether you learn control or, when you grow up, you calm down a little. Anyway, I was fat and depressed and I *was* crying out for help. (Lennon in *Playboy*, p. 187)

"HELP!" HAS THE desperation of "I'm a Loser" with none of the earlier song's countrified jollity. Lennon's first draft of the later song was slower, but since it was needed as the title track for an action film, they sped it up. What began as an introspective ballad gains urgency from the running-fast-to-stay-in-place tempo—where "I'm a Loser" has a margin of self-deprecation, "Help!" sounds spooked. (The introductory pseudo–James Bond music that is edited on to the front of the Capitol version of this album puts the song in huge nonthreatening parentheses.)

The opening is a breathless flurry: background vocals bark out "Help!" and Lennon answers with increasing delir-

ium—he sounds panicked, trapped. Paul and George interrupt his every cry, leaving him no room to breathe. As the
tension mounts and the backup voices go into the free fall of
the last "Help! _____," John drops out completely, as if
words escape him. The effect is one of joining an object in
free flight—George's concluding guitar lick and the drumroll
Ringo squeezes in a split second before the downbeat to the
verse only add to all the gasping. (The opening bars sequence
down from the initial B-minor exhortation of "Help!" to the
ultimate A-major tonality of the song.)

Since Paul and George anticipate nearly every line Lennon sings in the verse, the effect is of voices inside the same
head, prodding, goading. The call-and-response device has
been turned around again (backups preceding lead), but this
time to chilling consequence. By the time Lennon sings "open
up the doors," the voices are completely caught up in the
nightmare. The drums drive the verse into the refrain with
a determined, agitated fill that is at once constricted and
lunging.

The refrain follows the same harmonies as the introduction, and the beat opens up: Ringo switches from his high-
hat to his open ride cymbal, and a tambourine is added to
loosen up the suspense. "Help me get my feet back on the
ground," Lennon sings, before joining the backup vocals with
their leap to the falsetto free fall on "Won't you *please, please*
help me" (as the drums drop out completely). The whirlpool
of paranoia has sucked him in, and he chooses this moment
to soar into his high register—usually his most poignant range,
used here to express devastation.

The second verse follows the first almost exactly, except
for the final line, where Lennon forces too many words into
the phrase to heighten the sense of aggravation: "I-know-that-
I/Just-need-you-like/I've never done before."

Instead of the usual guitar solo for the third verse, the
aggravation fades and Lennon sings the first verse over again,
accompanying himself alone with his twelve-string acoustic

guitar. He's done this before for intimacy (the bridge of "I Want to Hold Your Hand"), but never with this much intensity. He sings it more directly without all the instruments going off around him, with sorrow as much as tenderness ringing in his delivery. As the band slowly rejoins him for the final refrain, the gears begin to churn again, and he gets caught up in the motion one last time. The forces he's crying out against are bigger—and more ominous—than even he can get a grip on.

Following the last refrain, the call-and-response sequence is reduced to just two lines: the backup vocals call "Help!" and Lennon replies "me!" in a moan too full of pain to be called singing. The final line, "Help me," is set up by the backup vocals ("Help") but concluded by all in a gliding motion that finally lands on the minor chord, ending where it all began. The voices linger on their note, holding it past the instruments' last chord, straining to hold it out almost at the cost of losing their breath. Instead of stretching the vowel "ooh," they switch to the more inward "nnn," closing up the word "me" with successively darkened tones, entrapping John's futile cries the way a movie screen freezes a frame and fades to blackness.

It might have been written as the title song for a James Bond parody, but "Help!" survives as a desperate cry for intimacy. John isn't the first to be stricken by pop-star neurosis, the angst of losing contact with the very everyday people and everyday life he wants his music to address. But "Help!" exposes it as a personal kind of nightmare. No other Beatles song about fame sounds as lonely: "Drive My Car" dodges the pain with sly innuendos; "I'm So Tired" conveys the weight of fame and the animosity it can harbor; "Carry That Weight" accepts fame's responsibilities with a majestic resolve. And the wish for innocence ("When I was younger . . .") is more softly expressed here during the acoustic section than it is later in the schizophrenic rhythms of "She Said She Said" (on the line "When I was a boy"). The immediacy of the performance brings the sense of isolation home so strongly that it's curious to think that it was probably not heard this way when it was released. The sense of unstoppable motion conveys not only Lennon's—and his audience's—personal growing pains but the public frenzy over his Beatle persona, which shows no signs of abating ("My independence seems to vanish in the haze"). As the masks in "I'm a Loser" suggest, Lennon feels trapped in his Beatle role—he's an avowed outsider confronting mass adulation, and stardom exacerbates his identity perplex. In "Help!" he sounds taunted even by his fellow Beatles.

"THE NIGHT BEFORE" is a piece of formula pop from Paul, with only small details of interest, nothing as rich harmonically as "Another Girl" on this side nor as precocious as "Yesterday" on side two. The background vocals sing tightly drawn "aah"s and "ooh"s behind the lead lyrics "When I held you near/You were so sincere" as the melody rises dramatically. During the bridge ("Last night is the night I will remember . . . you by"), Ringo varies his drum pattern, approximating a Latin rhythm (with a slight dip on four), and a tambourine is added. (Like "Yes It Is," the bridge pivots off the minor dominant and moves to the subdominant.) A Hohner electric piano is mixed into the right channel throughout. Paul's vocal performance is forthright and professional, peaking on the line "When I think of things we did/ It makes me wanna *cry*," and George's meager guitar solo is doubled at the octave, returning briefly at the final cadence to round things off.

MCCARTNEY'S ASSURED POP is followed by Lennon's reflective folk. "You've Got to Hide Your Love Away" doesn't owe as much to Dylan as some would like to think; it has more of Dylan's influence than his actual style. It's hard to imagine the master of deceit singing so direct a sentiment with such clear, distilled imagery. Although Lennon's delivery here is detached and somewhat restrained, it's still more personally revealing than most of the masks Dylan wears. Dylan is among the great singers of his generation, but his skill lies more in twisting meanings and snarling ironies; he sings with an ear for hidden inferences and innuendos. Although a lot of Dylan songs address the audience directly— explaining feelings, holding opinions, pronouncing injus- tices—it's not clear how many songs are meant in the first person. Who is the real Bob Dylan: the drifter in "Tangled Up in Blue" or the prayerful "tenant" in "Dear Landlord"? Lennon is never so detached from his subject. "How could she say to me/Love will find a way?" is the kind of sardonic line Dylan might write, but Lennon is singing more to himself than to the "clowns" he sees around him. There are more boundaries between Dylan the performer and his audience. Although Lennon is speaking to the world at large, what comes across is a sense of sober introspection, not a lesson on human relationships.

In a standard pop song like "Blue Skies" by Irving Berlin, melancholy wins out over the hopeful lyric by undermining it with a minor melody. In rock 'n' roll, these extremes are played with and inverted, often by positioning down-and-out words with whoop-it-up rhythms (Robert Christgau calls this "affirmation-by-negation"). "You've Got to Hide Your Love Away" takes this idea a step further: wrongheaded advice is renounced by the acrid tone Lennon invests in it. As his voice strains with feeling on the high note of "Hey," he suddenly sounds more determined, less vulnerable, even though the ad- vice the "clowns" are giving to him contradicts the nature of his personality. The images of isolation ("Turn my face to the wall") are accented by a lone tambourine on the offbeat; the flutes that carry all of verse three emphasize the tender more than the bitter. The irony in "You've Got to Hide Your Love Away" lies in Lennon's delivery—he sings it with scorn.

GEORGE'S "I NEED YOU" is built around the small gui- tar riff of its introduction. The verses play off its angles with antecedent-consequent (question-answer) melodic phrases: the first line ("You don't realize how much I need you") ends at a higher point than the second ("Love you all the time and never leave *you*"), which takes a small turn further downward. The middle section adds a cowbell and continuous background harmonies behind the lead voice, and ebbs and swells with a natural kind of arc instead of building to a pitch. George's voice sounds tired; and although he's improving as a singer and songwriter, he's still on his way to better things. This song doesn't measure up to "You Like Me Too Much" on the other side or "If I Needed Someone" on the next album.

THE LEAD GUITAR ambles into the right channel of the next track ("Another Girl") like a drunken commentary on the refrain. McCartney's playing sounds loopy, like he's tripping all over himself, and it gives the otherwise ordinary track a goofy subplot. Paul plays with the ambiguity between the major and minor inflections this blues melody has to offer, and saves it from becoming completely clichéd by moving into a different key area for the bridge. The shift isn't really drastic, but it adds a great deal of color and allows for some gorgeous vocals. (The verse is in A major; the bridge moves to C major. The blue notes in the verse flirt with A minor.) Thematically, the song is not as well worked out as the key areas of "Here, There and Everywhere" or the dramatic symbolism of "Penny Lane," but it does have a definite layout: the verses are all addressed to the woman he's about to drop; the bridge is a fantasy about his new conquest. But the song is a throwaway—and while the harmony singing is as tight and full as any the Beatles recorded, it is immediately overshadowed by what follows.

"YOU'RE GOING TO LOSE THAT GIRL" starts with Lennon uttering the title as a threat, daring his friend to an argument. The falsetto note on "lose" is used for all it's worth as the song progresses: at first it's set against the jeering background vocals, holding on as they pull away beneath it; during the transition to the bridge, the held note is used as a common tone to link up the two key areas of the song. This transition is richer than the one in "Another Girl": it makes "I'll make a point of taking her away from you" sassier, more cutting. For the link back to the original key area of the verse, Lennon uses a simple slide (from F down to E—a half step), suavely veering back into the groove of the verse.

The wit of the songwriting is the freshest since the title track—they're finding new ways of sustaining interest at every moment of a song. They did this with rhythm and texture in "I Want to Hold Your Hand," they do it here with the harmonic plan. (The chord progression of the verse varies just one chord from the progression of the refrain instead of remaining the same all the way through—E-G#-F#m-B7 becomes E-C#m-F#m-B7.) George's guitar solo, played to the music of the verse, is buttressed by the continuing background vocals (varying the fourths with thirds and mixing them all up in the bridge); and Ringo's bongos add a playful menace throughout. The final cadence visits the key area of the bridge again before resolving up to the home key.

If "She Loves You" was the best kind of news one friend could bring to another, "You're Going to Lose That Girl" is the most vindictive. The two songs are like inverse narratives of the same situation: a friend giving advice about a love affair. But where "She Loves You" was bursting with head-over-heels ecstasy, "You're Going to Lose That Girl" is tightly strung, and Lennon unleashes his vengeance not on the woman (as in "If I Fell") but on the man standing between them.

"TICKET TO RIDE" is the middle of a trio of guitar pieces, songs where the guitar lick is central to the whole track. Next to the assertive joy of "I Feel Fine" or the ultracool contour of "Day Tripper," it has its own modest incandescent glow.

The song is Lennon's, but Paul contributed the lopsided drum pattern, and this disrupted motion is the song's most intriguing feature. As if to dramatize Ringo's patterns, a tambourine's regular backbeat is set against it. When the bridge cuts loose in a standard rhythm ("I don't know why she's ridin' so high"), the contrast is palpable. And from the brief wah-wah cadence in the middle of the refrain ("ri-i-ide") to the sleek drum fills Ringo sneaks in after it, the arrangement fills up every second with sparkles of energy: none of Ringo's fills are ever the same twice, and each one propels the concluding line of the refrain with piquancy (before "She's got a ticket to ride/And she don't care!").

And there is variety within the varied format: the transition from the second refrain to the first bridge is anticipated by drums and tambourine as they shift to double time one measure ahead of the others; the transition to the second bridge has no such overlap. Usually handclaps are added to fill out the sound with the effect of several people being swayed by the beat; in this bridge, there is only one pair of hands clapping. The hands reappear during the fade-out, clapping the tambourine's part as it moves on to play a new pattern. The momentary swell of excitement that follows the bridge during Paul's guitar solo is given a shimmering backdrop by the shaken tambourine—a trick that Lennon will transform for the exultant surges of "Day Tripper."

Paul joins John in harmony at the end of the first line (on "I think it's *today*, yeah"). The swelling high note he hits is immediately outdone by the even higher one he leaps up to on the second line ("The *girl that's* drivin' me mad"). Paul joins him again in the bridge, and the duet they turn in could be their best since "If I Fell." Their voices bob along, harmonizing yet independent, each sensitive to the other's slightest nuance. Lennon's solo vocal is so cool it verges on anger, breaking down only on the second line of the refrain ("She's got a ticket to ri-i-ide"). The last time Lennon sings this line, Ringo's fill is a solitary flam on his snare, tripping the beat squarely for his final fill. The sliding moans Lennon adds going into the third and fourth refrains express disgust, while the falsetto-to-midrange melody he writes as the song's kicker laughs the whole thing off ("My baby don't care!"). As the song fades out to those words, Paul adds guitar commentary—the same goofy sound that he offered on "Another Girl." (These are the only two songs in the catalogue where he plays this way; and where the sound oils up "Another Girl," it makes the end of "Ticket to Ride" sound flippant.)

THE BAND STARTS the disappointing second side with a typecasting send-up: "Act Naturally" may be the broadest joke the Beatles ever pulled off. Ringo's favorable reviews in *A Hard Day's Night* led to his being cast as the protagonist of *Help!* (something of a joke in itself). The song, a number-one country hit for Buck Owens in 1963, is about a man with no talent getting famous by playing himself in a hard-luck movie. The cover works because it's self-conscious: it's the story of Ringo's life as well as the story of *Help!* By this point Ringo's unaffected demeanor is an essential part of the band's musical charm. Turning the record over from "Ticket to Ride" to find Ringo is like going from a sleek convertible to a pickup truck and affirming the beauty and value of each. If George's songwriting points up the greatness that surrounded him, Ringo's singing levels the whole heady experience of a Beatles album by reminding us of the virtues of being normal.

THREE WEAKER EFFORTS follow: Lennon's folky "It's Only Love," Harrison's vain "You Like Me Too Much," and McCartney's incidental "Tell Me What You See" (only "I've Just Seen a Face" and "Yesterday" keep the album afloat). Lennon made clear his distaste for "It's Only Love" to *Playboy* in 1980: "I always thought it was a lousy song. The lyrics were abysmal. I always hated that song" (p. 187). It is weaker than anything on side one, if not as chunky as "Baby's in Black" from the previous album. There are no group harmonies, only Lennon's double-tracked voice on the right channel for the refrain. The usual games are played with texture (tambourine only in certain sections, acoustic guitars on the left, electric on the right), but these decorations don't find much to prop up.

"You Like Me Too Much" captures the awkward Harrison persona better than anything since "Don't Bother Me"—it has a nervous charm, and the piano-guitar dialogue that is the solo defines cliché. The transition to the bridge ("I really do") has a nice pop feel to it; the harmonies are synchronized in the best possible way. But the transition back to the verse suffers because of the key change that earlier harmony has forced George to reckon with: the music to "If you leave me . . ." couldn't be less convincing, and the disoriented composer can be heard manipulating his way back to the verse hoping no one will hear. "It's Only Love" is better, even though George's song sits much better on the *Help!* album than it does on the Capitol's *Beatles VI* (where it lies between "Eight Days a Week" and "Bad Boy"). "You Like Me Too Much" is Harrison's low point until the arrival of "If I Needed Someone" on *Rubber Soul*.

"Tell Me What You See" is a working draft of "I'm Looking Through You." The electric piano that could be the signature of these sessions is put to one of its better uses here, though, in a spicy exchange with the drums after the refrain. Ringo's response to the piano's lick packs plenty of energy in the snap of his snare. The claves that perk away throughout give it a kind of lounge-act character, a domesticated banality next to the piano-drum exchange.

"I've Just Seen a Face" could easily have been written for Peter and Gordon, and Joan Baez would have done it better than "Imagine." It's the Beatles' most overt "folk"-inflected pop yet, the kind of generic song that sounds less distinctly Beatlesque than adaptable to numerous other treatments.

The introduction sets up the tonality of the song by falling into it, not establishing it. And it does the same thing with rhythm: instead of setting the ear up for a rhythmic pattern that will be used throughout, it glides into the swing by delaying it with triplet motion. (The rhythmic impulses of the intro are half what they are during the rest of the song.) The tune is sweet and lithe without getting saccharine, and works even though the ends of stanzas are wordless:

> *I've just seen a face I can't forget the time or place where we just met*
> *She's just the girl for me and I want all the world to see we've met*
> *Mmmmmmmmm (Di-di-di for the second verse)*

As if to stay completely country, there is no bass guitar, and the guitar solo is done on the low end of a six-string as Paul dances around it vocally. When McCartney performed this song during the acoustic set of his 1976 American tour with Wings, he gave it the right effect: of sitting around on a porch harmonizing to a good old rural favorite. The soft brushes that Ringo uses on his snare propel the song in a gentle way—drums could easily intrude—and the maracas added for the refrain divvy up the rhythmic texture the way the tambourine does in earlier songs.

If it weren't for "Yesterday," this would be Paul's best song on the album: there isn't one word out of place; neither the rhymes nor the alliterations sound forced; and the refrain is a wonder of a hook, with enough lyricism to contrast with the run-on verses. Even the wordless lines sound appropriate—they follow the wordy lines with a simple smile. The refrain is repeated three times to take the song out, and each repetition gains warmth as it clues the listener in to the song's close. On the final repeat, the vocals (Paul is double-tracked) take a slight trip on "Oh, falling" for a lilt just before the song comes around the bend to the finish line. It sounds as if it wrote itself, and it has the simple grace of a folk classic.

IF "YESTERDAY" ISN'T the most esteemed *recording* the Beatles ever made, it certainly is the most celebrated song they ever produced. Its universality guarantees cover versions for years to come, from Las Vegas singers to "Gong Show" contestants. The Muzak royalties alone account for a great deal in the Lennon and McCartney estates, even though Lennon admitted the song is solely Paul's. The landmark use of a string quartet on a pop song was immediately copied by several groups, notably the Rolling Stones on "As Tears Go By" later that same year.

The narrative is implied; the lyrics don't spell out the story the way Paul's other small dramas do ("Eleanor Rigby" or "Ob-La-Di, Ob-La-Da"). But the emotional impact is stirring—it's the kind of song that sounds immediately familiar and yet original, as if it already existed before it came to McCartney:

> I really reckon "Yesterday" is probably my best . . . I like it not only because it was a big success but because it was one of the most instinctive songs I've ever written. I just rolled out of my bed one morning and . . . just got the tune. I was so *proud* of it. I felt it was an original tune, it didn't copy off anything, and it was a big tune, it was all there and nothing repeated. (*Paul McCartney in His Own Words*, p. 17)

His gift for lyricism has never equaled this moment, and it follows through on the promises made in "And I Love Her" and even "I'll Follow the Sun." In the verses, a three-syllable melodic fragment ("Yesterday . . .") grows to two arching phrases: the first rises ("all my troubles seemed so far away"), the second gently falls ("now it looks as though they're here to stay") before returning to the opening word ("Oh I believe in yesterday"). The plaintive opening guitar introduction and solo verse from Paul establish a mood of complete loneliness, of being left behind in the starkest reality of all—where romance suddenly turns into a haunting illusion. As the strings enter for the second verse, everything swells with questioning heartache. George Martin's quartet arrangement is so tasteful that it barely draws attention to itself; all the focus is on the singer and the song. The way the viola pulls away from the voice's held note at the end of the bridge is so effective that Paul sings this viola line himself the second time around. The first violin holds a single note for the entire final verse; instead of soaring, it weeps. Where others try to wring buckets of emotion from the song, Paul's simple delivery winds up being the most effective; his poignancy is simple and direct. It is a great recording, then, because it frames the emotion without intrusion, capturing the honesty of the sentiment without affectation.

Paul's most famous lost-love ballad stands out in part because it's also his saddest, drawing on the same melancholy that laced "And I Love Her"—his seemingly boundless geniality becomes more three-dimensional in such songs. "Yesterday" received such wide acclaim as a result of its release on this album that it was subsequently chosen as a single, and Paul played it by himself in the middle of a full Beatles set on "The Ed Sullivan Show" appearances that followed its release. Thank you, Paul," John said after Paul sang it to respectful silence. "That was just like him."

FOR ALL OF Lennon's admiration for Larry Williams's singing and recording style (he also covered "Slow Down" and "Bad Boy"), he sounds defeated on "Dizzy Miss Lizzie," as though he doesn't feel up to fighting the same rock 'n' roll battles anymore. (The slower version off the Plastic Ono Band album *Live Peace in Toronto* some five years later has more meat to it.) Lennon's treatment of this Williams song is his first to suffer from a comparison with the original. Where

Williams sounds manic, Lennon sounds fatigued; where Williams lets the song carry him, Lennon drives it forcefully, inhibiting any sense of flow it might have had on its own. The rhythmic groove is well set, and some of Ringo's propulsive links into successive verses are charged; but the cover as a whole doesn't do much more than pay respects. The contrast between this Lennon album-closer and "Money" is striking—"Dizzy Miss Lizzie" lives up to the rock 'n' roll ideal without outdoing it. And with such a quirky follow-up to the beauty of "Yesterday," the problem seems less artistic than it does commercial: they needed one more song to fill out the record, as they had on *Please Please Me*, so they leapt into "Dizzy Miss Lizzie" without much caring.

But it's nearly the last nonoriginal the Beatles would ever record (only the traditional Liverpool "Maggie Mae" on *Let It Be* would follow), and the problem could have been much larger. The Beatles were now in a position to record only their original songs; they had transcended speaking through the masters' material that had guided them this far. "Dizzy Miss Lizzie" doesn't sum up *Help!* the way earlier covers did for other albums—it points up just how uneven the mood of this record really is, and how ridiculous it would be to think that the Beatles could continue making the quality of recordings they wanted with all the touring that was still expected of them. Their unconventional recording ambition on side two (the strings on "Yesterday," the electric piano on "Tell Me What You See") isn't fleshed out by supporting material worthy of the same claims. It's to their credit that they follow up the disappointment of *Help!* and its closing number, which promises more than it delivers, with songs and production that still count among their best. *Rubber Soul* shakes free from the shackles of confined studio time and cinematic obligations—it follows through on the emotional ambiguities and musical kinetics that began surfacing as early as *A Hard Day's Night* and fulfills the artistic promise that persisted beneath the surface of Beatlemania's incessant demands.

STATES OF THE HEART

RUBBER SOUL *Released: December 3, 1965*

Day Tripper (John)/*We Can Work It Out* (Paul and John)
Released: December 3, 1965

WHEN THE BEATLES returned from their second major American tour in September 1965, they took a month off. August had been an endless series of mobbed airports and concerts, prisonlike hotel rooms (easier for fans to infiltrate than for the Beatles to escape), and in California, a "secret" mountain hideaway besieged with admirers. "How do you like America?" George was asked. "Well, so far, I've seen a room, and a room, and a car and a room and a room," he replied. Two days after taking acid with Peter Fonda and Byrds leader Roger McGuinn in Los Angeles, they accepted Elvis Presley's invitation for a visit at his Bel Air home. They broke the ice by launching into a three-hour jam session of Presley songs—sounds that must have been the most myth-infested rock 'n' roll ever made.

Once they were back in England, their singular position became clear: with Beatlemania confounding all expectations of its strength and staying power, there was no need to rush the next record. They must have felt relieved at not having to produce an album subject to the tight schedule that had marred *Beatles for Sale* a year before. With no obligations for a third film score, their slate was essentially clean. Free from the pressures of public commitments, they returned to the Abbey Road studios for two months of work in October and

November, pushing up the Christmas-market release date until December 3.

There's a new affection for recording on *Rubber Soul*: for the first time, the Beatles make music that they will never perform live. The genius lies in the balance between the spirited life of their ensemble ("Their records retained a bar band's spark," write Christgau and Piccarella) and its elegant tone. "If the emotional touch was harder, the musical touch was lighter," Greil Marcus writes. "This music was seduction, not assault; the force was all beneath the surface . . ." *Rubber Soul* intensified their bond with their audience (the way "She Loves You" had) as it fed the idolatry surrounding their fame—it drew them closer to their listeners as the frenzy of their tours continued to isolate them. The fish-eye lens they look down through on the cover elongates their heads and faces, as though they made music in another dimension.

T HE A MERICAN C APITOL version of *Rubber Soul* is a misguided rewrite of an artistic breakthrough. Where the Parlophone edition starts with the savvy rock of "Drive My Car," Capitol substitutes the harmless folk of "I've Just Seen a Face" from side two of Parlophone's *Help!* The rest of side one's lineup is the same except for the omission of "Nowhere Man." But what may look like simple changes alter the character of the record drastically, emphasizing the softer numbers with acoustic-based textures and omitting the two dramatic electric flourishes the Beatles included to balance things out ("Drive My Car" and "Nowhere Man"). Side two suffers from Capitol's edit as well: it leaves out Ringo and George and inserts "It's Only Love" (again from Parlophone's *Help!*) at the top of the set. The songs left off the American *Rubber Soul* would show up six months later on the singles-and–odds-'n'-ends review *Yesterday and Today*, a synthetic compilation to which there is no remotely similar Parlophone edition. This seemingly innocent ploy for profits (Capitol's record offers ten new tunes, Parlophone offers fourteen) is drastically out of line with the Beatles' original intentions and created some important differences between the way Americans respond to this record as compared to the British.

It's been suggested that Capitol's alterations were a vain attempt to plug the Beatles' latest album into the American folk-rock trend that was perceived by record executives at that point as a full-blown craze. The Byrds' electrified Dylan was hyped as "America's answer to the Beatles" by their publicist, Derek Taylor, former press agent and ghost writer for Brian Epstein.

But in 1965 the pop world underwent a major *rock 'n' roll* explosion. Dylan's electric set at the Newport Folk Festival earlier in the year, and his two seminal rock albums *Bringing It All Back Home* and *Highway 61 Revisited*, effectively derailed the purist folk craze. His best rock tour de force, "Like a Rolling Stone," capped a summer that had started with the Byrds' elegiac cover of Dylan's "Mr. Tambourine Man" and the seething disaffection of the Rolling Stones' "Satisfaction." Direct confrontation with a beat outsold watered-down protest: the Who's bombastic "My Generation" extended the implications of "Twist and Shout" and "Money"—Roger Daltrey's stuttered delivery made it sound as if he were stifling obscenities. The rock audience, written off as ephemeral by Capitol when it signed the Beatles in late 1963, was not only growing; its tastes were maturing. For the Beatles, as eager and discriminating pop fans, all this activity, which they helped set into motion, challenged their approach to their next record.

But the shaded musical color of *Rubber Soul* took everybody off guard. With Dylan's electric conversion and the Stones' hard-edged triumph, nobody expected the Beatles to go soft. It's a measure of *Rubber Soul*'s success that by slowing the beat down they draw attention to how much rhythm can do. The material is still powerful, but the tug of the record is intelligent and cunning, not brazen or manic. At the time, *Rubber Soul* was as much an unpredictable response to 1965's activity as it was a step toward a greater synthesis.

And yet *Rubber Soul* doesn't sound at all reactionary— it's their most forward-looking album since *Please Please Me*. (The "White Album" is prescient in a different kind of way: it hints at possibilities and leaves loose ends for others to carry through.) Dylan and the Stones inspire rather than influence their sound. The untold story of sixties rock is how these artists admired each other without ever stooping to imitation— the narrow barriers of the archetypical rock-'n'-roll formula sound vastly different in the hands of these central figures. The improvised narrative of Bob Dylan's "Talkin' World War III Blues" expands into the verbal shenanigans of "Tombstone Blues" the same way his poetic vengeance in "I Don't Believe You (She Acts Like We Never Have Met)" (first acoustic, then electrified with the Band) is heir to the embittered "Don't Think Twice, It's All Right." The Stones' rhythm-and-blues foundations (covers like Leiber and Stoller's "Poison Ivy" and Muddy Waters's "I Can't Be Satisfied") give way to original breakthroughs like "The Last Time" (which came out in April 1965) and "Get Off My Cloud" (which appeared in October) in much the same way the Beatles' self-taught apprenticeship leads to "Nowhere Man" and "I'm Looking Through You." Like Dylan's and the Stones', the Beatles' musical voice remains intact: they continue to strengthen each other's individuality without ever compromising their ensemble approach. Even though they sound completely transformed, there's still an unmistakable delight in what four people can do together that is uniquely Beatlesque.

WITH *RUBBER SOUL* the Beatles come of age musically as their subject matter matures emotionally. The latent ambiguities in "If I Fell" and "I'll Be Back" are the sounds of young people trying to make sense of feelings they don't understand, uncertainties that find release in startling rockers like "I'm Happy Just to Dance with You" and "Can't Buy Me Love." But as teenage anxieties turn into adult perplexities, experience begins to temper their naiveté. The first signals of this shift can be heard in songs about sour romances ("No Reply," "What You're Doing") and the fallacy of success ("I'm a Loser," "Help!," "I'm Down"). The sad moments on the *Help!* album ("You've Got to Hide Your Love Away" and "Yesterday") are deeper, more welling than before ("And I Love Her" or "I Don't Want to Spoil the Party").

At the top of *Rubber Soul*, "Drive My Car" 's smart groove announces that love isn't all it's cracked up to be, or at least not without its hitches. There's no way "Norwegian Wood" could be substituted for the "You've Got to Hide Your Love Away" sequence in the *Help!* movie—the film song is a coming-to-terms with innocence where the *Rubber Soul* track is decidedly more worldly. The loss in "Norwegian Wood" comes from the same vulnerability as in "If I Fell," but this time Lennon knows he's got only himself to blame for the emotional risks he takes. The only pledge of unqualified devotion here is "In My Life," which is so full of the pain of separation from family that its irony is profound. The idea of love in this music is not just tested (as it is in "I'll Be Back" or "Yes It Is"); it's a whole new continent of feeling.

"DRIVE MY CAR" has the smooth bravado of a Jack Nicholson performance, grinning on the surface with wheels spinning like mad underneath. The automobile, the American symbol of status and wealth, is also where pop lives—cruising, dating, jamming the radio on the way to the beach. Former truck driver Elvis Presley consummated his gratitude for fame—and his oedipal infatuation—by buying his mother a Cadillac. The Beatles instead satirize the ethics that such materialism implies and laugh at the drawbacks of their own success: the sleek tone touts the pleasures of fame to be as confounding and ephemeral as love itself. (McCartney's original phrase was "Baby, you can wear my diamond ring"; Lennon reputedly shortened it and reversed the sexual roles.)

In the opening moments a brash lead guitar (doubled left and right) is thrown off meter by Paul's deceptive bass entrance (right); the texture is spare, and the beat has a new freedom to it, a relaxed, engaging draw. The divided mix is the studio imprint that makes these songs so richly textured: all of a sudden we're aware of how many different parts fit together to make up the entire sound, instead of everything being stirred together into one high-velocity mass (as in "Long Tall Sally"). The stereo separation clarifies the vocals, cowbell, piano, and lead guitar solo on the right channel by keeping the rhythm track (drums, bass, and rhythm guitar) over to the left. The effect is expansive. Ringo slides a lopsided fill in an instant before the first real downbeat of the verse.

The singer is a hopeful lover, his prospect more interested in easy fame than in love—a subtle parody on the Beatles' own stardom and the status seekers it put them in touch with. The title line's vernacular slang is twisted with implications: the woman wants "to be famous, a star of the screen," but she's also teasing the singer sexually ("drive my car" means both "make me rich" and "turn me on"). "Working for peanuts is all very fine," she tells the singer, "but I can show you a better time." A continuous guitar riff is doubled in the bass for the verse.

A qualifying "but" sends the vocals into high, taut harmonies at the end of each verse (on the words "But you can do something in between" and "But I can show you a better time"); the drum fills underneath exaggerate the flirtation (it resembles a similar passage in their demo of "How Do You Do?"—after its bridge, on the words "But won't you tell me how do you do it?") Ringo plays every break differently, pulling a distinct tension from the beat each time out—the vocals pick up on it just before the guitar solo and during the fadeout with "beep-beep, beep-beep, yeah." During the minor refrain, a piano criss-crosses the ensemble on an added major chord (G major, the common harmony between the verse's D major and the bridge's B minor). The piano superimposes triplet quarter notes over the bar with just the right delay, giving the beat a drag that's as witty musically as the words (stressing the key words "car" and "star"). The coy concluding line of the refrain ("And maybe I love you") is underlined by Lennon's double-tracked vocal in the right channel—the only double-tracked stereo vocal in the song.

The final verse is the punch line, what the singer suspects all along: she's got no car, but she's found a servile driver, "and that's a start." Love may be as fickle and fleeting as fame, but the "beep-beep"s are the singer's hoots of conquest. Both lead guitar and piano return for the fade-out as Ringo rolls modestly into the downbeat of every two measures. "Drive My Car" 's musical intricacy is uncanny, but its ingenuity is never forced. The flirtation that begins as satire ends as seduction.

THE LIGHT WALTZ of the opening guitar to "Norwegian Wood" is deceptive—the undulating rhythm lures us in to a forbidden dance, a furtive encounter. The smoky ambience is acoustically lit, with only tambourines for a rhythmic pulse—the sound alone is more mature, more restrained than in "I'm a Loser," the first-personisms more distant than in "You've Got to Hide Your Love Away" (even though Lennon claimed he wrote "Norwegian Wood (This Bird Has Flown)" about an actual extramarital affair). The detailed lyric is finally allusive, the scene is conjured up by inference rather than by description—atmosphere outweighs drama. Lennon circles over the rejection of the woman skipping out on him, mulling over his insecurities musically with the hazy drone of the sitar (a less threatening usage than the Stones' in "Paint It Black," which followed in 1966).

The bitter opening line neatly combines her refusal and his resentment: "I once had a girl/Or should I say/She once had me." This cynical regret far outweighs the relative idealism of "If I Fell." The bridge (in the parallel minor) adds Paul's upper harmony and tambourine on the offbeats as John's biting humor trips the harmony back toward the verse at the end of the couplet:

> *She asked me to stay and she told me to sit anywhere*
> *So I looked around and I noticed there wasn't a chair.*

and

> *She told me she worked in the morning and started to laugh*
> *I told her I didn't and crawled off to sleep in the bath.*

The implied tease and his annoyance at having to sleep in the bath is secondary; it's her aloofness that he can't abide—it's repayment for his own flippant way with women. The tone conveys a completely different kind of longing than the comparably green "It's Only Love": something has been set off inside that he can't explain, and it hurts simply to admit that a woman can affect him so strongly; the intimidation involves something more than infatuation. In the last verse, "This bird had flown" implies her departure not just to work but forever, leaving him alone in her apartment. Lighting the fire at the end is the revenging kiss-off: he's not reminiscing about the previous evening's fireside conversation; he's fantasizing (at least) setting fire to her elegant decor. (Dylan's answer to this song, "4th Time Around," is either a highly derivative imitation or an overwrought self-parody.)

L E N N O N ' S S U P P R E S S E D A N X I E T Y is broken by the striking and incisive piano jerks that hammer out the frustration of "You Won't See Me." Coming from Paul, this antagonism can't help being tempered by melodic suavity, so he winds up sounding like an innocent victim rather than a co-conspirator in a love affair. Short, clipped lines contrast with long-held notes in both verse (in major) and refrain:

When I call . . . you up
Your line's _____ engaged
I am hurt . . . enough
So act _____ your age
We have lost . . . the time
That was so hard _____ to find
And I will lose . . . my mind

If you won't see me _____
                    (You won't see me)
You won't see me _____
                    (You won't see me)

As John and George add backup harmonies behind the second and third verses, they descend above Paul's lead (ooh-la-la-la), join him for the title line, and then invert their downward angles by rising as they echo his plea, retracing their steps backward.

The bridge (in minor) works its way back to major with the tug of "I wouldn't mind if I knew what I was missing!" The backup vocals that pull away from Paul's lead on that final line (singing "No I wouldn't, no I wouldn't") ease the bridge back into the verse. (The last verse adds a third voice on the high tonic note to intensify the other harmonies.) Paul's lead vocal track is kept over to the right and is sometimes swamped by the activity that surrounds him—the texture becomes more engaging than the emotion.

Even though it doubles the backup vocals an octave below, the piano on this track is central—it complements Paul's bass percussively in a way that guitars can't. Paul's playing takes a quantum leap on the album as a whole: without ever being intrusive, his bass emerges as an irreplaceable part of the overall texture. Because he virtually breathes melody, his bass lines begin to soar with inventive counterpoint to the rest of the band (a device that comes into its own on "Rain").

.   .   .

THE CHORAL STRAINS that introduce "Nowhere Man" are breathtakingly seductive—the voices have a brilliant sheen that vivifies the despondency they're singing about. The paradox is that while singing as a group, they're singing about loneliness. "I'd love to turn you on," the catch phrase of "A Day in the Life," is "the motivating idea" of "Strawberry Fields Forever," writes David Laing (p. 134), and it motivates much of "Nowhere Man" as well. But "Nowhere Man" empathizes more than it pities; and, like that of "Imagine" or "Nobody Told Me There'd Be Days Like These," its tone is deeply moral.

The band's entrance is slightly syncopated in anticipation of the downbeat; they slip perfectly into the groove that the vocals have set up—the invisible background that the singers seem to hear suddenly comes alive. Rhythm guitar, bass, and drums provide the accompanying track; lead guitar comments at the ends of phrases; Ringo adds a subtle snare roll before each bridge; and Paul's arching bass figures link the bridge back up to the verses (after "The world is at your command"). The vocal harmonies remain thick through the verse, and as Lennon takes the lead vocal for the bridge ("Nowhere man, please listen"), the others fall into complementary backups. They rise toward the end, stringing out their "la-la-la"s to the last instant before George's guitar takes over.

Harrison's solo blends practiced arrangement with inspired performance—he starts each phrase with a chord and follows with a lead line that inverts the verse's melodic direction (climbing where the words "point of view" and "going to" normally fall). After he slides down for the last note, he bounces off of it into a harmonic that rings from the left channel to the right. Just as he later injects a fleeting drama into "Got to Get You into My Life," here he encapsules the track's luster in one simple gesture.

The ironic contrast between the shimmering texture and the compassionate text is the opposite of that in "All I've Got to Do" and "Any Time at All," where Lennon sang upbeat words to anxious rhythms. In "Nowhere Man," he sings for the unsung, the people who have shut themselves off from life; but the glowing timbre is hopeful. The communal surge in the ensemble warms the sentiment with a rejuvenating interplay—no one can make it through life's difficulties alone, the music seems to be saying, and the best crutches are other people.

WITH ITS BITTER tone, George's "Think for Yourself" is a cousin to his first song, "Don't Bother Me," and the fuzz bass adds just the right guttural cynicism. It's a step beyond the flaccid "I Need You" and the forced amorousness of "You Like Me Too Much." The rhythmic impulse changes between the verse and the bridge, and the angular harmonic turns are offset by Paul's triplets (after "Go where you're going to"); but George doesn't practice what he preaches about self-reliance (he doesn't do much with "Although your mind's opaque/Try thinking more if just for your own sake"), and it's far from the melodic sonorities and layered texture that make side two's "If I Needed Someone" every guitarist's hook-bound fantasy. "Think for Yourself" is still George as contrast, providing odd relief to the Lennon songs he interrupts.

THE PIANO THAT stumbles into "The Word" is a quirky yank away from George's putdown. The song is a philosophical cousin to "Nowhere Man" and a spiritual source for 1967's Summer of Love; this sentiment will grow into the restraint of "Dear Prudence" and "Across the Universe," but here the band latches on to a medium-tempo groove that leaves little room for fooling around. Its punchiness places it above the wafting utopianism of "All You Need Is Love"; "The Word" is more rooted in reality: "love" can be found in books both good and bad. Ringo's accented kicks nail Paul's rising bass lines down behind the syncopated harmonies ("It's so fine/It's sunshine") and follows them up with tart little fills; vocal harmonies grow continuously toward the high end of the final verses; and Paul's brief bass flurry in the middle of the third refrain shows just how succinct all the motion is. This message has since grown trite, but it tapped an attitude that was then enlisting activists in the civil rights and antiwar causes; that the Beatles would soon publicly denounce Vietnam made this song relevant in ways pop had never been before. (By the time this sentiment reaches "All You Need Is Love," its self-righteousness is parodically exposed.)

"MICHELLE" SOUNDS as if McCartney were self-consciously writing another standard instead of letting the song inspire its own setting. It tries too hard, and it's a classic despite itself. ("Yesterday" works better; its music is as nostalgic as its words.) The language barrier between lovers might have been suggested by Chuck Berry's "La Juanda (Español)," about a man who pretends he doesn't understand a Mexican prostitute's price. But Paul aims more for charm and sophistication with his French, like Nat King Cole in "Darling, Je Vous Aime Beaucoup" (1955)—instead of developing the idea of lovers who speak in different tongues, he pines over it, and the conceit never achieves its potential. McCartney is still playing with the way major and minor can set different sections off one another ("Michelle, ma belle" is in major; "I love you, I love you" turns into minor), but it lacks the wavering indecisiveness of "Fixing a Hole" or the hopeful desolation of "Eleanor Rigby." His understated bass lines at the ends of stanzas ("until I do I'm hoping you . . .") nearly save the schmaltz from puerility.

THERE'S AN ASSURANCE in "What Goes On" that kicks the Beatles out of the nest of their exemplars—it pays respects to heroes like Carl Perkins and Jerry Lee Lewis not as a cover but as a rockabilly original. This Beatles equivalent of "Honey Don't" is all rusticity, emphasizing character instead of message through Ringo's innocuous, out-of-tune delivery. "That was an early Lennon written before Beatles when we were the Quarrymen, or something like that," Lennon told *Play-boy*, "and resurrected with a middle eight thrown in, probably with Paul's help, to give Ringo a song and also to use the bits, because I never liked to waste anything" (p. 188). Before they even became the Beatles they had absorbed enough rock-'n'-roll history to begin knocking off solid country beats on their own, which shows just how much they loved the form. Placing this track at the beginning of side two (the same position as the Buck Owens hit "Act Naturally" on the previous album) makes the commitment to original material more explicit: instead of dealing Ringo another surefire cover, they challenge themselves into reworking an old standby.

LENNON TURNS THE solo vocal opening of "Girl" into a heartfelt rhetorical quandary—before he can catch his breath he's caught up in memories and feelings of a woman who left an unshakable impression on him. "Is there anybody going to listen to my story/All about the girl who came to stay?" combines a dash of self-pity with a lingering infatuation; "came to stay" is a visitation, both physical and emotional. The way he sings the next line ("She's the kind of girl you want so much it makes you sorry/Still you don't regret a single day") enforces the longing by letting words lag just behind the beat.

Instrumentally, it sounds like a scene from the old world, something passed down from the previous generation—the high guitar resembles a mandolin, and the solo section turns the beat into an emotionally laden two-step dance. The refrain, a simple "Girl" (in major), is a fitful sigh after the breathy anticipation of "thththth"—the release on "girl" is one of regret. (The inhalation is slyly stretched out to "tit-tit-tit-tit" in the bridge.)

The guitar countermelody that accompanies the last verse (right) adorns it naturally, growing right out of the progression it springs from; its line is implied all along. During the two-step, this same guitar line joins a new counterpoint with a mandolin-style higher melody, the two interlocking parts outlining the harmony rather than filling it in.

"Girl" is a "good deal more sophisticated than Dylan's 'Just Like a Woman,' " writes Greil Marcus. Love's afterglow is mixed with a resentment for what the affair touches off inside. The story of the verse (in minor) and the relief of the refrain (in major) play out these opposing emotions. The old-fashioned atmosphere conveys desire and self-deception, and Lennon sings it as much to console himself as to make sense of its bewildering proportions ("And she promises the earth to me and I believe her/After all this time I don't know why"). It's the sympathetic side of the anger in "Norwegian Wood."

THE TENSION BETWEEN appearance and reality that Paul confronts in "I'm Looking Through You" resembles the self-examination he undergoes in "Fixing a Hole." Change is endemic in a relationship, and love "has a nasty habit of disappearing overnight." The cast of clichés Paul uses suits his subject perfectly—none of them mean the same thing beneath the surface.

> *I'm looking through you*
> *Where did you go?*
> *I thought I knew you*
> *What did I know?*

and

> *Your lips are moving*
> *I cannot hear*
> *Your voice is soothing,*
> *But the words aren't clear*

These lines play off each other in subtle, charming ways. Does her soothing voice sugar-coat her words, or is it just the way he's hearing them? In seeing through his lover's eyes, does he recognize himself? The music dances around self-awareness as it explores the changing emotional phases lovers go through. It's reputedly an autobiographical song Paul wrote to girlfriend Jane Asher after returning from an American tour. (An early draft on bootlegs is slower, almost sad.) His mind is wandering, the way it will in "Fixing a Hole," and he comes up alternately pleased and confused.

The music echoes the acoustic flavor of "I've Just Seen a Face," with only a simple rhythm patter on the right channel, but the blue note of "I'm looking *through* you" stirs up the harmony in the same way that words refract double meanings. The frustrated rise in dynamics at the end of each verse, where the electric guitar enters, works its way into the relative calm of the bridge, even though that's the only place where he asks a nonrhetorical question ("Why, tell me why did you not treat me right?"). Vocal harmony is used sparingly (only on the third line of the verse), and Paul's sincere lead delivery makes this song as much of a singer's breakthrough as it is a songwriter's.

IN THE MOSAIC of *Rubber Soul's* romantic themes—we get to know these songs in terms of one another—"In My Life" is the most encompassing, and the closest to its subject. It links a particular love affair with all the dreams and disappointments inherent in close connections throughout a person's life. (This song began as a look back toward childhood, the same inspiration as "Penny Lane" and "Strawberry Fields Forever." The early drafts of Lennon's lyrics, reprinted in Ray Coleman's *Lennon*, recount Liverpool landmarks—the melody is McCartney's.)

The opening melody distills the singer's experience into a poignant guitar line played with stirring restraint. Ringo's irregular drumbeat adds a perpetual hesitancy, backing Lennon's soulful vocal performance with stop-and-start timidity. For all the certainty of the singer's devotion, he sings from a place of discomfort—the discomfort implicit in love itself. Paul's melody rises to the end of the first line ("There are places I remember") and then falls off as the background harmonies sing "ooh" behind the lead (on "All my life, though some have changed"). Paul's upper harmony for the first part of the line is more cutting than soothing, and his blend is superb.

The verse is broken up into two parts, the second with a more lilting texture than the first ("All these places have their moments"). The title line winds around a minor harmony: "In my life I've loved them all." This minor inflection is the same harmony that added reluctance to "If I Fell" (the minor subdominant), and here the musical irony stresses the intuitive feeling; the joy of a new love touches off the hurtful separations from earlier attachments ("I know I'll never lose affection/For people and things that went before"). In the second verse, Lennon addresses the lover directly: "I've loved them all" becomes "I love you more"—he's searching for ways to tell his lover just how much she means to him.

The piano solo is more than a proficient baroque piece of styling. A classically trained musician, George Martin responded to Lennon's request for "something baroque-sounding here" with an authentic-sounding solo in the style of Bach. The counterpoint of this style is a conjunction of individual voices woven into a fabric of interplay and opposition, the way Lennon's remembrances intermingle in the lyric.

Since Martin was an oboe player, not a keyboardist, he recorded the solo at half tempo and then sped the tape up to get the resulting quickened decay of the piano to resemble a baroque harpsichord. It graces the song with the same old-world tenor that made "Girl" so effective. Inserting classical styles into the pop medium (as with "Yesterday" 's string quartet) is a statement all its own: it makes airs toward "legitimate" respectability. At the same time, it links the popular idiom up with the history of music in the same way that the lyrics link the present love affair up with past involve-

ments. (This is all done with astonishing aplomb.) The caesura ending, where the band stops and Lennon sings the final
title line in dreamy falsetto, ranks with the ending of "God"
on his first solo album as the most beautiful singing of his
career.

THE SENTIMENT OF "Wait" is harsher than that of "It
Won't Be Long"; the lovers' reunion has more anxiety than
euphoria goading the beat. (These two songs have the same
inverted relation as "You're Going to Lose That Girl" and
"She Loves You.") Lennon wrote the verses and the refrain
and relied on Paul for the bridge ("I feel as though, you ought
to know")—the same formula that makes "We Can Work It
Out" and "A Day in the Life" such revealing collaborations.
Rhythmic momentum carries the verse: a tambourine strikes
offbeats on the right channel and grows to shaken maracas
and full drums in the right channel during the second stanza.
The drums spill into the chorus with an unusual twist: Ringo
hits the crash cymbal *before* his roll on the tom-toms (a backward fill), and a guitar echoes John's cries of "Wait!" with a
flash of pain. At the end of the refrain, the swell subsides
with guitar and tambourine reverberations on the empty beats
beneath the lead voice (after the words "the tears we cried").
The whole texture-building process starts again with the second verse.

Paul's bridge picks up where the empty beats left off and
takes the band into a circle-of-fifths progression (moving from
key to key as naturally as possible). With characteristic promises—"I feel as though/You ought to know/That I've been
good, as good as I can be"—he winds up back where he
started on the words "will wait for me" (which the guitar
punctuates in the right channel). The guitar on the right plays
a rhythmic (instead of chordal) figure during the bridge to
emphasize the rise in the harmonic progression.

Where "It Won't Be Long" is expectant, "Wait" is doubtful, anxious, uncertain—the "trust" in Paul's bridge is forced,

if not faked; the jubilance of "It Won't Be Long" sounds irrepressible in comparison. "Wait" doesn't measure up as a song, either in spirit or in structure. There's more uncertainty in "If I Fell," more ambiguity in "I'm Looking Through You." "Wait" sounds dashed off, composed and performed with finesse but not as much commitment.

ONCE IT GETS GOING, the ringing hypnotic guitar texture of "If I Needed Someone" carries itself. The ensemble slips right into the groove as if in disguise; the blend with the rhythm of the guitar is perfect (it resembles the band's entrance in "Nowhere Man"). Paul's upwardly arching bass line doesn't push or prod; it settles back into the ebb and flow of everything else. George's musical personality is still awkwardly earnest, but at the same time his best song yet sounds relaxed and confident. He knows he's set up a fine riff, and all he has to do is ride it out.

By leaving well enough alone, the words are evocative without much fuss. The melodic line always pulls at the beat beneath it by carrying words over the bar—"if" is the only word sung on a proper downbeat during the verses. This rhythmic overlay doesn't overdo the tension; it merely strings it out to full effect—the syncopations are played close to the vest.

The music turns on the word "of" as the band rides out a different harmony that sways against the constant bass line (the guitars change chords, the bass stays the same). The tension in this simple gesture propels some fine musical drama from all the players, especially Ringo, who applies just the right amount of pressure to bring the guitar harmony back into place. (The guitar solo is simply an intensification of this hook, not an elaboration.)

The bridge has the same verbal syncopation but sounds more driven ("Had you come some other day then/It may not have been like this")—instead of suspending things, it sets things in motion. "Don't Bother Me" is protest-too-much refusal; "If I Needed Someone" is qualified flirtation—a romantic interest is set on hold because "now I'm too much in love." "Carve your number on my wall and/maybe you will get a call from me" rings patronizing, but the musical suspension conveys it all without bravado or malice, and the effect is more passive than aggressive. (The lick even survives the Hollies' pumped-up cover in 1966, with some extraordinary drumming from Bobby Elliott.)

"RUN FOR YOUR LIFE" lets off steam with good old-fashioned denial; the most paranoid Lennon track is a clenched macho fist that rings true now only as a dated piece of jealous anger. Lennon cites it in *Playboy* as "just sort of a throwaway song of mine that I never thought much of, but it was always a favorite of George's" (p. 189). For its tone alone it's the weakest song on the album. Where the rest of the record is open-ended, allowing room for indecision and change, this song hammers closed-minded distress home with petty clichés and insulting accusations (it makes "You Can't Do That" sound reasonable).

From the opening moments, a driving acoustic guitar sets a tone of unswerving obstinance that only accentuates the insecurity that stirs beneath it. The vocal harmonies are drawn so close they're disharmonious, stinging with accusation. The lead guitar line, double-tracked on both channels, actually sounds like a nasal "nah, nah, nah," anticipating the syllables Lennon sings during the fade-out. The second verse even acknowledges that the singer is a "wicked guy/And I was born with a jealous mind," but then denies any responsibility for it with the simplistic dominance tag: "And I can't spend my whole life tryin'/Just to make you tow the line." (The most inflammatory line, "I'd rather see you dead, little girl/ Than to be with another man," is copped from "Baby Let's Play House," which Elvis Presley recorded in a 1955 Sun session.)

The interesting thing about this song as the culmination

of this emotionally varied record about romance is just where Lennon is in 1965, and how far beyond that he will go before he dies. His violent streak can be traced to this starting point—it magnifies the angered outbursts of other songs ("Not a Second Time" and "No Reply"). This song epitomizes all the violence and selfish aggressiveness that Lennon would later come to terms with. His own manic temperament is never really "tamed"—*Double Fantasy's* "I'm Losing You" has its share of conflict—but his repressions become more eloquent as time goes on.

ON *RUBBER SOUL*, the formal mastery that informed *A Hard Day's Night* ripens into something that eluded both *Beatles for Sale* and *Help!* Where the Beatles' early sound was bright, *Rubber Soul* is dusky. There's a restraint, a supple fluidity of rhythms that allows their deft musical intelligence to flow through.

At the outset, a guitar snares the ear an unlikely cross-rhythm with the bass, and "Drive My Car" is tart but not aggressive; the instruments are spaciously drawn in the mix. The album prolongs this air of suspension: instead of driving the beat the way they do in "It Won't Be Long," they let it carry them. "Nowhere Man" has a buoyant irony; "Girl" sets interlocking melodic lines afloat over a gently swaying dance pattern; and a triplet piano figure counters the measured strategy of "Drive My Car." "The Word," "You Won't See Me," and Harrison's "If I Needed Someone" are progressions that travel of their own volition—any extra kicks would be intrusive (the kicks at the ends of refrains in "The Word" have more lift than squeeze). "I'm Looking Through You" and "Think for Yourself" pivot off rhythmically contrasted verses and bridges. The bridge of "Wait" reduces the motion to its elemental eighth-note pulse, alive and continuous behind everything else. The sitar's waltz is exotic in "Norwegian Wood"; the vocal harmonies glide into their cadences in "What Goes On." Ringo's perky backdrop to "In My Life" is assuaged by the gentleness in the falling vocal harmonies; his drumming becomes the singer's timidity at articulating a deep feeling. By comparison, *Revolver*'s rhythms are marked: the drive of "Taxman" is harsh; the guitar in "Doctor Robert" pulls at the beat; and "Tomorrow Never Knows" deconstructs it. *Rubber Soul* has less the musical distillation of *A Hard Day's Night*, and more intricately contained wonder.

Day Tripper (John)/*We Can Work It Out* (Paul and John) *Released: December 3, 1965*

ON THE SAME day that *Rubber Soul* was released (December 3, 1965) a new single was issued: "Day Tripper," Lennon's electric-guitar heaven, is backed by one of the more remarkable Lennon-McCartney collaborations, rivaled only by "A Day in the Life"—"We Can Work it Out." It went immediately to number one.

> ["Day Tripper"]—that's mine. Including the lick, the guitar break and the whole bit. It's just a rock 'n' roll song. Day trippers are people who go on a day trip, right? Usually on a ferryboat or something. But it was kind of—you know, you're just a weekend hippie. Get it? (Lennon in *Playboy*, p. 188).

Lennon's casual description of the song sounds as offhand as the guitar lick itself: brilliant yet coolly irreverent. In less than a verse, that guitar lick is embedded in your memory; and the longer it stays there, the stronger it gets. "Day Tripper" is another song about being awakened and jilted all at once. The singer is looking back on the affair with a knowing humility ("It took me *so* long to find out"). Everything is aimed toward self-justification and self-redemption, and it delivers that and more in the climactic rave-up, the first since "Twist and Shout."

The opening moments are a formal abbreviation—the naked electric guitar riff on the left channel implies the entire track's attitude and form in its initial statement (the same way the elegant riff of the Temptations' "My Girl," by Smokey Robinson and Ronald White, holds the whole song in its first utterance). As the Beatles enter, first bass and guitar on the right channel, then rhythm guitar and tambourine on opposite channels, the guitar riff rides double waves: one on each stereo track. The drums are the last to enter, capping off the buildup with the rush of coming up for air from underwater. The excitement of the intro mounts as each new instrument enters, and the drums clench it up, locking the others together with a slow drag after the cymbal crash as surely as something slipping back into its natural orbit. At that moment of sync, the tambourine shifts into a backbeat figure, securing Ringo's tug on the reins.

Paul sings the first line and is then joined by Lennon for the succeeding harmony lines in each verse. As Lennon takes the lead for the refrain ("She was a day tripper"), the high background vocals bring a whole new dimension to the texture—the held notes of the title line and the syncopated line that follows ("one way tick-et, yeah") all hover above the insistent pulsation of the guitars beneath for a new variation in rhythm. As this figure is repeated ("It took me so long") to even higher harmonies, Lennon shoots up to an exasperated falsetto at just the right moment. The harmony never so much as glances toward minor: the entire song is done with major chords and yet is so convincing that it doesn't lack for contrast or dimension.

The first refrain leads back to an abbreviated strand of the introduction and the second verse, but the second refrain leads into an instrumental bridge, the rave-up to end all rave-ups. It starts modestly enough as a guitar solo, adding layer upon layer of texture as the tension rises. A buried guitar line that devotes itself to single notes emerges from the left channel, rising slowly up the major scale on the offbeats. Vocals enter after the sixth bar, and then George takes off into a solo, ornamenting all that's going on around him. The return of the opening riff isn't just satisfying; it's inexorable. Without the screams and hoots of "Twist and Shout," it doesn't quite reach the same pitch of excitement, but it has a formal surge all its own, and it plunges down into the last verse like a wave crashing on the shore. The lift that that moment delivers is the lift of release, the singer's redemptive breakthrough. It sounds better each time, even though we know exactly what's going to happen.

The last verse rides out the wave of energy much like the last verse of "Twist and Shout" did, only with more authority. There is a curious lapse of the tambourine and guitar on the right channel just after the words "tried to please her," which has never been explained. (It's obviously a mistake, a moment some engineer accidentally erased, but technical flaws are so rare on a Beatles recording that its inclusion is strange.)

As the end approaches, Ringo takes over with fills, and he defines the final moments—guitar heaven becomes drum nirvana. The drumming he has been slinging into the sound at every entrance is like small pelts of compressed tension and release, and it's difficult to imagine the track without it. But the final drum spot condenses his other fills into a solo of imaginative breaks: triplets here, tom-tom rolls there, filling up each opportunity with rhythmic commentary on the riff that has driven the entire song. Even Paul's hidden bass ad-libs (left channel) don't match Ringo's ingenuity. His timing shows just what attentive drumming a track like this requires, and it is among Ringo's finest moments.

"WE CAN WORK IT OUT" exemplifies the Lennon and McCartney collaborative technique of joining two separate parts to form one larger whole. Only "A Day in the Life" is a better song in this vein, with their swan song "I've Got a Feeling" neatly reversed as a kind of teaser. Its structure is simple: Paul sings the verses, Lennon sings the bridges. It's the details that are telling: Paul's verses are hopeful, they're in major and have a steady backbeat; Lennon's bridge is in minor, the sentiment is frustrated, and the rhythm jumps into double time. The two are linked by a small triplet figure that comes at the end of each line in the bridge, an oom-pah-pah merry-go-round of a musical image that conveys the futility of the argument. Everything follows this basic design: the harmonium that Lennon plays throughout swells with optimism during the verse and holds single notes which unravel during the bridge. Paul sings his verses alone; Lennon sings his bridge with upper harmony. Where Paul is laid back, Lennon is impatient; where Paul is cheerful, Lennon is doubtful ("I have always thought that it's a crime . . .").

The tension between the two sections gives it ironic appeal: the song is about an argument, presumably in a love affair (although not confined to one), which turns into an argument between the two songwriters. "We Can Work It Out" is really about noncommunication, and it makes its point most strongly in the way it fends off its own resolution. The arguments go full circle: as a musical conclusion, the oom-pah-pah figure from the bridge is played in the verse's major. All their previous songs point toward this opposition of viewpoints, but nothing unites them in terms that so explicitly threaten a falling-out.

STATES OF MIND

Paperback Writer (Paul)/Rain (John)
Released: June 10, 1966

REVOLVER *Released: August 5, 1966*

By 1966, public demand for the Beatles seemed insatiable. They continued plans for a third full-length motion picture, to be called *A Talent for Loving,* and they toured Europe and America. But the crowds' constant din was becoming unbearable, and the Neanderthal amplification technology constantly prevented them from hearing themselves adequately. "Don't try to listen to us," John is quoted as saying in Germany, "we're really terrible these days" (Norman, p. 261). By not showing up at a Marcos state dinner in the Philippines, they were forced out of the country as embarrassments. In America, a furor arose over Lennon's "We're bigger than Christ" statement, and they received death threats on the road as their records were burned throughout the Bible Belt. Their notoriety was not only distracting, it had become dangerous. Their performances at San Francisco's Candlestick Park would be their last.

Revolver singlehandedly made Beatlemania irrelevant—there was no longer any need for touring to keep the idea of the Beatles alive. It is so clearly the work of *recording* artists that the idea of them running through their hits on that last tour now seems ridiculous, a compromise of all the creative progress they had made in the studio.

Paperback Writer (Paul)/Rain (John)
Released: June 10, 1966

THE LUST FOR FAME in "Paperback Writer" is stripped
of the innuendos that make "Drive My Car" a sporty come-
on. The singer needs "a break" and has ambition to burn, but
it's all for easy money; the plot summary gives him away as
a hack: "It's a dirty story of a dirty man/And his clinging
wife doesn't understand. . . ."

The choirboy spoof in "Doctor Robert" is self-reflective
in "Paperback Writer"—the vocal collage that blossoms from
Paul's centered lead and accretes from left and right is resplendent but self-centered and hollow, like the lyric. George's
delicious lick (the kind of rhythmically playful riff that "Day
Tripper" perfects) interrupts the hanging vocal reverberations, teased and driven by Ringo's suspenseful backdrop, and
the verse enters after a daringly brief bass fill as they all fall
into the first big downbeat. (Paul's bass is mixed left, allowing
him to play off of the ensemble's rhythm track on the right.)
The grandiosity of the opening cascade is so thrilling that they
bring it back after each verse. Like that of the Beach Boys'
"Good Vibrations" (released later the same year), the vocal
effect is so disarming that the words are almost beside the
point.

What first sounds as innocent as a "la-la" background
vocal behind the second verse slowly emerges as John and
George singing "Frère Jacques," a farcical backdrop to
McCartney's daft cynicism. The bass solo that Paul gives himself going into fade-out groove draws out his quick rolls into
a dramatic figure that accentuates by resistance; he slows to
pull back from the downbeat like a horse rearing at the tight-
ening of its reins, suspending the fall. The remaining title-
line dialogue pits Paul (double-tracked in the center) against
John and George (left) repeating the title in squeaky falsetto,
scooping up the fourth time for shape just before the sound
disappears.

. . .

LENNON'S B SIDE IS the first stirring of pop psychedelia. David Laing writes that "Strawberry Fields Forever" depicts a "landscape of the imagination," and "Rain" anticipates that setting musically the way "Lucy in the Sky with Diamonds" fulfills it visually. The beat is deliberate but never circumspect (it's slower than even "Eight Days a Week"), a dreamy tug that casts a lulling spell. "Rain" matches the Byrds' "Turn, Turn, Turn" for texture and thrashes it with instrumental authority.

Ringo's five pert raps on his snare drum (two plus three) coil the understated allure of the track into a commanding opening gesture: "My favorite piece of me is what I did on 'Rain,' " he told Max Weinberg. "I think I just played amazing. I was into the snare and high-hat. I think it was the first time I used this trick of starting a break by hitting the high-hat first instead of going directly to a drum off the high-hat"—the same device he uses in "Wait" (p. 181). The arpeggiated (as opposed to strummed) guitar gives the texture its space, creating a web of sound in the center that the bass hovers over in the right channel. Paul's bass is even more prominent that it is on "Paperback Writer": there it stood off on its own and took a couple of small breaks; here it's an essential part of the melodic fabric, playing off the guitar instead of the other way around. His perpetual interplay adds a third instrumental line to the dialogue between Lennon and his backup singers.

During the second verse, Ringo's drumming swells into inspired flourishes of rhythm, from the cunning reversals (high-hat preceding snare) to the way he plays right through a downbeat (on the repeat of the line "when the sun shines"), throwing the meter completely off. He hooks back up with the others just before the refrain.

The refrain sustains tension on the words "rain _____" and "shine _____" toward the relief of "I don't mind" and "the weather's fine." But the texture implodes: voices hold the word "rain" in harmony, dipping with every two beats as the music sways against the pedal point (similar to the kind of harmonic contrast Harrison uses in "If I Needed Someone"—bass static as the harmony shifts above it); Paul's bass pulses along as the lead instrument even though it's only playing one note; the guitar changes from arpeggios to straight strumming; and the drums drop out completely except for the closing high-hat. As the music glides into the nearest landing point ("I don't mind"), Ringo pulls the beatless undulation together with a fill that sounds like he's running to catch up—there's a slight drag that gives his arrival a thwarted accent the first time around.

The plateau they land on has so much give that Paul bounces off of it—the spacious texture and tempo turn into a springboard for his bass playing. At the top of the third verse (after the first refrain), the formula is set, and Paul simply takes off, filling up the second refrain with triplets instead of the steady one-note lead he played the first time around, adding extra pull to the already ebbing tug. After the fourth and final verse, the motion stops for an out-and-out bass solo with drums. It's not elaborate or virtuosic (the way his playing in the rest of the song is), but it highlights the role the bass can play in creating a rhythmic and melodic undertow. McCartney's vocal gift is supreme—his melodies seem effortless—and this lyrical temperament lends his bass playing an unparalleled sense of line. His bass turns into an independent part of their ensemble, and the Beatles' command of textures grows geometrically.

After Ringo and Paul's interruption, Lennon ornaments the closing fade with a new favorite sound:

I got home about five in the morning, stoned out of me head. I staggered up to me tape recorder and put it ["Rain"] on, and I was in a trance in the earphones, what *is* it, what *is* it. Too *much*, you know, and I really wanted the whole song backwards . . . so we tagged it onto the end. I just happened to have the tape the wrong way round. (Lennon in *Beatles Forever*, p. 55)

By running the vocal track backward at the end, Lennon gives the illusion of the track starting over again, only in the wrong direction—the rest of the band moves forward while Lennon spins the record against the needle.

Alan Watts, Lennon's favorite philosopher, writes that reality is a spectrum of wavelengths, and that our human senses limit us to "receiving" just five of them. But because we are able to tune in to only a very small portion of this larger network of living vibrations, Watts holds, everything beyond what we call "real" remains a vast illusion: "I can show you that when it rains and shines/It's just a state of mind . . . " "Rain" is as much about attitudes as it is about how nature strikes our senses—with a line as suggestive as "They run and hide their heads/They might as well be dead," Lennon isn't singing about the weather. During the sixties, every "they" implied an "us," an establishment and a counterculture. What "they" are running from (perceptive experience) and what "they" are missing (life) in the verses plays off the laid-back advice of the refrain: "I don't mind . . . the weather's fine . . ."

By pitting a backward tape against a forward-moving ensemble, Lennon demonstrates his philosophical message with a musical metaphor. The dreamy effect of running tapes backward enhances this aural illusion with contrary motion—two directions at once. Rain is just as much a "state of mind" as music is.

REVOLVER *Released: August 5, 1966*

Rubber Soul has a romantic astonishment, the echoing realization that teenage quandaries don't dissipate with age;

they dilate. Starker realities intrude on *Revolver:* embracing life also means accepting death. The first track to be recorded was "Tomorrow Never Knows," in April 1966, and it bore the working title "The Void"—an image each of these songs circles around. They link a disillusioned view of the modern world ("Taxman") with a belief in metaphysical transcendence ("Tomorrow Never Knows").

Harrison's "Taxman" dances on avarice that makes death ignoble; Eleanor Rigby and Father Mackenzie are chaste strangers cast off from the world by age and neglect, brought together only by the empty ritual of Eleanor's burial. "I'm Only Sleeping" waves off reality's nightmare; "Love You To" encourages spiritual awareness but contains the most bitter line on the record ("There's people standing 'round/Who'll screw you in the ground"). The intensity of "She Said She Said" is Lennon in a neurotic deadlock, mourning the passing of his youth as the wish for innocence continues to haunt him; it sums up three stages of life in rhythmic apposition. "Doctor Robert" equates narcotics with religion; "I Want to Tell You" makes an earnest plea for human connection; and "Tomorrow Never Knows" turns to spiritual ecstasy as the only way out.

But if the overall tone of *Revolver* is bleak, it is far from disheartening: "Here, There and Everywhere" and "Good Day Sunshine" are beams of romantic light shadowed by "For No One" 's sober awakening. "Yellow Submarine" reclaims childlike pleasures in a pretend underwater diversion, and "Got to Get You into My Life" grounds the experimentalism of "Love You To" and "Tomorrow Never Knows" in the affirmative pulse of rhythm and blues. In its progression from dismaying experience through romantic and comic asides, *Revolver* moves from Western practice to Eastern thought, from outward predicaments to the calming inner universe of the mind.

The Beatles' best album is also their most artistically

compromised by the Capitol edition. Only three songs from the British edition are omitted, but all three happen to be Lennon's. The result more than disrupts the intended flow of the record—it confines Lennon's presence to the last cut of each side. With five Lennon tracks on the Parlophone sequence (instead of just two), his side endings sound less extremist, part of a larger process instead of a sudden swing to the surreal.

The cover depicts the four Beatles' faces looking away from each other, connected in the middle with a cornucopia of black-and-white images pouring from the center of their collective consciousness. Klaus Voorman, their Hamburg friend and bassist for Manfred Mann, sketched the surrealism of psychedelia with none of its color. As on *Rubber Soul*, the four faces are "so instantly recognizable," Philip Norman writes, "it was not thought necessary to print their collective name" [p. 269]. The back photo shows full faces, shaded by the hip modesty of sunglasses and cigarette smoke.

GEORGE COUNTS OFF "Taxman" in a low sneer that cuts through the off-mike studio noise behind him: fingers on live guitar strings, coughing, the expectancy of a take in the air. George's forefront voice is just a fake, though—the real count-off comes from the background (left). The two tempos not only trip up expectations as to where the beat will land; they gives a sense of space to the recording: the tension between what's heard in the foreground and how it's actually produced behind the scenes. The opening count-off of the first record, *Please Please Me*, captured the essence of the Beatles' live sound; "Taxman" uses the same idea to announce the new studio aesthetic of *Revolver*. It's more than "a symbolic gesture underlining the loss of innocence—both musical and social—which had occurred between the two albums," as Terence O'Grady writes; the backstage moment gives the album's conceit away: the difference between live and recorded sound comments on the Beatles' own career as it evokes the detachment modern man feels from the world that surrounds him.

The opening kicks have more than a little edge to them; they're playing with real anger, and George's voice is poisoned with acridity. In a schoolmarmish tone ("Let me tell you how it will be") he mocks the taxman's rampant greed, with no hint of the delicate smugness he saves for "Piggies." The breaks after each line where the band anticipates the hook of "Taxman" are sharp, incisive jolts of energy that contrast with the matter-of-fact dryness of Harrison's voice—he's angry too, but the best he can advise the dead is to "declare the pennies on your eyes." The stop-and-start guitar part is melded with Paul's bass, giving the line motion where the other instruments click with mechanical precision.

A tambourine is added to this basic texture on the first part of the second verse, a cowbell during the second part. Paul's bass playing on this verse comes unhinged in a series of lickety-split riffs. The third verse is completely rewritten melodically to incorporate a call-and-response dialogue between the background singers and the lead ("If you drive a car/I'll tax the street") that builds to the frenzied intensity of the final "taxman!" they all sing together. The guitar solo that bursts out of all this fevered stress sears from the right channel with a vengeance, and the nondiatonic notes it bristles through leave a sour smell in the air.

After another refrain, the lead guitar on the right swings into the accompanying riff with the ensemble on the left, and the backup vocals chime in with swipes at Mr. Wilson and Mr. Heath (prime minister and leader of the opposition, respectively—Harold Wilson had nominated them for their Members of the Order of the British Empire [MBE] royal citations in 1965). Background "shoo-wop" nonsense asides are turned into darts thrown at two-faced politicians. Everything condenses near the end: lead guitar adds extra bite; background vocals rile every held note. The final "And you're working for no one but me" takes it into the fade-out, which trails off with the guitar wailing and writhing as the sound dies.

THE OPENING VOCAL strains of "Eleanor Rigby" greet the listener at point-blank range, the "ah"s aren't soothing, they're aching, and the sudden drop in the cellos after the first line sinks the heart along with it. The choice of a string octet weighs the sentiment down as it strengthens the tone— the lithe quartet of "Yesterday" darkens into pathos, expressing a loneliness far greater than heartache.

The imagery defines isolation: in the first verse Eleanor "picks up the rice in the church where a wedding has been"— a sad figure left out of a happy occasion, a fading woman sifting through remnants of a celebration of youth and new life. She "waits at the window, wearing a face that she keeps in a jar by the door." Father Mackenzie's life in the second verse is no less futile: writing a sermon for no one, "darning his socks in the night when there's nobody there" as the string arrangement elaborates slightly on its terse, marching staccatos. In the final verse, the two characters are brought together: Eleanor has died with nothing but her name, and after her burial Father Mackenzie wipes the dirt from his hands, thinking to himself that "no one was saved." The strings on the last verse reach a gorgeous poignancy: a high note rides over Eleanor's burial, joined in syncopation by the middle strings at accented entrances; the cellos comment on Father Mackenzie's grim expression as he walks from the grave, doubling McCartney's voice an octave beneath it. In the final refrain, Paul doubles his own voice in the left channel, counterpointing his lead with distant resignation to the despairing story he has just told.

As in Lennon's "Nowhere Man," the vocal refrains that erupt in major contradict the aching loss etched out in the minor verses, and there's a sadness and compassion for the world here that overwhelm the personal scope of McCartney's

"Yesterday" and "And I Love Her." Along with "For No One," "Eleanor Rigby" offsets his other *Revolver* songs ("Here, There and Everywhere," "Good Day Sunshine," and "Got to Get You into My Life") with a tragic realism and makes his optimism sound more well-rounded. The corruption of "Taxman" and the utter finality of Eleanor's fate makes the world of *Revolver* more ominous than any other pair of opening songs could.

THE DOWNWARD STRUM on the acoustic guitar that starts off "I'm Only Sleeping" occurs simultaneously with the vocal entrance. The delayed downbeat has no preparation: before we can blink we're well into the first verse, and the effect is of being awakened in the middle of a dream. "I'm Only Sleeping" captures the bleary-eyed mood of returning to consciousness after a midday nap, and everything about the song is drugged with weariness, from the laid-back drum-beat to the yawning bass solo at the end of each refrain. Even the run-on lines ("Please don't spoil my day/I'm miles away/ And after all I'm only sleeping") drag the beat down instead of picking it up (as syncopations normally do by building tension).

There are two worlds in this song: the dreamy desires of the subconscious that come with sleep, and the intruding consciousness of reality. The link between the two is a guitar, distorted and twisted to seem illusory—the surreal presence it takes on when heard backward. It enters in the second verse (during "Running everywhere at such a speed"). After a truncated "bridge" ("Keeping an eye on the world going by my window/Takin' my time . . ."), it re-enters for a hallucinatory solo. Lennon adds a drowsy gape over Paul's bass solo the second time around before the bridge returns with even more sluggish kicks. The backward guitar is brought back for the fade-out as Lennon drifts back to sleep. It's the album's first image of escape.

.   .   .

THE DREAM WORLD that "I'm Only Sleeping" wanders off
to is where George's "Love You To" begins: out of time, full
of space, and rich with unorthodox pop textures. The sitar
flourishes in the opening moments make the sitar in "Norwegian Wood" sound like a normal part of a rock band—it's
the first Beatles track where traditional Western instruments
aren't even alluded to. Building on the Indian musical raga
principle of repetitive droning that slowly grows into virtuosic improvisation, Harrison crams the Eastern philosophy of
time as a dimension to be passed through into the Western
economy of wit—the pop structure. The expansive introduction breaks into a brisk ⁴/₄ meter that accelerates with each
solo. The refrain melody ("Love me while you can") is answered in the sitar as the meter diminishes (from ⁴/₄ to ³/₄ and
finally ²/₄ before the verse returns). Integrating foreign musical cultures is a tricky affair, as some of Harrison's later work
demonstrates, but here the crossover is appealing. George's
obvious infatuation with Eastern values and sounds makes
"Love You To" a fresh invention. It's a bold move from him,
trading in the religion of Chuck Berry's guitar for Ravi Shankar's meditative sitar.

PAUL'S "Here, There and Everywhere" domesticates Harrison's exoticism with the record's first straightforward love
song, written with the conciseness of a Rodgers and Hart classic: the first verse is built around "here," the second verse
around "there," and the bridge leaps to a new harmonic
ground for "everywhere." The two key areas of the song are
parenthesized in the disarmingly simple four-bar introduction
("To lead a better life" in G major, "I need my love to be
here," in B-flat, returning to G for the first verse). Paul's
double-tracked vocal (on both channels) is supported by a
slight instrumental accompaniment on the right, but it's the
background harmonies that paint a smooth surface for his
voice to glide over during the verses.

On the line "I want her *everywhere*," the melody climbs

gracefully to the new key area for the bridge, and the background vocals drop out to emphasize the change in altitude. A brief mandolinlike guitar phrase shadows the vocal on the minor harmony (on the words "but to love her is to need her . . .") before the return to the verse, which settles back into the original key by altering that same minor back into major (again on the word "everywhere"). The turn from minor to major—and from the key area of the bridge to the original key area of the verse—is the simplest kind of musical pivot, the alteration of a single note (the B-flat of G minor becomes B natural for G major).

A low harmony is added for the last bridge, and finger snaps lead the song home into its conclusion, where the first words of each verse are joined together for the title-line codetta. The end melody is a subtle touch: a descending French horn figure is added in the right channel—its brief appearance anticipates the horn solo in "For No One." These sophisticated moves drape a seductive ease atop the underlying harmonic frame. It is the most perfect song that Paul has yet offered, and it remains a standard of measure for others of this ilk that will follow (like the relatively egregious "My Love," or "Warm and Beautiful" from his solo career).

From the grace of Paul's tenor to the nasal honk of Ringo's throaty baritone is a leap only the Beatles could make successfully, and the comic relief of "Yellow Submarine" adds to Ringo's playful appeal even on the heels of one of Paul's finer moments. Ringo sings his opening line flat, but with such literal relish that it punctures the romantic aura much better than the existential angst of "She Said She Said" would.

Paul was interested in writing a children's song, but he realized that "Yellow Submarine" was too arch to be sung straight (imagine any other Beatle singing this song and something less loopy springs to mind). Ringo carries it like he has every other track he sings, with humor and self-effacement; but this is really his first chance to take an original and plant his personality on it. On the first album, "Boys" is a self-propelling Shirelles cover: "I Wanna Be Your Man" is a token original thrown to him for the second album; "Honey Don't," "Matchbox," and "Act Naturally" are affectionate rockabilly covers; and "What Goes On" so resembles that style that it outcamps its American models only by being an original. "Yellow Submarine" sounds as though enough of Ringo's dopey simplicity had rubbed off on Paul for him to knock off something exactly suited to his drummer's humble charm.

The track is one big Spike Jones charade, from the oceanic sound effects to the underwater band and "Full speed ahead!" clowning. The jeering echoes that Lennon adds for the last verses turn it into a sailor's drinking song: there's so much Goon humor in them they become an irresistible part of all the jousting. And as light as the song is, the Beatles give the refrain a taut vocal arrangement that leaves the last syllable of each refrain dangling (the unresolved sixth on "yellow submar*ine*"). "Yellow Submarine" doesn't subvert *Revolver*'s darker moods; it provides joyous distraction from them.

THE RIDICULOUS IS suddenly shattered by the traumatic: the outwardly harnessed but inwardly raging guitar that unleashes "She Said She Said" has a commanding emotional weight. Part of the song's complexity is its primal urge: the wish for innocence. A woman glibly tells the singer she knows what it's like to be dead; the singer shoots back that she's making him feel like he's never been born. His thoughts become scattered, and the confrontation sets off nagging worries and renewed aggravation; the exchange is trivial, but what it summons up is overwhelming—her smugness makes him feel impossibly small and defenseless. The intensity is palpable; the singer is wrestling with feelings he barely understands—inadequacy, helplessness, and a profound fear. Because Lennon so obviously feels these emotions as he plays and sings them, the music is a direct connection to his psyche.

The beat is neither tight nor chaotic but constantly lunging between the two. Ringo's drumming takes the sting of the opening guitar and diffuses it behind Lennon's opening line— he settles into a loose groove for the downbeat preceding "I know what it's like to be dead." The kicks that try to bridle the surges for the concluding line, "And she's making me feel like I've never been born" (echoed in the lead guitar), wind up disrupting things even further: the syncopations across the bar draw attention to the beat as much as they seek relief from it.

Melodies intrude on each other with panicked circularity. The opening words of each verse ("She said") encase the interval of a fifth that the opening guitar outlines; phrases are extended from eighth notes into triplets ("I know what it *is to be* sad") to intensify the rhythmic stress, the thin line between confidence and anxiety. After the second verse ("I said"), the bridge suddenly overtakes the meter by shifting into a completely different rhythm: the pulse shortens to three as Lennon leaps to the climactic "When I was a boy" (mimicking the opening guitar scale). For a moment ("everything was right") the ¾ meter seems to stick; but just as quickly, and with no preparation, the backbeat (in four) returns with the verse. It's as drastic a musical equivalent as there is for a sudden shift in mood, and the effect is schizophrenic. Lennon will drop a beat to throw expectations (for fun in "Everybody's Got Something to Hide, Except Me and My Monkey"), but only in "Happiness Is a Warm Gun" does he take the beat further, pitting one rhythm in the band against another in the drums.

In "She Said," this literal idea is placed next to the colloquial phrase, he hasn't been born yet, meaning he's so naive and ignorant. And the meaning of this phrase gets a new equivocal dimension. We begin to wonder whether birth is just a physical event, or whether it's some spiritual leap into a higher wisdom. Then, a little further in the song comes the line, "When I was a boy, everything was right." This tugs us back into the physical temporal dimension in which he is born, and then is a boy and finally the man who is singing the song. The way in which the song moves from one kind of reality to another is like the way the pieces of a kaleidoscope form a new pattern each time you look at them. In the song as a whole, the traditional certainties of the love song's systems of metaphor have become ambiguous and begun to crumble. Standing beside them is a new mode of apprehension, using words (sometimes the same words) in fidelity to a different kind of experience. (Laing in *The Sound of Our Time*, pp. 127–8)

Laing's description of the song's temporal and spatial inferences are drawn by the beat: the instant Lennon sings the word "boy," the meter changes; and the instant he returns to the conversation with the woman in the verse, everything reverts to the initial (although unsteady) backbeat. The contradictory emotional states these rhythms conjure up—the frustrated pull between idealized innocence and the overbearing complexity of a deeply personal disillusionment—are framed by the inevitable stages of human life: birth, middle age (the singer/narrator), and death.

"She Said She Said" raises unspeakable fears from the subconscious (Is death a mockery of birth? Does life ultimately cheat us all?) and poses them as essential questions. In "Money," Lennon cried out for all the freedom that life can give; in "She Said She Said" he acknowledges all of life's chains. In expressing rage and conflict in such demanding terms, "She Said She Said" finds a certain liberation—a rush of amorphous feeling finds expression, if only briefly. At the core of Lennon's pain is a bottomless sense of abandonment, the same primal loss that gets recast in "Strawberry Fields Forever" and again in "Julia" and "Mother." All these songs have constricted façades and deep, irrepressible subtexts of hurt. None of the loose ends are tied up in "She Said She Said"; they're simply left squirming as vocal elisions fold into each other and the band jumps into double time. By ending side one with this song, the Beatles continue the moods of three earlier songs ("Taxman," and "Eleanor Rigby" and "Love You To"). The love song ("Here, There and Everywhere") and the romp ("Yellow Submarine") are concluded with animated despair.

SIDE TWO BEGINS with the expectant pulse of guitar and piano; before the drums usher the sound into the refrain, the mood is hushed, a spring waiting to be released. The exclamation of the refrain deserves such suspense, and it bursts through with all the warmth of the sunshine it describes. Unlike the unhinged giddiness of "She Loves You," the restraint of "Good Day Sunshine" is mature, and the soft-shoe verse that follows (in a different key area) has just the right amount of camp to it. Other Beatles songs that celebrate nature ("Here Comes the Sun," "Dear Prudence," "Mother Nature's Son") don't have the same playful soft focus. With pianos double-tracked on both channels, there's no need for guitar; the song points toward the pub-band charm of "When I'm Sixty-four," and if it weren't for the vibrant colors of the harmonies on the refrain, it would be positively as old-fashioned. The ragtime piano solo that caps off the second verse (replacing a second stanza) is round with Joplinesque pleasure.

The two-key layout resembles that of "Here, There and Everywhere," only simplified: the romantic verses in A major are bathed in the warmth of B major for the refrain (the last line hinges on E major, the common harmony between the two). Ringo's kicks gently prod more than they jerk at the motion—modesty is its ultimate appeal. The final refrain has one of the few modulations (up one step for effect) in the entire Beatles catalogue. Voices cascade over other voices as they enter from different directions, like sun peeping through the trees (first center, then right, and finally left). The cornucopia of vocal colors expresses all the unexpected pleasure of falling in love.

.   .   .

"AND YOUR BIRD CAN SING" pits a forceful rhythm behind a magnetic guitar riff—everything sticks to it—and the lyrics are at once patronizing and sympathetic. The sensory images from "Nowhere Man" have more bite, more assertiveness, and more groove. Lennon's voice is double-tracked onto both channels, and the bass counterpoint to the guitar's perpetual lead creates a texture that is both constantly in motion and handsomely controlled.

In the verses, Lennon cuts his subject down to size: it's a shaded putdown song, not far from Dylan's "Positively 4th Street" (1965). The vocal harmonies that join Lennon's lead on every title line add a shimmer to their pungency; the title line is mock singsongy, and Lennon's voice strains on the word "me," the implied rejection. He's upset about the lack of human connection the way George is in "I Want to Tell You," but he retreats from derision in the bridge (in minor):

When your prize possessions
Start to weigh you down
Look in my direction
I'll be 'round
I'll be 'round

As in "Nowhere Man," Lennon's compassion is never far from his anger. The song's subject possesses everything she wants, but she doesn't "get" (i.e., understand) Lennon; she's seen the seven wonders, but she can't "see" (or empathize with) him; finally, she can hear every sound there is, but she can't hear (or communicate with) John. The second verse links the sense of sight with the color of her bird (green—John's color code for envy; c.f. "You Can't Do That"); the third verse uses the sense of hearing, "and your bird can sing." The compression of images allows wordplay: "And your bird can *sing*" in the first verse follows the line about possessions ("Tell me that you've got everything you want"), but not the last, which alludes to hearing ("Tell me that you've heard every sound there is"). The first verse anticipates the final verse's region of perception and takes the sound associations one step further: "your bird can sing" is changed to "your bird can *swing*," from listening to music to dancing to it, Lennon's favorite image of freedom.

The guitar solo is fluorescent irony. In a song about joy this fluidity would be celebratory; in the context of Lennon's nose-in-the-air arrogance, though, it glitters with supremacy—the sonic equivalent to Lennon's uppity vocal attack. The texture's hypnotic lull owes something to the Byrds (whom John admired), but the Byrds never recorded an original of such sour allure (they actually smooth out Dylan's "Positively 4th Street" rather than tart it up). The unresolved (subdominant) chord on which this song ends lets all the tension ride off into the air as Paul stutters toward a stop on his bass.

"FOR NO ONE" makes the same jarring entrance as "Eleanor Rigby"—it's awake and melancholy with dread, the way its unsuspecting lover arises with a headache. The first verse, sung to a lonely harpsichord, conveys the solitude and regret of "Yesterday" with more disbelief, more longing. The narrator describes the man's dumbstruck loss in the first stanza, the woman's new life in the second, and the brittle emotion of rejection and disintegrating dreams in the refrain:

> And in her eyes you see nothing
> No sign of love behind the tears
> Cried for no one
> A love that should have lasted years. . . .

The elegiac horn solo, played by master hornist Alan Civil, comes in the second stanza of the second verse, expressing feelings too piercing for words. The final verse juxtaposes the two lovers in separate lives and then returns to the very first stanza to round the song off.

The lyrical melody plays off of the simplistic plano figure (oom-pah-pah-pah): Paul's voice rises in ever-increasing stretches of yearning until he reaches the peak of the line, which lands on a dissonant note, one that sits outside the harmony it sounds with, and resolves itself only by falling resignedly. The melody itself mixes hope with disappointment. The piano figure for the bridge is another ironic comment on the mood; its predictable broken eighth-note chords contain the emptiness of what the lover sees in his loved one's eyes: nothing. The suspended cadence that is resolved at the end of the bridge is the musical equivalent of a sigh, the sorrow and self-obsession of a lover left behind. The brief echo of the horn solo during the final verse lingers like a lost memory in the lover's consciousness. It ends on its dominant harmony (the same way the preceding song finished on its subdominant) with the same sigh, and its return is irreconcilable.

> There were other father figures in New York at that time—the acid doctors. A friend of mine—well, an ex-friend of mine— told me about this terrific doctor where you'd get these vitamin shots—Dr. Charles Roberts. . . . I went one night, got this shot, and it was the most wonderful shot in the world. I had the answer: I mean, it gives you that rush. There were vitamins in it, and a very strong lacing of methedrine. I'd never heard of methedrine or speed. They never told you what was in the shot anyway. It was a slow evolution. I went there first and got a shot. I went a week later and got another one. And maybe one week later I was feeling kind of down, and I went twice a week. Eventually I was going there everyday, and then I was going two or three times a day. Then I went four times a day. Then I started shooting up myself. (Joel Schumacher in *Edie: An American Biography*, p. 260)

IN JEAN STEIN and George Plimpton's oral biography of Edie Sedgwick, the Andy Warhol superstar, Joel Schumacher describes Dr. Roberts of New York City, on whom John Lennon based his song. The doctor was notorious enough—*real* enough—for the Beatles to get wind of his reputation. (This was in the same period when George's dentist dropped acid into after-dinner coffee without telling John, George, or their wives.) The mix has the glossy appeal of the rush of a good drug: it sounds shiny and sweet, like candy, and the lure is as intoxicating as in "And Your Bird Can Sing," only synthetic—the aural sheen is not real, not lasting. The harmonic progression slips and slides around in the same way; we're never sure where home base is because the harmonic ground is constantly changing (from A major, tonic, to F-sharp major, submedian, to B major, supertonic). The only stability comes in the bridge, when the voices gather around an organ to sing the praises of the good doctor. This penetrating satire implicates not only the doctor and his "patients" but the listener who gets seduced by the song's tease as well.

Lennon's lead vocal (again put through both channels) has the bleary, drugged-up feel of an addict. The rhythm guitar continually leans back on the flat sevenths of the chords it belts out, giving the beat a tart, aggressive bite. As in "I'm Happy Just to Dance with You," Lennon's rhythm guitar pushes the song even more than the drums do. McCartney's upper harmony on the second verse ("He's a man you must believe/Helping anyone in need") inflects the blasé melody with salesmanship, setting the stage for the choral refrain. A lead guitar (right) plays a small introduction to the refrain before the organ enters and everything drops to a pulsing drone.

The refrain has the glowing hue of the Beatles with halos around their heads. They're sending up their own image as incorruptible young men—singing at the altar of the drug doctor. The return to the verse is sudden: the harmonic transition from the refrain back to the verse is prepared, but the shift from High Church to the band happens without warning (the keys pivot off E major from B major back to A major, the same diagram as in "Good Day Sunshine"). Lead guitar remains to add commentary, ornamenting the top layer of sound while the bass remains static. The mockery of empty religious values is as severe as the poke at the medical profession, and the two are implicitly linked by the music.

The key angles in the closing fade distort the tracks' harmonic maze: they arrive at B major just as the sound is close to disappearing, blurring the line between proper cutoff and fade-out. It's the fourth Beatles song in a row that ends in a different key than it begins in, satirizing its own key scheme like the "Sgt. Pepper" reprise and "Piggies."

THE TRANSITION FROM the blurred ending to the asymmetrical guitar line that opens "I Want to Tell You" is as satisfying as the drift from "I'm Only Sleeping" into "Love You To," and together they point toward the integration of song segues that makes *Sgt. Pepper* a continuous stream of sound. George's guitar creeps out of the silence (the opposite of a fade-out), and his syncopated eighth notes and triplets deliberately trick the ear as to where the best will land. It isn't until the drums enter with the solid backbeat that a rhythmic pattern is established—it's the most disorienting introduction to a Beatle song yet.

The lyrics are concerned with communication—and, as David Laing points out, not necessarily between lovers or even friends, but perhaps between artist and audience. This song shuns the "modern" anxieties with time and seeks healthy exchange and the enlightened possibilities that lie outside fixed Western temporal boundaries. This is why the song both begins and ends with disruptive rhythmic figures, and why its pivotal climaxes are rhythmic and focused: the repetition of one note on the piano (on the words "slip away") penetrates the confusion, the uptight feelings that drag the singer down.

The guitar line is central, the backbone for the esoteric lyrics, and the piano's annoying dissonant figure at the end of each verse disrupts its stability. The piano conveys the frustration of the singer, and its single-note solo is the peace he wants to attain. The last line ("It's all right/I could wait for-ever/I've got time") is the transcendental key: the tension sur-rounding the exchange in the song need not rely on any rigid measurements of time. "I'll make you maybe next time around" admits different frames of perspective for different people.

These issues are not explicitly drawn out in the lyric; they rely on the music to help convey their message: "I've got time" is sung just after the backbeat stops; "Maybe you'd under-stand" is sung just before the single repeated note in the piano that signifies the wish for relief; and the second time the re-peated piano note appears, it's after the lines

> But if I seem to act unkind
> It's only me it's not my mind
> That is confusing things

The repeated piano note combines what Laing refers to as the "individualistic, selfish ego" and the "mind . . . the Buddhist not-self, freed from the anxieties of historical Time"—the dif-ference George suggests between "me" and "my mind."

For the repetitions into the fade-out, the line "I've got time" is repeated in an exultant deluge of voices, freely im-provising around the disintegrating beat (or time itself). The constriction of Western time is conquered only by the singer's release from it; and as the sound fades, a single wandering voice dabbles around in a new modality, awash with pleasure (the expressive opposite of the same nondiatonic stretch of guitar at the end of "Taxman").

REVOLVER'S MOST DERIVATIVE cut is "Got to Get You into My Life," and it captures the urgency of rhythm and blues so well that it sounds like a Beatles cover of an old Beatles cover. Everything about this track shows how much they learned from playing material like "You've Really Got a Hold on Me" and "Please Mr. Postman" and from listening

to concise hit-writers such as Berry Gordy and Smokey Robinson and teams like Norman Whitfield and Barrett Strong
(who penned Marvin Gaye's "I Heard It Through the Grape-
vine" and Edwin Starr's "War") and Eddie Holland, Lamont
Dozier, and Brian Holland (who churned out hits like "I Can't
Help Myself" for the Four Tops as well as numerous Supremes
classics). The vigorous horns, pulsating bass, knockabout
drumming, and, above all, the untamed Wilson Pickett
vocalisms in the refrain echo the charged brilliance of the
Motown and Atlantic labels' finest pop rhythm and blues.

A sharp brass passage opens the track with a flash of
bravura: with a complement of horns and saxes on the right
and the Beatles on the left, the brisk high-hat and tambourine
set a clipped pace. Paul's high notes that punctuate the ends
of lines are perfectly placed, the "ooh"s are ripe with feeling,
and the drum fills round off each verse with soulful precision—the gut physicality of Ringo's playing owes a lot to the
Motown style of Bernard Purdie. (Purdie played with James
Brown, Aretha Franklin, and others—and had the audacity
to brag that he overdubbed Ringo's rhythm tracks for the
Beatles.) When Paul rips into the refrain after the second
verse, he defines the moment for himself (the way he did in
"Long Tall Sally" and "I'm Down"): his timing is extraordinary, and the excitement of his emotion is invincible.

The absence of guitar for the first three verses reveals the
Beatles as soul purists, but the song's astonishing moment of
glory after the third refrain transforms them into futurists.
This could well be George's finest moment: the sound of his
guitar is dazzling, and the crimped energy he packs into this
brief display has angular jabs against the beat that summarize
the gritty motion it springs from. He hangs out for the next
refrain, laying down tasty ornaments to the jive that surrounds him.

As the track streaks toward its finish, Paul has the last
word with his ad-libs, which he economizes by singing the

very opening line of the song. The moment is charged—everyone drops out except Ringo. When the ensemble reappears for the fade-out, high organ is added up on top, and the brass players go nuts. Just as the lead trumpeter leaps up for one last high scream, everything disappears.

"TOMORROW NEVER KNOWS" fades in from that same silence, but it sounds as though it's touching down from a different galaxy. The only Beatles ensemble players are Ringo and Paul, who lay down a feverish groove beneath the chaos as noises, backwards guitars, and eerie bird sounds swoop all around them. The swirls of motion are the product of eight tape loops mixed randomly together for a blizzard effect, with only an occasional organ adding harmonic dashes to the mesh. Lennon's voice is put through a Leslie loudspeaker for a boomy, distancing effect.

The lyric is from a version of *The Tibetan Book of the Dead* prepared by Timothy Leary as a handbook for people wanting to achieve spiritual enlightenment by taking LSD. Leary's book espouses the drug as a mind-expanding substance, and the words to this song are part of the text Leary recommends reciting to people taking the drug to guide them away from a bad trip toward a good one. The values of transcendence from the material world are similar to those in "I Want to Tell You": escaping from the mechanically physical nature of time, the irrelevance of Western "games" (e.g., money), and a blissful union with the spiritual realm. The true essence of being is knowing and existing, not cheating, hoarding, or putting the make on other people—and Leary would add that it's quicker with LSD than with simple meditation.

Lennon achieves the transcendental bliss he seeks in aural terms—who knows how many bad trips it cost him in real life? The track relies solely on the tape effects for its collage of aural color and imagery, and Lennon's vocal delivery actually deflects emotion—he's meant to sound primordial, elemental. The backward guitar solo spins out of the mass of sound, rearranging temporal direction before gliding back into the ether. Lennon sings the final verse through a filter that distorts his detached presence even further; it symbolizes the transcendence through which he supposedly guides the listener. On the other end of reality, Lennon sings:

> *That love is all, that love is everyone*
> *It is knowing, it is knowing*
> *That ignorance and hate may mourn the dead*
> *It is believing, it is believing*
> *But listen to the color of your dreams*
> *It is not living, it is not living*
> *Or play the game's existence to the end*
> *Of the beginning, of the beginning, of the beginning, of the*
> *   beginning . . .*

During the fade-out, much of the noise finally drops out and a lone, out-of-tune honky-tonk piano takes the song into the abyss. This is less a self-parody of the message than it is one more random sound tagged on to emphasize the lack of rational hierarchies in the altered state.

The song's slant sharpens the message of the entire record, which moves from cynicism to withdrawal. "Tomorrow Never Knows" embraces an alternative Eastern "reality" as though everything flowed from it—the ecstasy it describes deliberately contrasts the disillusion it follows. In Western culture taxes are a scam, time and money in general are fraught with human corruption, romance and the possibilities of meaningful connections are imperiled, and the untapped galaxies of the mind are the only hope of deliverance from worldly evils. Lyrical and musical circles intrude throughout: the cyclical stages of life in "She Said She Said"; the turning guitar line of "I Want To Tell You"; the modular key schemes of "Good Day Sunshine" and "Doctor Robert." At the end,

"Tomorrow Never Knows" uses circles of tape loops and swirling sound effects to evoke the idea of death as transition, the end that becomes a beginning.

COMPARED WITH *Rubber Soul, Revolver* gives the beat more prominence, with quicker tempos and more daring harmonic schemes. The earlier record's tone was softer but its rhythms more involved; *Revolver*'s beat is direct. The guitar solo on "Taxman" is at once red hot and alien; the nondiatonic tones hint at the Indian colors of "Love You To" and the converging temporal zones of "I Want to Tell You." "Eleanor Rigby" 's strings are sharper, more accented than on any other Beatles string arrangement except for "Glass Onion." The fatigue of "I'm Only Sleeping" only points up how incisive the grooves are in "And Your Bird Can Sing" and "Doctor Robert." At the end of side one, the rhythmic assurance of "She Said She Said" grounds the entire record with a determined insecurity: the scalar melodies are backed by shifting meters, and as the beat goes from four to three and back to four again, it suddenly gets more powerful. "Good Day Sunshine" and "And Your Bird Can Sing" share angular key layouts, and "For No One" and "Doctor Robert" follow as a string of four songs that end on different harmonies than they began in. "Got to Get You into My Life" finds as much redemption in the beat as "She Said She Said" finds terror. Only two slow cuts ("I'm Only Sleeping" and "For No One") resemble the reflective climate of *Rubber Soul*. Part of what *Sgt. Pepper* lacks is a similar commitment to hard, purposeful rhythms—it dabbles more in textural colors and imaginative fancies than in spirited actualities.

Beginning with the celebration of innocence ("Love Me Do" and "I Want to Hold Your Hand") and moving through uncertainties ("If I Fell," "I'll Be Back") and progressively disenchanted poses ("Help!", "Yesterday," "Day Tripper"), the Beatles arrive at an impasse:

[After our concert at Candlestick Park in San Francisco] we decided, no more touring; that's enough of that. I'm not going to put up with it. And I was dead nervous, so I said "yes" to Dick Lester, that I would make this movie with him. I went to Almeria, Spain for six weeks, just to . . . because I didn't know what to do. What do you do when you don't tour? There's no life. Because I'd been on the road for . . . well, it wasn't that I wanted to tour so much, but I didn't know what to do. What . . . what the hell do you do all day, you know, I mean? *[Laughs]* So I went, I did the movie which was boring as hell and spent six weeks there. But I was really too scared to walk away. I was thinking, well, this is like the end really. You know, there's no more touring. That means there's going to be a blank space in the future. At some time or other that's when I really started considering what can one do? Considering life without the Beatles—what would it be? And I spent that six weeks thinking about that. What would it . . . what would it . . . what am I going to do, you know? Am I going to be doing Vegas—I call it now . . . but cabaret? I mean, where do you go? So that's when I started thinking about it. But I could not think what . . . what it would be, or how I could do it, or . . . I didn't consider forming my own group or anything, because it didn't even enter my mind. Just what would I do when it stopped. (*Lennon Tapes*, p. 11)

Revolver celebrates life mostly in terms of evasion—the dream world of "I'm Only Sleeping" or the childish foppery of "Yellow Submarine." "Good Day Sunshine" and "Here, There and Everywhere" sound like wishful fantasies of happiness compared with the despair of "Eleanor Rigby," "She Said She Said," and "For No One." The layout of their greatest work pronounces its place in the larger journey: from unassuming naiveté (*Please Please Me*) through experience and disillusion (*Rubber Soul, Revolver*) toward alternative worlds of escape ("Tomorrow Never Knows," *Sgt. Pepper*, and *Magical Mystery Tour*).

"I'D LOVE TO TURN YOU ON"

Penny Lane (Paul)/*Strawberry Fields Forever* (John)
Released: February 17, 1967

SGT. PEPPER'S LONELY HEARTS CLUB BAND
Released: June 1, 1967

S G T. P E P P E R is the Beatles' most notorious record for the wrong reasons—a flawed masterpiece that can only echo the strength of *Revolver*. There probably has been more written about *Pepper* than any other rock album, and even though now most critics claim either *Rubber Soul* or *Revolver* as their best overall achievement, *Pepper* was the record that made rock criticism worthy of its subject. Purists mistrust *Pepper*'s airs of respectability—there's no all-out rocker with the thrust of "She Said She Said" or "Got to Get You into My Life," and the psychedelic colors in its layered textures come close to flaunting their musical sophistication. It has a degree of self-consciousness throughout that primitive rock 'n' roll snubs in favor of urgency and raw energy. (Its proportions were immediately satirized: the Mothers of Invention put out the heavy camp of *We're Only in It for the Money*, and the Rolling Stones responded with the limp *Their Satanic Majesties Request*.)

The layout is a vaudevillian smorgasbord with something for everybody: songs about friends and courtship, an Indian diversion, a circus masquerade, a dance-hall charmer, and some sentimentality for the old folks. This album is not about ideas in conflict and a growing introspective awareness of life: it's a miragelike reaction to the complexities of both *Rubber Soul* and *Revolver*. A direct assault like "Taxman" would spoil the nonchalant tone of *Pepper*'s picturesque world.

Where *Revolver* witnesses corruption and mortality and turns toward withdrawal, *Sgt. Pepper* begins as light farce and moves toward a sober awakening: "Tomorrow Never Knows" is drugged-up mysticism, "A Day in the Life" is reluctantly despondent. Only "Fixing a Hole" turns indecisiveness into a lingering quandary; "She's Leaving Home" is high melodrama where "Eleanor Rigby" is suffused with adversity. The Lennon songs disrupt McCartney's light touch with increasing wariness: "Lucy in the Sky with Diamonds" is ultimately about escape, the disturbed "Mr. Kite" turns a traveling circus into a ghoulish orgy of the bizarre, and "Good Morning, Good Morning" plys real horrors to set up the finale (which functions as an epilogue), "A Day in the Life." When the vaudeville ends, Lennon and McCartney's most successful song montage sets the punctured dream against the overbearing reality to epitomize *Pepper*'s larger theme: the necessity of fantasies and the danger of indulging in them—the blurring of real and imagined worlds in "A Day in the Life" is finally confounding. The restrained power of the finale makes the record somewhat lopsided; Paul's guileless showmanship keeps the receding gigantic chord from sounding hopeless. Ironically, *Pepper*'s popularity is part of its appeal, and McCartney's entertaining accessibility accounts for its widespread acceptance more than Lennon's intrusive doubts.

Because of George Martin's lavish attention to detail and nuance, *Sgt. Pepper* remains a very engaging record. Sounds appear unexpectedly, favorite moments are continuously satisfying, and familiar phrases take on renewed freshness with repeated listenings. But the self-consciousness of the record seems to work against it; *Rubber Soul* and *Revolver* sound like miracles of intuition by comparison. Where its predeces-

sors sound born to the world, entireties greater than the sums
of their parts, *Sgt. Pepper* is tinged with conceit.

IN THE SUMMER OF 1967, *Sgt. Pepper* was the longest
and most expensive recording ever produced in the rock medium, and it is still the all-time grand slam of rock albums if
only because of the way it hit the world when it was released
on June 1: radio stations competed with one another to see
who could air it from start to finish and how often. All across
America and much of the world, the sound of the long-
awaited new Beatles record rebounded off the airwaves
through people's minds, a soundtrack for the Summer of Love.

> The closest Western Civilization has come to unity since the
> Congress of Vienna in 1815 was the week the *Sgt. Pepper* album
> was released. In every city in Europe and America the stereo
> systems and the radio played, "What would you think if I sang
> out of tune . . . Woke up, got out of bed . . . looked much
> older, and the bag across her shoulder . . . in the sky with
> diamonds, Lucy in the . . ." and everyone listened. At the time
> I happened to be driving across country on Interstate 80. In
> each city where I stopped for gas or food—Laramie, Ogallala,
> Moline, South Bend—the melodies wafted in from some far-off
> transistor radio or portable hi-fi. It was the most amazing thing
> I've ever heard. For a brief while the irreparable fragmented
> consciousness of the West was unified, at least in the minds of
> the young. (Langdon Winner in *The Rolling Stone Illustrated
> History of Rock 'n' Roll*, p. 183)

"*Sgt. Pepper* sounds playful but contrived, less a summing up of its era than a concession to it," Greil Marcus
writes. The music's psychedelia captures a sensibility, an aural picture of the way things used to be; it mirrors the era it
was conceived in better than it speaks through time (psychedelic revivals are still, after all, revivals). It spoke most directly to its immediate audience and drew people together

through the common experience of pop on a larger scale than ever before.

Pepper's childlike playfulness with images and pictures springs from the songs they began with: "Penny Lane" and "Strawberry Fields Forever," two reminiscences of Liverpool. In December 1966 they laid down basic tracks for "When I'm Sixty-four" and "Strawberry Fields Forever"; "Penny Lane" was recorded during the first two weeks of January 1967. All three were intended for the album, but "Penny Lane" and "Strawberry Fields Forever" were put out as a single to appease the record executives who wanted to bridge the lengthening gap between records, and these were the only three songs from which to choose. (*Sgt. Pepper* came out ten months after *Revolver*—a then-unheard-of stretch between releases.) As part of *Pepper*, these two songs might have relieved some of the artifice. Combined for a single, they became a riveting apposition, signalling the split between Lennon and McCartney implanted in "We Can Work It Out."

Penny Lane (Paul)/*Strawberry Fields Forever* (John) *Released: February 17, 1967*

L I K E "Day Tripper"/"We Can Work It Out," this single was labeled a double A side. The conceptual idea embraced by the songs was depicted on the record sleeve: one side pictures the Beatles with their new mustaches, bright lights flashing from behind; the other features photographs of the four of them as children. The two songs refract views of childhood, the same subject igniting two vastly different emotional worlds. This pairing compounds Lennon and McCartney's contrariness—they look at life differently because they experienced *childhood* differently. "Penny Lane" is Paul's wistful and somewhat quirky view of urban life; "Strawberry Fields Forever" is Lennon's personal reminiscence of abandonment and the struggle toward self-identity. Their coupling is complementary but in some ways incompatible—the sensibilities that were stitched together for "We Can Work It Out" now speak the same language in their own separate dialects.

IN THE CRYSTALLIZED setting of "Penny Lane," everything is idyllic and precious. The urban workaday life is drawn with characters—a barber, a banker, a fireman, and a "pretty nurse . . . selling poppies from a tray"—who symbolize a thrifty, hardworking ethic. The musical atmosphere surrounding them idealizes their provincial charm (the barber displays photographs "of every head he's had the pleasure to have known"; the banker carries "a portrait of the Queen"), but the tone is as odd as it is ordinary. The middle of each verse is interrupted—the drums drop out, the harmony shifts from the bright major of the opening to a quizzical minor, and a shadow is suddenly cast across the characters' quirks (on the absurdist line "The banker never wears a mac in the pouring rain," the boomerang sentimentality of "The little children laugh at him [the banker] behind his back," and the final clever turn of "And though she feels as if she's in a play/ She is anyway"). Like the zombie nine-to-fiver he becomes in "A Day in the Life," McCartney romanticizes these people as he measures the inanities of their day-to-day lives: "very strange."

With the three accented impulses that accompany those words, the tonality shifts down one key from the verses for the refrain (from B major down to A major). "Penny Lane is in my ears and in my eyes": the singer-narrator steps back from his story for a moment and tells us, as Laing puts it, that "the return . . . is one in imagination," in the ears and the eyes of the memory. The refrain becomes an aside from the older man remembering scenes from his youth; the verse takes the listener back to the remembered experience as it lives in the imagination. The same three accented raps, on the words "meanwhile back," return the music to the original key. The two key areas carry the shift in perspective.

The second stanza of the second verse is given over to a

trumpet solo—not an ordinary trumpet but a piccolo trumpet, the toy trumpet of the child (a "real" trumpet doesn't belong in this imaginative world). The refrain it follows has a different stanza than the first:

> *Penny Lane is in my ears and in my eyes*
> *A four of fish and finger pies—in summer—meanwhile back . . .*

Trivial associations can set off the most stirring childhood memories. "Finger pies" is slang for both filching and teenage heavy petting, schoolboy rites of passage; it's the kind of personal detail that McCartney sees himself in—he too feels as if he's in his own play anyway. (Penny Lane is a bus roundabout near where they attended school.)

The drama of "Penny Lane" follows the outline of "Eleanor Rigby": opening verses introduce types and paint their world, and principal players (the banker, the barber, the fireman) are set in motion together at the end (when "the fireman rushes in . . . [to the barber shop] . . . from the pouring rain," even though it's the *banker* who "never wears a mac"). As the final refrain approaches, there is a modulation—a musical device the Beatles rarely used as a way of punching up the end of their songs. Climbing one key higher to intensify endings is the musical equivalent of a forced encore, but in "Penny Lane," the modulation is actually a working out of the key areas that frame it: the adult perspective of the refrain (in A) arrives in the verse key (of B) as the piccolo trumpet returns, commenting on the transformation with brisk effusion. (On the promotional copy of the single, the one radios aired, the trumpet gets the last word by rounding off the phrase it only begins in the original. This version makes more musical sense.) The summing up of the small drama rests on the musical worlds that come together at the end: the past is brought to life in the present.

McCartney's command of the 45 genre in this song is masterful. From the initial bass flutter to the distant flutes, everything coalesces into a hazy tingle that speaks to the innocent in everybody—it's as perfect as pop gets. The Victorian dance hall overtones make it categorically British, combining an old-world flavor with the modernity of Ringo's cushioned backbeat. "Penny Lane" survives as a classic because its surface charm masks its structural intelligence—the appeal is as simple and sweet as the youthful glow it recaptures.

> "No one I think is in my tree." Well, what I was trying to say in that line is "nobody seems to be as hip as me, therefore I must be crazy or a genius." . . . I don't literally mean genius as the things we deify, but as the spirit of genius that can come through anybody at any given time. And if there is such a thing, well, I'm going to *be* one. . . . "I think it must be high or low." What I'm saying, in my own insecure way, is "nobody seems to understand where I'm coming from. I seem to see things in a different way from most people." . . . Surrealism had a great effect on me because then I realized that the imagery in my mind wasn't insanity—that if it was insane, then I belonged to an exclusive club that sees the world in those terms. Surrealism to me is reality. Psychedelic vision is reality to me and always was. (Lennon in *Playboy*, pp. 166–169)

"PENNY LANE" is detailed and dramatic; "Strawberry Fields Forever" is evocative and euphemistic—its meanings are cloaked in surreal images and overlapping musical textures. David Laing writes that the world of "Strawberry Fields Forever" is a "landscape of the mind, not of the world." Both songs have an imaginative glow, but where McCartney's recaptures boyhood memories, Lennon's is about a childhood nature irrevocably lost, and he sings it from some deep poetic part of his subconscious. The title is taken from a Salvation Army children's orphanage around the corner from Mendips, his home in Liverpool. He used to hop the fence to play in the broad green lawns, and his Aunt Mimi would take him

to the fête there each summer. It was a magical forest to him
as a youth, comforting the ominous sense of insecurity he carried around inside, the unrelieved effects of his traumatic parentage. "Strawberry Fields" is a never-never land where
"nothing is real," where there's "nothing to get hung about,"
but the music overwhelms the words—it's as much about
loneliness as "Eleanor Rigby," and is one of the few Beatles songs
that de-emphasize vocal harmony. "What was perhaps most
disturbing about 'Strawberry Fields,'" writes Geoffrey Stokes in
his biography (*The Beatles*, p. 195), "was the affectless quality
of John's vocals; it is as though he wasn't teasing us with a
hidden meaning, but was hopelessly confused himself.
'Strawberry Fields' is less a riddle than a mystery." Its sense
of dislocation is part of its expressive resonance.

A doleful Mellotron droops into the first downbeat bale-
fully. There is no story line, only John's lone voice, weary
and somewhat distant, meandering with a confused detachment. He's singing about himself while affecting a blasé,
matter-of-fact surrealism. The dream of innocence is the same
as in the middle section of "She Said She Said"—childhood
as a place where "everything was right." But he can't articulate his angst over the father who left him and the mother
who died on him; the vocal performance is painfully distracted in contrast to the assertive sense of self he gives to
earlier songs. The texture carries the emotion that the words
and the singer grope for, suffocating Lennon's normally un-
inhibited style. He sounds trapped inside his own emotions.

The music carries the burdens of the text's obliqueness:
the Beatles' sluggish electric treatment is transformed into a
cello-and-trumpet ensemble after the second refrain. This is
George Martin's ingenious splicing of two completely different versions they had recorded, the first with the band, the
second with the orchestral instruments. (The American edition of this track has the new ensemble enter dramatically,
swooping across the stereo spectrum. The splice is heard more
clearly in the change of drum timbre on the European mix.)

The imbalanced mood that Lennon was after meshes these two versions together as one—the shift in aural tone is as disjointed as the words it envelops, and the two different instrumentations are more troubling than one alone possibly could be. (Lennon's voice suffers more distortion from the new mix.)

His confessional is met at every turn by denial, and every denial becomes a lie. Every musical gesture seeks relief, from the shifting stanzaic patterns to the shrill trumpet accents, as the singer tries to talk circles around the hurt he's obviously feeling: "Always, no sometimes, think it's me/But you know I know when it's a dream." The play on "no" and "know" confuses the pattern of pitting "always" against "sometimes" and "know" against "think"; it's there in the next line as well separating "you" and "I." Either spelling sows disorientation. The last verse places the vernacular stumble of "I think I know I mean ah yes but it's all wrong/That is I think I disagree" next to an irregular cello pattern, making the words fit the music (or vice versa) as if through sheer willpower.

The cellos groan their lines, offsetting the high plucked arpeggio that links the verses to the refrains. A high-hat sound played backward accompanies the line "No one I think is in my tree," as trumpets play the Mellotron part from before. But this is a dissolution of musical elements, not a compression—instead of gaining on the hurt he sings about, he's slowly losing control. Even where Ringo links up empty spaces with wide-open fills, the beat seems to melt. The title is the only lifeline to hang on to: "Strawberry fields forever, strawberry fields forever."

As the lead guitar returns after the final refrain, another electric guitar plays off the cellos and trumpets. After the fade-out a new set of wandering noises comes back in: a snare drum marches judiciously onward; flutes flicker and sputter around a repetitive guitar note. "Strawberry Fields Forever" gives tentative form to unexplainable feelings, and the telling of the story affects the shape of the story itself (told narratively, the song would refract a completely different experience). The nagging sense of self-doubt just beneath the surface of "She Said She Said" is conveyed without self-consciousness here: there's no pretense of cohesion or intimidation. (Accompanied simply by acoustic guitar, as can be found on bootlegs, he sounds even more distracted, even more lost in feeling.) Lennon's vocal performance in "Strawberry Fields Forever" is spellbinding, and the overall effect is aching, desperate. The man gets lost inside the child, and the child can barely make sense of things.

SGT. PEPPER'S LONELY HEARTS CLUB BAND
Released: June 1, 1967

Peter Blake's *Sgt. Pepper* cover is one of the best-known works that pop art ever produced. He places the Beatles among the notorious figures and artists they compiled together from the past century, major—recognizable and semi-obscure—icons from G. B. Shaw, Edgar Allan Poe, and Aldous Huxley to Lenny Bruce and Mae West (Elvis Presley and several others were removed for fear of copyright infringement). Its declarative use of popular icons suggests Andy Warhol's pop art, but its eclecticism is straight out of collage-based British pop art. Where Warhol singled out objects like a Campbell's soup can, distorting size, color, and dimension for effect, British artists superimposed the iconography of the postwar commercial boom, romanticizing home appliances and images of success. They turned reality back into fantasy by flipping the commercial ads they parodied inside out. An ordinary kitchen became "the best of all possible worlds."

In *Pepper*'s funeral pose, art romanticizes the celebrity. If the Beatles weren't bigger than Christ, they were certainly as big as any of the people they posed with here. Their costumes are Victorian band uniforms; the host of immortals they stand with are posing at a grave; and the memorial they are all attending is for the Beatles' former image—they're paying their respects to their own late live career. Their former moptop images, from Madame Tussaud's wax museum, look down on the grave; their former selves become as much of an illusion as Sgt. Pepper's band. (At the far left, crowded from the center of attention, is Stu Sutcliffe.) To the right a large female doll wears a sweater that reads "Welcome the Rolling Stones"; Stan Laurel peeks out from behind comedian Issy Bonn; Johnny Weissmuller, the actor who played Tarzan, leers behind Ringo, as Oscar Wilde peers out in back of Lennon.

Crowd noise opens the world of *Sgt. Pepper*, a performance-within-a-performance that satirizes the Beatles' retirement from the live stage. *Sgt. Pepper* makes fun of its own eight-track wizardry: we're listening to a pretend audience that is pretending to listen to the pretend Sgt. Pepper's Lonely Hearts Club Band. The mood is expectant, and the opening charge from the band onstage is warm and celebratory. It's the same kind of self-consciousness that makes "I Saw Her Standing There" a ritualization of youth; here, they're celebrating show business, and the relationship between the musicians and the home listening audience, which they themselves can only imagine. By turning conventions inside out (an imaginary band, an imaginary audience) the Beatles achieve a scary comic awareness. Sharing this self-awareness with their audience is one of the underlying motives of *Sgt. Pepper:* dashing the illusions that make them famous by creating new ones. Like the Who's top-forty radio gags on *Sell Out* (1968), only far more subtly, they parodize the medium through which they speak.

THE TITLE TRACK begins with a razor-sharp guitar lead to a buoyant beat, all on the far right channel—the context is camp, but the tone is rock 'n' roll. Paul plays emcee during the first verse, before horns enter (left) with a Sousa-like flourish that wins an astonished gasp from the canned audience. Then Sgt. Pepper's Band greets us with a string of showbiz clichés ("We hope you will enjoy the show") punctuated by a grandiose descending horn solo (after "Sit back and let the evening go!"). As the harmonies rise to the quieter section on the words "It's wonderful to be here/It's certainly a thrill," the vocals travel from far left to center—by the time Paul's emcee re-enters, it's as though the band is center stage and Paul is addressing the audience from stage right. "I don't really wanna stop the show," he interrupts, more like a circus ringmaster than a pop singer, and throws the spotlight on Ringo ("the act you've known for all these years").

The move from fictive band to fictive celebrity (Billy Shears) is made as the screams of Beatlemania hail Ringo's appearance. The high camp gets linked to personal warmth with a single electric guitar that settles slowly into the new tempo of "With a Little Help from My Friends." Ringo's celebrity posture has always included an element of "this could be you," so his first lines, "What would you think if I sang out of tune/Would you stand up and walk out on me?," are more than a perfect opening—they're his most self-revealing moment as a Beatle. He's singing about himself both to his audience and to the band that's backing him up. (In Joe Cocker's gutsy cover, these Beatlesque overtones are lost.)

Paul's bass is a lead instrument on the right channel; and his fills are not only melodic, they're an essential part of the song—without him, the whole character of the tune would change. As he falls from the line "Do you need anybody?" he sets up a high end for Ringo to answer in his boomy low tom-tom fill after the first verse. Ringo's ride cymbal on the third verse is the only shift in texture for the entire song: no more is attached to it than necessary; its good nature is open and spacious. Compared with the extravagance that follows, "Friends" is simply put.

. . .

T HE STREAMLINED TRANSITION between "Friends" and "Lucy in the Sky with Diamonds" becomes a signature of the album: there is barely a thread of silence separating tracks.

"Yellow Submarine" is a children's song that adults can sing; "Lucy" is a kid's song sung to adults. The Mellotron introduction raises the curtain on a playground of ideas, with streaks of bright hues for a musical texture. Even though Lennon's voice is childlike, he plays the calm but awestruck storyteller, describing scenes he finds himself entranced by. The opening line's invitation ("Picture yourself on a boat on a river") makes us participatory observers in sustaining the illusion of Lucy's world. The musical colors have no gravity; the singer drifts aimlessly among the images and makes them float in the hazy atmosphere the music provides.

Paul's bass is again prominent (right), lending the subtlest interplay with the Mellotron (left) as the track's only rhythm section for the verses. All the other sounds are built on this foundation. A lead guitar (right) shadows Lennon's vocal on the second part of the verse ("Cellophane flowers of yellow and green/Towering over your head") as the Mellotron drops out.

The heavy two-three-four drum fill turns the light waltz of the verse into a backbeat refrain (in four) which celebrates the imaginative act itself. The liberating title line transforms everything—it exalts the artful happenstance of child's play. The pleasure behind this serendipity increases as Paul joins Lennon for the high harmony.

Surreal images like "newspaper taxis" (actually Paul's line) and "marmalade skies" are juggled as effortlessly as the musical texture. Lennon immerses himself in the joy of language: unlikely adjectives are coupled with common nouns, trading the despair of "Strawberry Fields" for dreamy frivolity. "Lucy" is his bright, magically escapist exploration of psychedelia, where "Fields" and "I Am the Walrus" are convoluted and thick. The enigmatic heroine herself disappears as soon as she reveals herself ("Look for the girl with the sun in her eyes/And she's gone").

The final verse is cut off early with some sitarlike debris hanging over the last drum call. The closing refrains are ornamented with leaps and rolls from Paul's bass as the sound fades away. At this point in the album, the material world is completely clouded in the mythical by both text and musical atmosphere. The breezy shadings of color in the openness of the mix engulf the listener as the journey from introduction through Ringo's mock autobiography continues into Lennon's looking glass. There's a sense of discovery in these textures that renews the Beatles' approach to sound as it explores ways in which phrases and instrumental images can be shaped by layers of overdubs.

THE CLIPPED OPENING chords of Paul's "Getting Better" are upbeat pop confection: he's in love and all is right with the world. There are two small trips in the high guitar (right) that give the intro a twice-four count (one into the second bar, another just before the last upbeat before the vocals enter—without these simple accents, the meter would be obscure). Tunes reign in this song, and the arrangement is tailored to suit the melodies: Ringo enters with the vocals in a mock military shuffle and then delivers a quirky high-hat/backbeat combination for the verse; the bass gives the track a lot of its lift, making octave leaps in the verses and anticipating the chord changes during the refrain by getting there early at each shift; conga drums season the last verse; and there are some fine guitar touches darting in and out of it all.

But vocals carry the day, and Paul sings with the same excitement that made "Good Day Sunshine" believably unclouded. Criss-crossing his lead with backups, a clever new vocal texture is found, with sly elisions: the background vocals cry "Can't get no worse" as McCartney sings over the "worse" with "Yes!" There's even a cool high "oooh" before the last refrain, a signature from the past. It's a silly love song, but it's his most refreshing—he doesn't drag it out into cloying sentimentality. What it lacks in sweep it makes up for with infectious lyricism.

T HE INDECISIVE MAJOR-MINOR intro to "Fixing a Hole" maps out its harmonic symbolism: the first part of each verse begins in major and slips quickly into minor, as Paul sings of how repairing leaks sets his thoughts spinning. In the second part of each verse, on the words "And it really doesn't matter if I'm wrong I'm right," the harmony shifts back to major, and a new outlook shines through: satisfaction, self-assurance, and positivism. This is the same kind of dual-key setup that marks both "Good Day Sunshine" and "Here, There and Everywhere," only here it's just one key in an artful dance between doubtful minor and absolving major.

Harpsichord, bass, and drums form the backdrop, and lead guitar is added sparingly, with a falling figure after the first section of the verse. The bass line during the first part of the verse (under the words "there I will go _____") gives it its syncopated rhythmic pulse; the rock-'n'-roll chord outlines that the lead guitar plays (behind "See the people standing there, who disagree and never win/Wonder why they don't get in my door") brings it to its pitch.

The guitar solo after Paul's "hey, hey, hey _____" is also in two opposing sections: the first part is high, arpeggiated, and ringing; the second is low, syncopated, and rhythmic—a musical play on the words "wondering" and "wandering." Vocals enter on the major section that follows, going from "ooh"s to "deep-deep" as the guitar returns to play its swinging rock 'n' roll triads. They remain for the final verse, backing up Paul as he makes his final gorgeous leap to falsetto on the words "and I still go _____."

The song fades on the minor section of the verse, drawing out the tension and uneasiness (as in "I'll Be Back") rather than neatly, optimistically tying things up. The misplaced emphasis on "Where it *will* go" gives the line a gentle tilt, playing out the off-kilter sentiment that's being sung. This is a different kind of doubt than McCartney has offered before: "Yesterday" is full of longing, and "I'm Looking Through You" is romantic bewilderment. As he matures, emotional ambiguity is couched in musical equivocation. Following "Getting Better" as part of *Sgt. Pepper*, it qualifies his upbeat positivism the way "For No One" tempered the abundant warmth of "Good Day Sunshine."

THE STRING QUARTET in "Yesterday," doubled to octet in "Eleanor Rigby," is seasoned with a harp in "She's Leaving Home" to symbolize the extra dimension of the parents in this song. Of the three, only "Yesterday" was written by Paul alone; "Eleanor Rigby" was a collaboration built around a McCartney drama. Lennon's presumed contribution to "She's Leaving Home" transforms the domestic drama by voicing the parents' worst fears which have suddenly come to life:

> *(She . . .) We never thought of ourselves*
> *(is leaving . . .) Never a thought for ourselves*
> *(home . . .) We struggled hard all our lives to get by*
> *Bye, bye*

and later:

> *(She . . .) What did we do that was wrong?*
> *(is having . . .) We didn't know it was wrong*
> *(fun . . .) Fun is the one thing that money can't buy*
> *(Something inside that was always denied for so many years)*
> *Bye, bye*

When the two lines intermingle at the end of the refrain, John's voice with Paul's, the two worlds of the generation gap are brought together in their voices: the high held tone of the title line contrast with the lower Lennon melody; Paul reasserts the young woman's independence above the parents' grieving "Bye, bye"s.

The string arrangement is by Mike Leander, whom Paul sought out due to George Martin's busy schedule, and it conveys both the shock of the loss (the brittle high notes behind "Our baby's gone") and the clipped expectation of "Waiting to keep the appointment she made/Meeting a man from the motor trade." There is a touch of heart-on-the-sleeve to such obvious emotional gristle, a conceit that Martin might have avoided had he scored the parts. But the extra dimension of the harp lifts the song from the ordinary just as its textual counterpart, the consciousness of the parents, graces the story. It may not have the cold briskness that gives "Eleanor Rigby" its stark alienation; but the long, weary sighs that are this song's refrain pack a sadness rich in dramatic interplay. It's a weeper.

"BEING FOR THE BENEFIT OF MR. KITE!" is twisted carnival burlesque, like Keith Moon's mad invitation to Tommy's Holiday Camp in *Tommy*. Lennon drew the song almost verbatim from a circus poster he owned, setting the bill of fare to a runaway merry-go-round organ.

Paul's emcee at the top of the record was dashing; Lennon's salesmanship is sinister, clicking the last *d* in "in his way Mr. K. will challenge the world!," emphasizing the ten somersaults to be undertaken *"on solid ground,"* and drawing out consonants: "The celebrated *misss*ter K./Performs his feat on Saturday." There's something demented about Lennon's ringmaster; his delivery is contorted, and he has a malicious grip on the song's gears. As he announces Henry the Horse's waltz, everything shifts into a whirling ¾ meter; lights and colors suddenly burst forth from the sound, and a labyrinth of organ textures intrudes, like spirits set loose in the house of horrors.

The oom-pah oom-pah drumbeat Ringo provides for most of the song between his bass drum and his high-hat sounds like a clumsy old one-man band, the fool in the traveling show. "Kite" has a Dickensian aura: the people and images he sings of are so thoroughly British they resemble the traveling theatrical troupe that Nicholas and Smike join up with in *Nicholas Nickleby*. But the sparse accompaniment is burlesque, and the odd characters dance by in the listener's imagination the way they did in "Lucy"—only here the old-fashioned is bizarre, the surreal downright spooky. The organ pile-up returns for the fade-out, and everything comes to a halt with the equivalent of a pipe-organ cymbal smash. The song darkens the *Sgt. Pepper* fantasy of fame—its characters aren't lovable old show-biz types but freaks and misfits. These performers live outside the real world and do stunts with animals for a living; the song suggests the lunacy of a marginal world rather than a child's idyll.

SIDE TWO BEGINS with a spiritual mirage, fanciful in Indian color and exotic in texture. Listening to "Within You Without You" some twenty years later, it's hard to believe that lines such as "Life flows on within you and without you" were taken seriously—it's now the most dated piece on the record. In its way it's just as slick as McCartney's hat-and-cane routine, but it hasn't worn as well. This should have been the link between "Love You To" and the better pop effect of "Inner Light," but it winds up having the same unintentional affectation as "Michelle" or "All You Need Is Love."

The sound that engulfs the listener during the opening moments is stirring: time is expanded, and until the tablas enter there is a sense of weightlessness, of drifting. George's voice wakes us from this state by setting a tone of pure omniscience. The line "The people who hide themselves behind a wall/Of illusion" doesn't "explicitly describe what side one was all about," as Joan Peyser claims (in *The Age of Rock*, p. 132); it sits outside the *Pepper* fantasy in its own self-contained musical temple. Harrison's track could easily have been left off with little or no effect to the larger idea at work on the record. He stretches phrases out as though they were oracular, but the monotony of sound is dulling. The laughter at the end punctures the bloated clichés the same way "Her Majesty" pulls the rug from beneath "The End" on *Abbey Road*. Where "Love You To" has some sense of rhythmic spontaneity, "Within You Without You" is directionless.

P A U L   W R O T E "When I'm Sixty-four" long before he ever had dreams of recording it; some sources say he waited until his own father reached the magic number. "I wrote 'When I'm Sixty-four' when I was about sixteen," Paul told Paul Gambaccini. "I wrote the tune for that and I was vaguely thinking that it might come in handy in a musical comedy or something. I didn't know what kind of career I was going to take" (in *Paul McCartney In His Own Words*, p. 17). The period the song evokes is wonderfully captured, and the stereo layout is well-balanced: clarinets on the right, bass and drums center, and Paul alone off to the left. A nimble piano, playing only a few chords, pounds occasionally in the center. Martin scored the low clarinets to glide along like a well-oiled Model T; the arrangement alone is mint: the "ah"s that follow "you'll be older too" sound like the knowing wave of an elderly finger. A pert clarinet chimes in as Paul sings "go for a ride," and then fills out the lead voice with harmony during the last verse.

The verse climbs from worldly-wise homey virtues and promises to the humble title question: "Will you still need me/Will you still feed me/When I'm sixty-four?" The bridge has a more expectant beat and shifts to minor, but the final line of the stanza always resolves whatever troubles may lie ahead—all worries are ironed out, all doubt laid to rest. Before returning to the main verse, a chime of happiness is duly rung.

The last verse ("Send me a postcard, drop me a line") turns the song into a charming elderly pass, and the self-effacing tone refutes Richard Poirier's overinterpretation: "They quite suddenly at the end transform one cliché (of sentimental domesticity) into another (of a lonely-hearts newspaper advertisement), thereby proposing a vulgar contemporary medium suitable to the cheap and public sentiments that once passed for nice, private and decent" (*The Age of Rock*, pp. 176–77). There's no cynicism in the pub band (as there is in the oversimplified "Ob-La-Di, Ob-La-Da"), only affection. "Sixty-four" is nothing more than a dressed-up love song, the McCartney side of Elvis's corny hokum. "Yellow Submarine," the song he wrote for kids, is complemented by a song for grandparents, kids' best friends. "Yesterday" may be Paul's most popular song, but more people sing along to "When I'm Sixty-four." The final kicking-the-hat-from-behind "hoo" that sends the clarinet tune home and tucks the song in has a soft-shoe delicacy. The production turns it all into a delicately baked trifle.

PAUL'S OPENING "Ah" at the top of "Lovely Rita" arches in a beautiful rainbow curve that hovers over an acoustic guitar before Ringo's full-bodied drum fill. The song is a cartoon, a rock-'n'-roll ragtime with a tongue-in-cheek narrative that brings the cardboard sitcom to life. Paul plays with his delivery, going for the pun on "boob" as he sings "filling in the ticket in her little white *book*," tripping over the line "made-her-look-a-little-like-a-milit'ry-man" as easily as he prances around the final backup vocal refrains, ad-libbing his heart out. The piano solo (right) that follows on the heels of Paul's ecstatic "Rita!" has more spunk than the one in "Good Day Sunshine"—it ends with a one-finger scalar flourish à la Chico Marx. (But the can't-figure-out-how-to-end-this jam is unnecessarily long; it doesn't add anything to the whimsical inconsequence of the lyric.)

. . .

A ROOSTER'S CRY leaps out from the final downward glissando of "Rita" 's piano, a startling reveille to "Good Morning" 's frightful pace. The gaga frenzy of contemporary urban pace finds its voice in a television jingle: the cornflakes
ad that was this song's inspiration becomes a slogan of derision—"Good morning!" turns into a curse. The cackle of Lennon voices blaring from the right repeats "Good morning" an
irregular five times, and the final pronounced "ng-uh" strings
the irritation out tauntingly. Everything is suddenly a jum-
ble, from jobs to memories of the old school to marriage to
television, and the onslaught is so real it's ghastly. This is the
strongest hint that beyond the fantasies of this record a workaday nightmare awaits—"Good Morning" enacts the constriction and conformity that aggrieves "A Day in the Life."
Ringo's snare-drum fill just before the verse pushes the aggravated rush to its limits.

The first lines of verses ("Nothing to do to save his life/
Call his wife in") are punctuated by an asymmetrical cymbal
smash, dropping a full beat before moving on—a rhythmic
booby trap. Meters are uneven, and the horns are quacky and
aggressive, not like the Sousa flourishes of "Yellow Submarine." From the start, it's obvious that this song is about more
than just a daily job hassle: it's about lives that are daily
hassles to live. Lennon sings it with the high-blood-pressure
pulse of the Nowhere Man, physically overworked and spiri-
tually undernourished. The tag line, "I've got nothing to say
but it's okay," is sadly ironic.

George's guitar solo bursts from the madness with even
more fury than the one in "Taxman" and rams head-on into
a new section that twists things up even further, with saxes
plunging away in double time at a monotonous riff:

People running 'round, it's five o'clock
Everywhere in town it's getting dark,

Everyone you see is full of life
It's time for tea and meet the wife.

The shriek from the guitar after that last line is a howl of neurotic pain.

As THE SOUND recoils into its own whirlpool of repeated phrases, a fox hunt descends into the fore, satirizing the mad dash of life. Then George Martin's most inspired piece of trivial genius turns a chicken's squawking into an electric guitar as the cacophony of animal noises recedes. The evening's entertainment is over, and the closing reprise of the *Sgt. Pepper* theme is launched.

Paul's hiccuped "One, two, three, four" is peppy with anticipation, and Lennon can't resist adding an insouciant "Bye" behind him. (It vaguely echoes his same moment at the beginning of "I Saw Her Standing There.") Ringo's simple drum solo is nothing but the primal beat in all its glory, so charged and spirited that any showy twist would lessen it. The energy it gives off is regenerative—when the band enters, it sounds as though they've been playing all this time and have warmed to a closing pitch.

Paul's bass leads the others in, and they hit their stride with even more grandeur than the drums had hinted at. The band answers Ringo's antiflash solidity by reveling in the sound of a simple one-chord riff for four full bars before the vocals enter. The reprise extends the show-biz fireworks of the opening by adding a full-scale modulation—their most obvious yet—up a step for the last go-round. (Hoisting the harmonies up one key for a dramatic last verse is normally a Tin Pan Alley cliché, but putting it to use in this song shows their respect for the genre.) The kick it gives propels wordplay: "Sgt. Pepper's one and only Lonely Hearts Club Band/ It's getting very near the end," as if they were worried about falling off the end of the record. George saves his best guitar fills for this last segment, backing the vocalists as they slowly step offstage. One last "Whew!" sends the tune home.

BEFORE THE FINAL chord has even begun to fade away, the acoustic guitar of "A Day in the Life" enters the left channel, and the parallel universe of everyday life intrudes. The curtain falls on Pepperland just as another is raised on the sobering stage of the real world. (The unadorned guitar chords shatter the *Pepper* illusion in much the same way that backward sounds subvert the direction of "Rain.")

Like "Tomorrow Never Knows" and "Twist and Shout," "A Day in the Life" redefines everything that came before. After the reprise regroups the mythical band and sends the audience home with a rousing encore, the real Beatles take us back into the world that greets us after the turntable platter stops spinning. As a postlude to the Pepper fantasy, it casts a shadow that sets all the other songs (and the Beatles' own career) in perspective. "A Day in the Life" comments on how listening to a pop record relates to what's happening when the show is over.

The slow guitar chords at the outset have a drag to them, and the piano that soon joins in is wearied as well. The sound is ominous, broad but not dense. Lennon's entrance on "I read the news today, oh boy" is pregnant with disillusionment; the gentle fall on the word "oh" alone is the sound of poignance. The simple surface gestures in the music and the voice gain deep feeling with repeated listenings. "And though the news was rather sad," he sings, "well I just had to lau-augh." The laughter isn't funny but a nervous response to an overwhelming despair.

Guitar, bass, piano, and gentle maracas carry the first verse. Lennon's delivery from the far left channel sounds distant, adrift in the burdensome events he's reading aloud, unable to make sense of the news that greets his day. The second half makes the anxiety clear: "He blew his mind out in a car."

Even the way Lennon phrases that horror—borrowing an image from the drug culture to soften the violence—tells us that he has a great deal of trouble accepting the reality itself. Ringo's drum entrance swells this image further, filling up the space with large hollow tom-toms. The crash occurred because "he didn't notice that the lights had changed," a pitifully small oversight.

During the last lines of the first verse, Lennon's voice moves slowly from the far right toward the center as the song becomes more aware of itself and the music gains intensity. The end of the first verse reaches the melodic height with Lennon's falsetto left hanging in the air, unresolved: "NobodywasreallysureifhewasfromtheHouseofLords." Half of the horror is in the victim's unrecognizable familiarity—he could have been anybody.

Ringo's drums comment on each line in the second verse, conveying the emptiness the singer fears in himself. "A crowd of people turned away" from the brutal scenes of the war movie, but the singer cannot turn away—"having read the book," he is impelled to watch, repulsed by the illusions on the screen but unable to turn his eyes from the awful truth it imposes. (The despair hints at atomic devastation.) By the end of the verse Lennon's voice has traveled all the way over to the far left channel, and the journey of awestruck disbelief is complete. As he sings "I'd love to turn you on," his voice fades into the debris of sound that will soon rise up and overwhelm its meekness. (The BBC banned this song from its airwaves because this line was thought to be a drug reference, when in fact it is probably one of the least drug-oriented on the record.) The cloud of confusion that has grown inside the singer's head since the song began now opens up, slowly at first, then rises toward a torrential downpour of sound. The storm reaches drastic proportions in a matter of seconds.

The conglomeration of noise made by over forty orchestral musicians playing without music evokes the image of a train speeding toward a head-on collision—it picks up speed from its own momentum. At the peak of the summit, the moment of reckoning, a breakthrough occurs—an alarm clock goes off, and a befuddled sleeper wakes up and begins his day, oblivious to his own nightmare. The simple snare-to-cymbal rousing that Ringo whips off on Paul's waking words completes the transition.

The new beat is chipper, industrious, and comments on its own corporate precision only briefly at the end of lines, where the marshalled bass is set loose for a contrasting harmony (on the words "comb across my *head*" and "in seconds *flat*")—the snare marches purposefully onward. The compulsion of the rhythm conveys his obsession with time; after looking up and noticing that he's late, he actually gasps for breath before moving on.

Paul's complementary section is the day in the life of a modern everyman who sets forth each morning unaware of the tragedy around him—a kind of rock-'n'-roll Babbitt. Lennon's agonized empathy surrounds Paul's blissful ignorance: as it did the protaganist of "Good Morning," life is passing this figure by; he is not of this world but *out* of it, preoccupied with his schedule and bland attire. Hopping on the bus "in seconds flat," he climbs to the top level of the double-decker (where smoking is allowed) and has his routine ciggy to start his day. The nightmare returns.

The blurring of the dream life and the real world adds to all the confusion. We're never sure whether Lennon's section is the "real" world or if it's merely the dream that Paul slips back into atop the bus. The alarm clock blurs these boundaries: is Paul waking from Lennon's nightmare, or is Lennon imagining Paul's generic day in the life? The song inside a song works like the play within a play: the interdependence of reality and illusion is telescoped into one setting. As Paul drifts further off into his "dream," his "ah" travels from right to left and back to the right again, very slowly, doubling the distance that Lennon took over the course of the first two verses. The rhythm softens to a comfortable backbeat by slicing the rigid military snare in half, allowing a smooth transition back to Lennon's final verse. In fact, the pulse is constant until the end, and the basic rhythm track was recorded live after days of rehearsals, even though bass, drum and vocal tracks would be overdubbed several days later. (The orchestra was added last.) A loud brass line announces the return, and Lennon appears way over to the left, where he had arrived at the end of the second verse.

This last verse goes by more swiftly than the first two; the forces that are set in motion for the first orchestral ascent are starting up again here, only much sooner. This time the train is a runaway from the very beginning of the verse, and the loss of control is apparent with each passing line.

The final image of the song is trivial: the "four thousand holes in Blackburn, Lancashire" are potholes that the local authorities had to count. (There is disagreement about this image: Richard Poirier writes morbidly of Scotland Yard searching "for buried bodies on a moor by making holes in the earth with poles and then waiting for the stench of decomposing flesh.") Lennon comments on bureaucratic absurdity wryly: "Now they know how many holes it takes to fill the Albert Hall." What all the holes refer to doesn't matter as much as where Lennon takes the image—by devoting attention to such a meaningless counting task, he emphasizes the disparity between this verse (and the warped values it implies) and the other two.

The second orchestral tidal wave is larger and more disturbing than the first. Instead of arriving at an alternative world, the roaring tumult crashes headlong into the defeat that was its fate from the very beginning. The tangle of instruments was never scored; each player was told to follow George Martin's gestures and reach a certain pitch as he conducted the ensemble. It is the sound of utter turmoil, an ocean of vexation, churning from beneath everyman's subconscious and ready to explode at any second.

When the climax is reached and the final declamatory chord hammers the song closed, it is bombastically hollow.

The sheer force of energy released from it is enormous, but the tension remains unresolved; it leaves the listener more disturbed than mollified. This final chord, struck mightily by the four Beatles at three pianos on a simultaneous cue, hangs in the air forever, echoing until the final strains disintegrate before our very ears. The aural image couldn't be more stark; it has a sense of tragic inevitability that haunts long after the record is played.

In the context of the album, the track begins as an encore and winds up a eulogy; it dismantles the illusory world the Beatles entered as Sgt. Pepper's Band. Because "A Day in the Life" sits next to an unabashedly fun set of songs, it sounds all the more stark. But the *Sgt. Pepper* journey isn't futile; its despair is ultimately hopeful. "I'd love to turn you on" is a motto of enlightenment, of Lennon's desire to wake the world up to its own potential for rejuvenation, not self-annihilation. If "A Day in the Life" were a single, it would be unbearably pessimistic; as the final track to the *Pepper* road show, it cools the freak-out optimism and challenges its listeners to scheme beyond the numbing ordinariness that daily life confronts them with. "A Day in the Life" affirms the imaginative landscape of the rest of the album by acknowledging our need for it. Because of the larger context, it's not "a song of wasteland," as Richard Poirier suggests. The final blow doesn't summon the fate of modern man; it decries the tragedy of the fullness available and denied in our culture.

THE LAYOUT OF *Sgt. Pepper*, combined with the pop explosion that Marcus holds as its promotional triumph, gave pop the artistic legitimacy it deserved at least as early as *A Hard Day's Night*. Most critics agree, however, that *Sgt. Pepper* is not the Beatles' finest album, even if it is one of pop's most important. In *Hi-Fidelity* magazine, Roger Lees complained of the praise being heaped on the Beatles for a simple recapitulation of the theme song. Because of its initial impact, *Sgt. Pepper* has attained the kind of populist adoration that renowned works often assume regardless of their larger significance—it's the Beatles' "Mona Lisa." *Revolver* remains a better work than *Pepper* for its sturdier material, though *Pepper* represents a creative leap in terms of formal design.

And even though *Pepper* is a model of psychedelic design, it lacks its predecessor's emotional core. The labyrinth of sound that hovers over "Lucy" and "Mr. Kite" doesn't have the same compulsion that guides "She Said She Said" or the philosophical release of "Tomorrow Never Knows." Too much of *Pepper* winds up as texture for the sake of texture, surface sliding around on light substance instead of enriching it. The vexing clouds of "Strawberry Fields Forever" have mournful cellos as agents of expression; the haze of "Within You Without You" only confirms the song's vagueness of thought. "When I'm Sixty-four" and "Good Morning" justify their colorful sound patterns: the emotions generate the music; unlike "Lucy in the Sky with Diamonds" and "Lovely Rita," these two songs rely on more than artfully woven musical turns surrounding fanciful ideas. *Sgt. Pepper* contains only one proper love song ("It's Getting Better"), but nothing with the elegance of "Here, There and Everywhere" or the soulful punch of "Got to Get You into My Life." "A Day in the Life" actually saves *Pepper* from being an indulgent studio etude; imagine this record without its stark finale and it becomes an exercise in levity.

AFTER PEPPER, the main themes that have been set loose on the Beatles' records start to reappear in different contexts. With the death of Brian Epstein in August 1967, the internal politics of the band begin to shift—Paul begins to assert himself more as a leader—and the unity of the three middle-period records never finds the same coherence in their remaining work (the "White Album," *Let It Be, Abbey Road*). The innocence and disillusionment they balance so well on the "Penny Lane"/"Strawberry Fields Forever" single is never achieved again, in part because no solution is possible and in part because such a delicate balance implies extremes that are irreconcilable—any further apart and they fall off the map (cf. "Hello Goodbye"/"I Am the Walrus"). If *Help!* was the beginning of their studio career, *Sgt. Pepper* is its apotheosis and the beginning of their solo careers: from here on out, there are fewer and fewer Lennon and McCartney collaborations, and the different paths they pursue until "The End" on *Abbey Road* delineate more than align their opposing sensibilities.

FOOLS ON THE BUS

All You Need Is Love (John)/Baby, You're a Rich Man
(John) *Released: July 7, 1967*

Hello Goodbye (Paul)/I Am the Walrus (John)
Released: November 24, 1967

MAGICAL MYSTERY TOUR *Released: December 8, 1967*

YELLOW SUBMARINE *Released: January 17, 1969*
[new tracks recorded mid-June 1967 and early 1968]

SEEN IN RETROSPECT, the alternative world of *Sgt. Pepper* works as an antidote to the encroaching complexities of *Revolver*. They make an interesting pair: *Revolver* dwells in poignant realities until the deliverance of "Tomorrow Never Knows"; *Pepper* sustains imaginative possibilities before concluding with the tragic actualities of "A Day in the Life." Like *Please Please Me* and *Abbey Road*, the conclusions are essential to the way each record works. But where *Pepper* has acknowledged its own excesses by the time the masquerade is over, everything that followed it in 1967 plays off *Pepper*'s weaknesses instead of its strengths.

Brian Epstein's death in late August (two months after the release of *Sgt. Pepper*) sent the business career of the band into disarray. They were beginning to establish their own company, Apple, but they didn't bother to hire another manager. Instead, film and recording plans launched forward as though business would take care of itself. But even before Epstein's death, their music had begun to meander. On their first summer off from touring, the Beatles performed for a worldwide satellite hookup ("All You Need Is Love") and sang out loud about questions that had been stirring for at least a year ("Baby, You're a Rich Man"). Not such bad notions in themselves, except that they sound spent.

Magical Mystery Tour is a paltry copy of the *Pepper* road show (and Ken Kesey's Merry Pranksters), enacted childishly on the screen in their first film with no director. "All You Need Is Love" is Lennon utopianism more kitschy than even McCartney's optimism; the "Hello Goodbye"/"I Am the Walrus" single diffuses the polarities of "Penny Lane": congeniality becomes meaningless, and the emotional turmoil of "Strawberry Fields Forever" turns incomprehensible. For the rest of 1967, they rode out the psychedelic trend instead of redefining it in fresh, original terms, even though some material—the title track—was recorded before *Pepper* was released. ("Hello Goodbye" appears only as a single on Parlophone; "I Am the Walrus" will be discussed as part of *Magical Mystery Tour*.) Throughout all these sessions, the worst of the batch were consigned to the score for *Yellow Submarine*. The best of them—"Hey Bulldog"—was not even used in the animated movie.

All You Need Is Love (John)/Baby, You're a Rich Man (John) *Released: July 7, 1967*

Hello Goodbye (Paul)/I Am the Walrus (John) *Released: November 24, 1967*

THE MUSICAL SARCASM of the French national anthem kicking off "All You Need Is Love" is one of the good moments amid the rubble—it lets the simple hook ("love, love, love") ring out that much more baldly. The internal contradictions (positivisms expressed with negatives) and bloated self-confidence ("it's easy") make it the naive answer to "A Day in the Life."

The first two lines of the verse are irregular (seven beats—four plus three—instead of the usual eight), but the dropped beat simply allows the song to move forward less awkwardly; there's less space to fill up after the words are sung. The refrain, a simplified turn of phrase, breaks through with a regular 4/4 pattern, the kind at which Lennon normally excels. Here it's obvious rather than clever: "All you need is love" becomes "Love is all you need." The music, though, is an ideal world built on the idea that love can truly save us. The quipping brass and ornamenting strings give the sensation of joy run amuck. (Paul inserts asides—"All together now" and "Everybody"—during the last refrain, the same way that Lennon did on "Yellow Submarine.") The fade-out is a musical funhouse that stacks a Bach two-part invention, "Greensleeves," and Razaf and Garland's "In the Mood" on top of Lennon's capricious retort "She loves you, yeah, yeah, yeah." It ends like its "Marseillaise" beginning, robbing pomp of its currency and asserting a chaotic charm. It's the aural equivalent to Peter Blake's *Sgt. Pepper* visual montage.

Happiness would win out if the technical quality weren't so poor—compared with the clarity of *Pepper*, the mix sounds amorphous. "All You Need Is Love" lacks the ardor of "The Word." It would take a generation's hard lessons to learn that it takes more than love to survive, never mind thrive. (When Elvis Costello revived the song for his Live Aid appearance in 1985, his vitriolic snarl implied how far there still was to go rather than how far we'd come.)

THE FOGGED-UP texture to "Baby, You're a Rich Man" stirs different concerns into the same formulas. Like "A Day in the Life," it's a "combination of two separate pieces, Paul's and mine, put together and forced into one song," Lennon told *Playboy* (p. 194). "One-half was all mine. [*sings*] 'How does it feel to be one of the beautiful people, now that you know who you are, da da da da.' Then Paul comes in with [*sings*] 'Baby, you're a rich man,' which was a lick he had around."

The onslaught of questions Lennon poses gives away the aimless qualities of the music. The answers are vague witticisms, empty enough to deflate expectations:

> *How does it feel to be one of the beautiful people?*
> *Now that you know who you are—what do you want to be?*
> *And have you traveled very far?*
> *—Far as the eye can see.*
>
> *How often have you been there?*
> *—Often enough to know*
> *What did you see when you were there?*
> *—Nothing that doesn't show.*

It's clear that they understand their position: if the Beatles are beautiful people, by extension their listeners become beautiful people ("Baby, you're a rich man, too"). What's unsettling is how lacking in purpose it all sounds. "You put all your money in a big brown bag inside a zoo/What a thing to do" is not only a clumsy trope, it's immodest. There's no center to this music, and its inchoate character never finds the expressive Umbres of "Strawberry Fields Forever." A snake-charming Clavioline (imitating an oboe) swerves in and out of everything else as the only point of musical interest. "Help!" and "Drive My Car" addressed the fallacies of fame from cynical impulses; "Baby, You're a Rich Man" flounders in privileged emptiness.

THE "HELLO GOODBYE"/"I AM THE WALRUS" single magnifies "Penny Lane"/"Strawberry Fields" from earlier in the year as a dual-sided character study: McCartney gets more innocuous and Lennon gets more obscure. "Hello

Goodbye" resembles both "Penny Lane" and "Your Mother
Should Know" as a tuneful piano-based whimsy, and tacks
on a Hawaiian return after a fake ending to try to save its
meager melodic dividends. It's the kind of song McCartney
can write in his sleep, and probably did.

MAGICAL MYSTERY TOUR *Released: December 8, 1967*

The Mystery show was conceived way back in Los Angeles. On the plane. You know they give you those big menus and
I had a pen and everything and started drawing on this menu
and I had this idea. In England they have these things called
Mystery tours. And you go on them and you pay so much and
you don't know where you're going. So the idea was to have
this little thing advertised in the shop windows somewhere
called Magical Mystery Tours. Someone goes in and buys a
ticket and rather than just being the kind of normal publicity
hype of magical . . . well, it never was magical, really . . . the
idea of the show was that it was actually a magical run . . . a
real magical trip.

I did a few little sketches myself and everyone else thought
up a couple of little things. John thought of a little thing and
George thought of a scene and we just kind of built it up. Then
we hired a coach and picked actors out of an actors directory
and we just got them all along with the coach and we said,
"OK, act." An off-the-cuff kind of thing.
(*Paul McCartney in His Own Words*, p. 48)

Magical Mystery Tour starts out with all the ambition of
Sgt. Pepper but none of its spark of originality. It's like the
band set out to repeat past glories by enacting the fantasies
that make *Pepper* so enchanting. The title song is a warmed-
over rewrite of *Pepper*'s opening without the same layers of
self-awareness; "Your Mother Should Know" is "When I'm
Sixty-four" in knickers; "I Am the Walrus" combines the loss
at the center of "Strawberry Fields Forever" and the disturb-

ing confusion of "Being for the Benefit of Mr. Kite!"; and "Blue Jay Way" picks up where "Within You Without You" leaves off—an even longer trip to nowhere. In addition, the set of six *Mystery Tour* songs seems to have nothing to do with one another: as a long-playing album it would have been tedious, and as double extended-playing singles (two 45s packaged with a picture booklet) it seems overwrought. Where their early records could be forgiven their boundless naiveté because they were so full of musical high spirits, *Magical Mystery Tour* underestimates its audience. For the first time, the Beatles' fun sounds contrived.

The opening trumpet flourish is wearing thin by now: on *Pepper* it was razzmatazz; on "All You Need Is Love" it was reduced to nationalistic farce; here it's the worst kind of musical cliché, deliberate instead of spontaneous. Ringo packs a wad of energy into his drums' energetic punch as Paul (ringmaster again) shouts "Roll up, roll up for the Magical Mystery Tour, step right this way!"

But it's a sure sign that things aren't flowing right when tempos fluctuate this drastically between sections of songs: each time Ringo returns to the verse section, he pumps up the beat by accelerating—he's trying to revive it. At one return, after the mock *misterioso* section, he falls back into the backbeat with a deliberate restraint, as though he needs some place to build up from that the material itself isn't giving him. The song's ending slowly lets the air out of its feigned majesty— the same kind of can't-get-out-of-this jam that deflated "Lovely Rita."

"YOUR MOTHER SHOULD KNOW" is a lesser version of "When I'm Sixty-four"; it's got plenty of Paul's hokey affection for old-time singalong pleasure but none of his flair for characterization. The harmonic turns are bright and clever: the bridge is a piano solo that disrupts the oom-pah-pah meter, but it suggests more than it actually expresses. With a new lyric in this section, he might have turned the song into a more wistful standard—a song within a song would work well here. As it is, the interrupting piano-and-organ bridge doesn't seem to have anything to do with the verses. They dress it up by putting Paul's voice to the right for the second verse, and the background vocals adorn the bright, plunky piano chords with parodic irreverence. But the wordless verses ("da-da-da") make it sound like a demo with dummy lyrics.

"I AM THE WALRUS" meanders; but unlike "Blue Jay Way," it actually seems to suspend normal time boundaries—it creates its own world of sound so completely that we forget what came before and what comes after. The simple police siren chord the organ trots out in the opening moments is immediately contorted by the cellos that follow—Lennon means to take the expected pleasures of a Beatles tune and invert them, set the characters in the looking glass chasing the innocent listener. What comes dashing out is not fanciful, like "Lucy in the Sky with Diamonds," but garbled. John's stream-of-consciousness becomes just as pretentious as Paul's heart-on-the-sleeve emoting. But because "Walrus" is so unlike anything that comes before, so original, it sticks out in their catalogue like an impenetrable nightmare—its shifting time signatures and unidentifiable instruments visit a foreign reality.

For the first time, Lennon sounds detached from the words he's singing, voicing other people's thoughts resuscitated from his subconscious. "Corporation teeshirt, stupid bloody Tuesday man you been a naughty boy you let your face grow long" is answered in the next verse with "Crabalocker fishwife pornographic priestess boy you been a naughty girl, you let your knickers down." This is recognizable Lennon gibberish, like the semantic illogic that trips up "Strawberry Fields Forever," but here his references are impersonal, and the tone is mock cryptic.

In the middle, after the first "GOO GOO GOO JOOB,"

everything stops for a mawkish cello cadenza, which sets up the wry wit of "Sitting in an English garden waiting for the sun/If the sun don't come you get a tan from standing in the English rain." There are typical Lennon stabs ("Man you should have seen them kicking Edgar Allan Poe") and word-plays ("See how they smile, like pigs in a sty, see how they snied"), as well as pregnant alliterations ("pornographic priestess," a seed for "Lady Madonna" and "Happiness Is a Warm Gun"). From within the recesses of imagery, "I'm cry-ing" is the only repeated line that alternates with the title refrain. The ending is a musical battle between two polari-ties, one traveling up, one traveling down, pushing and pull-ing at one another as they fade out. Radio dialogue appears above the rubble, culled from a BBC broadcast of Shake-speare's *King Lear*—Edgar's line "Sit you down, Father, rest you," can be heard just before the sound disappears.

The world of "I Am the Walrus" has no gravity (like "Lucy in the Sky with Diamonds," which it quotes), but it's less an imaginative fancy than it is an unselfconscious phan-tasm of sound. It inflates the moods set off in "Being for the Benefit of Mr. Kite!" and "Good Morning, Good Morning" and puts them through a mixmaster of starkly evocative tex-tures. The most revealing line, "Don't you think the joker laughs at you? Ha ha ha!" foreshadows the sour comic self-consciousness in "Glass Onion." (Except for "Revolution No. 9," it marks the end of Lennon's underbellied sprees.)

THERE'S A SAYING among actors that the easiest way to win awards is to portray a cripple or a slow person as broadly as possible—audiences love feeling sympathy for people needier than themselves. "The Fool on the Hill" pits the major-key area of the verse against the confused minor of the refrain, trying to set the natural head-in-a-cloud simpleton against the real world, which is constantly "spinning round." Naturally, he's misunderstood by everybody else, "they don't like him," so the primitive outcast leads a lonely life.

But the last verse has a catch: "He never listens to them."
McCartney takes himself too seriously here—the film setting
for this track is the only one to use outside professional pho-
tography. The honk-honk ding-dong grind organ and the
featherbrain flute signify something so bucolic as to be un-
touchable; the fairy-tale figure that sits alone on his hill is
supposed to understand the nature of things simply because
he knows how to let life pass him by. But what's to be learned
from this fool? Little or nothing, except how to pull the heart-
strings. The last verse plays up its own weakest moment: "He
never listens to them/He knows that they're the fools" is answered by the lazy "They don't like him." Fools in Shake-
speare do more than watch the world spinning round; they
often reflect back the most cunning insights to their masters.
Possibilities in this song outweigh its substance—it's the most
unworthy Beatles standard since "Michelle."

''FLYING'' is the only Beatles song credited to all four
Beatles, and it amounts to less than anything else they ever
recorded. With the band on the left, an acoustic guitar lays
down some licks on the right before the bassoon enters center.
It's a trivial blues-based throwaway that is immediately
mocked by low voices on "la-la-la." The odd whirring sounds
that enter before fading out are a sure sign that they don't
know what to do with what they've just done.

"Blue Jay Way" begins with an ominous organ on a single note which is skated on dissonantly by a cello (right).
When George starts singing, he sounds as tired and droning
as what he's surrounded by. Drums are left, the vocal is right,
and small snippets of backward singing and noises enter spo-
radically, punctuating phrases, "mystifying" the scene. But
all those filtered background voices echoing George's lines
don't evoke much of anything, except the boredom of the
lyric. In three minutes and fifty seconds, it goes nowhere
tiresomely.

YELLOW SUBMARINE *Released: January 17, 1969*
[new tracks recorded mid-June 1967 and early 1968]

Brian Epstein arranged for the Beatles' third feature-length film for United Artists to be a cartoon, one that would use prerecorded songs so that the demand for new material—and live Beatles appearances—would be minimal. The soundtrack album that was eventually released has only four new songs, all recorded before work on the "White Album" began and all considered unworthy of that project. Side one starts with the *Revolver* version of the title track, follows with the four new songs, and finishes with the resurrected "All You Need Is Love," the finale for the cartoon fantasy in the film. Side two contains incidental music written and conducted by George Martin, played by a full orchestra. The result is nothing close to a Beatles record. The album was slapped together to meet a contractual demand, with little or no care taken with the shape of the song sequence, much less the way the familiar tracks are reused.

"ONLY A NORTHERN SONG" has gained in irony over the years. George wrote it as a mock-modest satire of Northern Songs, their music publishing company, and Philip Norman calls it a "self-confessed nadir of his ability and [the Beatles'] interest" in the entire project. Harrison later was sued for echoing "He's So Fine" too clearly in his 1971 "My Sweet Lord," and 'Northern Song" sounds like a prescient confessional to the sponging practices of pop songwriting. Its texture confirms all suspicions about the psychedelic hubris of 1967, digressive filigree sprouting up for no other reason than to occupy space. This "fake" song rambles on terminally—it sounds even longer than "Blue Jay Way"—and it self-deprecating pose doesn't redeem its own excesses.

IN CONTRAST, "All Together Now" has a simpler guitar entrance, pumped up with chumminess, before Paul begins singing (right). It was motivated by the same simple idea as "Yellow Submarine": to write a jolly singalong. John's harmonica, which hasn't been heard since "I Should Have Known Better," is all insouciance. The long, gradual speeding up that sees the song out takes great control—once the momentum gets going, the tendency might have been to give in to its tug and speed up much sooner than they do. Here, the escalation in tempo is drawn out over a lengthy space, giving the track momentum (where a modulation would have been trite).

''HEY BULLDOG'' outclasses its surroundings with a randy camp; Lennon's sardonic rocker is based on a wry piano lick that coils back on itself like the piano-based "Money." As an experimental treatment of how his surreal lyrical tendencies could be set in purist rock forms, "Bulldog" is a neglected piece of work. To a distracting psychedelic landscape these lyrics would fall flat—they're no more outré than "I Am the Walrus." But in the rhythm-and-blues context in which John sings them, they work as rhythmic spoils to the natty melody. For the refrain, "You can talk to me" is repeated in escalating cadences almost like a threat; it concludes with "If you're lonely you can talk to me" sung so cynically that it purges its literal meaning—it contradicts itself the same way "You've Got to Hide Your Love Away" does (it's the only line of the song that comes from both channels).

Lennon's guitar solo is a daring piece of rhythmic work; it leaps in stops and starts, with crimped harmonies setting off high, screaming outbursts (it recalls his solo in "You Can't Do That"). During the fade-out, his double-tracked lead vocal goes into harmony, the low part on the left and the high part on the right. Paul's bass is center, and engagingly active—as in "Rain," it acts as a solo instrument throughout. The repeating title phrase fade-out erupts into a squabble, and Paul's bark gets John howling; his mad laughter is more a hoot than a wound. This twisted beat song restores whatever humor and self-effacement they lost credit for on *Magical Mystery Tour.*

A FLAMING GUITAR opens "It's All Too Much" with the resplendent surge of a Hendrix electric fireball. With Ringo's vast drum entrance, they seem to be defining as large a space as they can, and the title words describe the sense of awe George was after in the music. The beat isn't so much the backdrop as it is the design—clumping off-beats appear in both left and right channels. The words are mock inspirational, the opposite of the honed and delicate imagery George will use for "The Inner Light" (the B side to "Lady Madonna"), his best philosophical pop. "Show me that I'm everywhere/And get me home for tea" is the kind of line McCartney might throw away. It's George's version of "All You Need Is Love" (a song that he adored so much he mentions it in his 1981 Lennon tribute, "All Those Years Ago"). But a song over six minutes long need not be boring (as "Hey Jude" proves), and the relentless barrage of the irrational only clutters the lyric's search for mystery, richness, and beauty.

Instead of the self-propelling lick of "If I Needed Someone" or the memorable maiden voyage of the lanky, painfully self-conscious "Don't Bother Me," Harrison's psychedelic outbursts point up everything that can go wrong with such ventures. The textures that coat "Blue Jay Way," "Only a Northern Song," and "It's All Too Much" wilt. These tendencies will later be tailored for songs like "Long Long Time" and the better songs on his first solo outing, *All Things Must Pass.* But unedited, they suffer from run-on lyrics sung with swallowed vocal delivery. Subtleties are scattered, good ideas are reiterated to no good purpose, and nice thoughts are subsumed by a lack of immediacy.

MAGICAL MYSTERY TOUR and *Yellow Submarine* would be easier to write off completely if it weren't for what follows.

Just as *Pepper* can be heard as a flowered response to the bleak character of *Revolver*, the profuse psychedelia of post-*Pepper* work is answered in 1968 by another distillation of musical resources—the pendulum swings all the way back toward essentials. If this weaker material confirms our worst suspicions about Harrison's lack of focus, McCartney's superficial charm, and Lennon's self-indulgent bouts with his subconscious, it also serves as a helpful contrast to their best work of the coming year: "Glass Onion," although presumptuous, is less claustrophobic than "I Am the Walrus"; "Martha My Dear" fleshes out McCartney's whimsy with a musical sophistication; and "While My Guitar Gently Weeps" has more sincerity than any of these other Harrison songs. (Perhaps if Ringo had sung "Only A Northern Song," its conceit would be more believable.) As it is, the weakest period of the Beatles' career is best thought of as a necessary dip that charts psychedelia's pale fringes and rallies them for work ahead that still compares with their best.

FRACTURED UNITIES

Lady Madonna (Paul)/The Inner Light (George) [Harrison]
Released: March 15, 1968

Hey Jude (Paul)/Revolution (John)
Released: August 30, 1968

THE BEATLES ("White Album")
Released: November 22, 1968

THE MAGICAL MYSTERY TOUR EP was released on December 8, 1967, and the film premiered on BBC television during Christmas. The record was a hit, but after the television broadcast the Beatles received their first sound lashing from critics. Undaunted, they opened an Apple clothing boutique on Baker Street in London, decorated by the Dutch artists who called themselves the Fool. During the first six weeks of 1968, the band began work on several new tracks: George laid down the instrumentals for "The Inner Light" in Bombay, while "Lady Madonna," "Across the Universe," "Only a Northern Song," and "Hey Bulldog" took shape at Abbey Road. In mid-February they traveled to Rishikesh, India, for a ten-week transcendental meditation retreat with the Maharishi Mahesh Yogi. Joining them were Mike Love of the Beach Boys, Mia and Prudence Farrow, jazz flutist Paul Horn, and Donovan. But the retreat was soon disappointing: Ringo and his wife Maureen returned to England after only two weeks; Paul and Jane Asher left after six; and John and George eventually walked out feeling cheated.

By April, Apple Corps Ltd. had established its headquarters and taken an ad in the *New Musical Express* to solicit aspiring artists' material. Derek Taylor, Brian Epstein's former ghostwriter and the Byrds' promoter, was hired back to be their new press officer. John and Paul made a trip to America to promote their new company, and George composed the soundtrack music to a film called *Wonderwall.* John and Yoko began their experimental tape projects together, and in the summer their joint exhibition entitled "You Are Here" opened at the Robert Fraser Gallery in London. But it wasn't until July that studio work began in earnest for the next Beatles album and single. Without a performing schedule, they found themselves with more time to compose and more material than ever before to record. "Hey Jude," the first Beatles single with the inimitable Apple label, was released at the end of August; work on the album continued into October. By the time the release date rolled around on November 22, the Apple boutique had closed, Linda Eastman had moved in with Paul, and the first edition of Hunter Davies's authorized biography had been issued; and in swift succession just before the "White Album" hit the stores, John was arrested for possession of marijuana, he and Yoko released *Two Virgins,* and Yoko suffered a miscarriage.

SGT. PEPPER is the fantastical response to *Revolver's* despair. Even "She's Leaving Home," the only thing close to "Eleanor Rigby," is decorated with a sweeping harp, framing its sadness within the colorful parameters of *Pepper's* mythical dimensions. "A Day in the Life" pulled the curtain on the allegorical dream world to expose the illusions that all of us subscribe to in everyday life. *Magical Mystery Tour* fails as a concept in part because it has no equivalent touchstone; its fantasy has no antidote. Unlike "Strawberry Fields Forever" on the back of "Penny Lane," "I Am the Walrus" seems truly unreal—it bears no relation to a fixed viewpoint. Side one of *Yellow Submarine* is grounded by "Hey Bulldog," the only song in that context that doesn't sound forced. At their worst, *Magical Mystery Tour* and *Yellow Submarine* are self-parodic without being self-conscious.

Their next period of work veers away from these tendencies back toward basics. Although they're still knocking off songs for *Yellow Submarine* as this new ethic takes shape (George's "It's Only a Northern Song"), the direction is clear. Both McCartney's "Lady Madonna" and Lennon's "Hey Bulldog" are piano-based and lean, and signal a return to simpler rock 'n' roll. Harrison's "The Inner Light" improves on "Within You Without You," and everything that follows prunes away the aural crutches of playful noise. Only "Revolution No. 1" on the "White Album" has psychedelic overtones; their use of sound as colorful imagery is edited down and controlled, their image decidedly less flamboyant. Long before the idea for the *Get Back* project was proposed, the Beatles began to reinvestigate their roots.

Lady Madonna (Paul)/The Inner Light (George)
Released: March 15, 1968

McCARTNEY'S OVERT Presley imitation on "Lady Madonna" makes it the kind of double-edged parody that pays respects as it holds its own. In Elvis's singing, for every threat there's another chance—an appetite for real experience that is full of broad, engaging humor. "Lady Madonna" is sinful fun, a sassy Fats Domino piano figure gussied up with a natty horn section and flapper falsetto harmonies. The title is an oxymoron: she's a "lady," but she's also a virgin with a "baby at [her] breast." It's a smart play on how chaste spiritual doctrine doesn't account for desires of the flesh, on the hypocrisy of pretending that it does. Like Lennon's Mother Superior in "Happiness Is a Warm Gun," a pure woman is seduced by earthly temptations: "Lady Madonna, lying on the bed/Listen to the music playing in her head. . . ."

The bridge lists days of the week in nursery-rhyme sequence, trotting out contradictions with feigned innocence: "Sunday morning creeping like a nun" gives piety away as a guilt trip. The downwardly walking piano turns around to come back up after that line—devoutness is mocked as empty dutifulness. The stately conclusion of "See how they run!" is sung with giddy irreverence—it implicates the "run" in her stockings (large enough for intercourse) as it exculpates the kids she's forced to feed as a result. The groove dances all over the contradiction.

Paul's cryptic tone makes the stylized nostalgia hip. A growling sax solo exonerates guilty pleasures backed by the vocals' sarcastic "up-bah-bah-bah"s. With kids running about in the verses and the farcical nursery-rhyme bridge, prolonged innocence is hooted at as unnatural; sex is congenital. Like the corrupt choirboys in "Doctor Robert," the religious concept of purity is uncovered as a charade. (At least one biographer, Chris Salewicz, holds that "Lady Madonna," along with "Yesterday" and "Let It Be," are about Paul's mother, who died of breast cancer when he was fourteen.)

HARRISON'S "The Inner Light" appears only on the B side of the "Lady Madonna" single, and its spiritual popism is more rhythmically varied and easier to swallow than nearly every other Indian-style album track. It rivals "Love You To":

Without going out of my door
I can know all things on earth
Without looking out of my window
I could know the way of heaven

The farther one travels, the less one knows
Arrive without traveling

See all without looking,
Do all without doing

"Forget the Indian music and listen to the melody," Paul says of this song. "Don't you think it's a beautiful melody? It's really lovely" (*Illustrated Lyrics*, p. 108). George's philosophical musings are less condescending than those of "Within You Without You," and the fact that both are built from the same Eastern rhythmic principles only exaggerates "The Inner Light" 's success. When he sings "the less one really knows," he admits a degree of spiritual modesty instead of flaunting sanctimonious hype. The lyrics are sung to soft hues answered in sitar, and the meter accelerates to a quick dance-like rhythm with drums. "The Inner Light" says all it needs to say about the insight that meditation can offer its followers, the wisdom of mystery that George goes on too long about too often during his solo career

Hey Jude (Paul)/Revolution (John)
Released: August 30, 1968

With the "Hey Jude"/"Revolution" single, Lennon and McCartney's competitive edge reaches an apex: the duality of "We Can Work It Out" that splits for "Penny Lane"/"Strawberry Fields Forever" and "Hello Goodbye"/"I Am the Walrus" reaches its final height (the remaining "Get Back"/"Don't Let Me Down" pairs them without the same expressive rewards). McCartney's sentimental muse finds its noblest voice, and Lennon's internalized odysseys are pared down for a refreshing return to Chuck Berry guitar motion. These two songs are touchstones of their mature sensibilities, with McCartney at his most lyrical and Lennon at his most uncompromising.

"HEY JUDE" began as an improvised song of encouragement to Julian Lennon, John's son by Cynthia, as Paul was driving him home one day. The Lennons were getting a divorce, and Paul's compassion was directed toward the child who found himself caught in the middle. With unfinished lyrics, he brought the song in and played it for Lennon. The two of them remember the demo session differently:

> I remember I played it to John and Yoko and I was saying, "These words won't be on the finished version." Some of the words were "the movement you need is on your shoulder," and John was saying, "It's great! 'The movement you need is on your shoulder.'" I'm saying "It's crazy, it doesn't make any sense at all." He's saying "Sure it does, it's great." I'm always saying that, by the way. That's me. I'm always never sure if it's good enough. That's me, you know. (*Paul McCartney in His Own Words*, p. 23)

> Well, when Paul first sang "Hey Jude" to me—or played me the little tape he'd made of it—I took it very personally. "Ah, it's me!" I said. "It's *me*." He says, "No, it's *me*." I said, "Check, we're going through the same bit," so we all are. Whoever is going through that bit with us is going through it, that's the groove. (*The Ballad of John & Yoko*, p. 50)

John read himself right into Paul's song: his involvement with Yoko and the ensuing divorce with Cynthia happened at the same time that Paul split from his longtime girlfriend, actress Jane Asher. The lyrics are atypically self-referential in that way ("You're waiting for someone to perform with"), as Nicholas Schaffner points out. What's more telling is how Lennon insisted that Paul keep the lyrics just as they were—Paul introduced them as dummies (like "Yesterday"'s "scrambled eggs"), but Lennon stamped them completed. This documented instance of who wrote what and how the other responded shows just how sympathetic they were to each other's temperaments. They often doctored up one another's sketches, but "Hey Jude" was so good that Lennon didn't touch it.

As usual, the biographical concerns reveal only so much of what the record is all about; the high spirits resonate beyond any immediate personal references. The communal overtones that were atomized in "She Loves You" are expanded in "Hey Jude"; the singer is singing as much to himself as he is to Jude, but Paul hones in on the joy of that earlier thunderbolt and stretches it into an anthem. The beat is grand rather than manic, and the choral refrain coda outlasts the song itself. "Hey Jude" reflects a larger realm of experience, and conveys a richer vision of how good life can get.

Paul starts the song alone with an immediacy of feeling, an urgency he can no longer suppress. He sings with the hope that something just may come of his effort, and by the end a sad song *is* made better. Part of this transformation lies in the journey from a lone voice to a chorus of others singing with him—the implicit message is faith in other people, the rejuvenating effect of shared singing. But in trying to cheer someone else up, Paul discovers his own capacity for healing. The process of singing the song testifies that uplifted spirits are *earned*, not just willed: no peace is possible without struggle, "Hey Jude" tells us, and although the journey must be shouldered alone, the strength of community sees the singer through. Instead of escape ("Tomorrow Never Knows") or withdrawal (the alternative world of *Sgt. Pepper*), "Hey Jude" declares human experience as the only path toward enlightenment. (That it accomplishes this much on one side of a hit 45 makes it all the more encompassing.)

The solo vocal opening is Paul's balladic answer to Lennon's naked outbursts (in "No Reply" and "You're Going to Lose That Girl"). As with the solo vocal that trips "Penny Lane," the emotional tone is engaging from the first few seconds. The compassion lies in the gentle fall between the two title words, and the sound has a hue that radiates warmth and empathy. Paul holds the pedal down to let the simple piano chords ring fully; their rhythmic cadence is ripe with feeling. By the end of the first verse, the melody is an old friend.

The suppleness of Paul's voice couldn't be sweeter—he caresses the words, soaring through the contours of a line as if in free flight, hugging its curves and gliding on its plateaus. The cut-off delivery of "re-mem-bah" is soft, not clipped; he enjoys singing through the consonants as much he enjoys holding the vowels. Like all great singers, he invites the listener into the song without conceit; the artistry lies in the seeming ease with which he greets us.

The second verse adds guitar (left) and a single tambourine (center) as the understated grace gains fluency. The vocal harmonies ("ah") that enter during the second half of this verse (behind the words "the minute") hint at the glory to come and help ease the groove for the drum fill into the first bridge. As Ringo offers a restrained tom-tom and cymbal fill, the piano shifts downward to add a flat seventh to the tonic chord, making the downbeat of the bridge a point of arrival ("And any time you feel the *pain*"). The singer arrives a split second before the downbeat does, making the moment well up with anticipation. Paul's bass enters here, and the song bursts wide open, just as it will on a larger scale during the transition to the coda.

The downward bass motion that defines the harmony of the bridge settles the groove into a steady pace. The bridge consists of two stanzas, separated by the same piano figure that introduces them. As relief to the midrange of the verses, Paul's voice shoots upward: the bridge begins high and ends low; the verse melody arcs in a rainbow curve. At the end of the bridge (in the subdominant), the "na-na-na"s reorient the harmony for the verse as the piano figure turns upside down into a vocal aside (two steps downward become two steps upward toward the original dominant seventh, a musical question mark). The transition glows with feeling as it reorients the harmony.

To sustain interest in a four-verse, two-bridge song, details are added: tambourine on the third verse, subtle harmonies to the lead vocal. After he sings "Now go and get her," a distant but audible Paul sings "So let it out and let it in, hey Jude," telescoping the lyric of the second bridge in the background. John joins Paul beneath his lead on the line "Remember to let her into your heart" and leaps above him on the next line on the words "start to make it better." When these vocal lines intersect on the line "Remember to let her into your heart," the musical interplay jells into a full-bodied blend. The basic rock ensemble gets colorful long before the choir comes in.

Paul arrives a hair early again at the second bridge ("So let it out and let it in"), but by now he's more at ease with the music—he doesn't have to define this moment the way he did before, he just lets it happen. Like the stage metaphors McCartney sets up in *Sgt. Pepper*, expectation and obligation are weighed; "You're waiting for someone to perform with" casts Jude as a nervous actor overplaying the part. A guitar lick enters in contrary motion to the piano after the words "perform with" (the piano moves downward as the guitar shifts upward). This brief juxtaposition sets Paul off—he sings the next line ad libitum, free from the melody, inspired by the splendor of sound that surrounds him. This is where the most encouraging lines of the song come: "Don't you know that it's just you/Hey Jude, you'll do/The movement you need is on your shoulder"—a tidy compendium of pop clichés that expresses the value of self-reliance and self-trust. Since Paul is singing not only to Jude and himself but to his audience, the metaphorical message is larger: he's telling us that we all share an intuitive talent for living. After the "na-na-na" transition back to the final verse, Paul adds a modest "yeah" beneath the piano's echo to prepare for the final stretch.

The last verse arrives with a strong sense of return—it's like the song has come back home again. This is the last time Paul sings the title line in the verse setting, and he strings it out delicately, with real affection. The single-line harmony that John sings with Paul on this verse, a repetition of the first verse, is more expressive than the harmony he supplies in the third verse. It's their best duet since "If I Fell," not only for its sense of shared experience but for its similarly effortless intricacy—the harmony is just as affecting as the melody it complements. Lennon's presence on the last verse makes what would have been a great solo more of a *band* experience, strengthening the power of what would have been a solo tour de force.

As the last verse comes to a close, a mood of expectancy pervades—the song isn't ending, even though it's supposed to be. Something even bigger is around the corner; and as it slowly begins to appear, the anticipation heightens even further. When Paul begins his ascent on the repeated word "better," the whole mood is transformed from quiet reassurance to liberated ecstasy. The screams that send off the coda are the joy that has been building up throughout the entire song; all hesitation is set loose, and the coda springs to life from beneath the singer's cries with a new commitment. (The repeated progression [I–♭VII–IV–I] answers all the musical questions raised at the beginnings and ends of bridges. The flat seventh that posed dominant turns into bridges now has an entire chord built on it.)

For the remainder of the record, the three-chord refrain provides a bedding for Paul to leap about on vocally. The Beatles asked the thirty-six-piece orchestra to sing along for the chorus, making the seemingly nonsensical "na-na-na"s sound like the spontaneous anthemic climax Paul must have imagined. If ever a trivial pop snippet was apotheosized, it is here. "Yeah, yeah, yeah" may be the early Beatles' cries of romantic enchantment; "na-na-na" is the mature version of the same intoxication with life. Both spring from a desire to say more than can be said with words, and both convey far more than words could ever express.

The seemingly endless string of ad-libbed hoots, hollers,

screams, wails and asides that Paul turns in atop this communal glory speaks for his sense of the moment. He has a way of off-handedly inserting a lick or a phrase that gives everything around it a new shape, a new shade of meaning. This is no small talent. By recombining what has come before with new inflections, ornamenting the already sturdy refrain with lines of soaring beauty, he makes "Hey Jude" not only a masterpiece of melodic invention but a recording of unrivalled vocal ingenuity. It becomes a tour of Paul's vocal range: from the graceful, inviting tone of the opening verse, through the mounting excitement of the song itself, to the surging raves of the coda. In seven and a half minutes he goes from refinement to abandon in a continuous escalation of pitch. If the song is about self-worth and self-consolation in the face of hardship, the vocal performance itself conveys much of the journey. He begins by singing to comfort someone else, finds himself weighing his own feelings in the process, and finally, in the repeated refrains that nurture his own approbation, he comes to believe in himself. The genius lies in the way he includes the listener in the same pilgrimage.

We recorded the song ["Revolution"] twice. The Beatles were getting real tense with each other. I did the slow version and I wanted it out as a single: as a statement of the Beatles' position on Vietnam and the Beatles' position on revolution. For years, on the Beatles tours, Brian Epstein had stopped us from saying anything about Vietnam or the war. And he wouldn't allow questions about it. But on one of the last tours, I said, "I am going to answer about the war. We can't ignore it." I *absolutely* wanted the Beatles to say something about the war.

The statement in "Revolution" was mine. The lyrics stand today. They're still my feeling about politics: I want to see the *plan*. That is what I used to say to Jerry Rubin and Abbie Hoffman. Count me out if it's for violence. Don't expect me on the barricades unless it is with flowers. As far as overthrowing something in the name of Marxism or Christianity, I want to know what you're going to do *after* you've knocked it all down.

I mean, can't we use *some* of it? What's the point of bombing Wall Street? If you want to change the system, change the system. It's no good shooting people. (Lennon in *Playboy*, pp. 196–7)

Rock 'n' roll has always been a revolutionary force. It changed the way youth culture perceived itself on a wide range of issues: sexuality, freedom, self-worth, individuality. By the mid-sixties the radicals began to see new political possibilities in the form. And yet for all the rhetoric in the underground papers, there are surprisingly few good political rock songs from the sixties. Crosby, Stills, Nash, and Young's "Ohio" (1970), directed at the Kent State killings, is the most affecting ("Tin soldiers and Nixon coming . . . "). Dylan got more mileage by singing "Don't follow leaders/Watch the parkin' meters" with an electric guitar in "Subterranean Homesick Blues" (1965) than he did acoustically with "Only a Pawn in Their Game" (1964). As Ariel Swartley puts it in her article, "A Life in the Balance" (Boston *Phoenix*, October 28, 1986), "What Dylan offered listeners was the subversive delight of individual interpretation along with the heady solidarity of consensus." Songs like the Rolling Stones' "Street Fighting Man" were overread as political potboilers (when the motivating line is really "What can a poor boy do/But to sing in a rock and roll band"). But in general, rock stars shunned the political roles that their audiences demanded from them—they were more interested in being musicians than they were in writing movement manifestos. (This attitude has its abhorrences: the Stones' jaded response to the front-row killing at their concert in Altamont in 1969 was a manipulative film—*Gimme Shelter*—and the crude ironies of their next record, *Sticky Fingers* in 1971.)

Lennon was a natural leader in the eyes of the radicals, but his instincts told him something different than what the revolutionaries were preaching on the streets. He wanted change, but he refuted violence; he felt the world was at a political and cultural epoch, but he disagreed with the leading leftists who insisted on hearing disorder in rock as a metaphor for revolt. What Lennon understood better than the reactionaries at the time—and what makes "Revolution" a classic, a song that still has a relevant viewpoint—is the difference between ideas and action. The gap between utopianism and practicality was all too apparent in his eyes, and real change began with the individual in any case. But because the single was released during the same week that saw police club protestors outside the Chicago Democratic Convention, his message in 1968 infuriated many, including some influential critics: "It is puritanical to expect musicians, or anyone else, to hew to the proper line," wrote Robert Christgau in the *Village Voice*. "But it is reasonable to request that they not go out of their way to oppose it. Lennon has, and it takes much of the pleasure out of their music for me." Lennon was miffed over the fuss the song raised:

> I don't worry about what you, the left, the middle, the right or any fucking boys club think. I'm not that *bourgeois*. . . . I'm not only up against the establishment but you too. . . . I'll tell you what's wrong with the world: people—so do you want to destroy them? Until you/we change our heads—there's no chance. Tell me of one successful revolution. Who fucked up communism, Christianity, capitalism, Buddhism, etc.? Sick heads, and nothing else.

he wrote in *Black Dwarf* magazine in reply to a harsh attack.

The first version of "Revolution" to be released, the B side to "Hey Jude," is a sped-up version of the original (heard at the beginning of side four of the "White Album"). The distorted anger of the triplet guitar solo that ushers in the storming antimanifesto is accented by a single thunk from the band—it has the same simple command as the opening lick to "She Said She Said," only this groove is slower, funkier. As vocal screams invade and the band falls into the verse, the guitar wails (left) are perfectly timed, coasting into the rhythmic riff that is the track's backbone.

The progression is straight blues, broken only for the stop-time in each verse where Lennon delivers ultimatums:

But when you talk about destruction
Don't you know that you can count me out

But if you want money for people with minds that hate
All I can tell you is brother you have to wait.

The key line of the song is "You tell me it's the institution, well you know/You better free your mind instead."

Like that of "Instant Karma," the message of "Revolution" is to put your faith in people, not systems. Lennon knew that any alternate form of government would be as frail as the humans who would construct it. When he did get involved with political activism in the early seventies, he stressed individuals and causes (John Sinclair, the peace campaigns) more than radical ideologies. Even then, the agitprop of *Some Time in New York City* (1972) is musically stilted. In retrospect, "She Loves You" changed more heads than "Ohio" which, although pungent, basically preached to the converted. Lennon's political thinking is best summed up in the simple quote he and Yoko used: "Think globally, act locally." (The Thompson Twins' vapid 1986 cover of "Revolution" usurps its humanitarian overtones by being chic—all posture and no soul.)

THE BEATLES *Released: November 22, 1968*

Richard Hamilton's classic plain white design and formal inner graphics for the "White Album" mirror the music's range from farcical simulation to tour-de-force rigor. *Rubber Soul* and *Revolver* didn't mention the word "Beatles" on the cover; this record doesn't even show a picture of them, and the title proper of the record is branded crookedly on the bottom right-hand side of the jacket. By being overtly elitist, it sends up pop's anti-elitism the same way Blake's *Pepper* cover deliberately overstates pop-as-art. Hamilton conceptualized "the first definition of low Pop Art and made the first high Pop Art work," writes Simon Frith. The "White Album" jacket was "a limited edition of millions, hand-numbered on the production line . . ." (*Village Voice*, September 23, 1986). The music it contains walks the same tightrope between respectful emulation and high musical satire, what Wilfrid Mellers terms "serious parody."

As a form, the double album has offered up some of rock's finest moments: Dylan's *Blonde on Blonde* (1966) equals if not surpasses both *Bringing It All Back Home* and *Highway 61 Revisited* (both 1965) before it. The Rolling Stones' *Exile on Main Street* (1972) and Eric Clapton's *Layla* (1972) are irreducible explorations of the American blues on which these English figures built their sound. Bruce Springsteen's *The River* (1980) unites concerns from both sides of his career, from the romanticism of *Born to Run* (1975) to the desperation of *Nebraska* (1982); the Clash's *London Calling* (1980) epitomizes the furious kineticism of punk. In each of these cases, the double album signifies a major artistic accomplishment and comes to represent much of what a given artist is all about. Even Elton John's *Goodbye Yellow Brick Road* (1973), a noble failure, stands as a hallmark of his development as a pop tunesmith—with certain double albums, it's just as revealing to hear what tracks an artist might have cut as it is to hear the ones he chose to include.

The Beatles toy with the double-album form in different ways: the individuality of the songs overwhelms the sense of the four sides as a whole. George Martin still holds that he preferred paring the material down to compose one strong two-sided record, and yet the options for making a satisfying single record from this compilation seem limited: which songs would be lopped off? "Wild Honey Pie" certainly, "Rocky Raccoon" perhaps; "Long Long Long" is the weakest George track, but "While My Guitar Gently Weeps," "Piggies," and "Savoy Truffle" are essentials. There is no sequence that would satisfy the strictures of the forty-minute record without discarding not a few but many great tracks.

THE "WHITE ALBUM" downplays the self-conscious sophistication of *Pepper* while extending that record's use of musical caricature. By placing "Birthday" next to "Yer Blues" and "Revolution" next to "Honey Pie," it's as though the Beatles mean to pair each musical extremity with its own opposite to highlight both the polarities at work in the band and the catalogue of styles that rock has grown to encompass—the popular tradition it stems from and future directions it will move toward. Throughout the record, their intentions are constantly shifting: animals are used as allegory ("Piggies"), nicknames ("Rocky Raccoon"), cartoons ("Bungalow Bill"), and symbols of the human spirit ("Blackbird"). Traditional English female names are sanctified ("Prudence" and "Julia") or modeled as types ("Sadie" is sexy, "Martha" is a "silly girl"). If the simple chords at the top of "Ob-La-Di, Ob-La-Da" sound trite, the corresponding piano intro to "Martha My Dear" hides the melody in an unlikely harmony. In the single version of "Revolution" John sang "count me out"; on the "White Album" version he sings both "out" and "in," toning down the steadfastness of the original to make it more sympathetic.

Like "Lady Madonna," the McCartney songs straddle the ironic distance between genre treatments and fresh, inventive material that stands well on its own. "Back in the U.S.S.R." is Brian Wilson with sex appeal ("Honey, disconnect the phone"); "Honey Pie" sends up twenties sentimentalism at the same time that it finds an endearing lovesick optimism, much like "When I'm Sixty-four"; "Rocky Raccoon" is a cowboy song that works as a country-western counterpart to Ringo's "Don't Pass Me By." "Ob-La-Di, Ob-La-Da" outsimplifies "Yellow Submarine" as a kiddie classic; "Martha My Dear" is quaint but harmless, "I Will" is quaint but indistinctive; and "Why Don't We Do It in the Road?" has the same mock finality of Lennon's "Yer Blues."

But as McCartney gains facility with different styles, his partner walks a bitter course. The beauty of "Dear Prudence," a key Beatles song about nature, is thwarted by a disdain for his own listeners in "Glass Onion." The parodic impulse at play in the doo-wop ending of "Happiness Is a Warm Gun" is sarcastically cynical. "Julia" explores the core of his emotional hurt—the loss of his mother—and casts light on earlier identity songs (like "She Said She Said" and "Strawberry Fields Forever") as well as his jealous streak ("You Can't Do That," "Run for Your Life"). "Yer Blues" is at once satiric and genuine; the glib title reveals nothing of the pain in Lennon's howls. There are moments in "Sexy Sadie" where his voice reaches a poignancy as great as at any moment in his career; but the object of its vengeance, the Maharishi, seems beneath contempt. McCartney uses song forms as historical reference points; Lennon twists them to serve his emotional needs.

The effect they have on each other's writing is everywhere in evidence, and the layout accents how their tendencies rub off on one another. Where side starters "Back in the U.S.S.R." and "Revolution" seem suited to their separate impulses, the verses to "I'm So Tired" are Lennon at his most lyrical, and "Why Don't We Do It in the Road?" is the crude side of Paul's humor. McCartney's wrenching "Helter Skelter" comes after Lennon's meddlesome "Everybody's Got Something to Hide Except Me and My Monkey" in yet another competitive apposition—Lennon submerges in scatological contradictions while McCartney ignites a scathing, almost violent disorder. Both rock extremely hard. And while it's fair to say that McCartney would probably have come up with

"Martha My Dear" and "Ob-La-Di, Ob-La-Da" without someone like John Lennon as a partner, his influence on John's characterizations in "Cry Baby Cry" is unmistakable.

George gets one song per side and, except for the self-explanatory "Long Long Long," regains the promise of his *Revolver* tracks. Without "Savoy Truffle," side four would be far too Lennon-heavy, and "Piggies" is smug anti-elitism outdone only by the dourness of John's "Glass Onion" and "Sexy Sadie." "While My Guitar Gently Weeps" seems longer than it really is, showing that he did have a good sense of timing (a quality "Within You Without You" lacks). It became a seventies classic, competing with songs like Led Zeppelin's "Stairway to Heaven," the Who's "Won't Get Fooled Again," and Erie Clapton's "Layla" for heavy FM rock rotation status. Ringo turns in his first solely authored original, "Don't Pass Me By," which grounds side two in unaffected rural simplicity.

Much of the recording was done separately: Paul played drums on "Back in the U.S.S.R.," taped "Blackbird" by himself, made "Why Don't We Do It in the Road?" with just Ringo; John oversaw the strings to "Glass Onion" on his own; George used Eric Clapton to play lead guitar on "While My Guitar Gently Weeps." There are no vocal duets, and the overall feel is that of a group that plays together but no longer shares a common idea of what it wants to project as a whole. As Mike Evans points out in *The Art of the Beatles*, Hamilton's accompanying collage poster juxtaposes photos from every period in their career, but they're all individual poses instead of group shots. And the sessions were marked by at least two walkouts: first George and then Ringo.

A SEARING JET touches down as the album begins, swooping into the center of the mix as the lead guitar (right) coughs before the band starts playing. The device rips off noises from a sound-effects record, and it fades in and out of the song like an aural cartoon. Drums, piano, and lead guitar are mixed to the right; bass and rhythm guitar are on the left; and Paul's vocal is centered. The basic song is rollicking, and, like "Yellow Submarine," it's an open invitation to a party: the background vocals' falsetto "ooh"s during the bridge (behind "The Ukraine girls really knock me out"), the falling syncopations of the lead guitar that nudge every line of the chorus, and the comic double-takes on "back in the U.S." before the second chorus.

"Back in the U.S.S.R." is most often referred to as a Beach Boys parody, the kind of fun-in-the-sun song the California surf kings did so well—it's a send-up of "California Girls" and "Surfin' U.S.A." It doesn't depend on this association to be delightful, though—as in "Drive My Car," the wit is happily tart. The more direct association is with Chuck Berry's "Living in the U.S.A.," a list of everything a black man like Berry *couldn't* have in America ("I'm so glad I'm living in the U.S.A." is more racially ironic than anything else, as Greil Marcus suggests). The commercialism that Berry immersed himself in is relocated and mocked—the joyous return to the Soviet homeland is sarcastic camp. (It had the desired effect of inciting the John Birch Society's editorial ire, which linked the song's sympathetic socialism up with Lennon's "Revolution," missing the point completely.) It's offered as a hoot and delivered as such, right down to the self-deprecation of "Georgia's always on my m-m-m-mind," repeating the *m*s as if mimicking their own earlier style ("Ask Me Why"). The lead guitar hovers over the last verse like the jet itself, playing a high single-note lead to take things home.

A s t h e f i n a l engine noises recede into the distance, John's guitar comes up in the far right channel with the elegiac falling riff of "Dear Prudence." The transition couldn't be more marked, but it works despite the extremity of the contrast between Paul's exuberant kickoff and John's inward and stirring ballad. The journey from parody to purity pits the fast-paced technological age against simpler evocations of a child's view of the world ("The clouds will be a daisy chain").

Lennon's opening words are punctuated by a delicate tambourine-and-bass accent in the left channel—the bass continues to play on downbeats, the tambourine reappears only at the beginnings of phrases. Ringo enters with just his high-hat on the first verse as the tone of the song is established, slowly quieting what has come before. The second verse gains in rhythmic activity, drums adding a full beat and bass rounding out a complete pattern that fills in the descending harmonies. When the background vocals enter behind Lennon after "See the sunny skies," the basic texture of the track is complete—the growth will be only one of energy.

For the bridge ("Look around"), these elements are enhanced by doublings: a short guitar section replays the opening riff with a new counterpoint; vocals are added (singing "round, round, round"); and a lead guitar on the left adds commentary. As the bridge draws to a close, a final "look around" swells in the voices as they sing a small musical circle, rising a minor third and ending where they began.

For the third verse, the same guitar intro is used, but it has gained in subtle authority: by now its restraint is gorgeous; the lull is charged with the simplest kind of truth. A lead guitar commentary on the left follows each line, and handclaps are added. As the whole thing mounts toward a swell into the final verse, everything blossoms (after the line "Won't you let me see you smile"). The drum fill Ringo provides is invisible, pulling the band along without drawing attention to himself.

The downbeat he hits at the beginning of the last verse as John sings "Dear *Pru*dence" sets all the restrained energy in motion: the lead guitar on the left begins playing a countermelody to the lead vocal, arching higher and higher with dramatic surges of brilliance. After the first line, a piano enters in the middle of the sound with downward arpeggios,

rippling and glistening with brightness, irradiating everything around it. Ringo's intro fill gradually becomes one solid
verse of a solo, accenting every other downbeat, then skipping one to draw out the tension. His varied timbres (snare
alternated with tom-toms) with his sure sense of time (no tri-
ples, only eighths and a few sixteenth notes) make the whole
mix jump with a beautiful undulating pulse. As they head for
the final cadence ("The sun is up"), the piano does a full
glissando all the way down the keyboard, and the lead guitar
on the left aims higher and higher for its peak, landing at the
top just before Lennon utters the final line.

The thwarted downbeat before this last line ("Won't you
come out to play") is the most satisfying resolution of all the
motion that has come before. There is a slight retard to buffer
the momentum, and the lead guitar echoes its own last note
in a distorted reverberation as it fades from the texture. The
last sounds of the solo guitar figure on the right complete the
larger circle the song travels in; it wanders off into the distance without arriving anywhere as the scene fades.

The life of the child and the celebration of nature are
familiar subjects for Lennon, but nowhere else does he sound
as composed as he does here, as infatuated with the innocence
he's singing about. He wrote it for Mia Farrow's sister when
they were both at the Maharishi's meditation retreat in
Rishikesh, but ultimately it's a song about sexual awakening,
the heady euphoria of natural pleasures wooed by a sublime
musical arc. It counts among Lennon's finest songs. (Siouxsie
and the Banshees' 1984 cover version is a surprisingly effective
distortion of the Beatles' elegiac original.)

AFTER THE HUSHED resolution of "Dear Prudence," the
opening drum and bass raps of "Glass Onion" are a rude
knock. Ringo's pert flams of anxiety set off verses that reach
a dead end with the title phrase, "looking through a glass
onion." John's "I" is explicitly first-person, and the verbal
attack is on his audience; it's an abusive version of "I Am the

Walrus." The texture is alienated and fragmented: sharp guitar accents above a thunky bass counter warping strings. The
condescension in John's voice is full of loathing as much for
his fans as for the boundaries that separate them from him;
like "Sympathy for the Devil," it imputes both audience and
performer. References to other Beatles songs are strung together implicatively: "Lady Madonna trying to make ends
meet, yeah," "the walrus and me, man," and "fixing a hole
in the ocean" (which refers to both Paul's *Sgt. Pepper* song
and the sequence in the *Yellow Submarine* film when the cartoon Beatles sail into the sea of holes).

As Lennon skeptically invites us to "another place you
can go," cellos slide up (like they do in "Strawberry Fields
Forever") and lead into the anticipatory kicks of the chorus—
every downbeat comes early, agitating the already anxious
beat ("*Look*ing through the bent-back tulips/To *see* how the
other half live"). The line "Here's another clue for you all/
The Walrus was Paul" comes a full year before the "Paul is
dead" rumors, foreboding the fanaticism of a last morbid
Beatles craze with an earned cynicism. When he repeats a
simple "oh yeah" in the bridge, he draws each one out further, gaining intensity at each repetition, finally screaming
out the last word until his voice breaks with disgust. It's like
he's putting his vocal cords through an emotional strainer and
all that comes out is lean acerbity. In the last verse, when he
sings "I told you 'bout the fool on the hill/I tell you man he's
living there still," he even brings in a shrill recorder (right), a
parodic echo of the simpy sounds Paul employed on his *Magical
Mystery Tour* track.

Instead of the external voices and surreal word-painting
of "I Am the Walrus," "Glass Onion" is an implosion of dis-
dainful self-references. It sounds like the whole Beatles mystique is paling for Lennon; he's weary of the role demanded
of him by the very people who buy his records, and he's looking for someone to blame. The betrayal is larger than in "No
Reply" or "Day Tripper"; as in "Help!," the band entraps

him as he sings about them. The resigning cello passage edited on after the last verse curdles the entire track.

THE RINKY-TINK PIANO chords that open "Ob-La-Di, Ob-La-Da" laugh off the bitterness of "Glass Onion" in an instant—all despair becomes frivolity. Paul's swinging bass underpins the offbeat chords in the piano, and the lift couldn't be sweeter—it out-simplifies "Yellow Submarine," with the kind of utterly convincing charm that people use to call "groovy." Paul's voice greets the listener from both channels.

Any fuss made over such a disarming romp would detract from its benign glint, so it rolls along harmlessly—saxes spurring the bridges along with syncopated nudges, background vocals doing what they can with their choruses, and tiny toy-piano flourishes sprucing up the final verse.

McCartney's solo career suffers from moves like this— anyone else performing a ditty this inane would get raked over the coals for it. But because it's self-deprecating, and sandwiched in with such fine stuff as "Dear Prudence" and much of what follows, it comes off better than Lennon's contemptuous sneer. Unlike "Wild Honey Pie" (a throwaway on the order of "Flying" from *Magical Mystery Tour*), "Ob-La-Di, Ob-La-Da" has an unforgettable, if insubstantial, hook. (In Britain it was immediately copied by Marmalade, whose single version reached number one in a chart life that lasted thirteen weeks.)

THE SPANISH GUITAR flourish that links "Wild Honey Pie" to "Bungalow Bill" sets up a tale of epic proportions, but the refrain breaks through with such reckless inebriation (in another key area) that the flamenco becomes a prop. In this episode of the ongoing radio melodrama, Bill and his elephants are "taken by surprise," and in the last verse Bill has to justify killing to the children who follow his exploits. "Not when he looks so fierce," Yoko (as "his Mummy") interrupts before he can answer. "If looks could kill it would've been us instead of him," she warns. It's comic-strip parody the way "Mr. Kite" made hoops and horses seem nightmarish, without all the psychedelia swirling overhead. The typical Lennon setup contrasts an uneven refrain (in major) with a half-time verse (in minor), linked by four thumps in the bass drum. The sportsman's whistling and self-important air tarts up the refrain, but, like "Rocky Raccoon," it sends up two-dimensional heroes and villains with a caustic subplot: what kind of brave adventurer would take his mommy along "in case of accidents"? Bungalow Bill would be helpless without Captain Marvel zapping the mighty tiger "right between the eyes." A lethargic bassoon enters on the repeat of final choruses, and the hunters erupt into applause.

The repeated piano notes (left) of "While My Guitar Gently Weeps" interrupt the rowdy hunters, flanked by bass and high-hat (right) and a single acoustic guitar (center) for the introduction. The repeated note climbs up into the melody as the progression gets rolling—Eric Clapton's entrance (left) just before the verse transforms the basic texture into a backdrop for his lead. It's a guitar track for and about guitarists, pushed along by Paul and Ringo's insistent support (right) and set off in the bridge with organ (left) (on the words "I don't know why nobody told you"). By the third verse ("I look at the world") the groove has grown enough for George to start harmonizing with himself, moving right into Clapton's solo for the fourth verse. They repeat a bridge and then a final verse pushed along with tambourine before letting the track glide out into vocal ad-libs and guitar musings. Things don't build to a raging pitch the way they might; the weeping tone is sustained by a constantly withheld intensity—the kind of blues that says more by holding back than it does by cutting loose.

WHERE "Dear Prudence" evokes a sexual pastoral, "Happiness Is a Warm Gun" is a squalid montage. Lennon starts it alone on his electric guitar—"She's not a girl who misses much" is sung despondently, not suggestively. As the band approaches from behind, its ominous swell is downright scary—its first downbeat utterly shrieks (before "She's well acquainted with the touch"). He's looking ugliness in the face: the sensation of the "touch of a velvet hand" is likened to the shiny underbelly of a "lizard on a window pane"; the dirty old "man in the crowd with the multi-colored mirrors on his hobnail boots" lies "with his eyes as his hands are busy working overtime" as vocal harmonies are added. A ringing guitar (center) is set against a clipped guitar (right) that injects incisive offbeat chords into the texture. In the opening sequence, a pervert looks up skirts with his boots' mirrors before masturbating—and then, bizarrely, "A soap impression of his wife which he ate and donated to the National Trust" (obscure British slang for toilet) shifts meters three times in three bars before landing in a drugged-up waltz.

A guitar solo links the first episode to the second with a dirty, pornographic grunge, and Ringo plays every other downbeat differently—first snare, then cymbals. "I need a fix cos I'm goin' down" has a junkie's dread to it, the burnt-out zone between coming down and the next rush. It's sung low, offsetting the high first scene, and conjures up a sordid street life of outcasts and perverts.

The next section gets no preparation: "Mother Superior jump the gun" combines an incorruptible fantasy status for a female with a munitions cliché—the nun has jumped the gun, fallen from grace. The meter disintegrates (three bars in $3/4$ answered by two bars of $3/4$ and one in $4/4$). Sex is inextricably bound up with the violent phallus of the gun, which plays off the junkie's "shooting up" and the dirty flasher "shooting his wad" before it lurches into the final episode.

The landing point for the unsteady rhythm settles into a new $4/4$ for a long fifties progression (I–vi–IV–V) that sends up the National Rifle Association slogan from which Lennon copped the title. To say that this section is parodic doesn't begin to describe its ferocity; the NRA line itself is a sick joke, a play on the "Peanuts" cartoon Broadway show song "Happiness Is . . . ," but after all the sexual ills it has touched upon and the extreme types it displays (from "girl" to "Mother Superior," dirty old men to young addicts), the feigned doo-wop euphoria effects a haze even more blinding than that of "Doctor Robert."

As Lennon sings "When I hold you in my arms," the already murky rhythmic waters get stirred up even more. Guitarists and vocalists go into ³/₄ as Ringo remains in ⁴/₄—a competing rhythmic tension that makes the stomach turn. All sense of the beat's gravity is suspended—no landing points, no steady repetitions, just two rhythms simultaneously fighting it out. Neither wins. The relish in Lennon's voice as he sings "when I hold you in my arms" makes the pleasure he's singing of too sick to enjoy.

After the caesura hold, where Lennon ad-libs a plainly insincere "Happiness is a warm, yes it is," he aims up to his high falsetto for the final coda. Instead of "shoo-op" and "be-bop," the background vocalists sing "bang-bang, shoot-shoot." The violent overtones are made even more ghastly in the way Lennon veils their presence; he doesn't have to spell things out; the terror in his voice tells a tale he doesn't have to describe explicitly. The surrealism that's used to paint the wandering identity denials in "Strawberry Fields Forever" is condensed to a potent realism here—it's about the seedy side of sex that springs from cultural repression. Lennon is barely in control of this story; it sounds like he's venting the hideously neurotic side of his sexual conditioning. Ringo's exhausted landing after everything is over is the dull thud of something dreadful.

SIDE ONE VISITS the extrenes the rest of the record will play out (only Ringo's drollness is missing). McCartney's gift for pastiche ("Back in the U.S.S.R.") and his charm ("Ob-La-Di, Ob-La-Da") sit next to Lennon's peacefulness ("Dear Prudence") and his violence, either the smugness of "Glass Onion," the black comedy of "Bungalow Bill," or the unrepressed anxiety of "Happiness Is a Warm Gun." George's song is a better relief from these contrasts than *Rubber Soul*'s "Think for Yourself"; "While My Guitar Gently Weeps" is expansive where the rest of the songs adhere to stricter forms. Like *Pepper*, side one of the "White Album" moves from a party to a nightmare, only the boundaries become exaggerated.

MCCARTNEY WROTE "Martha My Dear" in honor of his English sheepdog, and it gets side two off with a daft elegance. The snazzy piano intro (left) sounds like a drawing-room version of a dance-hall delicacy; the melody is lyrical and endearing, and deceptively engaging for the meter and harmony it trips up along the way. Strings complement the piano as chamber music during the first verse. The brass arrangement for the bridge ("Hold your head up") is tight and pert (it pivots off the minor seventh chord toward the supertonic on "Look what you've done"). The trumpet and tuba break in the second verse is done up with handclaps (center); it sounds like a windup marching band. For the second bridge ("Hold your hand out"), they play off Paul's lead contrapuntally. The three pulses of the tonic that reassert the home key for the verse wind up giving him some trouble when it comes time to bring the song to a close—the bass descends from the strings as they hold their last chord, but the effect sounds feigned, a compromise of harmonic home base (it might have worked better to set the toy band marching off into a fade-out).

"I'M SO TIRED" reverses that same bass motion, rising toward its tonic sleepily as Lennon enters in an insomniac's daze. The opening line droops down a half step with weariness, much like "Sexy Sadie," and the entire beat moves along grudgingly, sinking beneath the weight of exhaustion. A guitar makes sharp, jagged accents (right) as Lennon's delivery works itself into anger, his resignation rising to hostility on the line "I wonder should I call you/But I *know* what you would do." The hung-over pace of the players sounds as though they're trying to get through the track without knocking anything over.

Where the verse goes from listlessness to resigned indifference, the bridge starts with accusations and turns to pleas:

> *You'd say I'm puttin' you on but it's*
> *No joke, it's doin' me harm you know I*
> *Can't sleep, I can't stop my brain it's been*
> *Three weeks, I'm going insane you know I'd*
> *Give you everything I've got for a little peace of mind*

After that climactic last line, Lennon falls back into bleary-eyed annoyance—even the face on the cigarettes he reaches for makes him cringe ("Sir Walter Raleigh," the ciggy ad, "was such a stupid *get*"). When *Rolling Stone*'s publisher Jann Wenner wrote his commentary on the album in 1968, he called the heaviness in Lennon's voice the "weight of fame." The stop-again-start-again bass-and-drum exchanges after that key phrase the second time around only aggravate the calm that booze and cigarettes don't provide. Lennon goes out grumbling wearily.

''BLACKBIRD'' hasn't worn as well as some other Paul ballads, even though the simple elegance of the guitar writing rescues the extreme images of the words ("Into the light of the dark black night . . ."). It doesn't sound as imitative as "Mother Nature's Son" or "Rocky Raccoon"; but, as with "Michelle," there's a conceit at work that seems forced. A wounded bird, like a fool on a hill, is an easy target for sympathy, and Paul's double-tracked voice (center) sounds tentative for the "leap of faith" sentiment he's offering up. Compared with "Julia"'s "windy smile" and "seashell eyes," "Blackbird"'s "broken wings" and "sunken eyes" sound uninspired. Crosby, Stills, and Nash tried to make it their own at one of their perpetual reunion concerts, confirming its generic quality as a song best left for others to sing.

"PIGGIES" could be Harrison's "Son of Taxman," a self-righteous finger pointed at those who put money and social status before everything else. The harpsichord opening rivals "Martha" for musical taste, but it comes off as all the more condescending once George's intentions become clear. The blue notes that the harpsichord plays during its solo sound as odd as a violin might mimicking a guitar solo—it's twisted, the wrong instrument playing the wrong style, and it sticks out intentionally like swine grunting through an elegant drawing room. The final verse is a full piggy chorus, snorts and all, "clutching forks and knives to eat their bacon." Before a final grand cadence, wrenched up a half step by a string quartet, George snidely intones "one more time" in a thick scouse accent, smearing social elitists with their own symbols of "high" culture. (The tacked-on ending recalls that of "Glass Onion" and is no less brackish.)

"BUNGALOW BILL" is a Captain Marvel comic; "Rocky Raccoon" is a B-movie Western shootout that turns into a ragtime tap dance. Paul delivers the humorous narrative affectionately ("Her name was Magill/And she called herself Lil/But everyone knew her as Nancy"), and Ringo kicks the line "He drew first and shot" neatly. After Rocky's near-fatal duel with Dan, he tells the doc "it's only a scratch," making him the same kind of two-dimensional hero as Bungalow Bill. Ringo's "Don't Pass Me By," another rustic hillbilly charade with organ and hick fiddle, continues side two's acoustic-based set ("I'm So Tired" is the only song with electric textures), where side three is dominated by hard rock. Ringo's heartbreak actually turns morbid with a pass at "A Day in the Life": "You were in a car crash/And you lost your hair."

. . .

"WHY DON'T WE DO IT IN THE ROAD?" is
straight blues from Paul, who sings expansively—tongue in
cheek but all over the map vocally. The track probably would
have been edited from a single record, but its grit contrasts
nicely with the supple shine of "Martha"—it's good to hear
that Paul can be more than just dapper. It has a B-side quality to it, like Lennon's oldies favorite, Rosie and the Originals'
"Give Me Love"—all feeling and absolutely no finesse.

OUT OF THE FINAL cymbal smash, Paul's "I Will" makes
a humble entrance, and its acoustic romanticism is the polar
opposite of the blatant sexuality of what came before. Bongos
are mixed left, guitars center, and the bass track is an overdubbed Paul singing "dum" in the right—there is no bass
guitar. A simple countermelody from the lead guitar takes the
tune home in less than three minutes. As a brief encounter
with Paul's mushy side, it wins points by being quick.

"JULIA," JOHN'S balladic answer, is oedipally inspired—Julia is the name of his mother, who was struck dead
by an off-duty cop when he was seventeen. Like "Strawberry
Fields Forever," it speaks to us from a private part of Lennon's
subconscious; but the sentiment isn't groping, it's languid. He
sings to Julia directly, but he's addressing more the idea of
who she is and what her loss still stirs inside him. The double-
tracked vocal resembles that of "Any Time at All," new lines
overlapping the old as the song continues.

The first verse is sung slowly, as if in a dream, with guitar mixed way to the right and Lennon's fragile voice center.
The second verse enters on top of it, before the first has finished, with guitars spreading to right and left. The tenderness
in his voice is as far from "Glass Onion" and "Sexy Sadie" as
it can get, and the intimate personal tone that his primal solo
works adopt can be traced to this performance. The two-
word images resonate more poetically than the run-ons of

"Strawberry Fields": "seashell eyes, windy smile," "sleeping sand, silent cloud." There's a return to the minor subdominant harmony for the yearning of "call me" and "touch me"— the same harmony that brought doubt to "If I Fell" and "In My Life".

The high guitar line that feeds the voice its notes during the bridge ("Her hair of floating sky is shimmering") drops to lower counterpoint on the line "in the sun." The voice-and-guitar interplay is expert, independent yet complementary. As Lennon refers to the English translation of Yoko Ono's name ("ocean child"), he's connecting his yearning for the mother who died on him with the woman who now holds his heart (the sentiment "In My Life" attempted). "Julia" illuminates the mystery that the image of woman represents for John; the grief of loss and the insufferable longing he still feels for his mother better explain his earlier heartache songs— their jealousy and intimidation—as the result of some traumatic inner conflict. Like the sparse but evocative setting he uses on *Plastic Ono Band* two years later, the private world he reveals alone with his guitar is like a therapeutic confessional. ("Julia" even resembles "Look at Me" from that album; they were written in the same period.)

''JULIA'' and "Martha My Dear" are bookends on side two, but the distance between the two shows just how subverted the structure of the entire four-side layout really is. Songs lie next to each other in stylistic contrast, but there's less interdependence than there is complete independence. It's a measure of the emotional worlds these songs successfully conjure up that they sound more like entities unto themselves than parts of a larger framework. Side three's "Mother Nature's Son" could be exchanged with side two's "Blackbird" with little or no consequence to the general feel of either side.

RINGO KICKS side three off with a drum intro that resembles the reckless tumble into "She Loves You," and "Birthday" is an electric binge that's produced and performed for the sheer joy of dancing. It's some of the highest-energy rock 'n' roll the Beatles have played since "I'm Down." The riff that drives it along recalls "Day Tripper"; but instead of a steadily mounting ascent, the song visits different zones of excitement.

Song sections play off one another: after the main riff (in A major) with the bass echoing the rest of the band (center), Paul's lead vocal (doubling himself at the octave) enters on the far side of both channels. Ringo inserts a modestly short drum solo with tambourine after the first verse as background screams rise ("Come on," and finally "Yeah!!") to link the main riff up with the dominant (E major) rave-up. After the steadiness of Ringo's snare solo, the band returns with a new fervor, clinging to a single chord with all its might. Quick handclaps join John's vocals on both channels ("Yes we're goin' to a party, party"); and on the third and last repeat, Ringo kicks each eighth note, propelling the momentum toward a deceptive cadence (into C major) where a gritty-voiced Paul sings "I would like you to dance," answered by Yoko's high "birthday." The band plays a simple derivative blues riff outlining the alternating harmonies between the new tonic and dominant (C and G), and the sound opens up with a bright piano that flies out of the low guitars from before. As Paul repeats "dance, dance," a small linking section (moving from G through E major) stretches the harmony out to point things back to the main verse as the lead guitar jams in three high lead notes from above.

For the second verse, the band plays the same riff as in the first verse, echoed by chords way up high in the electric piano as the bass continues to echo way down low—it's a dialogue between the midrange and the sandwiching upper and bottom. At the end of this verse, Ringo drops out for a syncopated lick from the guitar and the bass, which he answers; guitar and bass respond before swerving into the "I would like you to dance" section again. This last episode takes them into the final verse, with all of these elements combined for a huge, jumping mix of sound: handclaps on the offbeats, piano and bass echoing the main riff, and Paul's vocals screaming along from both ends of the stereo horizon.

The effect of all this mayhem isn't as charged or rampant as the sweat that drips off of "Long Tall Sally," but the formal arrangement of these different episodes never detracts from the song's celebratory height. The rotating harmonies add direction that gives each new transition its own lift— especially the way E major is transformed into C major as the "party, party" rave-up moves into "I would like you to dance." By the time they reach the last verse, the texture smolders with energy and the song hits a pitch of accumulated hilarity. The siren noises that are left wagging once the final anticipatory kicks send the tune home give the effect of a huge train blistering past, the listener left gaping at the force of its motion.

"YER BLUES" saunters in immediately with Lennon's lead guitar on the right countering Ringo's drums to the left— Paul's bass thunks along with a fuzzy tone in the center. The beat is tired again, Lennon's guitar line first spicing the sound with rhythmic jabs and then falling, hanging on to the beat for dear life. The assertive lick Lennon plays at the end of each verse (after "If I ain't dead already") vents a sprawling, bluesy agony.

Ringo fills up the spaces in the second verse with big gestures; and the texture as a whole has a hollowness to it, not just because the instruments are spread out but because there's so much room in this blues lick that every player can afford to piddle about without sounding busy. The second verse starts out with "In the morning, wanna die/In the evenin', wanna die." Lennon pushes the word "evenin' " beyond the breaking point, his voice wrenched with pain. For him, the act of singing the blues becomes an act of struggle in itself; it brings on even more angst than he first feared. For the third verse, a stop-time break squeezes things even tighter:

> *My mother was of the sky*
> *My father was of the earth*
> *I am of the universe*
> *And you know what it's worth*

The band rejoins him at the end of that second line, jolted by the resentment in his voice. The next verse uses the same break to emphasize Lennon's reference to Dylan's paranoid journalist in "Ballad of a Thin Man":

> *The eagle picks my eye*
> *The worm he licks my bone*
> *Feel so suicidal*
> *Just like Dylan's Mr. Jones*

The third time he takes this solo vocal break, the band re-enters with a swinging blues, quicker than the beat of the rest of the song but even more distressing. This chorus follows what Lennon sings as the most disenchanting fear he knows how to express:

> *Black clouds cross my mind*
> *Blue mist round my soul*
> *Feel so suicidal*
> *Even hate my rock 'n' roll*

A guitar solo follows, and an extra snare is added to the mix to intensify the backbeat. The first round of guitar solos simply rocks off the beat—it sounds warped, as though we're hearing it from underwater. The second guitar solo (probably

George) is more melodic, even though its brittle tone is tense and pinched. At the end of its stinging assault, a compressed drum fill takes the band back into the original slow groove. On the last verse, John's voice is off in the distance, wailing at the lyrics even though his voice mike is off, overpowered by the band's relentless throbbing. The emotional angst in this music belies the parodic title.

P A U L ' S   M U S I C A L   M I M I C R Y continues with "Mother Nature's Son," where he targets Donovan's foppishness as he unwittingly outlines a career for John Denver (who actually covers this song). The singer is the innocent simpleton, pure beyond belief, a plastic pastoral. A measured brass choir enters (right) at the second verse, and the picture of wholesome, natural, back-to-the-earth sentimentality could not sound more pristine. He "doo-doo-doo"s his way through verses, amioably humming out his carefree existence. On the final verse, the brass drops out for Paul to hum over a fine guitar counterpoint (right). As he finishes things off, brass re-enters and plays a flatted seventh on the final chord, mocking the song's literal intentions like a deliberately satirical question mark.

T H E   G U I T A R   L I C K S that announce "Everybody's Got Something to Hide, Except Me and My Monkey" are only the barest outline of what will follow—set off by handclaps and drums, the guitar calls to the rest of the band from the far right channel, rousing them into the song but letting the listener in on none of the force that will soon invade the sound. The downbeat of the verse, where the band enters, is instantly frenzied; two lead guitars inject rhythmic licks (right)—one plays fragments of the intro, another pulsates madly around one note. Lennon sings in the center, and Paul's bass and Ringo's drums are augmented by a huge ringing cowbell (left). After the title line, the lead guitar again fills in two bars alone, as in the intro, but this time with a new lick that twice snarls the melodic line it follows.

The verses play suggestive opposites against one another:

> *Your inside is out when your outside is in*
> *Your outside is in when your inside is out*
> *So come on*

and

> *The deeper you go, the higher you fly*
> *The higher you fly, the deeper you go*
> *So come on.*

After the third verse and refrain, the band drops out, and a multi-tracked cacophony of Lennon voices jabbers "Come on, come on, come on, come on" at different speeds and with different inflections. A huge bass (right) lassos them all together and brings the band back in for a tidal-wave return—the repeated groove they brand into the end of the song goes around six times, instead of the usual four or eight, and it makes the return of the original verse texture startlingly swift and powerful. The six-time groove dams up the energy of the entire song; and when it bursts open, the band comes rushing through with irrepressible force, cowbell clanging like gang-busters. The "Come on" voices persist into the fade-out. (Like "Bungalow Bill," "Everybody's Got Something to Hide, Except Me and My Monkey" shares a comic tone with Chuck Berry's "Jo Jo Gunne," a song with a "meddlesome" monkey hero. "Monkey" is also said to be cryptic doubletalk for Yoko. The Rolling Stones' satirical self-portrait, "Monkey Man," uses the same imagery to laugh at their own use of "jungle" rhythms.)

DYLAN'S BITTEREST SONGS deliberately keep their subject vague. Some say "Positively 4th Street" is about the folkies who stiffly opposed his shift to rock; "Like a Rolling Stone" snarls at innocence itself. "Sexy Sadie" is a thinly veiled kiss-off to the Maharishi, Lennon's bitter hate letter to the Indian meditation master. The spirit captured in the piano's bare opening is touched only by a tambourine, and as Ringo leads the band in, John utters the title line with mock breathy sensuality—there's nothing sexy about it. The rising piano lick that arches overhead as he sings "You made a fool of everyone" makes the sarcasm deadly.

Lennon plays the butt of his own jokes, but he reels back in horror at getting duped—it feeds his paranoia. The serenely contemptuous background vocals chime in with "wa-wa-wa-wa"; and after the line "You'll get yours yet!" the piano answers with a tense repeated figure, singeing Lennon's already tart revenge fantasy. The cynical humor makes the sour taste that much more scathing.

With "She's the latest and the greatest of them all," Lennon soars into his bitter falsetto to bring home the sting of the betrayal. The atmosphere of this track makes it sound like a rehearsal run-through before the real take, as if the band resents the energy it takes John to answer a conniving meditational swindler. Music as disturbed as this implicitly belittles Lennon's overextended spiritual expectations and hints at the insecurity he tries to take out on his audience in "Glass Onion." Like Dylan's, Lennon's exaggerations reflect back on himself as much as his subject.

THE GUITAR (left) that demolishes the silence at the start of "Helter Skelter" resembles the lead of "Revolution," only there the figure leaned upward into its notes; here it falls into them from a high, piercing vantage point, the quick descent accenting the repeated notes that follow. Paul meets the guitar's pulse head-on and tears the opening line apart—by the times he reaches the end ("till I see you AGAIN _____!!!") he's way out of breath, and he pulls himself back in with a quickly caught "yeah, yeah, ye-ah." Ringo joins him in mid-flight on snare (right), and by the time the band enters at the start of Paul's descent, the sound is savaged. The guitar that's mixed center, behind Paul's voice, is out of tune and grating, and the track itself is more of a basher than a rocker. Ringo flails away mercilessly on the drums, heavy on the cymbals, and the bass (left) plods through the mix with a muffled thunk, like it's treading through mud.

On the first chorus, a second lead guitar joins the bass on the left for a lick to follow the title line; on the second chorus this guitar appears on the right. The beat is huge, wide and deep, but, as in "Sexy Sadie," somehow not full. As the final verse rolls around, John plays octave hops on his bass to dramatize the vast proportions that have been set plodding. At first the song goes out with weird traveling guitar noises into a ringing limbo, then they re-enter, hacking away into the fadeout. An infamous fade back in lets the listener eavesdrop on the whole thing falling apart, the band driving the song into the ground at the end of a long jam. The mix finally fizzles and stutters to a stop with random piano noises, then rises for one last gasp with Ringo's jam-slamming drum fatigue: "I've got blisters on my fingers!!!"

EVEN THOUGH the smoke and ash are still settling from "Helter Skelter," "Long Long Long" creates its mood quickly; Harrison's guitar invites the ear into a completely settled musical state. An organ adorns the top with brooding lines and two-note chords, and a simple piano enters at the bridge. Ringo's drum fills are big and round, contrasting with the quiet soul in George's voice. The song's reserved tone calls to mind the indulgences of *All Things Must Pass* two years later, but it works better unhampered by like-minded company. The track dissolves into not-so-eerie organ doodling and strange vocal cries.

AT THE TOP of side four, "Revolution No. 1" leaves on its false start, John yelling "Okay!" as his guitar gets going (left).

There's an unidentifiable crackling noice (center) before the verse, and once John's voice enters, it stops; the texture expands into a new web of sound—what might be called "mature psychedelic," lit with musical color but well-supported rhythmically. Instruments jump around, but they're controlled, arranged, and spaced with an ear for variety—because this version is slower than the single it turned into, there's more space to fill up. The main ensemble is centered, spreading into brass (right), lead guitar outbursts (left), and background vocals ("Bow-oom, shoo-be-doo-wa, bow-oom, shoo-be-doo-wa"), ancient girl-group snippets over the top. Lennon reaches for a climactic falsetto in the refrain "It's gonna BE"—and falls back into chest voice for "—all right." At the end of the final refrain, the band hammers the closing punches down an irregular three times to set the wandering grunts and traveling lead guitars off rambling, competing for attention in the fade-out.

PAUL GETS OUT his top hat and cane again for "Honey Pie," recasting the vaudevillian ham of "When I'm Sixty-four" as twenties swank. After the first phrase ("She was a working girl, north of England way"), a needle hits an old 78-rpm record (left), and Paul apes an old-fashioned melodramatic crooner ("Now she's hit the big time!"). It's not only a record inside a record; it's original-version-meets-respectable-parody as Paul the Beatle answers resignedly "in the U.S.A." The caesura they hold out for the lead guitar's upward slide (right) is impossibly long—they're playing up the suspense before Paul nudges the piano entrance downward.

Paul's sense of style is impeccable. His delivery is dapper, and he overdoes the "t-t-t"s with relish—even Ringo gets into it. The band tightens up for the guitar solo (center): Ringo gives each accent a silenced cymbal, and the clarinets and saxes (right) take the second half with a glistening swing. Paul intrudes with some uninspired scatting—"I like this kinda hot kinda music, play it to me, play it to me, honey, with blues"—

before one final scurry from the winds for the final bridge and verse. Instead of playing it smooth and letting the band finish alone, he gets carried away with himself way up high over the final cadence. (He loves this persona so much he made a fool of himself with it in "Gotta Sing, Gotta Dance," a number he wrote for his *James Paul McCartney* television special (1972), and again in "You Gave Me the Answer" from *Venus and Mars*.)

> "Savoy Truffle" is a funny one written whilst hanging out with Eric Clapton in the sixties. At that time he had a lot of cavities in his teeth and needed dental work. He always had a tooth-ache but he ate a lot of chocolates—he couldn't resist them and once he saw a box he *had* to eat them all. He was over at my house and I had a box of "Good News" chocolates on the table and wrote the song from the names inside the lid: Creme Tangerine, Montelimar . . . . I got stuck with the two bridges for a while and Derek Taylor wrote some of the words in the middle . . . "you know that what you eat you are . . ."
> (George Harrison, *I Me Mine*, p. 128)

RINGO ALWAYS finds the best groove for a song, using just the right touch by giving each track its own rhythmic propulsion, cymbal sounds, and tom-tom arches. The run-in snare that ignites "Savoy Truffle" is perfectly timed (left). George's vocals are mixed way to the right to play off the lead guitar on the left and the saxes that belt their sassy lines throughout. An organ warms up the bridges, and the saxes-and-lead-guitar (right) dialogue in the solo section makes for rousing rock-'n'-roll confectionery. In terms of sheer feel, it's the best George song since "I Want to Tell You": the rhythms are snug and his vocal doesn't wallow.

LENNON SINGS "Cry Baby Cry" from way to the left for the opening refrain, with his guitar (right) and George Martin on harmonium (center) circling around the melody to set up the verses, which have a completely different cast: guitar stays put, vocal joins a piano center, and bass putters about to the left. For the second refrain, the vocal goes back to the left, and drums and tambourine join the piano center. By the time they hit the second verse, the mix fills out completely—organ up top, drums all around, and bass busy over on the side—but the vocals keep alternating between center and left, with weak background harmony flanking later refrains (right).

The aristocratic adults in the verses goad their children into spiting them. For the last verse, Ringo taps his cymbal lightly (behind the words "At twelve o'clock a meeting round the table for a seance"), and everyone storms the end of the phrase ("in the dark"). The prank gets sent home by a great downward glissando on the piano ("With voices out of nowhere put on specially by the children—for a lark!") As a metaphor for the fear the youth culture's sounds instilled in their parents, "Cry Baby Cry" is an underrated Lennon royalty satire; it's his most accomplished Lewis Carroll pastiche.

THE HAUNTING SONG-SNATCH that finds itself wedged between "Cry Baby Cry" and "Revolution No. 9" is a piece of leftover Paul, a patch of melody that he never put to use. It flaunts the band's wealth of material the way "Wild Honey Pie" on side one does—they have enough music to fill four sides and then some.

THE TALKING BEFORE "Revolution No. 9" is hushed, furtive, finally argumentative; and before it expands into an aural stream-of-consciousness, a piano wanders plaintively behind an engineer's voice that swings from side to side. The track slowly casts a myopic shadow across the four sides it consumes. There is a danger in taking Yoko Ono's inspired avant-garde experimentalism too seriously, but its antecedents are clear—it's "I Am the Walrus" cubed, or "A Day in the Life" as a Joycean aural stew. And yet it can be very rewarding: new sounds jump out with each listening; the edited landscape has hidden pockets, sudden glimpses of light and several stretches of unresolved tension. It brings a sense of play to the obvious—the absurd is made significant—and it recedes back into the parallel universe it came from with a football crowd chanting "Block that kick!!" There is no musical structure to generate the noise, but the track has its own inchoate logic: things stem from other things; waves of noises ebb and flow across the stereo tapestry; and a single voice arches across, back and forth, intoning the only link with reality—"Number nine." Edgard Varèse experimented with electronic tape and synthetic sound collages as early as the 1950s, but Lennon's sound-piece is made up of identifiable media sounds jumbled as if in a dream. You can almost hear right through them.

Many of the noises are live musical performances, from the weary piano playing that underlies a good deal of the space to the huge orchestral climaxes—with chorus—spun backward at certain junctures. A marching band even intercedes before a striking dramatic pause when Lennon interrupts with "Take this, brother, may it serve you well." Although the journey is random and extreme, there's a musical ear guiding it. It's aurally abstract the way unidentifiable images on canvas are. There are moments of delineated rhythms, clarified speech—through voice filters, tape distortions, and male-versus-female dialogues—and whooshing onslaughts of several tapes spinning at the same time. At one point, Lennon fades the miasmic backdrop out, leaving himself listing various dance steps from the past generation (the watusi).

The result is experimental, but it's not just a free-for-all—no musical novice would have arrived at just this set of combinations. The fact that chance in art played a major role in the modern era by no means reflects a nonartistic consciousness selecting its parameters, sources, and material.

Lennon's touch lies in the humor of how things are juxta-
posed: tape loops, radio noises, honking cars, cocktail parties,
crowds, and choirs are strung together in tentative rhythms
and then smashed.

"REVOLUTION NO. 9" fades down into the softness that
becomes the lush string divertimento of "Good Night." It re-
capitulates the contrast that got things started way back on
side one, from technological rush to sentimental intimacy—
except that here the shift is only from Lennon's arty intellect
to his soul. Going out with Ringo singing also undercuts the
difficulty of "Revolution No. 9"—if that track had closed all
four sides, it would have a more ominous presence. "Good
Night," easily the smarmiest mush John ever penned, is also
among his most loving (along with "Bless You" and "Grow
Old Along with Me").

There is a tendency to write this song off as a parody,
but even though it works as one (with its female chorus), a
close listen reveals an open heart at work, not a hack, and
Ringo's genuine humility makes it a fervent plea for peace as
well as a lullaby offered to the record's audience after the
Beatles' longest—and most taxing—album. When he repeats
"Dream sweet dreams for me," drawing out the tension in
the dissonance, the calming effect of the resolution is gorgeous. The drums on George's "Long Long Long" (the only
comparable side-closer) give it a resistance, a rumbling beneath the surface that rises with eerie howls and the clatter-
ings that see it out. "Good Night" 's farewell is softer—calm,
serene, and incantatory. It has the classical feel of a standard
that speaks through the ages, like "Good Night, Irene."

THE "WHITE ALBUM" defies structure. Where *Revolver*
and *Pepper* had self-conscious beginnings and endings, the
compilation of songs here is less formally arranged; its totality
is not as central as the idea of any given track. There's a
governing irony throughout: the tendency to be supercilious

("Ob-La-Di, Ob-La-Da," "Piggies," "Revolution No. 9") is redeemed by rich instrumental interplay and sheer vocal virtuosity.

Each of the Beatles' solo albums would draw upon sounds that first appeared here: "Julia" captures a sense of fragility and loss that John would intensify on his first solo record; "Ob-La-Di, Ob-La-Da" could have appeared on McCartney's *Ram*; "Long Long Long" has the restraint of Harrison's *All Things Must Pass*; and "Don't Pass Me By" is Ringo's original country-and-western honk that sets the stage for his Nashville album, *Beaucoups of Blues*; "Good Night," the Lennon song Ringo sings to close the album, resembles his *Sentimental Journey* record even more.

In fact, that is the chief criticism this album lays itself open to: it sounds as though the Beatles have become mere accompanists for one another. But even this flaw has its merits: the varied stereo mixes make them sound like a different band on each track. In moments like the relentless groove of "Everybody's Got Something to Hide, Except Me and My Monkey," the lazy upbeats of "I'm So Tired," and the tight grip of the bridge to "Birthday," their sense of ensemble is as strong as at any other point in their career. The disparity between songs is linked only by the musical currents that still flow between them.

ROLL OVER, GEORGE MARTIN

LET IT BE *Released: May 8, 1970*
[recorded January 1969 and January 1970]

Get Back (Paul)/Don't Let Me Down (John)
Released: April 11, 1969

The Ballad of John and Yoko (John)/Old Brown Shoe
(George) [Harrison] *Released: May 30, 1969*

L ET I T B E is the Beatles' anomaly. It began as a tribute to their roots entitled *Get Back,* a documentary record and film that would capture them at work on songs and conclude with a live concert, the way *A Hard Day's Night* had. Along the way, the usual session jams of old rock 'n' roll numbers (like "Suzy Parker," "You've Really Got a Hold on Me," and "Bésame Mucho") would be left in to show how their new material connected with their beginnings. But *Let It Be* ended up as a shadow of these original intentions. After they had shelved the project for over a year, Allen Klein convinced them to mix and release the tapes for some quick cash, and Phil Spector was hired to turn the sessions into an album (the spring after *Abbey Road* was released).

Work on the project had begun on the second day of 1969 at the Twickenham Film Studios, with Michael Lindsay-Hogg's cameras rolling on rehearsals of new songs. (Lindsay-Hogg had just completed shooting the Rolling Stones' *Rock and Roll Circus* in December 1968, in which Lennon sang "Yer Blues.") At the completion of these sessions, a live appearance was planned, possibly at the Royal Albert Hall, where the formative strands of the practice sequences would coalesce in front of a live audience. But McCartney's yen for performing was greater than the others'. As the film makes apparent, his constant rallying had become unintentionally grating. In a conversation with Lennon in the middle of the film, McCartney says he thinks the reason the others are unwilling to go back to live playing is nervousness, and he recounts the mounting self-confidence they gained by performing in their early days. Lennon looks at him as though he's gone crazy—nervousness isn't the issue.

At the end of January, a compromise was reached: instead of an advertised appearance, the Beatles decided to appear impromptu on the Apple rooftop for a lunchtime concert, the kind of midday excursion they used to play at the Cavern. This is where Lindsay-Hogg's "documentary" turns into fabrication. In cutaways from the windy stage, his cameras get man-on-the-street double-takes as the sound echoes through London's garment district. The police arrive in response to complaints of noise, and several scenes are edited in to give the appearance of unexpected bobbies being ushered up to the roof to stop the concert.

The rehearsal sequences have some knockabout moments from the original *Get Back* concept: McCartney greets Ringo with a barrel-house piano boogie; George debuts "I Me Mine" alone on guitar for Ringo and George Martin and assists Ringo at the piano with the chords to "Octopus's Garden"; and Lennon introduces "Across the Universe" while Paul suggests an opening falsetto harmony. For our only glimpse of an album-in-progress, Lindsay-Hogg's cameras capture how songs shed several skins before they reach their final form, and how different rhythms are tried out before the band latches on to the one that works best. What starts out as rhythm and blues ends up as acoustic folk-rock in its final form ("Two of Us"); what starts off as a rocker turns into an uptempo shuffle ("Get Back") as musical ideas are batted about and discarded. Some·

footage shows just how rewarding trying out various settings for a song can be for a band.

But the emotional undertow is an impenetrable dance of egos: Lennon is noticeably silent except when singing, and waltzes with Yoko to "I Me Mine" as if oblivious; McCartney is unsatisfied with Lennon's falling lead on "I've Got a Feeling"; and at another point George glibly answers Paul's musical directions with low-voiced recrimination ("All right, I'll play whatever you want me to play, or I won't play at all if you don't want me to play. I'll do anything you want in order to *please* you . . .").

By the time they gather on the roof, the mood is tense—until they start playing. The live set is striking: with the sessions behind them, they ride wave after wave of redeeming rhythm, astonished at the vitality of their own ensemble work when performing. They find a surprising renewal back in front of an audience, and it must have genuinely lifted them, for although they shelved all the filmed and taped material for more than a year, they didn't throw it away—and while none of them bothered to approve the final mix, they didn't block its release, either.

By the spring of 1970, Allen Klein's profit interests may have motivated them more than musical considerations—they needed cash to stay afloat in order to afford breaking up—but they had plenty of other outtakes in the can and could have had a gold record with "Mary Had a Little Lamb" (as McCartney went on to prove). Phil Spector was called in to mix the *Get Back* tapes and prepare the record for release—George Martin was essentially snubbed. (Lennon had been impressed with Spector's work on "Instant Karma," his solo single from February 1970, and all of them admired Spector's early-sixties work with the Ronettes and the Crystals.)

Originally, *Get Back* promised to reorient listeners to the tradition that the Beatles helped keep alive—the invincibility of the young Elvis Presley, the scatterbrained audacity of Little Richard, the smug condescension of Jerry Lee Lewis, the unsophisticated charm of Buddy Holly and Carl Perkins. In its best moments the film reclaims these intentions, but the Spector album provides only disconnected glimpses of it—the way Lennon barks out the record's welcome in mock literary pomposity before the humble "Two of Us" even starts, or the stage patter between songs on the roof. The string productions of "Let It Be," "I Me Mine," "The Long and Winding Road," and "Across the Universe" might even have worked had they sounded more like the schlock strings of the late fifties and early sixties—like Spector's own grander hits, such as the Ronettes' "Walking in the Rain" or Ike and Tina Turner's "River Deep, Mountain High"—instead of grafted-on afterthoughts.

Still, the record's patched history looks worse on paper than it sounds on vinyl. The band's mood is more centered than it is on the "White Album," and sharing the formulative process of writing with their audience is open and intriguing; *Let It Be* doesn't play parodic games or manipulate images of public identity. Beneath Spector's uninspired textures a group is at work, and on the live tracks that remain ("I Dig a Pony," "I've Got a Feeling," "One After 909," and "Get Back"), the Beatles' distinctive joy in playing together remains palpable.

IN AN EARLY sequence of the movie, the Beatles try "Two of Us" out as a rocker with train rhythms, and Paul leaps into his arresting impersonation of Elvis Presley. In this final form, it's a country song, a good-humored celebration of the travails of a relationship, with the same unaffected appeal as "I've Just Seen a Face." Lines start with witty homilies ("Two of us riding nowhere, spending someone's—") that rise to stretched-out held notes ("—hard _____ earned _____ pay . . ."). "Home" refers more to the emotional space the couple shares together wherever they travel—the sense of adventure along the way rather than the destination ("not arriving"). The simple pleasures of wordplay ("burning matches, lifting latches") are balanced in the bridge, where the shared experience ("You and I have memories/Longer than the road that stretches out ahead") alludes to John and Paul's partnership as songwriters. The bureaucratic innuendo—"You and me chasing paper, getting nowhere"—hints at the ironies to come in "You Never Give Me Your Money."

There is a sense of expectancy in the silence at the end of each verse when the band drops out, leaving the two voices holding the word "home." The first time, the humble guitar reappears to start up the second verse. The second time, the bridge grows out of the held chord they land on through a solo snare-drum fill—a series of escalating eighth notes—that connects the refrain up with the bridge. When Ringo lands on his downbeat, the bridge begins in the new harmony, and Paul sings solo. (The bridge leaps to B-flat and passes through more minor chords; the verses are in G major—the same verse/bridge keys that hold "Here, There and Everywhere.") The last line ("The road that stretches out ahead") is strung out for a swelling return to the verse, Paul and John carrying the rest of the band in tow.

Although John and Paul perform it as a duet, "Two of Us" is a Paul song almost exclusively. The art is in the way John accompanies: he knows how to bring out the best in Paul's whimsy, and the two of them sound more different together here than on any other duet they sing. There is no bass, and the only electric guitar shadows the ensemble; drums are minimal, with few cymbals. Lennon whistles nonchalantly as the song fades out; but rather than simply turning the dials slowly downward, the band softens up on its own, receding into the distance like images on the horizon. The homemade warmth resembles the feel of McCartney's first solo record.

THE FALSE START that's left on "I Dig a Pony" is Ringo caught mopping his brow in the middle of their rooftop concert. It's fun to hear the Beatles make a mistake with such a loud thunk—Spector captures a moment of real spontaneity by keeping it on. Ringo's galloping circular figure (in three) brings the song in, and the verse reduces the meter to one beat per bar instead of three. (The lick is gleaned from the refrain, the guitar line after "All I want is you" that accelerates with bass into the dotted figure beneath "Everything has got to be just like you want it to.") This opening figure generates the song—and outlines the refrain's harmonies—like the sardonic blues lick of "Hey Bulldog." It's forceful and instantly appreciable as a musical hook, allows various possibilities in pulse for different sections, and the band plays it with verve and punch.

As John settles into the verse, "I-hi-hi-hi-hi . . . dig a pony" resembles the vowel reiteration in "I Should Have Known Better" ("And when I ask you to be mi-hi-hi-hine"). But the words free-associate instead of narrate; images leap out in unexpected ways, and John sings it tongue-in-cheek. It's as though the imaginative rambling of "I Am the Walrus" has been cast in a frame as sturdy and tidy as that of "I Call Your Name"—it's implicative musically without making much literal sense. The imagery is strung together to intensify the love relationship it describes ("You can radiate everything you are") coupled with a sense of playfulness ("Syndicate every boat you row" or "Feel the wind blow . . . where you can indicate everything you see"). The song is about the affection and the heights of feeling two people can share. By approaching the emotions tangentially, Lennon expresses a sense of the impossible made possible, the liberation of ideas set off when love rushes through the imagination. (There's even a backhanded allusion to an early Beatles name, Johnny and the Moondogs, when Lennon sings "I pick a moondog. . . .")

Everything points toward the refrain, where Paul's upper harmony joins John for the exultant "All I want is *you* . . . Everything has got to be just like you want it to _____ . . . because." Lingering on the word "to _____," they reverse

the blend they achieved on "Two of Us": even on the reiterated vowel phrases, when he rises in perfect symmetry with
John, Paul complements his partner more than he defines
his own space in the sound. Again, it's unlike almost any
other blend they reach together—Paul makes himself almost
invisible.

The beat has a terrific sense of gravity to it, as though
the direction embedded in the central lick carries the band.
Downbeats land with a satisfying give, and the transitions
have an inevitable pull to them. They rise to the swell at the
end of the verse with the line "I told you so," and it swings
them right into "All I want is *you!*" The whole song comes to
a halt as John and Paul finish the refrain and Ringo starts
things up again (after the final "Everything has got to be just
like you want it to . . . because"), playing out the energy
implicit in the silence the singers take between their words.
(They haven't had a caesura like this since the end of "She
Loves You.") The second time, when the break leads them
into George's guitar solo, the two of them hoot openly.

After the last refrain, they return to the opening lick to
take them home, and play the revolving figure out to the end,
landing on that last chord with all the bounce and oomph
that has accumulated. Fiddling with their final notes and
holding out faint "oohs," the Beatles dissolve into chatter
("Thank you, brothers," John says) as if they were playing it
just for themselves. These rooftop moments help give the record the intimacy of the film, the sense of eavesdropping on
closed sessions.

PHIL SPECTOR'S VERSION of "Across the Universe" is
unnecessarily hampered. Where Lennon's original demo
(available on *Rarities*) aspired to the sublimity of "Dear Prudence," Spector's souped-up strings and female choir make
saccharine sentiment out of Lennon's stirring pastoral. What
was intended as a childlike acoustic song is suddenly trans-

formed (at the first refrain) into a glitzy Hollywood production number: a choir of nymphs singing from the trees, a heavenly orchestra casting a benevolent glow upon the scene.

The first thing Spector does is slow it down, which in itself may have been a reasonable idea; but once familiar with the faster original version, the ear prefers it.

Lennon lets the words determine the meter of his lines, so no two verses follow the same rhythmic patterns. The first verse outlines the inspiration that set things in motion:

> *Words are flowing out like endless rain into a paper cup*
> *They slither while they pass, they slip away*
> *Across the universe*
> *Pools of sorrow, waves of joy are drifting through my opened*
>   *mind*
> *Possessing and caressing me. . . .*

The free-floating imagery determines the musical flexibility—the words evoke the creative process as much as a creative state of mind. The lulling effect explores the idea of music as meditation, and the refrain is a mantra ("Jai Guru Deva, Om/Nothing's gonna change my world"), the repeated phrase said in the rhythm of one's own breathing to calm the mind into higher consciousness. Lennon's rhythmic melody dances inside the harmonies lithely; the song almost overcomes its grandiose setting.

AN OMINOUS ORGAN broods behind George's opening guitar lead to "I Me Mine," making the opening moments sound like a horror movie takeoff. The waltzing verse begins rather humbly in comparison, and the song turns into an ode about self-pity, solipsism about solipsism. The chorus in four breaks out with all the joy and revelry of old-time rock 'n' roll, a lead guitar rejoicing (left), mocking the hubris of the verses. Spector's female chorus (right) and orchestral brass (left) don't play up these ironies; they virtually drown them.

As unfettered rock 'n' roll with acoustic verses, Harrison's song answers greed with a crude groove; with Spector's ornaments, the track is a washout.

"DIG IT" FADES in with Lennon at the helm singing the first thing that pops into his head—the kind of off-the-cuff riff with which musicians warm sessions up (the unedited jam is insufferably long). It fades out to Lennon introducing "Let It Be" with the same scorn with which he offered up "Yesterday" on "The Ed Sullivan Show." Here, he rolls the carpet out for Paul's latest ballad with a doll-like falsetto: "That was 'Can Ya Dig It' by Georgie Wood. And now we'd like to do 'Hark the Angels Come.' "

"LET IT BE" is the third in a series of songs by Paul alluding to his mother (following "Yesterday" and "Lady Madonna"). It has a more resigned tone than the dramatic rise of "Hey Jude," a gospel resolve that conveys a simple nobility of spirit.

George's guitar solo on the album is more polished than the one on the single—it arches more dramatically toward its highest note and was obviously added long after the original recording. (In the movie, the guitar solo rambles, still searching for its voice.) It returns for the final refrains, draping over Paul's vocal as the textural layers accrete. Spector's orchestra is mostly brass here, sounding regal and dignified, more tasteful than the gushing fake upholstery of "The Long and Winding Road." And Ringo's irregular drumbeat—trailing high-hats, reactions to downbeats—saves it from clichéd balladry. The falling cadence that sets up the guitar solo and sees the song out inspires some juicy organ playing from Billy Preston. (An organ solo proper might have made this song sound *too* reverent.) "Let It Be" doesn't have the climactic burst of ecstasy that "Hey Jude" promises (and then delivers), but it became the Beatles' epitaph.

· · ·

AFTER THE SOLEMNITY of "Let It Be," "Maggie Mae" has the irreverence of the laughter after "Within You Without You," the same wink-wink "bellyful of wine" that "Her Majesty" assumes after the grand finale to *Abbey Road*. "Maggie Mae" is a whore song from Liverpoool, about the legendary Lime Street tarts who used to walk the town (described by the Beatles' first manager, Alan Williams, in his book *The Man Who Gave the Beatles Away*). The song slides uphill to its conclusion, with members dropping out along the way until the bass is the only thing left. Whether this is a Beatles move or not is hard to tell, but it works, puncturing Spector's self-righteous setting of Paul's catholic ballad with spontaneous ribaldry.

SIDE TWO BEGINS with two live cuts from the Apple roof, the first a late Lennon and McCartney collaboration, the second an early Nurk Twins revival. "I've Got a Feeling" harks back to the singular blend of "We Can Work It Out," each singer contributing a distinct part of the song's tone. It's mostly Paul, even though he's out of character—singing about his own feelings, exposing his inner commotion, and finally screaming in frustration over the very angst of love during the bridge. John's reply is atypically detached, and Spector combines the two for a splendid irony in the final verse.

The simple guitar riff that gets things started has a supple restraint to it, relishing the pure major harmonies it dwells in. By the time the drums enter on the second phrase, the song has set itself up as a disarmingly natural melody built around two chords, simple but solid. When Ringo's fill brings the rest of the band in for the surmounting conclusion, the beat pops with a penetrating ring—at the end of the run, when they all pause for Paul to sing the concluding "I've got a feeling," the verse has been rounded off in the best kind of old-fashioned curve: pointing toward a goal, hitting it, and falling away from its charge naturally. John joins in for harmony on the second verse ("Oh, please believe me"), and they both play around with the different ways the tags ("Oh, yeah" and "Oh, no") can be sung—from a distance, hard and cutting, even jokingly.

Paul's bridge cuts loose from the sturdiness of the rest of the song with a raging frustration. Where his verse moves along smoothly, the bridge stumbles and lunges, and gains an anxiousness that finds as much discomfort in the groove as the verse finds pleasure:

> *All these years I've been running round the world*
> *Wondering how come nobody told me*
> *All I been looking for is somebody who looks like you!*

He's not prone to such outbursts of self expression, and his voice breaks into such earnest passion that it's an entirely believable personal statement, as gut-wrenching as "Oh! Darling." Rising from the supple alternating chords that give the track its expectant opening moments, his outbursts twist the song from an affirmative smile into a tormented howl. Lennon's guitar, which links the bridges back up to the verses, tilts downward slowly, pulling hard against the beat before Ringo's fill sinks it deftly back into place. Bending his strings to avoid exact delineations in pitch, it's like one wailing guitar left squirming in pain from all the hollering that came before.

John's verse flips his typical perspective around as well: Paul is singing about his feelings, so John describes events in a free narrative, an outsider looking in. In a conversational tone, he sings about the small pleasures, "wet dreams," "putting your feet up," "letting your hair down," "putting your foot down." The phrases are plays on clichés that center around relaxing, letting nature take its course, permitting things to happen with their own logic—the side Paul usually takes. Lennon also contrasts McCartney's shorter lines, employing the words rhythmically for the kind of play against the beat a good set of Lennon consonants provides.

For the final verse, Phil Spector mixes these two vocal lines on separate channels, John and Paul singing different interlocking melodies with different words, expressing their inverted personality traits at the same time. The song is summed up in this section the way "We Can Work It Out" never is: the contradicting personalities are sounded together, linking the implications of their role reversal with the music. It shows us how self-conscious they are of their traits, and how they enjoy playing with our expectations of their roles. On this record, it's Spector's best expressive touch.

THE BEATLES RECORDED "One After 909" in 1963, but John and Paul wrote it as far back as 1957 and were never satisfied with the lyrics. Spector's inclusion of it makes it the only remnant of the original *Get Back* concept: the Beatles romping through their roots. On the preferably slower 1963 version (on bootleg), George plays some stunning train noises as an introduction; here they just lean right into it with a brief guitar fill. Once the song is set off, the rush of remembrance and the joy these men feel toward this rare original is tangible. It's probably as corny as anything they threw out, but on this record it comes to mean much more—you can hear the thrill they find in it together, and you can see it in their faces in the film. It's hard to tell who's happier: Paul in front of a live audience again or John blushing at the immature lyrics that George answers with every line.

Their harmony sounds as rapturously open and bright as in "Please Please Me" and as self-mocking as in "Misery" ("Come on, baby, don't be cold as ice"). For George's guitar solo they slip into a fresh twist on the groove, leaning harder on its contours, reveling in the breaks they have him fill in (the "Move over once . . ." passages). At the end of the bridge, after John sings "I got the number wrong!," Ringo sways against the bar, nudging the beat to emphasize the humor.

The repeats of the unfinished title line see the song out by winding the hook up even tighter and letting it roll home of its own volition.

Hearing where it all began revives the innocent life of their ensemble, a musical bond that goes beyond brotherhood. Just at the song's end, Lennon starts singing "Danny Boy," conjuring up what stage patter at their Hamburg shows must have been like—ridiculing old songs, talking gibberish German to the drunken throng at the Star Club. That pop artists of this proficiency can throw themselves wholeheartedly into this rollicking aside tells us just how much the simple forms are still worth, and how everything they do stems from the thrill of unadulterated rock 'n' roll.

SPECTOR COMMITS HIS crimes early in "The Long and Winding Road." The initial vocal statement with piano has a tender grace to it; Paul invites us into the song with the same ease as in "Let It Be." But as soon as that phrase is finished, a full orchestra accentuates it and smothers whatever meekness it might have had: all of the sudden it's as if we're in the showroom of a large casino, and Paul is cruising into a schmaltzy ballad. Not that he can't croon—he could still outdo Linda Ronstadt with a singer's album of other people's material—but following the sheer directness of "One After 909," the veneer sounds applied rather than inspired.

> I'm not struck by the violins and ladies' voices on "The Long and Winding Road." I've always put my own strings on. But that's a bit of spilled milk. Nobody minded except me, so I shut up. When we first got it, Linda and I played it at home. It was a bit rough after *Abbey Road* had been very professional. (*Paul McCartney in His Own Words*, p. 20)

The film versions of both "Let It Be" and "The Long and Winding Road" still offer more intimate music-making—Paul sings them directly to his audience. With just the band, and

John and George adding backup harmonies for the refrain, the effect is quieter, more gently reassuring. With both tracks, Spector fiddled with subtleties and exploited McCartney's weepier tone; the Beatles gave them simple humility and longing. In their original versions, they're minor classics.

''FOR YOU BLUE'' is a slight boogie from George, with John playing slide guitar and Paul on honky-tonk piano. It's harmless, the kind of song that gets batted around for a while and then left off a record. The best thing about it is the enticingly brief but deceptive acoustic guitar intro.

BEFORE THE ROOFTOP finale, John sings a gibberish version of what is about to come: "Sweet Loretta fat she thought she was a cleaner/But she was a frying pan." "Get Back" has become a rock classic: Elton John launches into it on his live *11/17/70* album alongside Elvis's "My Baby Left Me." But it makes no pretense at being anything more than a pleasant romp, and Ringo's gentle snare shuffle, eschewing cymbals except for the kicks, trots the song along with a perfect pace. Paul writes high for his voice, reaching up for the note on "Jo-Jo was a man who *thought*," then scooping down for "but he knew it couldn't last."

On the first chorus only, John joins Paul for a low harmony, and for the rest of the time Lennon concentrates on his lead guitar part (left), commenting with a lower lick that's accentuated by an upper rhythmic figure. Billy Preston's piano solos are tightly drawn restatements, the perfect answer to Lennon's extremes. The alteration between the taut, focused groove (during the harmonized chorus) and the explosions into a punched-up version of the same thing two refrains later make the kicks fly that much higher. They go out soaring through the same accents as Paul ad-libs on top of them. Lennon steals the last word with mock humility: "I'd like to say thank you on behalf of the group, for ourselves, I hope we passed the audition..."

. . .

SPECTOR'S KITSCHY STRINGS make the ear appreciate George Martin's modest English touch—compared with the one on "The Long and Winding Road," the orchestra on "Good Night" sounds positively curt. But even the abominations of the Spectorized "Across the Universe," "I Me Mine," "The Long and Winding Road," and "Let It Be" don't seem to ruin the record as much as they play up the contrast between the live set and the reworked studio sessions. Side two begins with two rooftop cuts, then breaks for Paul's second ballad and George's throwaway, then returns for the rooftop finale. If side one had sequenced "Two of Us," "Across the Universe," "Let It Be," "I Me Mine," and "The Long and Winding Road" next to the complete live set on side two (including "I Dig a Pony," both film versions of "Get Back," and "Don't Let Me Down"), omitting "For You Blue," the album's form would have better reflected the sessions. Spector's layout lacks the sense of direction that gets taken for granted on their best records, and points up just what good hands the Beatles were in with George Martin.

Get Back (Paul)/Don't Let Me Down (John)
Released: April 11, 1969

THE SINGLE VERSION of "Get Back" sounds identical to the album version except for the tag at the end, a coda that Spector leaves off *Let It Be*. This single was released before the *Let It Be* album—the first thing the world heard from these sessions. The B side is Lennon's "Don't Let Me Down," the most stirring love blues he ever wrote.

An artist's B side used to be throwaway songs—the ones that didn't make it onto the album. But largely because of the Beatles, the album form eclipsed the single as the main unit of commerce, and since they gave their lesser material to other artists, their B sides are uncommonly good. A great B side is a shared secret to those who give it a chance (from

"Thank You Girl" and "I'll Get You" to Harrison's "The Inner Light" and "Old Brown Shoe"). Bruce Springsteen's *Born in the U.S.A.* B sides from the 1984–85 singles are mavericks of similar dimension: "Johnny Bye Bye" is a stirring one-minute-and-fifty-eight-second history of rock 'n' roll and the quaking dimensions of Elvis Presley's death; "Shut Out the Lights" makes the heaving irony of "Born in the U.S.A." a personal plea for sanity; "Pink Cadillac" is more Presley myth with Bible-busting humor; and "Janey Don't You Lose Heart" could be his best pop ever.

"Don't Let Me Down" belongs on the *Let It Be* album as part of their live set—the film version even includes some priceless Lennon gibberish when he forgets his own words. It's an ironical cousin to "Help!," a song about fame that decries robbed privacy; "Don't Let Me Down" is a pledge of devotion that writhes in the fear of loss. His first ode to Yoko is a cry of paranoia so honest and heartfelt that it strikes as deep a pathos as "In My Life."

The opening downbeat is warm and full, and George's guitar lick rises out of its sound invitingly. With his guitar landing accented by bass and drums, John's first entrance is commanding; the song becomes a vehicle for his vocal expression. (On a bootleg, at one point during rehearsals John asks Ringo for a big cymbal crash before this entrance, "to give [me] the courage to really scream.") But as in "Hey Jude," it's not the singer alone that makes the song great: this number ranks among their best individually meshed mosaics, coming together in one various yet complementary whole.

Billy Preston's electric piano fills in the ends of phrases with soulful restraint, and Paul's vocal harmony adds just the right touch of edge to the top end—there's no smoothing over the tension in John's voice. For the solo breaks ("Nobody ever loved me like she does") the band gives Lennon's vocal arc an extra beat to fit all the words in—five instead of four—and the elongation pulls on the already broad rhythm with an understated delay. The rhythm for the verse that follows swings just ever so slightly, and Ringo kicks accents in threes across two bars, the same way that the chorus's "don't let me down" is syncopated in quarter triplets over half a bar. George adds a descending octave guitar lead to the right channel.

When the refrain returns the first time, Ringo kicks it with his high-hat instead of his cymbal, and Paul accents his bass note twice. With a more declarative vocal break that follows from Lennon ("I'm in love for the first time") they move into the bridge. The bass and electric piano (right) play a simple but arresting descending motivic counterpoint to the vocal, this time carrying groups of two in delayed rhythms over the bar. The subtle interplay sets the song's bottom afloat *beneath* Lennon as he climaxes toward his most assured expression of the song: "It's a love that lasts forever/It's a love that has no past." Like the charged commitment in the middle of "All I've Got to Do," the bridge redeems the uncertainty of the refrains.

When the refrain comes back after the first bridge, Lennon's delivery intensifies—the next verse ("And from the first time that she really done me") is sung intimately, the breathy sensuality conveying something keenly felt. He storms into the following refrain with the sound of a man moved by both love and fear, still driven to paranoia by forces he can't understand. Lennon howls out one last falsetto "please" to go into the final ad-lib refrain, interjecting pleas and "Can ya dig it?" asides behind Preston's keyboard solo. The song ends on the same warm, deep chord it started on. "Don't Let Me Down" accepts the tenuousness of true love that he once could only fear ("If I Fell").

The Ballad of John and Yoko (John)/Old Brown Shoe (George) Released: May 30, 1969

JOHN AND YOKO'S wedding symbolized much more than just another pop star's coupling, and they knew it. "The Ballad of John and Yoko" recounts their dashes around the continent, pulling stunts to manipulate the press as much as to send up the frantic attention they received. The 1968 drug bust got in the way of their wedding plans: they had originally wanted to get married in Europe ("tryin' to get to Holland or France"), but settled for the Rock of Gibraltar because of visa problems. The wedding ceremony was private, but the honeymoon was public: a week in bed in front of the press, promoting peace (". . . the Amsterdam Hilton/Talking in our beds for a week"). (Their first solo single together, "Give Peace a Chance," was recorded live in their hotel room in Montreal, where they held a similar Bed-in six months later.) The refrain is directed at the press—

> *Christ! You know it ain't easy*
> *You know how hard it can be*
> *The way things are going*
> *They're gonna crucify me*

—a cynically light-hearted reference to his "bigger than Christ" quote, the flap that earned the Beatles death threats in 1966. The last verses capsulized John and Yoko's Bag event in Vienna and the Acorns for Peace campaign.

John's lead guitar echoes itself, played in the right channel and resounding in the left. Piano glissandos spill into the bridge ("Saving up your money for a rainy day . . ."), where the paparazzi pace is contrasted with the private wisdom that keeps them sane ("Last night my wife said/Oh boy, when you're dead/You don't take nothing with you but your soul _____"). The end of the bridge drops two beats after the word "soul" for Lennon to shout "THINK!" Paul's harmony for the last verse adds the same supportive dimension that Lennon's did on the last verse of Paul's "Hey Jude"—the way he drags out the last "the way things are *goin'* " turns it into a Beatlesque duet.

This single points up the degree to which the Beatles

thought—or didn't think—of themselves as a band by this point. The only two Beatles on this recording are John and Paul (who handles drums, bass, and supporting harmony). In six weeks, John would release "Give Peace a Chance" and credit it to the Plastic Ono Band, his imaginary new group. In this way, Lennon's solo career really began before the Beatles finished, and he claimed the authority of a solo artist long before Paul released his first solo album, at the same time *Let It Be* came out.

GEORGE'S "OLD BROWN SHOE," the B side, is at least as good a rocker as "Savoy Truffle." Paul's bass ignites a perky piano before the band enters in the verse, and Ringo supplies a quickly moving set of dotted rhythms that make everyone else jump. The lyrics are a witty and oblique look at love, delivered with sardonic flair:

> *I want a love that's right,*
> *Right is only half of what's wrong*
> *I want a short-haired girl*
> *Who sometimes wears it twice as long*

The bridge has an inside bow to Ringo ("wearing rings on every finger"), and leads into a daring guitar solo George's best since "Got to Get You into My Life"—that rises and falls with astonishing fluidity and control. Recorded in the spring after the "Get Back" sessions, it's the kind of piquant effort that *All Things Must Pass* lacks.

A TWO-HEADED ORACLE

ABBEY ROAD *Released: September 26, 1969*

ALTHOUGH THE "White Album" lays bare the forces of disintegration at work within the band, the intuitive musical flow still overwhelms the factionalism of the songs; you can hear it in the way Ringo second-guesses Paul's bass lines, or the way Lennon reads a vocal space they leave open for him ("Happiness is a warm, yes it is—"). Less than four months later, Michael Lindsay-Hogg films the Beatles' encroaching incompatibility, but the album *Let It Be* disguises the conflicts with Phil Spector's omissions and orchestral facelifts. (George Martin might have captured the band as John had hoped, "with [their] trousers off.") But regardless of the fatigued sessions that led up to it, the rooftop sequence sounds like the Beatles in their prime.

Their corporate harmony was another story. The spring of 1969 saw the mismanagement of Apple and the Beatles' publishing interests become public news. Lennon wanted Allen Klein, an American businessman who won owed royalties for the Rolling Stones, to represent the Beatles' affairs. McCartney preferred his soon-to-be father-in-law, Lee Eastman, who headed a New York firm that eventually turned McCartney into the richest man in show business, with holdings of up to $500 million. On Eastman's advice, Paul had been buying up shares of the Lennon-McCartney publishing company, Northern Songs, behind the others' backs to increase his holdings, and he continued to listen to Eastman while John, George, and Ringo sided with Klein. In February, Brian

Epstein's brother, Clive, sold NEMS, Brian's original general-interest management company, to Triumph Investment Trust; and the next month Dick James, the Beatles' publisher, sold his interest in Northern Songs to Associated Television Corporation (ATV). With three Beatles on his side, Klein attempted to buy out the rest of Northern Songs with stock from Beatles companies and some of his own holdings. But a third consortium of investors resisted Klein's tough bargaining and Lennon's obstinacy. They insisted on autonomy, and by May ATV had gained a controlling share of Northern Songs, leaving the Beatles only part owners of their own catalogue. By the end of 1970, the only way to divvy up their collective interests was to dissolve the partnership in court; Paul sued the other three. (Eventually Klein himself was countersued, in litigation that lasted well into the seventies.)

In between business negotiations, the Beatles were all busy with outside projects: Ringo appeared in the Peter Sellers film *The Magic Christian*, whose hit song "Come and Get It" was written by Paul McCartney and performed by an Apple discovery, Badfinger. Harrison's *Electronic Sound* was released on Apple's experimental subsidiary, Zapple. John and Yoko heard about Dick James's sale at their Amsterdam Bed-in, and the "Ballad of John and Yoko" single, featuring just John and Paul, came out at the end of May. Paul produced records for Mary Hopkin and Jackie Lomax and played bass with James Taylor, another Apple find, on "Carolina in My Mind."

Still, venturing out into solo careers was a daunting notion, especially when the itch to make more Beatles music wouldn't go away—perhaps the rooftop set had been so promising that they felt the need to reconcile the musical loose ends on the unreleased *Get Back*. If the Beatles were still a band, they owed their audience a follow-up to the "White Album." George Martin remembers a phone call from Paul in July asking him to help make a record "the way we used to do it." Martin was skeptical of reliving past glories: "If the album's going to be the way it used to be, then all of you have got to be the way you used to be" (Norman, p. 378). But Paul persisted, hoping that a musical reunion would help assuage the animosity of their financial entanglements, and Martin returned to the recording console for sessions in the summer of 1969.

LENNON WANTED a straightforward rock-'n-'roll album, songs laid back-to-back the old-fashioned way, nothing fancy or elaborate. McCartney and Martin were interested in playing with form: they wanted to create an album that would combine pop hooks with classical recapitulations—a kind of pop symphony, something more conceptual than a collection of songs. The sizzling blues of Lennon's "I Want You," cut short abruptly at the end of the first side, severs the record in half: side one gives each Beatle his requisite track; side two links a series of episodes into a developed song montage. In contrast to the "White Album" 's independent strokes, *Abbey Road* has one overall sheen of sound. The playing is polished bordering on slick; the production is punctiliously detailed and clear. There are no bleary, first-take tracks, like "I'm So Tired," and nothing with the brazen punch of "Birthday" or the spontaneous live aura of "I Dig a Pony."

The efficiency of *Abbey Road* is as far from the gripping immediacy of *Please Please Me* as seven years' development can be. But where their first record gains credibility by its unabashed candidness, *Abbey Road*'s masterful professionalism doesn't work against it. The opening track, Lennon's "Come Together," is a recasting of Chuck Berry's "You Can't Catch Me" (copping a couplet and guitar figure), a delicate piece of textural modernity with a rooty subtext. Both of George Harrison's songs are uncommonly strong: "Here Comes the Sun" is the sweetest Beatles track about nature (dwarfed only by "Dear Prudence"), and "Something" has earned its status as a standard alongside "Yesterday" and "And I Love Her." The vocal gymnastics on "Oh! Darling," which

Paul prepared for with a week of screaming, is his closest stab at a gut-churning roof raiser since "Long Tall Sally." "Maxwell's Silver Hammer" is ersatz comedy decked out in arch studio trickery; "Octopus's Garden" is Ringo's feeble rewrite of "Yellow Submarine," complete with underwater effects. "I Want You" is a varied rhythmic exercise that draws from the basic blues form of John's failed parody "Yer Blues."

The first side etches the same kind of lines between tracks that the "White Album" does; the second side virtually erases them. The songs were connected only after they were written and recorded, but they make more sense when heard together, and the emotional impressions they create make their extended linkage implacable. The common ground is musical, not narrative. The song suite resonates at both ends of the Beatles' career. Like the major-minor motif they discover on *A Hard Day's Night*, the entire second side pivots on a series of connected harmonies (hinging on C and A major). The dangling chord at the end of "Because" sounds like a premonition of "You Never Give Me Your Money," and the end of "Polythene Pam" unwinds into the entrance of "She Came in Through the Bathroom Window." The side progresses from George's opening acoustic guitar through electric guitar and vocal textures ("Because") toward piano and orchestral timbres ("You Never Give Me Your Money" and "Golden Slumbers") and climaxes with a drum avalanche and a guitar duel. The conclusion ("The End") recombines these instrumental colors less as a summation than as a circumstantial axiom; "Her Majesty" goes out with a nudge and a wink.

While the Beatles were embracing blues forms ("Yer Blues," "Why Don't We Do It in the Road?," "Oh! Darling," "I Want You"), others reverted to the country styles the Beatles had already covered. After his motorcycle accident and eighteen-month sabbatical (during which he recorded the fabled *Basement Tapes* [1975] with the Band), Bob Dylan's response to psychedelia was the rustic mysticism of *John Wesley Harding* (1968). Jimi Hendrix turned "All Along the

Watchtower" into a storm of impending cultural doom, but Dylan himself followed his musical instincts back to Tennessee (where he had recorded some of *Blonde on Blonde)* to croon *Nashville Skyline* (1969), a loving set of country songs. Conversely, as the Beatles camped their way through "Rocky Raccoon" and "Don't Pass Me By," the Rolling Stones delivered their most stirring blues testimonials, "Prodigal Son" on 1968's *Beggars Banquet* and Robert Johnson's "Love in Vain" on 1969's *Let It Bleed.* At the same time, they inverted their electric smash "Honky Tonk Woman" into a rural-guzzling "Country Honk" on *Let It Bleed,* tattered and worn with fiddle. On the same record, their musical ambition vaulted toward the other extreme, with the Bach chorale on "You Can't Always Get What You Want" (the same way that the Beatles joined forces with an orchestra on "Golden Slumbers" and "Carry That Weight").

T H E B A S I C Chuck Berry guitar riff Lennon recycles for "Come Together" resembles the ones in "Revolution" and "Get Back," but the surrounding texture is spare and elemental: Ringo sticks to his tom-toms, Paul repeats a querying bass line, and Lennon's voice echoes on top of it all, the detached observer pondering his latest self-portrait (the irony is that he sings it himself). This distance separates his singing from his self-references; the impersonal, detached first-personisms of "I Am the Walrus" combine with the carping self-consciousness of "I'm a Loser" and "Help!" Like "Strawberry Fields Forever," it's an attempt to forge an identity from amorphous feelings.

The album's opening moment sinks a muffled "Shook!" into the first downbeat, which springs into an eerie bass leap and fall as Ringo catches up on tom-toms. Ringo (left) goes from cymbal to hi-hat to tom-tom roll in a swirl of drum textures that gives the heartbeat of the song its contour; Paul's bass line (center) obscures the faint guitar (left) and slides into each downbeat with a questioning upbeat on the heels of Rin-

go's swells. When John's lead vocal enters, Ringo holds fast
to his tom-toms, and the guitar goes into an alternating riff
that provides the only harmonic backdrop.

The lyrics cop their opening couplet and narrative bent
from Berry's "You Can't Catch Me," a flying car fantasy
which Lennon eventually covers on *Rock 'n' Roll*. Lennon
puts the title of his source to work implicitly, by unraveling
separate strands of identity couched in contradictions and
cryptic asides:

> *Here come ol' flattop he come*
> *Groovin' up slowly he got*
> *Joo joo eyeball he one*
> *Holy roller*
> *He got hair down to his knees*
> *Got to be a joker he just do what he please*

As Lennon takes his solo vocal break on that last line,
Ringo's pulsing bass drum pushes him along from behind to
set up the sexual innuendo of the tag ("Come together, right
now/Over me"). Just before the band returns after the last
word, fingers slide atop guitar strings, squeaking like finger-
nails across a chalkboard.

Paul's lower harmony during the second verse is atypical
of their duo singing. As the music rises to the title line after
the second vocal break ("One thing I can tell you is you got
to be free"), Ringo heads for his snare to kick the sudden burst
of guitar sound, and the contrast breaks through on the
downbeat of the title words. The spare texture exaggerates
the veiled low profile of the verses, making the shift to the
refrain dramatically charged. It's a process of delayed grati-
fication, and the two contrasting sections fit together snugly.

In the link back to the third verse, a repetition of the
intro, Paul adds a small improvised lick to the final repeat of
the basic ruff instead of his usual drop into the downbeat,
settling down into the self-generating texture.

> *He Bag production/He got/walrus gumboot/He got/Ono side-*
>   *board/He one/spinal cracker/He got/*
> *Feet/down below his knees . . .*
> *Hold-you-in-his-arms-till-you-can-feel-his-disease*

The references to his Bag press stunts with Yoko, now his constant companion (his "sideboard"), and his notorious abrasive humor ("spinal cracker") lead illogically to the clap-trap humor of "feet down below his knees." The last line cuts through the myth and conveys a real sense of inner pain: the "disease" he carries is his own overbearing self-consciousness, his ever-present sense of insecurity and longing. (Some transcriptions mistakenly substitute "Hold you in his armchair" for "Hold you in his arms till"—either way, the line is addressed to a lover, and the issue is intimacy.) A deeply felt "Right!" hangs over Ringo's impulsive drum fill that takes the band into the solo chorus.

As the piano repeats a rhythmic figure (left), Lennon punches the center up with short, breathy "heh"s, and leans into a healthy groan as the high guitar solo enters (center). Ringo opens up to his ride cymbals as the sound gains momentum for the guitar's cries, and he fills in the empty spaces with dark tom-tom flourishes. After the guitar trails off on its last piercing note, there's an astonishing linkage back to the verse: electric piano carries most of it (moving to center), but after repeated listenings, bass and guitar criss-cross in their midrange, suspended together out of time before falling back into sync. In a spontaneous juxtaposition, the band (minus Ringo) reaches a magical blend of confusion and interplay in the small space between the guitar's last cries and the impending last verse. Paul finishes it with a decorative upper mordent on his bass.

The fourth verse is more calculated doggerel, with Paul shadowing his partner vocally from behind as in the second verse. "He roller coaster" pinpoints John's fluctuating emotional extremes; "He want mojo filter" refers to his affection for Italian ciggies; and ". . . one and one and one is three/ Got to be good-looking cos he's so hard to see" parodizes his evasive logic and the self-deprecating hippie mask his long hair and beard affect. For the last "Come together" refrain, Ringo lays off the snare for no apparent reason.

In the final outro (a literal repetition of the intro), the piano plays a single chord (left) as a flapping noise and high lead guitar upsurge are added (center) to emphasize the hanging mystery in the middle of the swell. As they go into the repetitive last section, Lennon comes forward with an unrestrained "Oh!" atop Ringo's directional fill that sets off John's title-line dialogue with the guitar solo. The coda flows on languorously, piano and rhythm guitar repeating the harmonic riff and Ringo cutting loose on his ride cymbal to play up the release at the end of this tightly-woven ensemble piece. The lead guitar rises above the rest to trade ever-heightened utterances of the main melody with Lennon's falsetto, and just before the sound dies away, Paul begins puttering about more freely on his bass.

RINGO'S CALCULATED tumble into "Something" sends off the lead guitar with large hollow tom-toms before George's soft vocal entrance. Compared with the restrained first verse, the entrance is grand and conventional, almost staged. Paul's bass (right) plays a solo role from the start, balancing his duties between providing a harmonic foundation and injecting a lyrical counterpoint; his rhythmic impulses are always informed by a strong melodic sense. Because the song is a ballad, it's slow enough to create large spaces for the players to fill in: Ringo's drum fills are purposeful, pulling the others into downbeats with tasteful restraint. When George sings "I don't wanna leave her now," Paul leaps up on his bass for a lick of dashing beauty. Strings enter quietly behind this line and grow into a backdrop for the others to play off of by the second verse. Unlike Spector's string arrangement for "The Long and Winding Road," Martin's strings sneak in to complement the band rather than overwhelming it with gush.

A high keyboard figure enters at the end of the second verse to enlarge the textural spectrum, and the three-pronged intro motif that sets the whole thing off returns to take things into the bridge (the verse has been in C major, the bridge drops to A major).

As they hit the new harmony at the end of this link, a flush of color bursts through (to set up the words "You're asking me will my love grow"). Paul fills in the harmony with an arpeggiated figure (defining the outlines of the chord), and the rhythmic underpinning for the change of key is spurred by Ringo's new high-hat patterns for the wordier text. Vocal harmonies are added on the first lines of stanzas ("You're asking me will my love grow" and "You stick around, well it may show"), climaxing with the added harmony on the concluding line, "I don't know!" Strings play a low countermelody to George's vocal in this section, and stanzas conclude with step-wise descending passages, the first in the key of the bridge, the second paving the way back to the key area of the verse. Near the end of this second fall, low piano octaves are brought up (center) to emphasize the change in color.

Landing in the solo verse area, George's lead guitar (center) is understated rather than virtuosic. By this point, the band has reached a comfortable pace with the well-worn grooves the song has to offer. Ringo's drum fills pull with more weight, and Paul's perpetual bass solos propel the others with just the right touch of control. After a tasteful high triplet, when George's lead arrives at the phrase sung to the words "Don't wanna leave her now," Paul leaps up as before, this time providing a breathtaking *upper* counterpoint to George's lead: George's guitar plays low, repetitive notes which soon arch into a final cry that leads back into the verse; Paul's bass is high and soaring, ornamenting the lead with an inspired dialogue. It rivals Paul's performance in "Rain," without stealing too much attention from the solo it supports.

After George sings "Something in the way she knows" in the final verse, Paul's line adds a new lick, extending what he's already set up for himself. Heading into the final cadences (the first deceptive, pointing toward the bridge harmony, the second resolving), the strings assume the melody, and the lead guitar peaks over the top of Ringo's drum fill with a towering arched curve above the rising step-wise intensity of Paul's bass. The final utterance of this cadence ends resolutely on the three pulses from the opening moments, spaced to emphasize their finality.

For all the predictable dismissals the schmaltzy tone baits, the high drama between George, Paul, and Ringo is the sound of intimacy itself. George's romanticism has a stately touch, and this survives as his strongest song since "If I Needed Someone." (At Allen Klein's suggestion, the Beatles release it as the A side of their first single from this album, backed with John's "Come Together," the first Harrison A side to a single.)

"Ob-La-Di, Ob-La-Da" has an insouciant frivolity; "Maxwell's Silver Hammer" is mega-camp: it dresses its dark comedy up in such bright clothes that there's a disappointing lack of irony between what Paul sings and the music that surrounds him. "Maxwell" tries to justify itself with textural games—no two verses or refrains don the same instrumental patterns—and the linkages between sections are fussed over in a way that steals attention from what they're supposed to ornament. The simple trio that backs Paul's lead vocal up for the first verse (piano and bass left, drums right) is soon so decorated and awash with other sounds that it becomes unrecognizable. Such gimmickry is a sure sign of weak material: it doesn't generate its own setting, so one has to be designed to keep it propped up.

Another reason the song falls flat is its square rhythmic sense: the one-two punch of "Bang bang" on the refrains gets predictable, and when Paul fills in the ends of lines with "oohs" instead of words ("Jo-oh-oh-oan . . ."), the syncopations don't find any friction with the beat they could rub up against. With an anvil on every "bang," the effect is literal instead of cunning. Maxwell, the medical student who murders people with his hammer, might have been a spoof antihero like Bungalow Bill or the Paperback Writer, but his elaborate musical character makes him a contrived Loony Tune. The song sounds refined and almost luxurious in tone where it should stay cute and forgettable.

The first chorus adds a bright, tasteful lead guitar figure (center) before a reverential synthesizer passage links the refrain back up to the second verse. A single synthesizer line plays a countermelody to Paul's lead on the second verse, and a guitar comments after the first stanza. There's such a big deal made out of the obligatory step-wise motion up to the chorus (piano and bass play it, drums kick it in), that it promises much more than a simple repeat of that refrain can deliver—even though this time the arrangement blossoms: acoustic guitars flesh out the lead guitar line, which follows with its own solo refrain (complete with "doot-doot" backups). The second linking passage bedecks the upright-sounding piano (which has been piddling away on the left) in concert-grand formal tails, arpeggiating chords as though they mattered. You can hear McCartney wanting to sucker you into this charm, but he relies so completely on his devices instead of his melodies and humor that these moments become manipulative. The modesty in the low tom-toms and bass that round out this link sounds out of place.

The last verse has a spooky synthesizer shadowing Paul's lead vocal, beginning in the far left and traveling all the way over to the right by the end of the verse. Rainbow curves work better when they're expressive: the distance Lennon's voice travels in "A Day in the Life" is truly ominous, outlining a distance that the singer takes inside his own head; it becomes the consciousness of the song itself. Here it's just another decoy to substitute musical radiance for a banal lyric. The heavyhandedness reaches its most unnecessary forced aside when the background vocals rejoin McCartney, playing the parts of Rose and Valerie in mock falsetto ("Maxwell must go free," left). As he goes into the final refrain, a wa-wa synthesizer sound effect darts off (right), and the song begins to wind down.

The last chorus has a lot of motion to it, and all the colors introduced throughout the song take on a warm glow; but the mix bustles with an activity that can only approximate the natural, happy impetus of earlier farcical singalongs like "Yellow Submarine" or "All Together Now." "Maxwell" has no real giddiness; it's virtuoso pulp. A final synthesizer solo precedes the choral last rites to the words "silver hammer," before the track is finally hammered shut with two final rings on the anvil.

JOHN'S ARGUMENT THAT the Beatles were worthy of better material than "Maxwell" is confirmed by what follows. "Oh! Darling" is a masterful piece of singing from Paul, his most spine-tingling vocal assault since "Long Tall Sally" and "I'm Down." Beneath a motorized banging piano (left) and blistering chopped guitar chords (right), he gives himself a swaggering bass line that swerves and pivots, mitigating the angered surface with a constantly swaying bottom. The heated rhythms of "Got to Get You into My Life" are slowed to a simmering gospel blues torched with Ray Charles vocal melodramatics, sacred inflections redeeming secular heartache.

In addition to the angular bass line that undergirds the verse, Paul writes himself a walloping solo vocal break at the top of each verse. Like Elvis Presley in "One Night" (1957), McCartney crams more into every new title outcry, making each one more charged than the last—it's the kind of break that allows a great singer to unleash the very essence of what the song is all about. By seizing the moment completely, Paul defines it, shapes it in his own terms; his vocal authority commands all the other players. He makes these moments unignorable the same way he makes the feverish ad-libs in "Hey Jude" so compelling—by letting his guts tell him where to land, and trusting his spontaneous sense of what sounds right to guide him toward the most riveting spontaneous phrasing. Nothing sounds planned because it isn't, and the gripping sense of emotion in the rising and descending swells at the end of each verse helps ground his flights as they set up his next entrance.

The bridge transcends the lift of the verses: as he sings "When you told me/You didn't *need* me anymore," Paul's voice comes unhinged, and the clipped guitar of the verses balloons into huge arpeggiations of the harmonies (right). It's one long scream of pain, and Paul sustains the tension right up to the last solo plea, "I nearly broke down and di-i-i-ed, oh, darling!" as he links the final desperate cries of the bridge up with the return of the verse. The escalation of harmony in the bridge is almost secondary to the way he contorts the word "need" (from A major, the band jumps from D7 to F7 on that word to intensify the basic blues progression). In these moments he nearly leaves everyone else behind, and his focus dares the others to match his emotional pitch.

The third verse is all warmed up: Paul takes more chances stretching words ("I'll never *maaaake* it . . . alone"), and lets silences spew their own inner tensions. The second time they move toward the bridge, Paul ad-libs "Believe me, darling"; we know what's going to happen, and they know that we know, so they're forced to make even more out of it the second time. As the second bridge comes around the bend, the sense of excitement is inescapable: the persuasive piano rumble that gets going in the left barely hints at the explosion of energy that takes place once they land on it. The end of the band's fuse suddenly ignites Paul's voice: "When you *told* me—whoo—woo!!"

That single ad-lib takes the whole track into hyperspace—you can hear it in the way the piano's octaves get manic throughout the succeeding bridge, and the way it reluctantly cools to the unsettled determination of the final verse ("I'll never le-e-et . . . you down"). (With energy like this in the air, there's no need to dress things up with roving synthesizers and sly backup-vocal jokes.) The last line Paul sings has all the sorrow of rejection and the resolve of not caving in that the entire song has sustained: he grieves over his loss, convinced that he doesn't deserve it. A guitar frames the track with bristled notes as the band holds the final chord.

WE SEE RINGO trying out "Octopus's Garden" in *Let It Be*, with George offering some optional harmonies for the second half of the verse. By the time it reaches *Abbey Road* six months later, John and Paul may have dabbled with it as well; all the simple charm has been produced out of it. There's nothing worse than to hear Ringo take himself too seriously: when he leaps up for the minor harmony on "We would be so happy, you and me," with piano banging away fitfully behind him, his singing sounds coached, like he was talked out of the village-idiot goofiness that made "Act Naturally" so disarming. It's bad enough that Paul tries to be Ringo on "Maxwell"; when Ringo tries to be Paul, his aplomb turns into bathetic self-parody. (If they had omitted Ringo's rewrite of "Yellow Submarine" and had him sing "Maxwell" instead, it would have saved the side some of its overdone charm.)

McCARTNEY'S EMOTIONAL URGENCY on "Oh! Darling" is out of control; he throws himself into his outbursts without hesitation. Lennon's "I Want You (She's So Heavy)" carries the weight of holding back—he gets even more mileage from the rhythmic reins he puts on his considerable screaming than he does from the screaming itself. The shifting swing patterns disrupt the primacy of the lyrics, and the band's changing tempos become the main musical force, keeping the combustive texture in check until the emotional buildup overwhelms them in the long coda that sees the song out. In the end, the tension is chopped off rather than resolved—Lennon seeks absolution and finds only continuous struggle.

The intro is a slow-moving arpeggiated guitar riff with a zigzagging bass line, held together by firm tugs from the overarching lead guitar (in D minor). After the band lands on the unresolved held chord, John sings a blues duet with his guitar (in A minor). He takes his time with it; the band lightly accents his every line with three raps, then four, then three again before they join him with an accompanying figure in a quicker tempo than the intro. This juxtaposition of tempos and harmonies is part of what gives this song its spark—the repeated vexation of the vocal is played out more dramatically in the rhythms than in the words.

The texture is basic: the bass on the right fills in spaces handsomely beneath a purring organ; Ringo's drums lean toward the left with George's fuzzed-up, sporadic rhythmic figures; in the center are John's voice and guitar. What's striking about this vocal performance, compared with that of "Yer Blues," is the complete lack of affectation: there's no self-consciousness as he sings; the consequentiality draws its force from an even starker, less inhibited style. As in McCartney's slow track on this side, there's enough space for everybody to move around—things come together in random moments of creative chance rather than in predetermined hooks. At the end of the second verse, John hauls into a repeated tag line to the verse ("It's drivin' me . . .") that sends the band into a rip-snorting exclamation (on a dominant E-7 with added b-11 chord), answered in Paul's vaulting bass solo.

Lennon wails "She's so . . ." after Paul's second-verse bass solo, and the band breaks into the tempo from the intro, a slightly slower and more measured $^{12}/_8$ groove (returning to D minor) that pulls on the rising tension with the force of backed-up counterpressure. The long delay before he sings the word "heavy" compounds in the line's repetition as vocals layer on top of one another in mounting swells. The organ is brought forward, and Paul's bass steadies to anchor the guitar's circular arpeggios. Lennon's lead guitar is left trailing over the last chord, and just as the feedback starts it pivots into its solo verse.

The next verse is a guitar solo; Ringo adds a Latin-tinged beat (tom-toms on two, snare on four) to give it more direction, and the organ offers a new accompanying lick. John was right when he assessed his guitar playing for Jann Wenner: he does more than just play notes, he "makes a guitar speak"—his instrument takes on human inflections. For the second bass break at the end of this verse, Paul adds a small rhythmic trip. The organ breaks open the world of the slower section this time out with even more heat than before. (With its sharp rhythms, it improves on the jaded-cum-existential Los Angeles blues of the Doors.)

After the second bridge, the fourth verse resumes its cool: the tempo is the same, but Ringo repeats his Latin patterns and the feeling relaxes—Lennon is singing the blues, but on this verse he's boogieing more than he is crying. The downward fall that Paul can't resist going into the second stanza in this verse plays up the happier spirit. Lennon's wailing "Yeah!!!" at the end brings the slower section back with a vengeance.

This last bridge repeats itself into a coda, gaining strength from the sheer repetition of changes (the same D-minor progression of the intro). You can hear Ringo pulling the others into sync during the first few moments, holding back their tendency to rush. The expressive power gained from reiteration is among the most powerful devices in rock: in "Hey Jude" the three-chord coda works as redemption; in "I Want You" it acquires a sustained apprehension. Paul leaps up and down the neck of his bass, dramatizing the highs and lows Lennon's singing has embodied, and a fog of white noise enters in the background, enveloping the sound. The singer disappears completely, drowned by his own self-absorption.

As in "Don't Let Me Down," the love described has as much to do with the pain of longing as it does with the joy of fulfillment. John's yearning has a long history, but his relationship with Yoko conjures up the most profound fears—anxieties about closeness that were first heard in "If I Fell" and "Girl," and later more imposingly with "She Said She Said" and "Julia." By making the simple declaration of "I Want You" a testimonial of faith as well as a howl of doubt, with none of the parody he tried to hide behind in "Yer Blues," he transforms his idiomatic blues into a statement of purpose. (In 1986 Elvis Costello's "I Want You" uses the same album position, the end of *Blood and Chocolate*'s side one, for a similarly consumptive effect.)

THE SUDDEN-DEATH EFFECT makes the unevenness of this side unsettling; it sounds as though the needle has jumped off the vinyl. The colliding passions of the two main songwriters still seek extremes, with Lennon's and Harrison's tracks exploring group dynamics while the others' smooth over musical inequities with slick production values—McCartney's deeply felt "Oh! Darling" only dramatizes the shallow waters it lies between. What side one does not do, in fact, is prepare the listener for the rest of the record.

Side two eases into its song suite after Harrison's "Here Comes the Sun" and Lennon's "Because" with McCartney's "You Never Give Me Your Money." By then, the syncretic instrumental textures are established: basic rock 'n' roll (guitar, bass, and drums, with added synthesizer) expands into piano balladry with orchestra; rich vocal textures ("Because," "Sun King") coalesce into unison ("Carry That Weight") and back into harmony again ("The End"). The silence before "Golden Slumbers" separates the memories and imaginative fancies that are set off in "You Never Give Me Your Money" from the closing ruminations and majestic resolve of "Carry That Weight."

THE SUPPLE ACOUSTIC GUITAR that greets the day in "Here Comes the Sun" shares some of the purity that fills Lennon's falling electric entrance to "Dear Prudence." Its gentle, inviting melody shapes syncopations that will mark the song's irregular bridge; but although the lick outlines disruptions in the beat, the effect is simple, not intricate—it hints at what lies ahead without giving anything away.

The guitar enters demurely on the left, and a synthesizer joins its simple repeat of the melody. Another synthesizer appears overhead (center) to fall toward the right, where a window opens on George's vocal surrounded by strings and background vocals. His opening refrain is delicate; he bounces lightly on the "doot-n-doo-doo" tag, and by the time the drums come in for the concluding syncopated riff (grouped in threes over the bar), the song's (and the side's) awakening is fresh and inviting. (After four groups of three, Ringo's fill squeezes two triplets in one-third the space—two beats—before landing on the downbeat of the verse.)

A synthesizer shadows the second verse; drums and bass mind the center with guitar touches here and there before the acoustic guitars (left) break away to introduce the shifting meters of the bridge (which moves from C major down to A major). As the vocals (right) repeat "Sun, sun, sun, here it comes" four times, extra guitars, synthesizers, and handclaps are added one by one until the texture blooms into a vivid array of colors. The transition back to the verse sequences a climbing melody above a dominant chord, spilling into the last stanza with a new synthesizer lead (center) to counterpoint George's voice.

The arrival at the final verse isn't climactic (like the one in "Dear Prudence"); it carries the momentum of the bridge into a pleasantly rolling pace. The band repeats the last refrain for the sheer pleasure of it, singing "It's all right" at the end as the music rejoins with the two-bar riff in groups of threes. On the final line, the synthesizer holds the concluding note as the opening acoustic guitar alludes to the bridge before finishing as it began—a trim, implicative solo, containing the seeds to all the song's syncopations in its endearing melody.

LENNON LIKED TO SAY that the arpeggiated synthesizer harmonies at the start of "Because" are Beethoven's "Moonlight" Sonata played backward, which may make good copy, but the progression bears only a small resemblance, even though it's in C-sharp minor (a relative harmony to "Here Comes the Sun" 's A major). "Because" is essentially a vocal harmony piece, engaging the ear with rich but transparent harmonies throughout.

The synthesizer arpeggiations (left) are joined by guitar (right) before the voices enter the bass on "Ah _____" (center). By the time they enter the verse the mood is hushed, and the pristine voices solemnly intone the undercutting wordplay of the lyrics. As a result, lines like "Love is all, love is new/ Love is all, love is you" don't sound as clichéd as they should. McCartney's voice flutters the high point of the last verse ("Because the sky is *blue* _____"), and the effect is elegant and refined, a strangely beautiful setting that doesn't take itself at all seriously. A synthesizer solo sings the melody on top of the voices to see the song out, leaving the last harmony hanging in anticipation of the piano to come.

AFTER GEORGE'S GARDENING ode and John's mood piece, Paul's "You Never Give Me Your Money" begins poignantly and ends dynamically, outlining the shape of the song suite it sets off. The suite tells several imaginative stories at once, beginning with Paul's shattered love affair and moving through heady nostalgia toward sober reflection: the love song becomes a metaphor for his feelings toward the Beatles. It

ends with a wistful English nursery rhyme, the same descending progression that gets recapitulated in "Carry That
Weight"; and once that association becomes clear, the soured
romance tells the Beatles' own story.

The suggestive melancholy of the piano chords (left) are
answered by a richly toned electric guitar at the end of the
first phrase (right) which dips into the downbeat of the verse
with a tasty lick inside the piano's brief silence. Paul's tender
first verse is joined by bass (center) and soft cymbals (right)
for the second, which grows slowly toward the tumble into
the next section as vocal reverberations echo above Ringo's
accelerating tom-toms. The financial metaphors allude to the
Beatles' business troubles ("You never give me your money/
You only give me your funny papers"), the theme that gets
played out in group terms by "Carry That Weight" and
"The End" (which reverses this song's solo-piano-to-band
direction).

As Paul pushes his voice into an almost unrecognizable
baritone for the following episode (right), the piano (left)
erupts into honky-tonk ragtime, as though thumbtacks had
instantly been applied to its felt hammers (it resembles the
boogie-woogie in "Lady Madonna"). The lyric is a reminiscence of salad days when life seemed simpler ("See no future,
pay no rent"). By the time the rhythm halves and Paul sings
"But oh, that magic feeling, nowhere to go," his voice has
traveled all the way up over the center to sit as far to the left
as it had started on the right. The song moves from the im-
perfections of a love relationship to the fond memories of
carefree unemployment; the vocal journey across the stereo
horizon traces the leap of imagination that the singer takes
from adulthood back to wishful naiveté.

The fantasy grows into a longer vocal refrain on "ah,"
which is spurred along by a guitar lead (right) that soon swells
into a doubled solo (right and center), arching toward higher
harmonic ground as Ringo responds to every rising sequence.
Landing in A major (the parallel harmony to the opening A-

minor chords), a soulful rock-'n'-roll guitar texture emerges: "One sweet dream . . . Pick up the bags and get in the limousine" conveys the sweeping rush of early fame. "One sweet dream came true today/Came true today," flushed out with high bass rolls and tambourine accents, subsides into a goodnight prayer: "One, two, three, four, five, six, seven/All good children go to heaven" (recalling Lennon's bridge to "She Said She Said," with "When I was a boy/Everything was right"). A guitar lead dances around the singers as bells (left) and crickets (right) begin to roam, eclipsing the daydream that "You Never Give Me Your Money" drifts into; the nocturnal opening of "Sun King" is telescoped into the fade-out.

From the left, a hushed cymbal roll sets off a dark, mellow guitar; a cymbal rings (center) and carries Ringo's drums all the way over to the right before a second arpeggiating guitar appears (center) and wanders between channels (toward Paul's bass on the left, then back toward Ringo's drums). The atmosphere is pitch black, lunar and echoing, and as the choir of voices enters on a stop-time break ("ah _____") everything is brought to a momentary halt on a dangling Dm7/G chord (the harmony in between E major and C major, the key area of the verse). They fall back into the undulating rhythmic pattern that gives this song its flowing draw—it would be positively mellow if it weren't for Ringo's gently insistent bass drum. An organ joins in with a countermelody during the repeat of "Here comes the sun king," and as John takes the lead for the following lines ("Everybody's laughing, everybody's happy"), the song lulls with a tidal expanse. On the final repetition line, everybody leaps up into a gorgeous elaboration of the melody.

The link to the next area reverses the step-wise motion of the first transition (from F major up to A major, the subdominant of E major). The vocals sing an inferential Spanish gibberish above the opening instrumental texture, parodying the copped Harrison line with lilting syncopated patterns. The rhythmic inflection the singers give this nonsense kneads the motion, stretching the words as far across the bar as possible, always lagging just behind the beat.

The last chord rings suggestively, but the drums (right) immediately puncture the mood with a linking fill to set up two Lennon character sketches: "Mean Mr. Mustard," a "dirty old man," and the androgynous "Polythene Pam," who is "so good looking but she looks like a man" (she might be Mr. Mustard's sister). These short, punchy rock 'n' roll sketches contrast with Lennon's two slower songs on this side ("Because" and "Sun King") and are answered by Paul's "Bathroom Window."

A randy piano (center) spurs the beat; synthesizer provides the bass (left); and a tambourine (center) shakes up the motion. "Mean Mr. Mustard" describes a homeless bum, with lines sung over the bar to disrupt the meter: "Mean Mr. Mustard sleeps/in the park, shaves in the/dark, tryin' to save paper."

The music is grungy; the sounds low and guttural; and Paul's expert parallel vocal harmony tarts up the second verse: his sister Pam is a "go-getter," she "takes him out to look at the Queen," where he "always shouts out something obscene." At the end of the second verse, the "dirty old man" tag goes into 6/8 to connect with the opening chords of "Polythene Pam."

Without any warning, the song is over—the opening acoustic chords to "Polythene Pam" tear a hole through the last bar. The booming guitar has a vicious edge; to get this much sound from a nonelectric instrument, Lennon thrashes at it with the same commanding effect that Pete Townshend gets on "Pinball Wizard." The whole band answers back (both channels) as best it can with repeated eighth notes in the second bar, but the guitar dominates. As if to emphasize this, Ringo's drumming stresses tom-toms, giving the whole texture a compulsion that relies less on the electric guitar that answers every line (right) than on the sheer energy of the propulsive rhythm itself. Lennon's delivery is clipped; he spits his words out quickly to fit them all in, supported by tight, weaving vocal harmonies on "ah." The first verse ends with a declamatory "yeah, yeah, yeah" echoed in the acoustic guitar, which has moved over to the left.

John sings in a thick Scouse accent, deliberately blurring the words as they rush past ("She's killer-diller when she's dressed to the 'ilt."). As in "Hey Bulldog," the words are secondary to the groove that's set in motion: three chords and a burning band doused with flippantly clipped absurdity. When Lennon sings "yeah, yeah, yeah," he's referring to much more than just the girl in the song; he's reminiscing the way McCartney did when he sang "that magic feeling—nowhere to go." Even their trademark early hoots bob to the surface: a "yeah, great!" sets the guitar solo off (right). Ringo sticks to his tom-toms and punches up the ends of two-bar phrases with large accents; tambourine and extra percussion fill in the gaps.

The acoustic guitar is still ringing (left), and as everything approaches a conclusion, the guitar also descends into the lower register and everybody pulls back a little on the momentum. Two descending bars link the end of "Polythene Pam" to the beginning of "She Came in Through the Bathroom Window." In anticipation of the change in meter, John can be heard chuckling "heh-heh," and Paul shouts "Oh, look out" just before the impending downbeat.

The new song breaks forth with a jarring drop into half-time (like the "magic feeling" shift)—the beat gets twice as big. As the first huge downbeat lands, all that resounds is the lead guitar that led it in (right) and the tambourines that signal the new beat's pulse. But the downbeat itself is simply a platform for Paul to leap off vocally, and he seizes the moment as only McCartney can, forging his presence onto everything else in the mix. As he finishes his dramatic opening title phrase, backup vocals glide upward from behind (on "ah-ooh"), and Ringo slides into the next bar with a drum fill,

dragging just enough to make the verse downbeat pulveriz-
ing. It's one of the focal points of the side.

The flirtatious hustler in "She Came in Through the
Bathroom Window" is McCartney's sister to John's "Polythene Pam," and it sounds as though both songs were cut
during the same take. Acoustic guitars ring out brightly (left);
lead guitar offers up commentary on each phrase (right);
background vocals flank Paul's lead (left); handclaps interrupt the motion of odd offbeats during the second verse; and
Ringo piles menacing drum fills on top of one another to keep
everything moving forward. When they hit the bridge
("Didn't anybody tell her"), the stop-time break adds a vocal
harmony—as always, they're aware of the music's direction,
and a repeated break demands more interest than the first
one. (The bridge alters D major to D minor, and twists the
song around from A major into the C major to which they
modulate—after "Tuesday's on the phone to me"—before
heading back to the second verse. The closing moments wrap
the key areas of the bridge and the verse up in one neat turn,
moving from C major back to A major for the final surprise
cadence: "oh yeah.")

These three songs that follow "Sun King" have a textural
relationship that invokes the good old days in "You Never
Give Me Your Money," when they made rock 'n' roll for fun,
not for pay. All three emphasize guitars as rhythmic instruments and turn on playful ambiguities, the singer in different
slants of condescension toward his subject. In the last song
the money issues are more corrupt: "She could steal, but she
could not rob . . ."

A SMALL SILENCE follows to set off the broken piano
chords of "Golden Slumbers" (right). Its poignancy evokes the
earlier piano intro of "You Never Give Me Your Money," and
its lyric comments resignedly on that song's fantasies of youth:
"Once there was a way to get back homeward." The orches-

tral gloss that is laid on after that line signals the passage of time: the texture is no longer that of a simple rock 'n' roll band, it's a full-bodied orchestral wall of harmony, stratified by Paul's scooping bass (center), whose off-bar accents give the strings their rhythmic foundation.

"Golden Slumbers" also picks up on the lullaby ending to "You Never Give Me Your Money": the words are borrowed from Thomas Dekker's sixteenth-century "Golden Slumbers Kiss Your Eyes," and are offered up as a farewell to altruism. When the drums (left) come crashing in, we hear just how pressing these lost ideals are. The refrain is a big-chested line of grand, nostalgic drama that breaks away with determined conviction after the yielding sadness of the verses. (In contrast to the songs that it follows, this song emphasizes piano even in the larger, drummed-out refrain.)

The second verse repeats the first to a more seasoned orchestral dialogue, strings juicing the singer's plaintive tone with countermelodies, and an added horn part underlines the emotional plight. As he reaches the end of this verse, Ringo's fill ushers in "Carry That Weight," and the longing and tenderness of "Golden Slumbers" grow into the larger implications of fame and notoriety—obligation and commitment—that weigh in the singer's heart.

A unison Beatles chorus sings the declamatory refrain of "Carry That Weight" to a slightly slower beat, with rhythmic bass impulses surging from beneath and a snare drum doubled to the right. At the end of the first phrase, piano and drums fill up the space between exhortations with a determined punch; after the second phrase, the brass heralds the re-emergence of the melody from "You Never Give Me Your Money." The lead guitar's response (right) to the orchestral statement is charged with the earlier song's pathos and nostalgia—it's a short dialogue of rock textures with "mature" orchestral symbolism. When the voice returns, we hear the last verse sung among musical forces that symbolize the burdens of maturity and the pressing responsibilities of fame. It is here that McCartney utters the most intimate line, shunning the financial language:

> *I never give you my pillow,*
> *I only give you my invitations*
> *And in the middle of the celebrations*
> *I break down*

As the others join for a final chorus of "Carry That Weight," the ironies become palpable; the love song Paul sings to the Beatles spells out the price that fame has exacted from their friendship. The same guitar arpeggio that saw the end of the original "You Never Give Me Your Money" out (to the children's rhyme "One, two, three, four, five, six, seven/All good children go to heaven") returns for two statements (moving again from C major to A major). Then, without warning, the beat shifts gears, jump-starting the band on a new pattern ("The End").

The ascent to this final section is an exchange between the three guitarists and Ringo: the band plays ascending chromatic chords, then drops back down to the tonic. Ringo fills in the empty space with tom-toms that spread across left and right channels, kicking the band into a repeat of its phrase before his drum solo. "Oh yeah! All right! Are you gonna be in my dreams tonight?" Paul sings, with all the anticipatory gusto of their early rockers.

For Ringo to take a drum solo is a special event—he never has taken one so exposed before, and has built his reputation by shunning virtuosic display. His entire career with this band has been devoted to rhythmic frameworks for songs rather than technical showboating. Given the spotlight for one final flourish, however, he turns in eight bars of pure rhythm that seems to define what his drumming is all about as its breathless tension lifts the whole side to new heights. In his introductory solo to the reprise of "Sgt. Pepper," he reveres the beat above all else; here, every little gesture that strays from it gets tugged right back into the commanding magnetic thump of the bass drum. The thrills come with the way he disrupts the regular meter of eight beats to the bar: injecting three sets of four sixteenth notes separated by one eighth to a measure, he throws the ear's expectations off, making the band's exultant re-entrance a triumph of sustained anticipation and expectant release.

The simple groove that the drum solo sets in motion is as enticing as any rock 'n' roll the Beatles have ever delivered. Something is approaching a climax, but we don't know just what, and the refreshing neatness of the two alternating chords (A and D) makes the resulting guitar exchanges ripe with implication. They're playing straight, pure rock 'n' roll to emphasize how much they love the unadulterated form, and how much this simple idea can generate—like "One After 909" on *Let It Be*, it comments not only on its own record but the entire career it looks back on; the idea of the group gets even bigger than the idea of the album side that's climaxing. The vocal chanting (either "love you" or "yeah, you," depending on whose lyric sheet you follow) plays up the celebratory side of the sound (it starts out on the right and moves to the far left just before the guitars enter). As on any other classic groove from their past ("Money" or "I'm Down"), they sound like they're enslaved by the beat, responding to the repetition's natural currents of tension and relief.

There is a little break where Paul plays, George plays and I play. And you listened to it. And there is one bit, one of those where it stops, one of those "Carry That Weight" where it suddenly goes boom, boom on the drums and then we all take it in turns to play. I'm the third one on it. I have a definite style of playing. I've always had. I was overshadowed. They call George the invisible singer, well, I'm the invisible guitarist. (Lennon, in *Lennon Remembers*, p. 56)

The jam is a three-way conversation between the three guitarists. The exchanges are telling: if Lennon's summary is correct, Paul's lines are typically melodic, George's are soaring and virtuosic, and John's are intensely rhythmic. Paul and George turn in rhythmic lines, but both of them get out of the rhythm they set up with lyricism; John drives his patterns into the ground. On the final, distorted guitar entry, John pushes the momentum that has built up to its breaking point: the band suddenly disappears into a void, leaving only a repeated A-major piano chord.

The piano's simple triad springs unassumingly from the collective motion—it would sound affectedly coy if it weren't preceded by such a dramatic buildup. The effect captures a regained innocence that this side has pointed toward since the opening guitar of "Here Comes the Sun," and with the piano introductions of "You Never Give Me Your Money" and "Golden Slumbers."

Paul's simple vocal line "And in the end . . ." is answered exquisitely by two guitar licks, the first from the right, the second echoing symmetrically off to the left. John and George join him for the next phrase, "the love you take," answered by the right-channel guitar only, before the easy sway of the melody leads them all down into a resolving downbeat as they conclude "Is equal to the love . . . you make" (in two dotted quarter notes to the bar, changing the meter momentarily from 4/4 to 6/8, echoing the triplet patterns in "Here Comes the Sun" and the end of "Mean Mr. Mustard").

When they hit the words "love you make" (and the meter changes back to 4/4), the orchestra reappears, and a one-bar drum fill from Ringo helps buffer the subsiding motion (the harmonic transition moves from the piano triads on A major to the final destination of C major, the central key relationship of the entire side). The music settles down into a grand march of uncovered truths, the arrival of a more elaborate and complex journey than the one "Hey Jude" made. A guitar lead climbs the distance of two octaves above a vocal bedding, and Ringo tugs at the final bars to make sure the brakes are applied toward the finish.

When all these elements—orchestra, guitar, and vocals—combine for the final cadence, the concluding line has enough veiled irony to bring these conflicting tensions together, if only to admit their existence. It's sung both from Paul to the other Beatles and from the Beatles to their audience.

If the conclusion is too nicely tied together, the loose ends of these personalities too patly tucked away in a wash of orchestral luster, the record's encore puts all the apocalyptic overtones in perspective with a grinning gesture of self-deprecation. McCartney's "Her Majesty," which travels from right to left across the stereo spectrum (a reverse image of the rainbow arc the synthesizer played at the beginning of "Here Comes the Sun"), recalls the closing grooves of *Sgt. Pepper*, whose British edition emitted high-pitched sound waves that only dogs could hear. It sounds like the pub song the band hears after knocking off a day's work in the studio—slightly bawdy and somewhat soused. Without this lusty aside, the grand finale would have sounded like uncharacteristic pomposity. The track is cut off (just like "I Want You" on side one), leaving a final dominant note unresolved, wanting its tonic resolution but never getting it.

ABBEY ROAD is more coherent musically than it is conceptually. The spook of Paul's bass line in "Come Together" becomes the lyrical alter ego to George's lead guitar in "Something"; Ringo's drumming holds the same two songs with expert stylistic contrast. The album is a model of fluent ensemble work, vocal personas, and brilliantly shaped guitar textures. But the line between parody and sincerity blurs: "Maxwell's Silver Hammer" is a catchy annoyance; "Because" and "Sun King" can't be taken at face value; and the two halves lie at an even greater distance from each other than the sides of *A Hard Day's Night* and *Help!* (Even the musical unities are ironic: when they write different versions of the same song ["Oh! Darling" and "I Want You (She's So Heavy)"], Paul and John sound worlds apart—the way everything coalesces near the finale only exaggerates their remoteness.)

Side two works better as a set of distinct but related tracks (like the Who's *Tommy*) than as a lengthy single song; it revives different stages of their career for a remarkable nostalgic resonance and comprises an ingenious manipulation of rock 'n' roll textures. The pauses (before "Sun King" and "Golden Slumbers") intensify the climaxes—the driving guitar rock sounds more energized next to the more reflective piano. It has McCartney's and Martin's signature (some call it Paul's best solo album), but the effect is of a collective swan song. The guitar exchanges delineate the band's personalities the way song choice and vocals did on *Please Please Me,* and the ensemble finale returns to the dance floor possibilities of "I Saw Her Standing There."

But as much as this album looks back, it sets creative standards for the production values and the longer concept treatments of the seventies. The Beatles integrate the synthesizer into their group texture as naturally as they do string quartets and brass; like Pete Townshend's masterful use of the new technology on *Who's Next* and *Quadrophenia,* their expanded musical vocabulary never loses sight of the music's origins and purposes. As a musical statement, the record is more rewarding to return to than *Sgt. Pepper* but more difficult to read literally. It closes their career equivocally.

THE DREAM IS OVER
THE SOLO CAREERS

WHEN IT LOST the Beatles, pop lost its hub. They symbolized the ultimate integration—outrageous yet accessible, varied yet whole—and their breakup made the period that followed sound irrevocably splintered. The best Rolling Stones and Bob Dylan records of the seventies ignored trends more than they set new standards: *Exile on Main Street* and *Blood on the Tracks* (1974) are grounded in the experience of the sixties, enigmas to the pop climate they greeted (a dilemma Dylan wrestles with in "Idiot Wind"). By 1978, with the Stones' disco pander "Miss You" and Dylan's conversion to Christianity *(Slow Train Coming* [1979]), they began to sound like Presleyan parodies of themselves, especially compared to the ethic of reinvention practiced by punk and new wave ascendants—the Ramones, the Talking Heads, Elvis Costello, the Sex Pistols, the Clash. Only Steely Dan, the most strategically innovative group to follow the Beatles, won mainstream commercial favor, while going straight over most listeners' heads. Singer-songwriters like James Taylor, Cat Stevens, Joni Mitchell, and Jackson Browne suppressed the beat and wrote almost completely in the first person. Heavy-metal forebears like Led Zeppelin and Alice Cooper dispensed with subtleties and exaggerated the beat by slowing it down, spelling out a mass-cult style with its own rituals and sacred cows. Stevie Wonder, Marvin Gaye, and Sly and the Family Stone applied album concepts to soul and funk better than art-rock bands like Emerson, Lake and Palmer, Jethro Tull, and Yes did. And yet some sixties hangovers went on to make good records based on the frameworks of their original sounds instead of buckling under to the prevailing trends; and several of them produced their most remarkable work: Rod Stewart on *Every Picture Tells a Story* (1971), Eric Clapton's (Derek and the Dominos') *Layla* and his own *461 Ocean Boulevard* (1974), Paul Simon on most of his solo work, and the Who on *Quadrophenia* (1973). The two seventies figures to emerge as eighties superstars, Michael Jackson and Bruce Springsteen, were in many ways the guardians of the artistic tradition, Springsteen with his herculean concerts and albums, Jackson with singles. The fact that Dylan's heir apparent, Elvis Costello, didn't win over a deserved large audience says more about the fickle masses than about his formidable songwriting invective. With the measured California rock of the Eagles and Fleetwood Mac, and Elton John's and Billy Joel's bright melodic hits, the wake of the Beatles sounded more neutralized than artistically centered.

In the midst of it all, Beatles imitation bands (John dubbed them "Sons of Beatles") inevitably sprang up. Paul McCartney wrote Badfinger's first hit, "Come and Get It" (1970), and George Harrison went on to produce them; "No Matter What" (1970) made terrific use of the expectant Beatles silences in "Love Me Do" and at the end of "She Loves You." Two years later, the Raspberries, led by Eric Carmen, debuted with a rapturous single, "Go All The Way," that was almost as artfully sexy as "Please Please Me." Later in the decade, the Knack was hyped as the next Fab Four with the smash "My Sharona" and the *A Hard Day's Night* TV-set pose on their debut album's back-cover photo. (Capitol Records, their label, went so far as to revive the rainbow inner label

to make the connection explicit.) Almost predictably, spurred
by a backlash of star worship that would go so far as to immortalize McCartney with a fake death, a Beatles-reunion
rumor ignited surrounding the Canadian group Klaatu's
eponymous album and helped push their debut, a watered-
down mechanical retread of faintly Beatlesque formulas, into
the top forty. Naturally, Klaatu's label, Capitol, did nothing
to squelch the gossip. In the eighties, the taut harmonies of
the Bangles, a Los Angeles female quartet, were labeled the
successors to the great vocal ensemble tradition, and the
Smithereens won praise for their unabashed retranslations of
Beatlesque song forms. Some of the groups that most deserved
the Beatles analogy, like the British Squeeze and XTC, never
found the larger audiences they deserved. American outfits
like the Rubinoos found brief cult status with faithful encore
covers of "I Want to Hold Your Hand," and Cheap Trick
borrowed Beatles-isms like self-parody (and covered "Day
Tripper"); but none of these displayed consistent songwriting
skills or the compelling personalities to live up to their models, and few backed their singles up with solid full-length
records. All suffered immensely from the weight of the comparison. The Beatles dominated rock by their absence almost
as much as they once had by their involvement.

As soloists, all four Beatles worked outside the mainstream of pop's prevailing currents, making their records curious echoes of a better place in the past rather than engaged
dialogues with the pop life around them. The memorable solo
hits—"Maybe I'm Amazed," "Give Me Love," "You're Sixteen," right up through "Starting Over"—usually had nothing in common with the charts they topped. The exceptions
are telling: Lennon's "Whatever Gets You Through the
Night," his first number one, was a duet with Elton John that
danced on its blatant commercialism where McCartney's
"Goodnight Tonight" succumbed to it. Their Beatles work

grew in stature as time went on and re-entered the charts with the slightest of pretexts: Elton John peaked with "Lucy in the Sky with Diamonds" in 1974; a Capitol re-issue campaign put "Got to Get You into My Life" in the top ten in 1976; and as late as 1986 the Beatles' 1963 recording of "Twist and Shout" (featured in the films *Ferris Buehler's Day Off* and *Back to School*) blitzed past McCartney's solo "Press."

The Beatles' unfailing sense of ensemble points up how rare it is for four players to find a common voice. When these gifted collaborators hired studio musicians, the dynamic of interplay took a backseat to the material; and only striking and varied music can carry a single voice for an entire album. (This put Ringo and George at an obvious disadvantage.) Where together the Beatles could redeem lesser tracks by getting up inside of them to make the idea of the group more persuasive than the idea of the song ("What Goes On" or "All Together Now"), on their solo records they sound trapped—even when McCartney credits his players in Wings, the sidemen are always subsidiary, the records padded with filler. Solo Beatle singles outdo their complete albums, and their music always uses their sixties work as a reference point.

With the strained musical camaraderie already at work as their business disputes progressed, it's no wonder their early individual efforts touched on the animosity they left behind. The utopian dream of Apple Corps as a haven for struggling artists crumbled into a rock 'n' roll Jarndyce and Jarndyce as their lawsuits with Allen Klein stretched into the seventies. A series of songs they sang to one another from their separate islands of creativity became a sideshow to the creative fallout. Ringo started with the B side to his first hit, "It Don't Come Easy"—a wishful reunion epistle called "Early 1970." Then, in typical confrontational fashion, Lennon wrote a scathing renunciation of the Beatles myth in "God," a nulling but vain attempt to slam the lid on the reunion rumors that persisted until he died. Paul's "Too Many People," on *Ram*, snubbed

Lennon's hyperactive politicking. Lennon retorted with "How Do You Sleep?" on *Imagine*, a knife-twisting indictment of Paul (the album was packaged with a postcard of John manhandling a pig, a direct satire of the sheep on the cover of McCartney's *Ram*). On *Wild Life*, Paul offered up "Dear Friend," a saddened rebuttal to the acridity of "How Do You Sleep?" which nonetheless brought the exchanges to a halt until Lennon's death.

Their solo careers marginalized their independent strengths. The maxim that their whole was greater than the sum of their parts seems true beyond description. By the time the jet-set pop scene of the seventies was deliberately fractured by punk and new wave in 1977, Ringo and George's solo careers were basically over, Paul's work had turned sadly formulaic, and John had gone into retirement to raise his new son, Sean. At one point during his five-year sabbatical, Lennon got a visit from McCartney in Manhattan, and they watched together as Lorne Michaels of NBC's "Saturday Night Live" comedy show offered the Beatles a whopping three thousand dollars to reunite on the air. Lennon recalls that they "were watching it and almost went down to the studio just as a gag. We nearly got into a cab, but we were actually too tired. . . . [We] went, 'Ha ha, wouldn't it be funny if we went down?' But we didn't" (from *Saturday Night: A Backstage History of Saturday Night Live* by Doug Hill and Jeff Weingrad, pp. 134–5).

John Lennon's comeback album with Yoko in 1980, *Double Fantasy*, was heralded as the promising answer to 1970's tormented *Plastic Ono Band*; it bolted to the top of the charts the month before he was killed. In the spring of 1987, Ringo Starr returned to recording studios in Memphis, and George Harrison was at work with former Electric Light Orchestra member Jeff Lynne. As of this writing, Paul McCartney continues to produce records regularly and hints at more live appearances.

RINGO STARR:

The Act You've Known for All These Years

Ringo was always the Beatles' own biggest fan. His signature song, "A Little Help from My Friends," plays up his dependency on the others and makes the possibilities of the ordinary seem not only entertaining but rejuvenating. The breakup appeared to leave Ringo stranded, virtually unimportant in the legal imbroglio over songwriting royalties and creative control. As a drummer, he couldn't very well join another band without taking a step down. So he decided to sing.

His early releases succeed on the same extramusical terms as his Beatle persona: his charm is irresistible, so much so that whether he's singing big-band standards or a maudlin collection of country and western, he wins listeners over with the musical character realized in "Act Naturally" and "Goodnight." *Sentimental Journey* (1970) is a crooner's record of nightclub staples, arranged by contributors like Quincy Jones, the Bee Gees' Maurice Gibb, and Oliver Nelson. Backed by full jazz band and occasional strings, Ringo poses as a Liverpudlian Jack Jones, with surprisingly good results. *Beaucoups of Blues* (1970) is affectionate country recorded in just two days with Nashville cats under the direction of veteran steel guitarist "Sneaky" Pete Drake. Both these albums have a deceptively easy feel, and the strongest moments from each ("Dream" and "Blue Turning Grey Over You" from the first and "Woman of the Night" on the second) confirm his fundamental appeal as a personality.

Staying active in session work with people like Leon Russell and blues heroes Howlin' Wolf and B. B. King, Ringo followed up these lovably odd ventures with two fine hit singles that he wrote himself: "It Don't Come Easy" in April 1971 (which won a big ovation when he sang it at George's Concert for Bangla Desh) and "Back Off Boogaloo," in March 1972.

It wasn't until 1973's *Ringo* that he recorded his first rock album, supported—albeit separately—by the other three Beatles (and by the Band on one track) for a committed return to harmless pop. The cover drawing by Hamburg friend and bassist Klaus Voorman parodies *Sgt. Pepper:* Billy Shears is finally getting a record to himself. Ringo doesn't have to do anything to Lennon's megalomaniacally uproarious "I Am the Greatest," which lets the audience know that Ringo knows that the laugh is on him—it's a middle-aged answer to "Act Naturally." McCartney's contribution ("Six O'Clock") is a tasteful ballad with an elegant synthesizer duet. The record gave Ringo three top ten hits: "Photograph," his collaboration with Harrison, became his first number one; "You're Sixteen," a 1960 Johnny Burnette cover complete with a "mouth sax solo" from Paul, repeated the same feat; and "Oh My My," written with his seventies songwriting partner Vini Poncia, followed at number five. This semi–Beatles reunion is the closest they ever came to getting back together, and Ringo's role in drawing the others back to support him emanates from an undying fondness for their musical companionship.

Even though Ringo stuck with producer Richard Perry, the same formula—hiring bigshot friends to write and duet with—mars 1974's follow-up, *Goodnight Vienna*. Technically, Ringo has the same problem as George: his voice doesn't have the range to carry an entire record—he is only as good as his material. Unlike *Ringo*'s unfeigned lightheartedness, these contributions from crack songwriters (Lennon, Harry Nilsson, Elton John/Bernie Taupin, Hoyt Axton, Allen Toussaint, Roger Williams) sound more thrown away on Ringo than tailored for him. Even so, the Platters' 1955 debut hit, "Only You," which Lennon suggested for him, reached number six; and Hoyt Axton's embarrassingly square "No No Song" scored as a kind of novelty item at number three.

Blast from Your Past, a greatest-hits collection released for Christmas of 1975, combines Ringo's staples with would-be hits without reverting to Beatles tracks (the way Harrison's collection does). It includes the B side to "It Don't Come Easy," a touching Beatles epigram called "Early 1970"—the first ex-Beatles song sung to the others, with a verse devoted to each—it survives as the most hopeful reunion rumour.

McCartney's well publicized no-show at the Rock and Roll Hall of Fame awards that saw the Beatles inducted as lifetime achievers in early 1988 was only the latest incident in the ongoing legal squabble over publishing rights and royalties. Even Ringo's lawyers refused Knopf permission to reprint the lyrics to "Early 1970," one of his best songs, saying it would allow this book to profit off of his original material. And yet for a drummer of Ringo's caliber, to get shut out of creative royalties from Beatle records underscores how unfair the authorship issue in rock really is. Lennon and McCartney were undeniably the chief songwriters of the four, but Ringo's contributions especially are at a much higher level than the average studio hack they might have recorded with (if Martin had had his way originally). McCartney may have suggested the drum pattern that accents the guitar line's hanging triplet in "Ticket to Ride," but no one else could have gotten the sound down with just the right punch, the way Ringo does. His varied fills before the final line of each refrain only extend this ingenuity.

RINGO'S REMAINING SOLO work suffers the ex-Beatles burden rather than using it (the way *Ringo* did); the supporting-cast routine begins to wear thin. Hollywood film composer Arif Mardin produced 1976's *Ringo's Rotogravure* to distraction, making meager contributions from both Lennon and McCartney sound even weaker than they should. (The back cover pictures the former Apple offices at 3 Savile Row in London, ravaged by graffiti.) Mardin repeated these mistakes on *Ringo the 4th* (1977), even though moments like the inebriated glint of "Can She Do It Like She Dances" beg for more inspired playing from pros like Sneaky Pete, Don Grolnick, and the incomparable session drummer Steve Gadd (only Ringo could credit Gadd's playing and not appear shamelessly modest). *Bad Boy* (1978) is virtually irredeemable. McCartney's and Harrison's material on *Stop and Smell the Roses* (1981) suffers the ignominy of being upstaged by dismissible Nilsson pap like "Drumming Is My Madness" and the spontaneous goodbye rap Ringo gives in the title song.

Lennon's tired goodbye to *Rock 'n' Roll* rebounds as a self-confessional—he remarked later that it was a moment when he realized he would be leaving the record business. Like Lennon, Ringo could never make a weak record without evincing self-consciousness: it's curious that the group's most recognizable everyman should also understand the charade that most of his solo records fail to sustain. He knows his career has to stop; "everybody wants it to stop," he ad-libs into the fade-out. As usual, the gesture is friendly, but the admission is somewhat galling. To date, this Ringo farewell capsulizes the ex-Beatles' declining estimation of the audience they once ennobled and empowered. (There's even talk of a Ringo TV sitcom, God help us.) Still, Ringo being Ringo, he gets it both ways: his delivery has the same bracing self-effacement as "With a Little Help from My Friends," and it gives the record its only worthwhile humor. Not even the requisite covers ("You Belong to Me," the 1962 hit by the Duprees featuring Joey Vann, and Carl Perkins's inimitable classic "Sure to Fall") can save this album.

Naturally, Ringo's musical decline got reflected in sales (his last single, Harrison's "Wrack My Brain," barely crept into the top forty, halting at thirty-eight), and his market appeal faded to the point where much of his catalogue is now out of print. *Old Wave*, the 1983 record produced by Joe Walsh, was released only in Germany, even though it stacks up better than Ringo's previous three records—notably Leiber and Stoller's "I Keep Forgettin' " and Walsh's own "Goin' Down," an unpretentious jam with a small drum solo.

Ringo's best drumming is found on Lennon's *Plastic Ono Band* and in the astonishing time he keeps doubling Jim Keltner on *The Concert for Bangla Desh*. He sits in on sessions with friends like Keith Moon and Harry Nilsson and does what he can on a number of McCartney's and Harrison's records; and this studio work proves his rhythmic feel is more of a prize than his songwriting ambitions with Poncia on later solo albums. He dabbled in film (Frank Zappa's *200 Motels*, Marc Bolan's *Born to Boogie)*, and his most notable work on screen is as David Essex's co-star in *That'll Be the Day*, where he plays a ducktailed carnival tough in the late fifties who doesn't follow his own advice. His marriage to Barbara Bach in 1981 reoriented his family life, and now he shows up in television movies and talk shows as well as the odd promotional campaign (Sun Country wine cooler). When his legendary status beckons, he still takes part in celebrity benefits (he appeared in Miami Steve Van Zandt's antiapartheid benefit "Sun City"). But his biggest dream goes unfulfilled. As he told Max Weinberg in *The Big Beat* (p. 189), "My one ambition was to have been in the audience when the Beatles played. It must have been great."

GEORGE HARRISON:

Don't Bother Me

HARRISON'S BEATLES songs helped offset the brilliance of Lennon and McCartney. His singing on "Do You Want to Know a Secret" and "Don't Bother Me" made him sound like a scrawny younger brother to the clan. These early, half-out-of-tune gems, like Ringo's, helped form a bond of commonality with their audience and kept Lennon's and McCartney's cockiness in check. His apprenticeship on guitar traces a growth in skill from the willful "Roll Over Beethoven" solo to the commanding leads on "Taxman" and "Got to Get You into My Life." But as a songwriter, he scrambled just to keep up; and as a singer of other people's songs ("Chains," "Devil in Her Heart," "I'm Happy Just to Dance with You," and the laconic "Everybody's Trying to Be My Baby"), he relied on the others' support more than he inspired them.

Harrison's best Beatles tracks place modest lyrics above guitar-based textures. Only a handful of songs hold their own: "If I Needed Someone" and his three sturdy *Revolver* tracks; "The Inner Light" ("Lady Madonna" 's B side) and "Love You To," the only Indian excursions that survive as more than curiosities; "While My Guitar Gently Weeps" and "Piggies" on the "White Album," held together more by guitar playing and wit than by George's vocals; "Savoy Truffle" and "Old Brown Shoe" from the same sessions, which relegate his voice to a secondary position beside randy guitar licks and hard rhythmic kicks; and "Something" and "Here Comes the Sun," which couple vocal maturity with a promising new songwriting finesse. But the weak spots surrounding these better moments are prescient: for every "Inner Light" there is a ponderous "Within You Without You"; for every harmless "I Need You" there is a strained "You Like Me Too Much"; and virtually all of his psychedelic musings ("Blue Jay Way," "Only a Northern Song," "It's All Too Much") are misguided and pretentious. The dark-horse mystique that once surrounded his early solo efforts seems unfounded in retrospect.

WHEN HARRISON TEAMED with Phil Spector a few months after *Abbey Road* to record *All Things Must Pass*, his ambition outweighed his creativity; a double-record debut solo album is the height of conceit. The fact that he repeats the dourest track, "Isn't It a Pity"—at an even slower tempo—points to a larger problem: the monotonous material doesn't provide enough variety in tempo and mood. It's typical for artists to record many more tracks than are needed to fill up a forty-minute LP; Harrison's problem, at least with this record, is editing. Tracks like "What Is Life," "Beware of Darkness," "Apple Scruffs" (an affectionate ode to Beatles groupies), "All Things Must Pass," "The Art of Dying," and the best of the lot, "Run of the Mill," on a single record would have made for a much less sprawling album; as it is, these better cuts get buried among turgid studio exercises ("Let It Down") and light treacle ("The Ballad of Sir Frankie Crisp [Let It Roll]" or "Wah-Wah").

Even though the record garnered him a double-sided number-one hit ("My Sweet Lord"/"Isn't It a Pity"), and "What Is Life" went to number ten, *All Things Must Pass* remains the least durable of all the ex-Beatle solo debuts; it wound up at the top of John Swenson's 15 Most Boring Classic Albums in *The Book of Rock Lists*, beating out such dinosaurs as Chicago's *At Carnegie Hall, Volumes I–IV* and the Moody Blues' *Days of Future Passed*. (The extra record of jam outtakes Harrison included might have brightened things up with some scalding exchanges between demanding players like Dave Mason, Eric Clapton, Jim Keltner, and Billy Preston; instead, it rambles aimlessly.) To seal this record's historical blight, Ronnie Mack, composer of the Chiffons' 1963 hit "He's So Fine," took Harrison to court for stealing the basic progression of that song on "My Sweet Lord"—and won.

GEORGE BROUGHT TOGETHER a host of fine performers on very short notice for the Concert for Bangla Desh in August 1971, and the live album he and Phil Spector mixed afterward contains four songs from *All Things Must Pass* mixed with three Beatles tracks ("While My Guitar Gently Weeps" with Eric Clapton, "Here Comes the Sun" with Badfinger, and "Something") and "Bangla Desh," composed specifically for the event. It includes a difficult Indian set from Ravi Shankar; a Leon Russell medley; a song each for Billy Preston and Ringo; and a startling five-song acoustic set from Bob Dylan (accompanied by George on guitar, Ringo on tambourine, and Leon Russell on bass), the only worthwhile music on the entire six sides.

·   ·   ·

THE ELEGIAC "Give Me Love," Harrison's best single (from *Living in the Material World*), saturated the summer of 1973, a soothing piece of radio taffy that's as easy to tune out as it is to tune into (it made a like-minded companion to Paul Simon's "Kodachrome," a similar piece of nose-on-the-face pop). But as a starting point for the album it sets up, it makes almost everything that follows a letdown. "Sue Me, Sue You Blues" recounts the Beatles' legal problems with a hurry-up-and-wait tag line ("We're gonna play those") before an instant of silence, making the title line hesitant instead of forceful. (This song was later unwittingly co-opted by Lionel Ritchie in the theme to the movie *White Nights* as "Say You, Say Me.") Even with the compressed—and somewhat innaccurate—Beatles history in the title track, the continuing stream of devotional numbers ("The Light That Has Lighted the World," "Who Can See It," and the over-orchestrated "The Day the World Gets Round") makes Harrison sound increasingly insulated even as he sings of spiritual involvement.

GEORGE WAS THE FIRST ex-Beatle to embark on a full-length tour—to promote his 1974 album on his new record label of the same name, *Dark Horse*. The record continues the series: a couple of modest hits clouded by poor excuses for surrounding songs (on "Hari's on Tour" he wisely lets his slide guitar do the talking; "Simply Shady" quotes "Sexy Sadie" for an atypically gnarled track). By comparison, the tour was a humble success, even though his voice wore thin and Billy Preston's hits "Nothing from Nothing" and "Will It Go Round in Circles" interrupted George's devotional restraint with danceable excitement. As Ben Fong-Torres wrote in his *Rolling Stone* cover story:

> On paper, without mentioning the drive of Andy Newmark's drumming, the color of Emil Richards' percussion work, the solidity of Willie Weeks' bass, the vocal (and sweeping key-

board) help rendered by Billy Preston, the exuberant rock and blues guitar of Robben Ford, and the brilliant horn work of Tom Scott, the concert sounds pretty dreadful. But it wasn't quite that bad.

Harrison was reluctant to perform any Beatles songs, relenting only with "Something," "While My Guitar Gently Weeps," "Here Comes the Sun," and a sincerely charged reworking of Lennon's "In My Life" (singing "I love God more" instead of "I love you more"), which actually gained resonance with the brotherly overtones, when sung by one ex-Beatle to another. But overexpectant audiences had to sit through an entire first set of Ravi Shankar's Indian music, and while Harrison's new material sounded better in concert than on record, the act seemed to confirm his stature as a sideman more than show him off as a leader.

The remainder of Harrison's catalogue has only a smattering of good moments. "You" is an unassuming and pleasurable guitar lick stretched out to a diffident single from 1975's *Extra Texture—Read All About It,* which also contains a feeble answer to "While My Guitar Gently Weeps" entitled "This Guitar Can't Keep From Crying." 1976's *Thirty-Three & 1/3* contains the lukewarm hits "This Song" (a response to the "My Sweet Lord" lawsuit) and the foppish "Crackerjack Palace." On *George Harrison* (1979), he resuscitates "Not Guilty," a track the Beatles left off the "White Album," even though he doesn't alter the arrangement, and pens yet another unnecessary answer song (to "Here Comes the Sun") with "Here Comes the Moon."

LENNON'S DEATH INSPIRED good songs from some improbable sources. Elton John's "Empty Garden" draws from "Dear Prudence" with sadness and respect, reworking Lennon's "come out to play" line with a genuine swell of feeling that he rarely achieves in his Taupin collaborations. "The Late Great Johnny Ace," Paul Simon's tribute orchestrated by Philip Glass, appears on the wistful *Hearts and Bones* in 1983. And Loudon Wainwright III, the sardonic folkie, sets down a meekly despondent response in "Not John," from his *I'm Alright* LP (1985).

Harrison recruited Paul and Ringo together to play on his Lennon memorial, "All Those Years Ago," and although he doesn't rank with Elton or Simon as a perennial underachiever suddenly overachieving once again, his kid-brother tone recaptures the approach he took on "I'm Happy Just to Dance with You," the song Lennon wrote for him. Like Elton, he addresses Lennon directly, but the bounciness of the synthesizer overdubs and "doo-wa" background vocals are breezy, and he sounds upset only in the wedged lyrics of the bridge:

> *Living with good and bad*
> *I always looked up to you*
> *Now we're left cold and sad*
> *By someone the devil's best friend*
> *Someone who offended all*

"The Late Great Johnny Ace" brings Simon's *Hearts and Bones* to a dead standstill, with Glass's embryonic strings casting a ghastly pall over the dread that the song—and album—have witnessed. McCartney's "Here Today" centers *Tug of War* at the end of side one with stirring personal memories. But Harrison undermines any cathartic possibilities "All Those Years Ago" might have held as part of its 1981 album, *Somewhere in England:* "Baltimore Oriole," the lifeless aside that follows, simply defuses it.

Gone Troppo (1982), Harrison's last record before a five-year hiatus, is easily his most dismissible. He appeared as a news interviewer outside the pillaged Apple offices in Eric Idle's television film *The Rutles*, a bull's-eye Beatles parody, but did better at producing Monty Python–related films (notably *Life of Brian*, the underrated *Time Bandits*, and Terry

Gilliam's acclaimed *Brazil)* than he did with composing. With Derek Taylor, he wrote his autobiography, *I Me Mine* (1980), a slight recollection of his life (less than seventy-five pages) fleshed out with pictures, photocopies of handwritten lyrics, and explanatory notes to his songs. Until the quaintly dull comeback of *Cloud Nine* (1987), he retreated increasingly from the public eye, his interviews dwindled, and his interests wandered to car racing and gardening. In late 1985 he made a rare appearance with Carl Perkins in London for a cable television special, looking trim and happy, offering up "Everybody's Trying to Be My Baby" as earnestly as ever.

PAUL McCARTNEY

The Working-Class Hero

The moment was temporary like everything is. Nothing in life really stays. And it's beautiful that they go. They have to go in order for the next thing to come. You can almost add beauty to a thing by accepting that it's temporary.
(Paul McCartney in *Life* magazine, April 16, 1971)

FROM THE BEGINNING, McCartney rarely personalized his songs the way Lennon did; he had a keener commercial instinct, and in some cases helped put Lennon's more challenging work over with a smile and a wink. The sexual directness of "Please Please Me" is smoothed over by McCartney's high, arching harmonies; and "Strawberry Fields Forever" rode the popular coattails of "Penny Lane." Where Lennon challenged his audience with lofty ideas like the illusory nature of reality ("Rain") and acute anxiety ("She Said She Said," "Julia"), McCartney satisfied pop expectations, whether covering "Till There Was You" penning dandy stories like "Lady Madonna" and "Ob-La-Di, Ob-La-Da" or reassuring ballads like "Hey Jude" and "Let It Be." Once they became solo artists, these tendencies stratified: the profundity of *Plastic Ono Band* lacks the comic self-effacement McCartney might have provided; and *Band on the Run*'s layout and casual feel could use some of Lennon's clever acidity. Their best albums epitomize their strengths as they delineate what an intriguing match of sensibilities the two of them once were.

McCartney's ambition to get back on stage again was realized early on with Wings, the new band he formed around him. He taught Linda to play keyboards, and the band's constantly shifting personnel revolves around the two of them. (In whatever form, Wings were always a better band live than they were on record.) All his records are riddled with the snatches of bright humor and deft musical turns that make him almost supernaturally popular, but as a series of moments they get dragged under by an overall lack of discipline; there is little, if any, extended growth from one period to the next, and when McCartney starts to copy trends instead of inspire them, his commercial savvy quickly turns predictable (the disco pap of "Goodnight Tonight," the techno-pop of "Coming Up"). His good moments argue for the lesser songs to be weeded out.

But even his best songs are self-derivative in ways that only recall his earlier triumphs. "Every Night," one of his first album's best tracks, steals its refrain from "You Never Give Me Your Money"; "You Gave Me the Answer" retreads "When I'm Sixty-four"; "Call Me Back Again" mimics "Oh! Darling"; and *Band on the Run* is largely a compendium of reformed ideas worked out to better effect: "Bluebird" recasts "Blackbird," "Mamunia" is a second-generation "Rain," and "Picasso's Last Words" simply turns the episodic inanities of "Uncle Albert/Admiral Halsey" into a poignant montage. By around *London Town*, McCartney began to suffer the same insularity as George, only without the spiritual excuses—Linda's domestic influence on Paul was even more worrisome than Yoko's avant-garde influence on John.

McCartney's ten-day imprisonment in Japan for attempting to smuggle in a suitcase full of marijuana in 1980 appears to be the logical extension of how much his musical standards have withered; he tests how much he can get away with more than how much he can still challenge himself. Without Lennon's expressive prongs, McCartney's professional approach evolves into uninspired vocation. The spontaneous charm of his early work takes on a glow once his later work begins to falter; what were once inspired melodies start to sound forced, and his lyrics become hackneyed. As happened with Elvis Presley, putting out records and performing have become his job, and he works assiduously, often without emotional incentive or purpose.

His singles, however, are consistently strong, especially the ones that aren't lodged inside spotty albums—"Hi, Hi, Hi," "Live and Let Die," "Helen Wheels" (which was added to *Band on the Run* after the fact), "Junior's Farm," "Mull of Kintyre" and its underrated B side, "Girls' School". These moments of slapdash excitement and wry absurdity seem to spring from him effortlessly.

THE HUMBLE TONE of *McCartney* (1970), his first solo effort, has a homey appeal that makes up for some of the half-written tracks. It's not a major effort, but like its one-man-band counterparts, Pete Townshend's *Who Came First* and *Scoop* and Todd Rundgren's *Something/Anything*, the piddling about that goes on behind records is fun to take part in; the listener casually overhears an album-in-progress that would normally get edited down.

> Yeah, I'd say "Maybe I'm Amazed" was the most successful song off *McCartney*. You've got people who say "Oh, I love 'Lovely Linda,' " and silly things that were just little asides on the album. Or "That Would Be Something." They were almost throwaways, you know. But that's why they were included— they weren't quite throwaways. That was the whole idea of the album. *(Paul McCartney in His Own Words, p. 69)*

Four songs would have fit on any of the last three Beatles albums: "Maybe I'm Amazed," the single, finds an uncommon ensemble groove considering McCartney is playing all the instruments himself; "Every Night" is a gently melodic love song; "Junk," a sweetly lilting waltz, would have made an affectionate title track (it gets an unnecessary instrumental repeat); and "Teddy Boy," a tune that was batted about during the *Get Back* sessions, is an intuitive mother-and-child scenario that follows revolving harmonies.

To make a public announcement of the end of the Beatles, McCartney released *McCartney* a month before *Let It Be*, which quickly nudged it off the top of the charts.

The frivolous tone of his second effort, *Ram* (1971), makes it the Beatle solo album that most resembles *Sgt. Pepper*, even though its orchestral conclusion, "Back Seat of My Car," resembles "Two of Us" more than "A Day in the Life." (It's preceded by a harmless, melodic single, "Another Day," backed with a thumping rocker, "Oh Woman, Oh Why," that echos "Why Don't We Do It in the Road.") *Ram* combines the homemade tone of *McCartney* with Paul's notorious pop perfectionism—he hired crack studio musicians (Dave Spinozza, Hugh McCracken) to play insipidly cheerful tracks like "Three Legs" and "Monkberry Moon Delight" and declined to play bass even on the two concluding cuts that deserve it ("Back Seat of My Car" and "Too Many People"). "Dear Boy" is an underrated piano song sung to Linda's ex-boyfriend(s), and the smoldering "Smile Away" pulverizes "Uncle Albert/Admiral Halsey," the innocuously rambling single it follows on side one.

But it wasn't until 1973's *Band on the Run* that McCartney returned to the kind of album-making he built his reputation on, and he was almost forced into proving himself by the intervening releases: *Wild Life* (1971), the first Wings record, sports only one worthwhile track, a deliciously funked-up cover of Mickey and Sylvia's 1957 hit, "Love Is Strange." "Dear Friend," his answer to Lennon's temper-baiting "How Do You Sleep?," is mawkish. Three hit singles followed in 1972: "Give Ireland Back to the Irish" counters Lennon's agitprop with rollicking daftness; "Mary Had a Little Lamb" satirizes charges of simplemindedness as it implicates itself; and the rip-snorting "Hi, Hi, Hi" sat beside Elvis Presley's lascivious "Burning Love" on the charts without apology.

McCartney's tours of Britain with his new musicians in 1972 (drummer Denny Seiwell, guitarists Henry McCullough and Denny Laine) demonstrated his natural talent for live performances, some of which were captured on film for his 1973 television special, *James Paul McCartney*. On this tour he unpacked Little Richard's "Long Tall Sally" and Presley's "Blue Moon of Kentucky" from his chest of covers, and still sang them daringly. *Red Rose Speedway* (1973), the first and only Wings record with this lineup, is barely a notch above *Wild Life* in terms of quality: the hook to "My Love," the smarmy surefire-hit single, is sung to "wo-wo-wo-wo." The closing medley ("Hold Me Tight/Lazy Dynamite/Hands of Love/Power Cut") shows how many unfinished songs he has lying around instead of how many he cares about polishing off.

DENNY SEIWELL and Henry McCullough dropped out of Wings just before the next recording sessions were due to take place in Lagos, Nigeria, so Paul wound up drumming for *Band on the Run* (1973). It's McCartney's sturdiest set of solo songs, even though they fail to live up to the critical praise that first greeted them. *Ram* included a halfhearted reprise of its ukelele title tune; *Band on the Run* fades the title cut back in after the pseudo-apocalyptic conclusion, "Nineteen Hundred and Eighty-five," making the concept sound faintly *Pepper*esque. "Jet" and "Helen Wheels" are propulsive yet still melodic, and "Let Me Roll It" is a gauntlet tossed at the bath-tile vocal echo Lennon and Spector developed for *Plastic Ono Band*. But the customary asides, romantic and otherwise, are all too familiar: "Bluebird" is a second-class "Black-bird"; "Mrs. Vanderbilt" apes "Monkberry Moon Delight" with the ultimate Paul hook ("What's the use of worrying?"); and "Mamunia" is a pale rewrite of Lennon's "Rain" despite its smart two-key framework. With "Picasso's Last Words," McCartney adapts the "Uncle Albert/Admiral Halsey" formula to weave in song fragments from "Jet" and "Mrs. Vanderbilt" in the same way that "Golden Slumbers" visits the last verse of "You Never Give Me Your Money."

Coming after the wandering quasi-epic muse of "Picasso's Last Words," the straight rock 'n' roll of "Nineteen Hundred and Eighty-five" tries to get the record up to a higher level before closing—the nimble major-minor piano lick the song centers itself on seems to slyly laugh away the pretension of what came before. But the bridge doesn't follow suit; the ominous organ and "ooh" vocals resemble the middle eight of "Your Mother Should Know," and when the getaway of the title track is reprised to send the album into its last fade-out, it sounds even more enticing than the opening.

In his *Rolling Stone* review, John Landau lauded *Band on the Run* for being neither a "collection of song fragments *(McCartney, Ram)* nor a collection of mediocre and directionless songs *(Wild Life, Red Rose Speedway).*" For upholding the mythic rock tradition in McCartney's own terms, Landau dubbed it "the finest record yet released by any of the four musicians who were once called the Beatles." But these comments read like overextended hopes in light of how this record has aged. Play it alongside *Plastic Ono Band* or even *Sgt. Pepper* and it sounds leveled. Like *Tug of War*, *Band on the Run* suffers from its own admirers' misappropriated praise.

VENUS AND MARS (1975) follows *Band on the Run* more promisingly than *Red Rose Speedway* approached it; it feels like Wings' arrival. Combined with *Wings at the Speed of Sound*, it provided most of the material for his 1976 live dates (when drummer Joe English and guitarist Jimmy McCulloch replaced Seiwell and McCullough). New Orleans pianist Allen Toussaint roughs up "Rock Show" for a rousing jam, and the band crashes in behind him with a deep, heavy beat; saxophonist Tom Scott turns in a masterful first-take solo to the single "Listen to What the Man Said"; McCartney insists on yet another twenties crooner, "You Gave Me the Answer," and tries to make up for it by screaming his way through "Call Me Back Again," a close cousin to "Oh! Darling." But even including Jimmy McCulloch's "Medicine Jar" (the only non-McCartney track besides the closing instrumental, "Crossroads Theme"), McCartney underestimates his new band's presence, especially in "Magneto and Titanium Man," his latest cartoon ditty. They grasp for more than the material can give them, and they wind up overplaying.

WINGS AT THE SPEED OF SOUND (1976), the record before the big tour, fared less well on stage; only four cuts were chosen to perform live: "Let 'Em In," a coy brass and marching-drum number where Paul tips his hat to Phil and Don Everly; "Time to Hide," a token Denny Laine number; "Silly Love Songs," where Paul, à la Presley, invites his audience to have a laugh on him; and "Beware My Love," patterned after the ranting and raving of "Helter Skelter" with none of the oblique panache. "Cook of the House," Linda's culinary puffball, is a feminist's nightmare. (The closing "Warm and Beautiful," a potentially gorgeous ballad, could still be revised and saved from its unfinished limbo.)

WHEN MCCARTNEY FINALLY put together his major tour with Wings after years of scheming and working out his visa status (which was complicated by drug busts), he did it as well as any former Beatle could have. Ever the showman, he noted Harrison's disinclination to play Beatles songs and made sure his act included the best of his solo singles (the high point was "Live and Let Die," his 1973 James Bond movie theme) as well as a few monumental classics. He was probably tired of "Yesterday," which by 1976 was eleven years old, but it had grown into a standard he couldn't *not* perform. He sang it alone at the end of an acoustic set that included Paul Simon's unlikely "Richard Cory" as well as "I've Just Seen a Face" and "Blackbird" (he also considered doing "Hey Jude" and "The Fool on the Hill"). He closed with "Band on the Run," encored with the lickety-split "Hi, Hi, Hi," and threw in a new number, "Soily," a sweltering finish.

Wings over America (1977), the three-record compilation from this tour, captures the spirit of these concerts handsomely and still ranks with other fine live sets (Elton John's *11/17/70*, the Band's *Rock of Ages*). Almost all of the Wings material fares better when punched up with the adrenaline the delirious audiences provided; "Lady Madonna" is still sassy after all these years, and "The Long and Winding Road," minus Phil Spector's strings, lives again. Even with a new phony ending to "Maybe I'm Amazed," this onstage version returned to the charts.

There is a memorable tag to the film of the tour (available on video as *Rock Show*), shot during the final concert in Seattle. After the last encore, Ringo embraces Paul backstage; they exchange modest compliments, engage in small talk, and generally play down what's happening around them. Although brief, the meeting has a very keen sense of where these two men have been together, all they have accomplished, and the irretrievable past that looms over their mock humility. In this moment, Paul's solo career seems quite removed from his enormous musical significance as a Beatle, and Ringo's ceaselessly good-natured air turns bittersweet.

"MULL OF KINTYRE" (1977), a ballad complete with bagpipes and marching drums that celebrates the McCartney home near the Hebrides, became one of Paul's all-time biggest hits, largely because of its instant local popularity in the British Isles (even though it never broke the top forty in

America). The insuppressible "yahoo"s in the final verse make it an inebriated pub standard. "Girls' School," the B side, is another charged rocker in the style of "Junior's Farm" and "Hi, Hi, Hi."

Beginning with *London Town* (1978), all semblance of the group Wings began to disintegrate—on this record, Denny Laine is the only surviving member, and even he left after its release. Along with *Back to the Egg* (1979), it revamps familiar McCartney themes with technically flawless productions: "With a Little Luck," the first record's musically lame (but smash) single, tries to update the optimism of "We Can Work It Out," "Fixing a Hole," and "Getting Better." The simplistic screamer "I've Had Enough" and the willfully sulky "London Town" became relatively successful follow-up singles, but the overlooked track is "Name and Address," another affectionate Presley imitation.

Back to the Egg auditions a new lineup—Steve Holly on drums and Laurence Juber on guitar. Their playing is more than competent, but the material is again sorely lacking. Some songs never seem to get going ("We're Open Tonight"); others try too hard ("Getting Closer"). "Spin It On" is the only clue that Paul has been listening to the punk explosion happening right under his nose; it bolsters its energy with sheer velocity. The "Rockestra Theme" is a bloated piece of instrumental trash, and "Baby's Request" sounds so much like another song that it probably is. His first album for his figure-busting Columbia contract hangs out on the charts briefly before getting sentenced for life to the budget bins.

In between records, the brightly textured disco of "Goodnight Tonight" (1979) reaffirms Paul's commercial instinct for another top ten hit, although not much else. By the time he compiled his set for the *Concert for the People of Kampuchea* (1981), a benefit he helped organize in Britain, he had reverted to several Beatles standbys as if admitting his own watered-down muse. The live horns on "Got to Get You into My Life" reinvigorate his singing, but the arrangement sticks so closely to the original that even when he ad-libs at the end he sings along with his former self. This contradicts his own pop ethic of prizing the spontaneity of the moment; instead of seeking out new spaces for excitement in this vocalist's showcase, he relives what it once was. There's more formal acuity when the band rips into "Lucille," the Little Richard song he used to play with the Beatles on BBC radio; and the live gospel feel that supports "Let It Be" makes this version almost preferable to Phil Spector's single mix: his little piano fill before the guitar solo is sprightly without being irreverent. (When Paul, at Bob Geldof's request, closes the 1985 Wembley Live Aid show with "Let It Be," his flippant delivery and pompous air detract from the song's heartfelt sentiment.)

His second single-handed effort, *McCartney II* (1980), shows a disappointing lack of growth from the first, considering that ten years separate the two. Ten years is a long time in pop—enough time for some to forget, others to grow up. One of the wrenching ironies of Paul's story is that young fans start to buy McCartney's and Wings' records without the slightest knowledge that he used to be a member of a sixties band called the Beatles. Like *McCartney*, *McCartney II* has its moments: "Coming Up" survives as a quirky texture piece but found greater commercial favor in its "live at Glasgow" rendition, despite its musical limitations; "Waterfalls" is an ambitious song about risk and loss with a haunting melody; and "Nobody Knows" is a scrappy rocker with a flawed lyric that streaks in at under three minutes, which helps. But nothing stands out like "Maybe I'm Amazed" or captures the endearing homespun demo charm of "Junk" and "Teddy Boy." The contrast between these two records is disappointingly telling: Paul should still throw away more songs than he uses.

BOTH *TUG OF WAR* (1982) and *Pipes of Peace* (1984) reunited McCartney with producer George Martin and capture Paul grappling with his weakness of abundance, even though both albums fall short of their high aspirations. *Rolling Stone* proclaimed the first his "masterpiece" (the same year that magazine misguidedly compared Elvis Costello's *Imperial Bedroom* with *Sgt. Pepper*). But despite the seamless production (the taut saxes on "Take It Away," the snazzed-up mix of "Ballroom Dancing," the coin clinking on "The Pound Is Falling"), the filigree keeps popping up ("I Know How You Feel," "Dress Me Up As a Robber"), and the stronger songs are forced to carry too much of the burden. The grunting noises on the title track are too literal, and his promising duet with Carl Perkins on "Get It" is saccharine countrybilly, the worst kind. "Ebony and Ivory," his duet with Stevie Wonder, is a single verse that Martin stretches out with the help of a key change. McCartney simply steps aside for Wonder's funky "What's That You're Doing?"—it's a Wonder track that sounds phoned in to someone else's record.

So it's paradoxical that Paul's Lennon tribute, "Here Today," is sadly stirring. The "Yesterday" guitar-plus-string-quartet arrangement sounds derivative at first but soon grows effectively poignant. Paul shares his *personal* memory of Lennon, a risky poetic conceit that works even though Lennon doesn't need McCartney to immortalize him. What Paul offers his audience goes far beyond what he usually offers up as sentiment—there is a fragility to this emotion, no matter how precious he makes the "playing hard to get" first meeting sound. For the first time since side two of *Abbey Road* (or since the impulse behind "Dear Friend"), McCartney reveals himself in a manner that speaks through the predictable setting—the voice that used to be raised in exultant harmony with his partner now wobbles with feeling.

"Wanderlust," side two's fulcrum, is the kind of stately piano ballad that makes it impossible to dismiss the record entirely; along with "Here Today," it makes one wish for so much more from McCartney. Its tune rests snugly above its three simple chords, and soon a countermelody enters that sounds as inspired as its foundation (it outdoes the contrived bit of three-part singing in "Silly Love Songs"). Martin's

tasteful horns are all decked out and at attention for Mc-
Cartney's vocal; the sound is majestic, round and satisfying.
It begs for better company.

"WONDERFUL CHRISTMAS TIME"/ "Rudolph the
Red-Nosed Reggae" (1982), Paul's Christmas single, contains
a forced round that makes "Silly Love Songs" sound like inspired counterpoint. Who would have thought that Paul
would wind up stealing from George ("ding-dong, ding-dong"
on side two of *Dark Horse)*? "Rudolph" is a play on an old
Beatles joke from the 1963 Christmas message, where John
erupts into "Ringo, the Red-Nosed Beatle."

PIPES OF PEACE suffers from its overly simplistic title track
and goes downhill from there. In "Average Person" the common touch McCartney would still like to affect is finally condescending; the pointless tribalism of "Tug of Peace" is a
contrived return that elevates *McCartney*'s finale ("Kreen-
Akrore") to the unselfconscious primitive. Since neither really
needed the extra exposure, the two Michael Jackson collaborations ("Say Say Say" and "This Is the Man") come off as
limp commercial moves. "Through Our Love," the closing
song, is out-and-out Muzak.

By the time McCartney filmed his own movie, even his
most fervent admirers had lost some faith in him. Instead of
developing a partnership with Britain's finest playwright,
Tom Stoppard, Paul sacked him early on to make *Give My
Regards to Broad Street* (1984), a self-written, updated *A
Hard Day's Night*. What's most disturbing are Paul's recasts
of two of his best Beatles songs: Ringo should have talked him
out of the stuffy Dickensian "Eleanor Rigby" film sequence,
never mind the weak vocal recording on the soundtrack;
"Here, There and Everywhere" becomes a mere skeleton of
its original beauty. Elaborate makeup spoils any pleasure that
might have been taken in watching crack sessionist (and Toto
member) Jeff Porcaro play drums on "Silly Love Songs." The

better moments come during a rehearsal scene, when Mc-
Cartney cuts loose with Chris Spedding, Dave Edmunds, and
Ringo for ensemble footage that might have approximated
the rooftop finale to *Let It Be* if not for the material ("Not
Such a Bad Boy" is unbearably prudish). Although "No More
Lonely Nights" redeems his stock on the charts, the movie is
a washout.

> I really dig myself as a bass player . . . I kind of fancy myself.
> As a singer I do, you know, and as a songwriter. Probably
> comes in that order. But then I can kind of play a bit of key-
> boards. It just depends on how I'm doing, really, I can play
> lousy keyboard, too (*Paul McCartney In His Own Words*,
> p. 39)

What's disconcerting about McCartney's estimation of
himself is his accuracy. Like Barbra Streisand and Michael
Jackson, he shortchanges his own potential as a vocalist by
demanding complete control of his work—his singing is still
peerless, but his material rarely lives up to what he can put
into it, and his bass playing never reaches the same virtuosic
lyricism he displayed on *Abbey Road*. He remains as gifted
as he is undisciplined. Some of his better post-Beatles songs
were written for others: for Peggy Lee, "Let's Love," a return
compliment for the obvious inspiration she provided him on
"Till There Was You"; for the Everly Brothers, "On the Wings
of a Nightingale." But "Spies Like Us" (1985), the title tune
for a Chevy Chase/Dan Aykroyd comedy thriller, sounds like
a discarded Queen arena anthem. McCartney's latest ven-
ture, *Press to Play* (1986), falls into the same traps despite a
new producer (Hugh Padgham) and a harder edge. In the
video to the single, "Press," Paul mugs for the camera as only
he can, getting lost in London's underground railway, be-
nignly unaware that getting lost on the subway only points
up how much he gets chauffeured around. When he runs
through "Get Back" and "I Saw Her Standing There" with

Tina Turner, Phil Collins, and other eighties superstars at Prince Charles's annual charity concert in 1986, he becomes a kind of kindhearted benefactor, beloved for what he once was more than for what he is now. Instead of building on his Beatles past, he lets it overwhelm him.

JOHN LENNON:

We All Shine On

> When two great Saints meet it is a humbling experience. The long battles to prove he was a Saint.
> (Paul McCartney, dedication to *Two Virgins*)

EVER SINCE HE made *How I Won the War* with Richard Lester in 1966, Lennon had trouble imagining himself apart from the band—his first wife, Cynthia, put it to him best: "You seem to need them even more than they need you." When John and Yoko began collaborating during the period surrounding the "White Album," it immediately provoked Lennon to turn away from the aimless profusion of "I Am the Walrus" and leap back onto his beloved Chuck Berry rhythms for "Revolution." In addition to forging a new partnership, the transition from Paul to Yoko became a deliverance; he gleaned greater insight and redemption from his first great love, rock 'n' roll, and he put it to work for the rest of his Beatles career (from "Everybody's Got Something to Hide, Except Me and My Monkey" up through the "One After 909" revival and "Come Together"). The flip side of this return to rock 'n' roll was an expansion of the experimentalism of "Tomorrow Never Knows" and "I Am the Walrus," which he continued outside of Beatles records ("Revolution No. 9" notwithstanding). Long before the band came apart, John and Yoko immersed themselves in their own gallery shows, films, lithograph projects, duo recordings, and performance experiments, all of which catalyzed his individual work and opened creative doors the other Beatles saw no use for.

Yoko seems to have convinced Lennon that rock 'n' roll really could be art if he wanted it to be. Where McCartney's popular solo work can sound aloof, Lennon's most revealing introspections are deliberately noncommercial. The craftsman in Lennon was almost always at the service of the artist; his hits ("Instant Karma," "Imagine," and "Starting Over") are more remarkable than McCartney's because of their searching emotional power.

In the early avant-garde records, there is a sense of adventure beside all the playful squeaks and squawks, as though he needed to vent the endless stream of ideas that roamed his imagination in order to settle his pop instincts down for his first independent solo project. *Plastic Ono Band*, his anguished goodbye letter to the Beatles in 1970, remains as difficult and challenging to some as the tape layers of "Revolution No. 9," but it remains his most deeply felt work, and it informs everything he did with the Beatles.

From there he reverted to *Imagine*'s brighter tone— "candy coated," as he called it—and added strings, which have a completely different effect on his material than they do on McCartney's. Afterwards, his solo work wandered, although the sense of personal struggle is always at play in the music. *Mind Games, Walls and Bridges*, and *Rock 'n' Roll* trace his midlife crisis until his self-imposed retirement in 1975, while his extremes as a Beatle magnify: what sounds uneven in McCartney sounds radically temperamental in Lennon; he rarely has the objectivity to distance himself from his records. Where Beatle Paul often threw Lennon's radical departures into high relief (the way "Hello Goodbye" floats astride "I Am the Walrus"), on his own Lennon can sound disconcertingly nostalgic ("Mind Games"), impassive ("Nobody Loves You When You're Down and Out"), and out of touch with his own roots (the embarrassing "Slippin' and Slidin' " and "Bony Maronie" on *Rock 'n' Roll)*.

Without McCartney, Lennon's sense of proportion sometimes falters. If Paul rarely sounds risky after the Beatles, John can sound all too risky, in unattractive ways. He can't seem to adopt any pose without taking it to extremes: *Some Time in New York City* is well intended but strident; *Rock 'n' Roll* is ambitious and somewhat overwrought; longer tracks like *Imagine*'s "I Don't Want to Be a Soldier Mama, I Don't Want to Die" are unpredictably comfortable in tone; and the larger tragic irony is not that Lennon was murdered on the eve of a comeback full of promise, but that *Milk and Honey*, the posthumous outtakes from the follow-up to those sessions, poises a more delicate balance between wistful sentiment ("Grow Old with Me") and humorous incredulity ("Nobody Told Me").

Like McCartney's, Lennon's singles tend to work better than his albums as totalities (except for *Plastic Ono Band*), but for different reasons. To begin with, he put out fewer of them (McCartney has released over thirty, Lennon has exactly fourteen), and except for the first four ("Give Peace a Chance," "Cold Turkey," "Instant Karma"—his best—and "Power to the People"), he lifted them all from albums instead of making them separate pieces. (McCartney is the only Beatle who continues making singles as separate entities well into the era of the mega-platinum multisingle albums in the eighties.) Lennon's growth wasn't as much musical as it was personal, for although he wrote his version of "Hey Jude" in "Instant Karma," he never penned another song that will be remembered as well as "Imagine"; and even though he got better at expressing his manic mood swings (his last hits, "Woman" and "Nobody Told Me," rank among his best), his partnership with McCartney seems to have provided him with a musical reckoning, the same way he intimidated Paul lyrically.

HE BEGINS WITH three avant-garde records. *Unfinished Music No. 1: Two Virgins*, his first collaboration with Yoko, came out alongside the "White Album" in November 1968, an extension of "Revolution No. 9" 's tape dialogues. The cover shows the naked couple standing by their strewn clothes, with gently naive expressions on their faces. The pictures were inflammatory—EMI refused to distribute the album, and thousands of copies were confiscated in New Jersey as obscene—but now seem relatively harmless, like the sounds inside: Yoko screeches, murmurs, cries, and wails, and John counters with scatterbrained asides ("It's just me, Hilda, I'm 'ome for tea . . .").

Unfinished Music No. 2: Life with the Lions (1969) features "Cambridge 1969," a long, severely atonal improvisational dialogue between Yoko's voice and John's guitar. Yoko twists and mangles her long "eh"s to mimic the antic distortions Lennon gets in his feedbacks, and his own engaged metalism winds around her vocal effects as if it wants to be human. Even the silences get eerie. Side two contains sounds recorded in Yoko's hospital bed before her 1968 miscarriage: "Baby's Heartbeat" is the sound of a microphone pressed up against her womb; "Radio Play" finds John spinning a radio dial, creating rhythms out of the static (the way rapmasters will use turntables later on to punch up rap music). The cover photo captures the Lennons surrounded by fans in front of the Marylebone registry after being arrested for possessing dope.

Their *Wedding Album* of the same year collects newspaper clippings and photographs for a souvenir album of pop's most notorious peaceniks, who invited the press into their honeymoon suite to promote the "War Is Over" campaign. Side one is another extended dialogue: John says "Yoko," Yoko answers, "John" for over twenty-two minutes. But the range of emotion they evoke with these two words transcends the self-indulgent framework: when Yoko erupts in piercing screams near the end and John responds in kind, the moment is ripe with pain and desire; at another point, they become deeply erotic. It ends as simply as it began, with a slight smirk of a question mark in their voices. Side two's "Amsterdam" is a day in the life of John and Yoko's Bed-in that begins with Yoko's opening prayer for peace and ends with "good night" mumblings. Their speeches to the press restate the hippie rhetoric of the left they mean to brighten with humor, but their intentions are lighthearted, and they clearly enjoy baffling the world's media.

THE HIT SINGLES that follow consign Yoko's relatively inaccessible art songs to B sides. "Give Peace a Chance" (1969) was recorded in their Toronto hotel room during one of their Bed-Ins for peace and captures an impromptu sing-along. Timothy Leary, Tommy Smothers, Derek Taylor, and a host of journalists join in the choruses, while John fills in the verses with run-on lists of "-isms" and "-tions" (shades of Chuck Berry's "Too Much Monkey Business"). Its comic overtones simplify the message underlying "Revolution": it doesn't talk down to radicals; it forms a coalition among its singers (like 1971's "Power to the People"). A few months later, "Cold Turkey" (1969) appeared, a brutally painful enactment of heroin withdrawal. John takes "I'm So Tired" 's key line ("I'd give you anything I've got for a little peace of mind") and unloads it into a scorching howl of self-torture ("I'll promise you *anything*/Get me out of this hell!!"). As the song fades, John's gut-pinched screams are surrounded by distressed guitars, using Yoko's vocal techniques as a model of invention.

Two weeks before the release of *Abbey Road* in September 1969, Lennon flew to Canada at the invitation of the Toronto Rock 'n' Roll Revival Festival to perform with a hastily assembled pick-up band: Eric Clapton, Klaus Voorman, and Alan White. Choosing fifties standards, they rehearsed on the plane, and the performance was captured on *The Plastic Ono Band—Live Peace in Toronto, 1969.* "Okay, we're just gonna do numbers that we know cos we've never played together before," Lennon says in apology before launching into Carl Perkins's "Blue Suede Shoes." The playing is heavy at first, almost hesitant, but Clapton pulls things along with his first solo, and Lennon seems to gain confidence from him—his second verse is more intense. "Money" sinks more into the gravity of the lick (piano traded for guitar), weighing the frenzy of John's *With the Beatles* version with angst. "Dizzy Miss Lizzie" is actually quick where the first two songs tend to drag. By the time Lennon settles into it, he lets out a few ad-libs of enjoyment, hoping to recapture the manic spirit of his all-night Hamburg sessions with these songs. (He was physically ill with nervousness before he took the stage.) But Clapton, Voorman, and White are still feeling each other out, and as good as they are, they never quite peak over the crest of the wave they all know is there.

To supplement his rock 'n' roll set, Lennon chose three solo numbers, all of them personal blues-based takes on the songs he had just sung. The weighty trudge of "Yer Blues" becomes the arrival point of "Blue Suede Shoes" 's resentment, "Money" 's determined punch, and "Dizzy Miss Lizzie" 's ego-scorching plea, and adds paranoia to all the emotional desperation. Yoko's high, birdlike calls above the band help give "Cold Turkey" the brittle texture of the single. John offers up "Give Peace a Chance" by saying, "I've forgotten all those bits in between, but I know the chorus, so . . . ," and he delivers a rousing chant of acceptance that works at redeeming all the blues this side has witnessed. (Side two is a long stretch of Yoko's grating dissonance—"Don't Worry Kyoko [Mummy's Only Looking for her Hand in the Snow]" and "John, John [Let's Hope for Peace].")

O N   T H E twenty-sixth day of the new decade, John woke up with a new song bouncing around in his head, and by evening he had written and recorded "Instant Karma" with Phil Spector, his answer to "Hey Jude," and the rock 'n' roll antecedent to the softer "Imagine." "I wrote it for breakfast, recorded it for lunch, and we're putting it out for dinner," Lennon quipped. The crude, obviously hurried mix does a lot for the message—that pop's impact can be instant, its force penetrating and incorporeal. It starts with the "Some Other Guy" lick that trips Richie Barrett's 1962 single, the jealous revel that Lennon sang with the Beatles on their live BBC broadcasts. With a sudden slink of Alan White's drums, Lennon turns this brief Barrett cop into a rousing piano-based testament to the power of pop. Quoting from one of his own favorites, he links his work up with the possibilities that early rock 'n' roll once held out for him.

Stephen Holden writes, "He turned the pop cliché that everyone's a star into a rousing, pro-life anthem":

> *Why in the world are we here?*
> *Surely not to live in pain and fear*
> *Why on earth are you there*
> *When you're everywhere, come get your share*
>
> *And we all shine on*
> *Like the moon and the stars and the sun. . . .*

"Revolution" said, "Don't put your faith in systems"; "Instant Karma" holds out exactly where faith is best invested: in ourselves. As in "Hey Jude," this vision is put across with more than just words; the tentative lone voice that counts off "Three, four" is joined by the end with a choir of unprofessional voices—people were recruited whimsically from a nearby nightclub, and George Harrison was dubbed choirmaster. The sound is rough, not grand, and White's two drum breaks that answer Lennon's rhetorical questions ("Why in the world are we here?") punctuate their spaces with dauntless, lopped-off sprints—the mood is compelling, the immediacy gripping. "Cold Turkey" reveals an impoverished morality by trying to reclaim it; "Instant Karma" finds enlightenment through the darkness it confronts, and rings that much truer as a single, a context unto itself.

.   .   .

DR. ARTHUR JANOV'S primal scream therapy, which John and Yoko experienced during the summer of 1970, influenced *Plastic Ono Band*, Lennon's first real solo album, to a marked degree: these confessional songs seek out the idealized state of childhood, the pain of individuation, the fragility of fantasies and the very real power of illusions. The directness of his late-period-Beatles blues ("Don't Let Me Down," "Yer Blues," and "I Want You [She's So Heavy]") fuses with the gnarled emotional cores of "Strawberry Fields Forever" and "She Said She Said." Minimal ensemble settings (Ringo on drums, Voorman on bass, occasional piano from producer Spector and Billy Preston) punctuate the album's stark musical landscape, carving beauty from buried pain—the simplest of gestures glean chilling effect from their modest means, and the act of reduction increases the import of everything Lennon sings about. The soul-bearing leanness of the sound embodies the crux of what rock 'n' roll is all about: a restlessness with the status quo, a hopeful dissatisfaction, and a gnawing sense of encumbrance that finds release as it expresses itself.

The music hinges on elemental contrasts: verses sit in different meters than their refrains ("I Found Out," "Isolation," "Remember," "Well Well Well"), Ringo's drum patterns shift quixotically, and distorted guitar effects taunt and tease the extraordinary vocal inflections. (The vocal resonance throughout resembles the kind of reverb Jerry Lee Lewis got on 1957's "Whole Lotta Shakin' Goin' On.") Everything promulgates the contradictory impulses in Lennon's personality, from the allegiance to rock's early spirit (quoting the opening line to Sam Cooke's "Bring It on Home to Me" in "Remember") to the sudden yelp of "Cookie!" that interrupts "Hold On" (after "Sesame Street" 's Cookie Monster). The intensity is offset by frail laments ("Hold On," "Look at Me," "Love "), making the conclusion, "God," a chimerical mixture of denial and hope, a meditation on truth and conceptualization that strips pop formula to essence. Like "A Day in the Life," "God" overwhelms the world it follows. The postlude, "My Mummy's Dead," echoes the faint sing-songy tune that was slowed for "Mother," a bookend that makes plain the loss behind all the other songs, the pain at the center of the record. As Robert Christgau wrote in his *Record Guide* (p. 224):

> The real music of the album inheres in the way John's greatest vocal performance, a complete tour of rock timbre from scream to whine, is modulated electronically—echoed, filtered, double-tracked, with two vocals sometimes emanating in a synthesis from between the speakers and sometimes dialectically separated. Which means that John is such a media artist that even when he's fervently shedding personas and eschewing metaphor he knows, perhaps instinctively, that he communicates most effectively through technological masks and prisms.

THE SOMBER BELLS in the opening moments are foreboding peals of mourning; Lennon's voice suddenly breaks free from them in an impossibly high held note, as gorgeous as it is distressed, and he soars above ominously struck piano chords that slowly decay beneath Ringo's framing drums. The melody is a child's lullaby decelerated to a dirge.

With his aching falsetto hitting notes he has no right to hit, Lennon's vocal performance turns "Mother" into an agonized exorcism of parentage as well as an omen. The shadow of his abandonments, so long hinted at behind his Beatles group identity (jealous outbursts like "You Can't Do That," "I'll Get You," "No Reply," and "Run for Your Life"), breaks through with a deeply felt realism. "A lot of people thought it was about my parents," he says during his introduction to this song at the One to One benefit concert, "but it's about ninety-nine percent of the parents, alive or half-dead"—and by extension, the longing for closeness that touches everybody's life. Each verse changes subjects while exploring the same hurt: "Mother" is first, "Father" is second, and the last verse addresses his audience directly with a concise metaphor for his years inside the bubble:

> Children don't do what I have done
> I couldn't walk, so I tried to run
> So I just gotta tell you
> Goodbye, goodbye

"Mother" has a hollowness to it that nearly swallows Lennon's gnawing delivery in its desperation. The music doesn't rise or swell—it contracts, relenting from its tightly drawn spaces only in the final triplet syncopations where Lennon sings "Mama don't go/Daddy come home . . ." Even then, the syncopations don't lift the beat; they twist things together. He shrieks convulsively into the fade-out.

W HEN LENNON WAS killed, he was eulogized by those who didn't know better as a "Working Class Hero," an image he knew to be false even though he did little to clarify it when he was alive. The song itself is a resentful riot act read to the bourgeois social system that spurs competition as it smashes creativity and promotes alienation (he sings alone, accompanied only by his dry, Dylanesque guitar). It has such a bitter flavor that it might have been banned as an antiestablishment diatribe even without the obscenities:

> *They hurt you at home and they hit you at school*
> *They hate you if you're clever and they despise a fool . . .*
>
> *Keep you doped with religion and sex and TV*
> *And you think you're so clever and classless and free*
> *But you're still fucking peasants as far as I can see*
> *A working class hero is something to be*

Lennon prized the impact of extremes, whether it was pledging his love to Yoko ("I Want You") or venting his anger at the Maharishi ("Sexy Sadie"). "Working Class Hero" is harsh; but for all the finger pointing, his detached sarcasm on the line "If you want to be a hero then just follow me" admits a certain degree of culpability; as much as the Beatles wanted to shake the world up, they too were seduced by the wealth and prestige of fame. The serenity of "Imagine" sounds all the more hopeful when measured against the cultural neurosis Lennon sketches here. "Silly Love Songs" can actually typify Paul's approach; "Working Class Hero" operates as a stringent backlash to the flower-power optimism John and Yoko's Bed-Ins unwittingly epitomized.

SIDE TWO BEGINS with "Remember," the quickest groove here, and the most perpetually frightening. The subject is looking back, but not as nostalgically as in "Penny Lane"— the remembrances here are oppressive, an adult trying to make sense of early hurts, and only the bridge tries to put things in perspective:

> *And don't feel sorry* _____
> *'Bout the way it's gone*
> *And don't you worry* _____
> *'Bout what you've done*

The meter gets chopped in half for those lines to allow Lennon a sweeping vocal, and for a moment the tension relaxes. But the return to the verse is inescapable; experience gets trapped by time.

Adultism is the first prejudice, the most unintentional seed of resentment. "Remember when you were small/How people seemed so tall" seems naively obvious until the tag line: "Always had their way." Parents' dreams for their children ("Just wishing for movie stardom") dissolve into unrealized images of selfhood: "Always playing a part." Lennon keeps the other players on their toes by taking his time before spitting out lines, disrupting the regular meter as he goes, and forcing bassist Voorman to constantly second-guess where to land. In its first-or-second-take feel, it captures the rush of memory with a momentum that seems to feed on itself: only the bridges let the players expand with relief from the relentless beat; the overall tone is hastily out of breath.

Coming out of the second and last bridge, Lennon throws everything away—"Remember . . . remember . . . / The fifth of November." Guy Fawkes Day is a national holiday in Britain: Fawkes is a celebrated antihero because he failed to burn down the Houses of Parliament in 1606—a monument still stands there to commemorate his inefficacy. It's the only way Lennon can get out of what he's set in motion; the song pulls so strongly back into the pulse of the verses after each bridge that aside from fading it out (which would sound mannered), the only way to finish it off is by blowing it apart. But the image of Guy Fawkes is a curious one—a failed revolutionary, England's Benedict Arnold, an annual historical scapegoat for nationalists. It's appropriately absurd for Fawkes to trigger the jarring end of this song; it reinforces the lunacy of empty tradition.

LIKE ''IN MY LIFE,'' "God" (the finale) finds promise and renewal only by acknowledging the separations implicit in new beginnings. After the repeated, awkward opening line ("God is a concept by which we measure our pain"), Lennon renounces a string of heroes, gods, leaders, and gurus, building toward the rock myths that once held his own imagination—Elvis, Zimmerman (Dylan) . . . the Beatles. He reverses the direction of "Hey Jude" by moving toward a declamatory silence (after the climactic line "I don't believe in Beatles"), which falls toward Lennon's timorous but resolute falsetto on the concluding lines ("The dream is over . . .") to convey his individual redemption. The litany is spellbinding: the musicians push and pull against the major and minor axes that ensnare the words, and both the introduction and conclusion brace the denunciations with the simplest doo-wop progression (I–vi–IV–V, a slower version of the "bang-bang, shoot-shoot" refrain to "Happiness Is a Warm Gun"). The effect is strangely nonsatirical, uncannily straightforward and direct, and conveys both how easily pop myths are created and how resistant they are to disassembly.

Plastic Ono Band outstrips the other three solo Beatle debuts with a brutal but still romantic honesty and a chilling but compelling rhythmic undertow. With Springsteen's *Nebraska* (1982), it holds an iconoclastic position in the sphere of superstar albums: it was obviously anathema to commercial tastes, but it managed to succeed on terms entirely foreign to popular standards. (Both albums broke the top ten easily, *Nebraska* peaking at number three, *Plastic Ono Band* at number six.)

I N T H E D A Y S A N D W E E K S after Lennon's stupefying murder, "Imagine" acquired an unbearable sadness; future generations will never be able to appreciate it in its pure form. But the song is strong enough to survive nearly any context: as the opening track on the eponymous 1971 album, it sets the tone for a brighter, more accessible record than *Plastic Ono Band;* as a single its chart life gave off a radiant hue, the seventies equivalent to "She Loves You" or "I Want to Hold Your Hand."

"Imagine" sounds born to the world, not invented. It feels ageless, and has become as sure a classic as "Yesterday," even though it's much harder to pull off; Lennon's presence in the song itself is so strong that anyone else's version—a Joan Baez's or an Elton John's—seems irrelevant. Unfortunately, its utopian spirit gets diluted when it sits outside the rest of his catalogue. Lennon's hope for the world is inseparable from the despair he expressed; "Imagine" simply wouldn't be as much of a song if it didn't spring from the same unsettled spirit that gave us "A Day in the Life" and "Happiness Is a Warm Gun." Its universality is at once embracing and specific; the deceptively facile musical surface has a deeply personal inward tone.

The rest of the album clings to brighter colors and thick mixes even when the lyrics probe fundamental conflicts. "I Don't Want to Be a Soldier Mama, I Don't Want to Die" has a Spectorian scope and impenetrability to it, and without the randy sax solo "It's So Hard" might have fit on *Plastic Ono Band.* "Give Me Some Truth" pits Lennon's angered demand for justice against a high, ringing guitar line that anticipates that of "Mind Games"; "Jealous Guy" recalls the confusion and timidity of "If I Fell" and "Yes It Is" with a mature frankness (Bryan Ferry sang a regrettable tribute cover in early 1981).

"How Do You Sleep?" is a cutting open letter to Paul, which starts out with *Sgt. Pepper* hemming and hawing, the studio players sitting in for the fake audience:

A pretty face may last a year or two
But pretty soon they'll see what you can do
The sound you make is Muzak to my ears
You must've learned something in all those years . . .

The strings that swarm those words are embittered Muzak, the kind of hateful scorn that reveals the insecurity about what it lashes out against (as in "Run for Your Life" or "Sexy Sadie"). Lennon's viciousness underscores the closeness of their partnership, despite the denials he was then dropping to the press in his interviews. (McCartney's reply, "Dear Friend" on *Wild Life,* sounds almost at a loss for words.)

Imagine closes with a carefree 1968 love song to Yoko, complete with robust harmonica. In many ways, this album works as a respite from the raw fear and vulnerability that move *Plastic Ono Band*—the pain is still there, but it's made more accessible with lighter moments ("Crippled Inside" and "Oh Yoko!"); it becomes part of a larger sensibility. Ironically, it's the one Lennon solo album where McCartney's influence is overt. Together, these first two records represent Lennon's best work alone.

IN AUGUST OF 1971, a month before the release of *Imagine,* John and Yoko moved to Greenwich Village in New York City, where they met up with Jerry Rubin and flung themselves into radical politics: an American Indians' civil rights protest in Syracuse, New York; a John Sinclair rally in Ann Arbor, Michigan; and in October, the recording of "Happy Xmas (War Is Over)," a heartfelt seasonal jingle recorded with the Harlem Children's Choir. (The B side, Yoko's "Listen the Snow Is Falling," is her prettiest and most soulful ballad.) In early 1972, they guest-hosted "The Mike Douglas Show," where John sang "Memphis, Tennessee" and "Johnny B. Goode" with his idol Chuck Berry.

In the spring of 1972, John and Yoko hired the Elephant's Memory band to record their *Some Time in New York City* album, an almost repellent string of agitprop songs that came out in June. The musical flavor is sour, the tone that "Revolution" overcomes; and only "Woman Is the Nigger of the World" and "New York City" stand out as political ideas that work well as songs. It's as though they decided to produce an entire record built around different versions of "Working Class Hero" and "Give Me Some Truth" with all the attendant leftist clichés; their hearts are in the right place, but their intentions constrict their better musical instincts. (An immodest extra record pits "Cold Turkey" and "Don't Worry Kyoko" from a 1969 Lyceum Ballroom performance with a 1971 Fillmore East jam with Frank Zappa and the Mothers of Invention.)

Elephant's Memory served as his backup band in August for a benefit performance for handicapped children called One to One. The show was filmed for television, but an album wasn't released commercially until 1986, as *John Lennon: Live in New York City.* Lennon's apologies ("Welcome to the rehearsal") key the in-house nature of the project—it's a lesser live album than even *Live Peace in Toronto*. Only "Come Together" compares with the original Beatles version; lyrics fly all over the place, but the basic rock 'n' roll lick stands up well, and the vocal breaks are severe and punchy.

I N 1 9 7 3 , Lennon was ordered by the U.S. Immigration authorities to leave the United States, ostensibly because of drug busts in England dating to 1968 but ultimately part of the Nixon administration's paranoia concerning his political activities (detailed in Jon Wiener's *Come Together*). While appealing his visa status, he separated from Yoko and settled in Los Angeles, where he hung out with Keith Moon, Harry Nilsson, and Ringo, drinking heavily and recording simply because he had nothing better to do. Three records came out of this period, which Lennon called his "lost weekend"; and although each has a particular flavor—each stronger in its way than *Some Time in New York City*—they all sound lackluster, with only an occasional dash of insight. The first of these, *Mind Games* (1973), is the least memorable. Its best songs—the title single, "I Know (I Know)"—can't carry the dross of "Tight A$," a throwaway, or the near-hit "One Day at a Time." There's a lack of focus in the writing that draws attention to the lack of interplay among the studio musicians, and it sounds as distant as Lennon will ever get.

Without a moment's pause, John began work on a lifelong dream: to sing an album of oldies with producer Phil Spector. The project started in late 1973, but because of intervening projects (his production work on Nilsson's *Pussy Cats*, Spector's notorious crackups, and the ongoing immigration hearings), the album was delayed for another year before John returned to work on production himself at New York's Record Plant. By the time it was released in 1975, only four Spector tracks remained (Chuck Berry's "You Can't Catch Me" and "Sweet Little Sixteen" plus "Bony Maronie" and "Just Because"). Ben E. King's "Stand By Me" gets the best reading and produced a hit single. But *Rock 'n' Roll* suffers when compared with oldies collections like the Band's *Moon-dog Matinee* (1973). Lennon's usually assured delivery comes out in fits and starts; even "Bony Maronie," the only Larry Williams cover, doesn't have half the resolve of his early Williams treatments, like "Dizzy Miss Lizzie" and "Bad Boy."

You can hear what Spector was trying to do with Lennon: cast him as a producer's "singer" in his huge sonic firmament. But these massive, echoing arrangements—the same formulas Spector relied on for his sixties masterpieces (the Crystals' "Da Doo Ron Ron," the Righteous Brothers' "You've Lost That Lovin' Feelin'," among others)—tend to surround lesser vocalists, who rely on the surging waves of sound to cushion them. Though Spector had a gift for making fair-to-good singers sound incredible—you come away from the Ronettes' "Walking in the Rain" thinking "What a record!" not "What a singer!"—Lennon doesn't get a chance to declaim in this setting; he simply sits back and lets the music float by—it robs him of his unguarded drama. When he dares himself to reapproach Spector's own "To Know Her Is to Love Her," the wondrous ballad of devotion he used to sing with the Beatles, he lets Spector stretch it out into a gaudy display of glitzy vulnerability (it winds up on *Menlove Avenue,* among outtakes from these and other sessions that Yoko released in 1986). When Lennon makes the undulating tempos work for him (in an enthralling—and enthralled—version of the Ronettes' "Be My Baby"), it doesn't make the final cut. *Rock 'n' Roll* winds up less the must-do project it began as than the rush-release it became. (Morris Levy's *Roots,* an illegal bootleg of these sessions, forced a hurried completion schedule.)

Lennon's appealed citizenship trial required his presence back in New York City come 1974, so he continued work on *Rock 'n' Roll* as he began his next solo work, *Walls and Bridges,* in order to keep apace of court costs (his Beatles assets were frozen by numerous Allen Klein suits). Even though *Walls and Bridges* is a more depressed record than *Mind Games*, it's closer to its subject and has more committed song craft in its favor. Elton John's appearance on "Whatever Gets You Through the Night" is an unusual reversal of favors—the new hitmaster helping out the seasoned veteran for his first number-one solo single. (Lennon returns the gesture by playing guitar on Elton's versions of "Lucy in the Sky with Diamonds" and "One Day at a Time"). Elsewhere, "Bless You" is a haunted lullaby sung to Yoko that sees through jealousy to find an undying love; "Scared" and "Nobody Loves You When You're Down and Out" are frightened texture pieces in the mold of *Imagine*'s "I Don't Want to Be a Soldier"; "#9 Dream" is a visionary piece that recalls "Across the Universe"; and "Surprise, Surprise (Sweet Bird of Paradox)" and "What You Got" are two upbeat confections that work as danceable foils to the surrounding uncertainties.

Although the self-portraiture of "Steel and Glass" sounds bleak and nearly hopeless (especially on *Menlove Avenue*), the most disturbing track here is "Nobody Loves You When You're Down and Out," which works as the inverse of "Imagine." It matches his signature single's hope with regret and jaded ambivalence; when he sings "it's all show biz," you know he doesn't want to believe it, but when he stumbles into his own epitaph ("Everybody loves you when you're six feet in the ground"), you know he's not just getting sentimental. This is the burnt-out side of the monstrosities in Lennon—aghast at his own celebrityhood—that most people leave out of their eulogies.

Lennon appeared on stage with Elton John on Thanksgiving of 1974 at Madison Square Garden to play "Lucy in the Sky with Diamonds" (which had reached number one), "Whatever Gets You Through the Night," and "I Saw Her Standing There," which he introduced as "a number by an old estranged fiancé of mine called Paul." Backstage after the concert, he and Yoko reconciled. ("I Saw Her Standing There" appears on the B side to Elton's 1975 disco salute to Billie Jean

King, "Philadelphia Freedom.") The following January he collaborated with David Bowie on his *Young Americans* album, penning "Fame" with him and contributing guitar to Bowie's glam-rock rendition of "Across the Universe." *Rock 'n' Roll* was released in February, but it wasn't until the next fall that a U.S. Court of Appeals overturned the deportation order and Lennon was granted citizenship. On October 9, his thirty-fifth birthday, Yoko gave birth to Sean Ono Lennon, and John's long legal battle ended. "I feel higher than the Empire State Building," he said. *Shaved Fish*, (1975), the Christmas collection album that starts with "Give Peace a Chance" and moves through singles up to "#9 Dream," came out later the same month.

THE LAST FIVE YEARS of Lennon's life were spent with Yoko, raising Sean in their New York apartment. When he re-emerged with *Double Fantasy* in 1980, "Watching the Wheels" described his disengagement from the pop world, a dizzy existence that Lennon was happy to be rid of. The entire record has a clear, open texture that revives the optimism of "Imagine." The bells that tick off "Starting Over" sound like kitchen timers, domesticating the morbid gongs at the top of *Plastic Ono Band*; it became his second number-one single. When he sings "But when I see you, darlin'/It's like we both start fallin' in love again," he openly parodies the tongue-in-cheek charm of Brian Wilson's "Don't Worry Baby" (it resembles Wilson's melodic sequence in that song on the words "when she makes love to me"). It's the kind of wit that Lennon's solo career too often lacks, and it signals a newfound comfort with life.

The record is an alternating duet between John and Yoko, with songs sung to each other and to Sean: Yoko's "Kiss Kiss Kiss" is an intensely passionate coitional workout; "Cleanup Time" is a playfully gentle gibe at household chores that works as an adult song about addiction; John's "I'm Losing You" is answered by Yoko's "I'm Moving On"; John's lullaby to Sean, "Beautiful Boy," is countered by Yoko's love song to both of them, "Beautiful Boys." (John leaves behind his own vocal treatment of Yoko's "Every Man Has a Woman Who Loves Him" for her fiftieth birthday present, a collection of her songs sung by various artists released under the same name. In the drawn-out phrases, he finds his own personal space in Yoko's spacious contours, and she trades roles from the *Double Fantasy* version, shadowing his lead elegantly.)

"Woman" is a medium-tempo guitar-textured single with Beatlesque vocal harmonies that restores Lennon's gift for musical joyrides (it's a mature version of "I Should Have Known Better" or "Eight Days a Week"). And even though "I'm Losing You" is a frightened exercise in loss, it fills the darker moments of the record less severely than *Plastic Ono Band;* the prevailing mood is warm and generous. "Beautiful Boy" uses a delicate Oriental pentatonicism to convey a fatherly adoration; McCartney still calls it one of his favorites. The lyric contains the most penetrating line of Lennon's late career: "Life is what happens to you while you're busy making other plans."

ALTHOUGH MILK AND HONEY (1983) is comprised of unfinished tracks, it hangs together extremely well—the incompleteness has its own sense of possibilities. "I Don't Want to Face It" is a raunchier version of "Watching the Wheel," and "Nobody Told Me" is a scrappy return to basics with a lyric that decries the anomie of the eighties almost before they got started (it was presumably written in the pall of the first Reagan landslide). "Grow Old with Me" may not turn out to be the wedding standard Lennon intended it to be, but its disarmingly simple melody stands up well, the kind of intuitive songful grace that informs "Jealous Guy" and "Love." There's an intimacy to this recording—done as a demo on their house piano with a rhythm box—that makes it the mature answer to *Plastic Ono Band*'s nightmarish "My Mummy's Dead."

These last two records overcome the midlife crisis of Lennon's solo career (*Mind Games* and *Walls and Bridges*)—a new partnership is finding its way in the music, sharing experience and a common purpose. The hopeful direction they were pointed in made his death impossibly cruel and canonized him as the kind of pop martyr he never wanted to be. It's clear that by the end he had made a certain peace with himself and his family, and if his mid-seventies efforts sound strained and deliberate, his final recordings return to the uncalculated sense of expression he found so easily with the Beatles. He wasn't creating for other people (the way McCartney can still seem to); he was reclaiming his personal musical language as an artist.

Between *Plastic Ono Band*'s barren and scathing deliverance and *Double Fantasy*'s gentle acceptance, there's an undeniable personal growth that defines Lennon's songwriting. Where Paul conceived his music more and more as craft, and eventually as product, John used his skill to make sense of his feelings. Paul deliberately set out to write hits ("Junior's Farm," "Girls' School," "Goodnight Tonight"); John's commercial success was more a consequence of his musical intuition ("Instant Karma," "Imagine," "Woman"). The distance measures the difference between the ways Paul and John worked and helps explain what they discovered as partners: even at their most incompatible ("A Day in the Life"), they completed one another.

POP IS STILL catching up with the Beatles. By the time punk paved the way for more lasting talents like the Talking Heads to emerge, it was clear that any significant pop inheritors would have to shatter the model and make claims to greatness on their own terms, just as the Beatles did. There simply isn't any way to "top" what they accomplished—the next pop thunderbolt will necessarily take a completely different shape. Bruce Springsteen is beginning to be touted as Presley's legitimate heir, but his music works on less innovative terms: his mature songs are topical, but hard-boiled and reductive; he acts persuasively as though punk, disco, first-person and singer-songwriters never happened and weren't important. As a child ·star and a reclusive adult, Michael Jackson may already have played out his hand; his records will probably not survive as long as his videos.

The Beatles will always be tagged sixties artists, but it's remarkable how well their songs step around time. Their music still projects a sense of engagement with the world, because very few lyrics rely on topical issues ("She's Leaving Home," perhaps). "Revolution" was actually misheard as solely about current issues in 1968, but it survives as universal. Even the names they gave their characters seem antiquated, almost Victorian: Eleanor Rigby, Father Mackenzie, Lucy, Henry, Rita, Jude, Prudence, Martha, Julia, Sadie. The bulk of their catalogue operates on images of continuing pertinence; they struck nerves that were both immediate and lasting, so much so that twenty years later their records fit snugly into radio segues in and out of contemporary hits without sounding the least bit dated.

That the tone of Beatles records—the emotional space these four players could summon up together and the heights of feeling they committed to tape—continues to enthrall us is a comment on more than just the music itself; like the limits that Elvis Presley's voice overcomes, or Rosie and the Originals' inspired bad joke, the Beatles' expansive artistry exists as metaphor as much as music. All great music symbolizes integration; the Beatles sharpened that dynamic by making it a drama of personalities as well as sounds—the fluid reciprocity they achieve as writers and players signifies much more than musical analysis alone can get at. And the games they play with their audience make it clear how much the Beatles enjoyed being the Beatles: at the height of their popularity *(Sgt. Pepper)*, they were still confident enough in their abilities to stay lighthearted about their success.

The mass catharsis that the entire world experienced in

the days after Lennon's death demonstrates the power of their music to bring people of vastly different attitudes and outlooks together. They became the world's family, and their music continues to both embody and enact procreative interplay; when they covered "Twist and Shout," they wanted to get everybody dancing, not just on the dance floor but in everyday life. They play up this central idea in as many ways as possible: confronting harsh realities with shared fantasies; acknowledging the tension between life as it could be and life as it is; relishing the peculiar thrill of emotional intelligence ("Hey Jude," "Instant Karma") and the cleansing effect of shared despair ("Eleanor Rigby," "Don't Let Me Down").

It's reassuring how boldly and irreverently their catalogue flies in the face of postmodernism, squelching the ethic that art is exhausted, that existence is meaningless. The idea of undiscovered possibilities between people is the biggest metaphor on Beatles records, and in this sense they inspire us all. The opposing sensibilities that they weaved into invigorating harmonies still argue that their similarities were far greater than their differences. By extension, the world's continuing embrace of what they produced demonstrates that our collective strength lies in emphasizing what we have in common. It's our connections with people that make us most human, the Beatles seem to be telling us; our interaction with others fulfills the biggest part of our humanity.

EPILOGUE TO THE
SECOND EDITION

Albums
1. Parlophone catalogue on CD (EMI/Capitol/Apple), released 1987–88
2. The Complete EP Collection (EMI/Capitol), released 1992
3. *Live at the BBC* (EMI/Capitol/Apple), released 1994
4. *Anthology* CDs Vols 1–3 (EMI/Capitol/Apple), released 1995–96
5. *Yellow Submarine* (EMI/Capitol/Apple), released 1999

Books
1. *The Beatles' Recording Sessions*, by Mark Lewisohn (Harmony, 1988)
2. *The Complete Beatles Chronicle*, by Mark Lewisohn (Harmony, 1992)
3. *Many Years from Now*, by Paul McCartney with Barry Miles (Henry Holt, 1997)
4. *The Beatles Anthology*, by the Beatles (Chronicle Books, 2000)

WHEN THIS BOOK first appeared in 1988, the Beatles' career was a closed subject. Unless you were a bootleg scavenger, the arc that went from 1963's *Please Please Me* to 1969's *Abbey*

Road and 1970's *Let It Be* had enough thoughtful curves to exert anxiety of influence over generations of bands to come. The arc is now classic: early idealism followed by middle-period maturity—and as Mark Moses pointed out in the *Boston Phoenix*: "conceptual coup [*Sgt. Pepper*], renunciation of conceptual coup [*White Album*], roots move, fall to pieces." You could scour post-career compilations like *Rock 'n' Roll* or *Reel Music* for touchups to mixes, "fixed" mistakes, and the odd remaster, but basically the story was over, the solo careers were half-hearted apologies to expired greatness, and Lennon's death precluded any real reunion talk.

Several major, Beatle-driven developments have since blown their story apart, changed its meanings, and altered the band's glow for future generations. For starters, simply the choice of Jeff Lynne (the former Electric Light Orchestra frontman, then George Harrison's mate in the Traveling Wilburys) over original producer George Martin (who oversaw all the CD transfers) as producer of the new mid-90s reunion singles on the *Anthology Vols. 1–3*, gave the updated Beatles a vastly different color than before. The death of George Harrison on November 29, 2001, made the reunion project seem more justified, even if it grew from a mixture of emerging rock fatalism, sullied reputations, and financial incentives than any magical spark of inspiration. After all, in the midst of reunions by the likes of Supertramp and Kansas, would the Beatles remain the only major rock group *not* to reunite in proof of their relevance to rock's enduring audience? Several external factors played into reunion fever, extending its effect and imbuing it with more respectability than it probably deserves. In the aftermath of Harrison's death, the *Anthology* acquired a bittersweet finality.

On a ceremonial level, the Beatles have long since passed into High Respectability, above and beyond their 1965 MBEs[1]. Thirty years later, in June of 1996, producer George Martin was honored with a knighthood, and at the end of that year, after the *Anthology* video and CD package enriched England's tax coffers, Paul McCartney became the first Beatle honored with a knighthood; he is henceforth known as Sir Paul McCartney. The actual knighthood ceremony was held March 10, 1997. In a statement, Paul said he accepted the honor ". . . on behalf of all the people of Liverpool and the other Beatles, without whom it wouldn't have been possible. So I hope I can be worthy of it." George and Ringo jokingly called him "His Holiness."

The larger context for the Beatles' reunion was steered by overlapping musical and legal twists; each of the Beatles needed to settle old scores for different reasons. McCartney's motive was largely aesthetic: as the richest man in show business (even without owning his own songwriting catalog), his ears still told him that his creative reputation would forever rest on his work with his first band. Amid a slew of lackluster solo albums with and without his '70s band, Wings, he commanded the world's stages as a renowned songwriter who wrote perhaps one solid song for every thirty that rolled out of him, and had little if no incentive to finish many of his more promising numbers ("Wanderlust," or even one of his biggest hits, "Mull of Kintyre," or the Super Bowl jingoism of "Freedom"). His defensive tone in his authorized biography, and during many interviews (where he berated Yoko Ono for refusing to give him top songwriting credit for "Yesterday"), led Mim Udovitch to write, "[He] makes you want to sit down and write him a letter saying, " 'Dear Sir Paul: Anybody who really knows recognizes that without your superb musicianship, the Beatles could not have been. You are a fully a co-genius with the late John Lennon. Now please relax.' "[2] He twice triumphed merely by turning to other people's material, first one *Choba b CCCP (The Russian Album)* (EMI/Capitol, 1989), and then, after his wife Linda died of breast cancer, on *Run Devil Run* (EMI/Capitol) in 1999. Each fallback move proved exactly how much McCartney still had in him, especially vocally, and how much he'd thrown away by acting as his own Executive Producer. *Run Devil Run* especially disarmed fans and critics by being some of the best work of his post-Beatle career, and stands alongside much of his cover tracks with the Beatles as well.

Ringo Starr sobered up and ran his semi-annual summer touring camp for has-beens, and Harrison popped in and out of the limelight, recording *Live in Japan* with Eric Clapton in late 1991, bopping on stage for a disarming "Absolutely Sweet Marie" at Dylan's 30th Anniversary Celebration (of his first Columbia recording) in New York. But McCartney's career was both the most bloated and the most uninspired—at least Harrison put out fewer records. McCartney could have taken a cue from Harrison, who triumphed with the Traveling Wilburys, a group of icons (Harrison, Roy Orbison, Bob Dylan, Tom Petty, and Jeff Lynne) that sent up the shared burdens of fame and aging on two deliberately low-key albums. The second contains an understated Harrison tribute to Orbison, "You Take My Breath Away." The Wilburys would be completely harmless if it weren't for Lynne's participation: his production is bland to the point of distraction, as if some of the more original voices in pop can't sound any more distinctive than the boldly derivative Electric Light Orchestra. As a sideline it's a forgivable lark; as prelude to Lynne's work on the Beatles' reunion, it's unthinkable.

TELL ME WHY hit stores just as this new story was getting started. In 1987, EMI/Capitol began reissuing the entire Parlophone album catalogue in the new compact disc format (with two discs devoted to singles' collections as *Past Masters I & II*, 1988) which was just then becoming the dominant medium. Early on, the controversy surrounded EMI's decision to release the first four CDs in mono only, claiming that the stereo mixes were "unavailable," and making George Martin the fall guy. Since one of the primary aims of *Tell Me Why* was to cue American ears to the original British sequences, this commercial repackaging was serendipitous, as future generations will most likely get to know the Beatles in digital form instead of vinyl. There are bootleggers and collectors who still prefer their Capitol sequences of *The Beatles' Second Album* or *Yesterday and Today*, but there is much wider agreement now about how the Beatles intended their songs to be heard, and not just because of digital technology's brighter, more detailed reproduction.

Around the same time that Albert Goldman published his hysterically tabloid life of John Lennon (*The Lives of John*

Lennon, originally *Nowhere Man*), Mark Lewisohn resurfaced from the basement of Abbey Road studios after listening to the entire library of master tapes. His book, *The Beatles' Recording Sessions* (and the subsequent calendar book *Chronicles*), represents the first new major primary source material to emerge from the story since the albums themselves (secondary source material will be discussed below). Comprehensive, detailed, and exacting, Lewisohn not only sheds light on the Beatles' work habits but their grueling schedule—seven years when the collective muse drove them all to new creative heights with each recording.

Obviously, Lewisohn's work would have been a dream reference for the type of work *Tell Me Why* aspired to be; as it is, I can only be grateful mistakes and omissions were not made any more blatant by his research. But there are several outstanding issues that deserve mention. For starters, McCartney plays drums on "Dear Prudence" (p. 264–65), which I had counted as among Ringo's finest moments. This recording occurred on August 28 and 29, 1968, sessions when Starr had quit the band and the others simply kept on taping. McCartney has never made too much of an issue about this, but it would certainly be interesting to hear Ringo's thoughts on it now that it's one of the few confirmed Beatle tracks without his backbeat (McCartney also drums on "The Ballad of John and Yoko").[3]

LEWISOHN'S RESEARCH IS INVALUABLE but not imperfect. If EMI had handed almost anybody the keys to its archives, few writers would complain. And yet Lewisohn is more the insatiable fan than keen-eared critic, and his descriptions of many of these sounds fall short of artful, evocative session summaries. For the most part, Lewisohn leans heavily on superlatives and adjectives like "brilliant," when what one really wants (since we'll never be able to hear all of it) is color, texture, and mood. And he was obviously not hired for his willingness to confront his employers with negative opinions.

For example, on page 49, he describes the "Eight Days a Week" session:

> "Eight Days a Week" was a landmark recording in that it was the first time the Beatles took an unfinished idea into the studio and experimented with different ways of recording it.

This overstatement disregards a lot of the work on "Can't Buy Me Love" that's now available on the *Anthology I*. There's all kinds of evidence that the band got more and more creative and experimental as they progressed, but they clearly opened themselves up to numerous ideas about tempo, arrangement, even meter before "Eight Days a Week." On *Anthology I*, for example, we hear them try "I'll Be Back" as a waltz.

> Although it was to become the first pop song to feature a faded-up introduction [what about Chuck Berry's "Downbound Train"?], the session tapes reveal that this was not the original plan. Take one was played straight, no frills, on acoustic guitar. On take two John and Paul introduced a succession of beautifully harmonized "Ooohs," climbing up the scale, to precede the first guitar strum. On take three they merged the first two ideas, "Ooohs" and acoustic guitar. On take four the "Ooohs" were altered to remain on the same pitch throughout [which pitch?] rather than climbing the register. Take five incorporated "Ooohs" at the end as well as the beginning. Take six took the shape of the released version but did not have the faded intro or outro. From then on, until the "best," take 13, the Beatles concentrated on perfecting take six, overdubbing a double-tracked Lennon vocal, for instance. . . .

This description completely evades the effect of the creative process, which was a stripping away of vocal harmonies to build tension and color. Where the takes begin with the harmonies you an hear on *Anthology I*, the final arrangement emerges from their absence (much the same way it did on "Can't Buy Me Love"). It gives the song its rarefied air of buoyant energy, and displays the Beatles as suspicious of any ornamentation that merely props up material at the expense of a song's truer, unfettered nature. In other words, the effects that these vocal harmonies are going for are completely discarded in favor of something simpler, less intrusive, and less ornate—which suits the track's helium lift perfectly. The creative process is one of peeling away, not addition; the poetry lies in the throwing away of all ideas extraneous to the song's core charm.

And this is only one of the few cases in which officially published takes are available for first-hand reference to compare to Lewisohn's notes. There are literally hundreds of other songs where his descriptions are less detailed and the number of takes more numerous. Early on, song takes numbered between one and ten or twenty; later it became more common to go through hours of takes of a song before a basic track was accomplished: one notorious example is the seemingly innocuous "Ob-La-Di, Ob-La-Da," which took up most of July 1968, alongside other songs. On July 8th, alone, twelve takes of the song were taped; a frustrated Lennon piano intro is suddenly "twice the speed" of previous renditions—which is quite a kick. The song's takes would ultimately number 23 (which by then was an average number). And then there are Lewisohn's offhanded references to things like: "Take six was aborted when Paul burped a vocal instead of singing it, take seven was complete but ended in uproarious laughter . . ." (p. 49, during "Every Little Thing"). Such comments cry out for fuller descriptions.[4]

To be sure, Lewisohn spent over a year listening to master tapes all day long; his notes on outside instrumentalists and instrumentation are thorough and dependable. And there is a way in which a strong point of view could have put precisely the wrong slant on this project. *The Beatles' Recording Sessions* is likely to remain the only reference book of its kind, and Lewisohn clears up a number of details that make it indispensable for close listening. Perhaps it is the curse of all things Beatles that any amount of information only leaves you wanting more.

NINETEEN EIGHTY-EIGHT BEGAN with the Beatles' induction into the Rock 'n' Roll Hall of Fame. The award came at a

moment when McCartney was in court against the others; he refused to attend the New York ceremony and issued a statement
that said, "I was keen to go and pick up my award, but after
twenty years, the Beatles still have some business differences,
which I had hoped would have been settled by now. Unfortunately, they haven't, so I would feel like a hypocrite waving and
smiling with them at a fake reunion." The acrimony of the
breakup had devolved into years of squabbling, first to clean up
Allen Klein's string of legal suits, and later to recoup royalties
from Capitol in America. Beatle camaraderie had long since
turned sour.

So it fell to George Harrison, typically more jaundiced than
McCartney, to address the occasion. His plastic nostalgia solo
record, *Cloud Nine* (produced by Jeff Lynne), and its hit single,
"Got My Mind Set on You," were getting heavy airplay, and Harrison's trademark sardonicism suddenly rang sincere. As he stood
on the stage with Ringo Starr, Yoko Ono, and Sean and Julian
Lennon, he gave this abbreviated speech: "I don't have much to
say, because I'm the quiet Beatle. . . . It's unfortunate that Paul's
not here, because he was the one who had the speech in his
pocket. Anyway, we all know why John can't be here, and I'm
sure he would be. And it's really hard to stand here supposedly
representing the Beatles . . . what's left, I'm afraid. But we all
loved him so much."

That evening, even insiders might not have predicted that
the biggest pop act of the 1960s would become one of the biggest
sellers of the 1990s. It began with their earliest recordings from
the BBC, which comprise some of the most intriguing and revealing work. *Live at the BBC* captured the Beatles in the act of
defining themselves: scoping out their version of rock's tradition,
submitting themselves to that tradition, and finally turning it into
a creative challenge to pounce upon and overtake. The group's
appearances on the BBC airwaves between 1962 and 1966 had
been on collectors' short lists of unpublished Beatle wonders
even before they were first resurrected for a radio series in 1982.
Beginning back when manager Brian Epstein began pounding

London pavement in search of a recording deal, this material stakes a claim in rock mythology equal to that of Bob Dylan's *Basement Tapes* (recorded in 1967, released in 1975) or Elvis Presley's comeback television special in 1968 (available as *One Night with You* on video). These projects tell secrets about these performers that are central to their greatness—Dylan's cockeyed intoxication with the early American west, or Presley's inspired notion of how to recreate himself in middle age by chuckling along self-consciously with his younger image, turning the later Vegas kitsch back on itself to a point at which sincerity flirted with irony. After you hear *Live at the BBC*, the entire Beatles catalog makes a different kind of musical sense, and their creative leaps seem less out-of-the-blue than essential.

The 56 tracks included on these two discs, interspersed with gaggles of between-song chatter, trace Lennon and McCartney's distinct vocal development, the seeds of their songwriting partnership, and the way these four instrumentalists learned to play off each others' strengths to create an unparalleled ensemble. Paradoxically, these tracks also show how the Beatles elevated the idea of covering other peoples' songs into an act of self-definition, a glossary of their own taste and aspirations, a bildungsroman of song. The Band's *Moondog Matinee*, Guns N' Roses' *The Spaghetti Incident*, and the spate of best-selling tribute albums in the 1990s, from the Eagles to the Grateful Dead, are all direct descendants of the Beatles' impulse to absorb, imitate, and expand on their models. To hear the Beatles perform before they were signed provides the most accurate picture of the band's character before Epstein tailored the act for television. Live and unvarnished (and rolling about giggling on the bathroom floor, as host Brian Matthews remembers), the Beatles made music as great as they would ever record once famous.

On the other hand, the BBC and EMI/Capitol contrived to make this two-disc release (clocking in at two hours, 13 minutes, and 40 seconds) an unnecessarily frugal sampling of the vast selection available. The rival nine-CD set (a 1992 bootleg) from Italy's Great Dane label, *The Complete BBC Sessions*, lasts well over ten hours; an updated (and speed-corrected) version of that set, *Complete BBC Sessions Upgraded*, from Purple Chick, recasts much of the same material, plus updates, across 10 80-minute CDs. The major-label defense for its paltry two-CD frugality is sound fidelity, which is poppycock. Although some of the digitally cleaned-up sound here is wonderful, sound quality is hardly what makes the collection as a whole so appealing. This music has already won over skeptics through hundreds of low-quality vinyl pressings. The supposedly superior quality of the meager "official" selection doesn't justify cheating fans out of even more revelatory material that's been making the bootleg rounds for over 30 years.

Granted, EMI/Capitol seems to take pains to irritate Beatle fans, whether it's putting out the right thing in the wrong format (the first four CDs in mono only), or the right thing in the wrong packaging (*Rock 'n' Roll*, 1976), or the wrong thing period (*Love Songs*, 1977), or the wrong thing done wrong twice over (*The Beatles/1962–66* and *The Beatles/1967–69*, a.k.a. the Red and Blue Collections, released as two CDs each in 1993, when the material could easily fit on one long-playing disc apiece). Given the track record, there's not much hope for the *Hollywood Bowl* CD, or the *Let It Be* session material, if and when such projects ever appear.

Even a "testing the waters" defense doesn't jibe with the enormous sales potential of this material, which certainly made EMI stockholders happy: The package debuted at number three in the final months of 1993, spent three weeks in the Top Ten during the Christmas spree, and remained in the top 40 for over six weeks. That makes *Live at the BBC* an anomaly in pop history: What other 30-year-old collection of covers ever did as well? All this would be overshadowed by successive Beatle releases—but it's easy to overlook the popular significance of this band's apprenticeship.

And still, this "official" version of the Beatles' formative history stacks up quite well in spite of everything (as usual). They were a generous and combustible live act before worldwide Beatlemania stirred their songwriting juices. And they knew more than a thing or two about how songs are put together before Martin began contributing to their arrangements. Though it's long been known that the Beatles had exceptional taste in cover material, what *Live at the BBC* reveals is just how abiding that taste was, and how fiercely they embraced rock history (at that point, barely a decade old) before anybody took notice. Even with the omissions, this song sequence presents a pretty balanced picture of how the Beatles defined rock style: as a mixture of rhythm and blues (Arthur Alexander), catchy guitar riffs (Chuck Berry), campy belters (Little Richard), novelty items ("The Honeymoon Song"), and more rockabilly and country than is commonly assumed (the Harrison-sung Carl Perkins number "Everybody's Trying to Be My Baby," Buddy Holly's "Crying, Waiting, Hoping," as well as the key early Lennon-McCartney duet on Perkins's "Sure to Fall").

The Beatles' quest to be original led to ingenious theft. Take their affection for girl group material, which they held in at least as much esteem as they did Elvis Presley or Buddy Holly. They start by completely reimagining the tacky gender roles in songs by the Shirelles and the Cookies. Manhandling Little Eva's "Keep Your Hands Off My Baby," Lennon bites into some possessive girl-talk and spits out an insecure macho threat. In the Shirelles' "Baby It's You," instead of a woman pleading to a man, the original's shivering feminine dependence turns to shuddering male vulnerability. When they get to the second verse ("You should hear what they say about you. . . ."), Paul and George chirp "Cheat-cheat," which lends the original Shirelles' gesture an early twinge of Lennonesque paranoia. Sung by men, the "sha-la-la-las" lilting behind the lead vocal turns precociously liberated and subversive. These nonsense words pitched in character behind the singer jack up the camaraderie alive in the playing.

Everything included on *Live at the BBC* points to numbers left behind, and conceals the more wide-reaching sources the Beatles heard in rock 'n' roll. On their set list in this period were such gems as Roy Orbison's "Dream Baby," which McCartney turned in at their very first BBC session in 1962. Other missing essentials include Carl Perkins's "Lend Me Your Comb," a bouncy duet from John and Paul (which appears on *Anthology I*), and the Coasters' "Three Cool Cats," a song that shows how self-consciously they were developing their group identity (recorded twice but never broadcast by the BBC, it's easiest to find on bootlegs of their Decca audition tape). With its totemic vocal climaxes, "Twist and Shout" would emerge as their ensemble signature, but only after they test-drove many alternatives.

Still, some important songwriting characteristics peek through: Lennon's swelling frustration in the bridge of "To Know Her Is to Love Her" sounds like a scrimmage for "I'll Get You." In the only Everly Brothers cover they ever released, "So How Come (No One Loves Me)," they show just how ineffable the Lennon-McCartney vocal duets promised to be. And included here for the first time is "I'll Be On My Way," an early Lennon-McCartney ditty that could be the Everlies singing Buddy Holly. (The key missing early rocker in their catalogue, perhaps even more intimidating to them than Presley, is Jerry Lee Lewis. We know Lennon sang "Fools Like Me," and McCartney did "High School Confidential" on stage, but not for the ages.)

The different things Lennon and McCartney heard in their favorite rock stylists dramatized their conflicting ideas about rock 'n' roll. McCartney idolized Little Richard. Lennon admired Chuck Berry's tight narratives, and heard in Berry's candid swagger an emotional directness that answered Richard's showmanship. When he wasn't singing about himself directly, Lennon preferred singing about characters; McCartney always seemed to be playing a character—a habit he can't seem to shake.

So the cultural significance of John Lennon singing "Johnny B. Goode" is considerable. To Lennon, the song's hero isn't as freighted with the racial baggage that Chuck Berry slyly concealed (some read this fable as a shadow biography of Elvis Presley, or a fantasy of Berry's own story had he been white). To Lennon, "Johnny B. Goode" was the Everyman statement: Lurking inside these enviable American heroes with their rock 'n' roll soundtracks there was a universal impulse waiting to be tapped. The sound was open enough for a Brit like Lennon to identify with, apply to his experience, and sing back to Americans as his own. Alongside the class identification, British rockers identified with how much noise American black musicians had to make to get noticed, never mind respected, in the pop music world. What we hear in retrospect is the man who wrote "Don't Let Me Down" singing a bar-band staple (talk about a song with legs). But at the time, "Johnny B. Goode" signaled how much the Beatles heard for themselves in this music, and how much they intuited in a style few took seriously.

Program your CD player to sequence all the Lennon–Chuck Berry covers, and you'll be hard pressed to argue that Lennon wasn't Berry's best interpreter. "Too Much Monkey Business," "Carol," "Johnny B. Goode," "Memphis, Tennessee" on disc one; and "Sweet Little Sixteen," "Rock and Roll Music," and "I Got to Find My Baby" on disc two. ("Johnny B. Goode" segueing into "Memphis, Tennessee" may be this collection's high point.)

For Lennon's summary of how rock's jealousy, obsession, and left-field humor could quickly turn callous, try this sequence: On disc one: the Ray Charles–cum–Elvis Presley "I Got a Woman"; Goffin-King's "Keep Your Hands Off My Baby" (originally done by Little Eva); Arthur Alexander's "A Shot of Rhythm and Blues"; Ritchie Barrett's obscure (except to Liverpool) "Some Other Guy"; the Shirelles's "Baby It's You"; Arthur Alexander's "Soldier of Love"; another Presley number, "I'm Gonna Sit Right Down and Cry Over You"; Smokey Robinson and the Miracles's "You Really Got a Hold On Me"; Phil Spector's "To Know Her Is to Love Her" (originally done by Spector's Teddy Bears); and on disc two: the Johnny Burnett Trio's "Lonesome Tears in My Eyes," and Larry Williams's "Dizzy Miss Lizzie" and "Slow Down." With these tracks in your ears, the insecurity that seeps from Lennon numbers like "I'm a Loser" begins to make a lot more sense. And, since he probably knew that Spector's "To Know Him Is to Love Him" was engraved on Spector's father's tombstone, could Lennon be singing that emotional black hole of a bridge in "To Know Her Is to Love Her" to . . . his mother Julia? Stu Sutcliffe?

Stringing together a programmed sequence also lets you concentrate on McCartney's better side and avoid the tired ritual of "Till There Was You" and "A Taste of Honey." Where Lennon heard humor, verbal acrobatics, and point-of-view tricks in Chuck Berry's writing, McCartney heard pure release in Little Richard (even if it doesn't sound as if he knew what a transvestite was): On disc one, Paul sings Presley's "That's All Right [Mama]," The Jodimars's arcane-but-great "Clarabella," Little Richard's "Long Tall Sally," and "Lucille"; on disc two, Chan Romero's "The Hippy Hippy Shake," Little Richard's medley of "Kansas City/Hey! Hey! Hey! Hey!" as well as "Ooh! My Soul." McCartney's impressive vocal swagger on such songs makes it clear why Lennon teamed up with him in the first place—for his giddy hellfire wail. (Cue up this track list: Chuck Berry: CD 1: 5–16–29–30; CD 2: 10, 21, 29; Lennon's emotional footsteps: CD 1: 4–6–9–11–14–17–20–23–24; CD 2: 12–23–33; McCartney's sequence: CD 1: 15–19–26–31; CD 2: 14–24–30.)

In fact, the best song sprint on these two CDs comes when these competing rock idealists go head-to-head trading favorites at the end of disc one, beginning with "You Really Got a Hold On Me" (Lennon), "To Know Her Is To Love Her" (Lennon), "Long Tall Sally" (McCartney), "I Saw Her Standing There" (McCartney), "Johnny B. Goode" (Lennon), "Memphis, Tennessee" (Lennon), "Lucille" (McCartney), and ending with the full-blown writerly confidence of "Can't Buy Me Love." Theirs is an argument between musical personalities that ping-pongs vehemence and desire, anger and exaltation, abandonment and fulfillment—with an embrace (not a rejection) of Tin Pan Alley ("The Honeymoon Song," "Till There Was You"). Of course, this is the internal debate the Beatles had, and rock had with itself, and has had ever since.

These jarring contrasts—from breathtaking excitement to jittery self-scrutiny to music-hall sentimentality—sum up the inclusive Beatle formula. Add a streak of country and western and rockabilly (something they're not famous for but plenty adept at), and you have the total Beatle embrace. For the hick touch they turn to George, who's perfect for the awkward narrator of the Lieber-Stoller-Pomus song, "Young Blood," the other Coasters' ensemble piece. His best moment is the Presley cover, "I Forgot to Remember to Forget," in which he embodies a sheepish teen almost too well. Missing is Harrison's droll streak through "The Sheik of Araby," a cover of a 1961 Joe Brown and the Bruvvers track, which would have rounded out his character (it finally pops up on *Anthology I*).

These are all qualities made manifest in later Beatle recordings, which makes it all the more flabbergasting to hear them this early, this unproduced. And yet there's more to learn here about Ringo than about any other member of the band. *Live at the BBC* forever clears Ringo's name as the luckiest man in rock and positions him as its most underrated musician. The Beatles did three appearances on the BBC in 1962 when the strapping but standard-issue Pete Best was still backing them up. "Sadly, no quality recording exists of this or their other three broadcasts of 1962," BBC producer Kevin Howlett writes in his liner notes. Note the evasive word "quality." These tapes were simply voted down. The qualities Ringo brought to the party, however, should hereafter be inarguable. He was breaking himself in as the Beatles' locomotive, and on each of these tracks, he proves himself a rhythmic wonder crucial to the developing Beatle sound. Acutely attuned to the nuances in Lennon and McCartney's songs as they began pouring out, Ringo combined a controlled rhythmic drive with a keen sensitivity to each number's overall shape and hidden detail. He was a developing songwriter's dream. Invisible (and thus underrated), his drum parts meld into songs as neatly as Lennon-McCartney's composed retransitions and rhythm guitar fixtures.

Listen to "Thank You Girl," done live in June 1963, and known then as the B-side to the brand new "From Me to You" single. Just as the band finds its groove and leans into one of its early songwriting peaks, Ringo holds back just slightly where lesser drummers would push; he pulls back for tautness instead of shoving ahead—you can even hear him steady the others' impulse to rush during the intro. This is the most important and difficult thing for any new drummer to do: impose a meter on his new bandmates. (The tendency to rush the beat is exaggerated in front of a live audience.) This withheld energy adds an extra stream of tension into the sound. Song after song, Ringo tugs the reins against the band's momentum, creating a backlog of energy that swells hard against his imposing rhythmic spine. On the heels of "Some Other Guy," from the same live spot, this toughened version of "Thank You Girl" makes the studio version sound coy.

And when Ringo takes his breaks on "Ticket to Ride" in a BBC session from May 1965, nothing he does simply repeats what he had already recorded. Not only is each verse-closing drum break varied, he alters each one subtly from version to version—he deliberately drags his fills behind the bar, and his anticipations are often simply breakneck silences (just after the brief post-bridge guitar solos) that pack even more tension than his fleet double-stick rolls. Starr's cunning modesty is as radically counter-intuitive to rock's vernacular as McCartney's liberated bass lines.

Because it's likely to stand as the only "legitimate" musical snapshot from this period, for most fans *Live at the BBC* will provide the best glimpse of the Beatles' early repertoire, and the most persuasive explanation of why they returned to these songs in early 1969 for inspiration. The *Let It Be* sessions may be the most bootlegged tapes in the rock catalogue, but they don't come close to conveying what the Beatles were seeking in this music— the heights they'd scaled a mere seven years earlier. What you hear on these BBC tapes is immediate, direct, and unselfconscious, a sense of how alive rock could be in the moment before the world caught on. No wonder they turned to this material as a release from the musical bickering and financial animosity that had, by then, poisoned their well.

For the Beatles, playing this music was more than a primer in rock history, it was an acting out of how much rock 'n' roll had to teach. Even their contemporaneous selections (like the Shirelles's "Boys," which Ringo sings with paradoxical conviction;

or Smokey Robinson's "You've Really Got a Hold On Me") testify to the music's unfailing purpose. (So much so that the coda of "Love Me Do" at the end of this set is an odd anticlimax to a string of revelations.) Rock 'n' roll had not only reached across the Atlantic and seized the imaginations of grammar school Teds, it had taught two promising young songwriters how to compose, and three self-taught guitarists and a replacement drummer how to divine a band. It was one of rock's key early triumphs to transcend its racial, class, and geographical roots to become a universal phenomenon.

WITH SALES POTENTIAL proven by *Live at the BBC*, the three ex-Beatles began shoring up their legacy in earnest, gathering in early 1995 to remake several unfinished songs offered by Yoko Ono from Lennon's private stash: "Free as a Bird," "Real Love," "Grow Old With Me," and "Now and Then." Because the demos were recorded on primitive home equipment and were at least 2nd or 3rd generation copies (the Lennon estate was looted in the days following his death), Jeff Lynne oversaw removal of tape hiss, clicks, and unsteady beats. Meanwhile, a video production team put together a 10-hour film of archive footage, radio interviews, TV appearances, home movie reels, and demo material for broadcast on American TV (ABC) in November, which included new videos for "Free as a Bird" and "Real Love," the two reunion tracks that made it through completion. This *Anthology* project brought three Grammy awards in 1997, including Best Pop Performance by a Duo or Group with Vocal, Best Music Video, Short Form (the "Free as a Bird" video), and Best Music Video, Long Form (the *Anthology* video).

"Free as a Bird" makes the Lester Bangs quote about how any Beatle reunion would likely prove ". . . the biggest anticlimax in history" seem generous. The material itself is not just lo-fi (in fact, if Jeff Lynne gets any credit, it should be for the technical clean-up he gives the Lennon demo), the song itself is unfinished. The bridge Paul McCartney writes for it is a conspicuous lift from the Shangri-Las' "Remember (Walkin' in the Sand)," accented by the first three words ("Whatever happened to the boy that I once knew/The boy who said he'd be true. . . ."). This direct song lift was widely heard at the time of the single's release, played on National Public Radio, but McCartney has remained mum on the subject. Aside from being an arch reference to an early girl-group staple, the kind the Beatles themselves might have covered (alongside "Chains" or "Please Mr. Postman"), it cheapens the entire effort. To have the remaining partner of the century's greatest and most popular songwriting team finish his dead partner's demo by stealing a bridge from a well-known favorite seems hinky, even for McCartney.

To add irony to the existing acrimony between McCartney and Harrison, the Shangri-Las' echo rubs Harrison's nose in the lawsuit he lost when the Chiffons filed against Harrison for sponging their "He's So Fine" chord sequence in 1970's "My Sweet Lord." That no suit took place in 1995 against "Free as a Bird" was a factor of the increasing sampling in pop culture by hip-hop, which by that point had gone far beyond what any court could keep track of, and evolved into an elaborate aural symbology of homage more than theft. When Coolio samples Stevie Wonder's "Pastime Paradise" (in "Gangsta's Paradise"), or Angie Stone builds a new song from the foundation to the O'Jays's "Back Stabbers" (in "Wish I Didn't Miss You"), the effect is of recontextualization, mining more from the source than simply sticking your name in the author slot. And Harrison's case, being among the earlier conflicts, predates digital sampling and served as a dissuasive benchmark against which future songwriters held as a standard. (When the Rolling Stones discovered they had inadvertently stolen kd lang's "Constant Craving," on a song called "Anybody Seen My Baby," they simply added her name to the composer credits.) But there's no way George Harrison didn't hear McCartney commit almost exactly the same crime Harrison had thirty years earlier and get off scot-free.

ALTHOUGH THE *ANTHOLOGY* PROJECT collects a lot of rare, personal footage, including studio exchanges and tour material, the overall motivation is spotty, its outtakes and demos a mixed bag—and the title is misleading. Certainly the Beatles deserved the chance to tell their own story and reap the profits they had so long shared with too many others. But as a document, neither the video nor the book can count as "definitive"; the Beatles and their crew are not always the best people to tell their own story. Neil Aspinall, originally a Liverpool roadie who now runs Apple, seems to get as much camera time as the Beatles themselves, and lacks any kind of charisma. Often whole sections of the story are omitted; other times, only three-quarters of the story gets told.

While the video production introduced a new audience to the Beatles' career, more than a few younger consumers picked up the accompanying CDs under the impression that this collected all of the Beatles' essential work. On the one hand, there are superior live tracks that count among some of the band's best performances (including "I'll Get You," and the Royal Command Performance in 1963). But Martin's editing process muddies the waters: "Yes It Is," for example, begins as a rough take, with Lennon doing a guide vocal (an early performance to be sung over as a diagram for the final version). This elides into the finished version as if to trace the professional transformation the Beatles give the number. It raises the question of how much sweetening is done throughout the project without explanation, and also seems beside the point: where the final version is widely available, this early mix is intriguing for its tentativeness, and betrays a unique strain of Lennon's vulnerability. Even when he's going through the motions for himself, his voice is uncannily expressive.

Like the BBC tapes, everything that's here points to more significant material that is still unavailable: the "Helter Skelter" excerpt on *Anthology II* only hints at the notorious longer jam session that was edited out of the *White Album* version, the most sought-after bootleg in the entire canon. And on numbers like "Revolution," from the David Frost show in 1968, the live-vocal-backed-with-canned-instruments version gets spoken over during the video documentary, spoiling any chance of unfettered access to this one-time version of the song (the only version where Paul and George chime in with "Bah-om, shoo-by doo-wop, bah-om, shoo-by doo-wop . . ."). It obliterates the notion that bootleggers won't keep trafficking this material for years to come.

Some numbers have long deserved official publication: McCartney's "That Means a Lot," a sprawling Brian Wilson–like arrangement from the *Help!* sessions that was abandoned and finally given to American export P.J. Proby, and Lennon's 1964 aggravated braggadocio in Little Willie John's "Leave My Kitten Alone," which stands alongside his greatest covers, including "Rock 'n' Roll Music," "Money," or "Bad Boy." A 1965 live set from Blackpool that includes "I Feel Fine" and "Ticket to Ride" is anything but flat; "Mailman, Bring Me No More Blues" (by Ruth Roberts, Bill Katz, and Stanley Clayton) stands out from the *Let It Be* sessions as a moment of inspired lethargy (it was originally the B-side to Buddy Holly's "Words of Love," from 1958). To stumble onto this of all songs during their prolific rehash of '50s favorites adds chilling commentary on their situation. (During one film outtake, Lennon stares blankly into the distance for what seems like hours before announcing dully: "Well, it's been a lot of fun.") And the closing remix of "The End," which spews sparkling guitar exchanges between Harrison, McCartney, and Lennon, segues directly into the final *Pepper* chord from two years earlier, which seems not just anachronistic but hackneyed.

Analogous video segments are gratuitous: does anybody really need a 1995 footage of McCartney singing "Eleanor Rigby" alone on the guitar, interspersed with glimpses of anonymous lower-class children? The accompanying *Anthology* book simply expands the video interview transcripts which cry out for judicious editing (although it sells more than two million copies). It's packed with private photographs and notes, lyric drafts, postcards, and all manner of back-of-the-drawer quips (Lennon writes to a friend "Do You Want to Know a Negro?"). And in general, the agonizing court cases that kept a bitter McCartney from joining his bandmates at the Rock 'n' Roll Hall of Fame ceremony in 1988 are smoothed over. The conciliatory tone tries to pass over the aesthetic wreckage of their solo careers, and the public relations damage done by the acrimonious *Let It Be* footage, but it doesn't hit its mark. In a way, this feigned harmony seems more of a letdown than the acrimony itself.

THE SUCCESS OF *ANTHOLOGY* led to the re-release and remaster of *Yellow Submarine* material for the new 5:1 Dolby Surround Sound home theatre format (minus 'George Martin's instrumentals). This reissue draws attention to many of the discrepancies in mixing that have changed through the years. Beatle mixes were often as creatively sharp as their writing and playing, with instruments in odd spaces or making sudden, strange movements, which is another reason why Lynne's reunion track production sounds stodgy. The new mixes were supervised by Ted Hall at Pacific Ocean Post, engineered by Abbey Road's Peter Cobbin, and overseen by the Beatles themselves. The ironies are abundant: for starters, the *Rubber Soul* CD edition of "Nowhere Man," keeps the left-right separations, but for the *Yellow Submarine* remix, the vocals are double-tracked to both channels. This makes for a "fuller," more "contemporary" sound, but along the way the echo gets enriched, and the effect has more sheen than the original—and part of the original's sheen was effortless. You don't *need* to add any reverb or echo to that rich a vocal part sung with such gusto, it carries itself. And where does the roaming guitar harmonic from "Nowhere Man" disappear to (it should occur at 1:01)? The final harmonic used to ring from channel to channel, and this mix has since disappeared from every single CD version of the track. (After so many different "official" renditions, there's no longer any meaning to the idea of "official" version of anything.)

The same with McCartney's priceless vocal crack on the second bridge of "If I Fell," which has been "repaired" on the mono master, and so appears "fixed" on both the *Hard Day's Night* CD (at 1:44), and The Complete EP Collection. Why does this get repaired and not the tambourine that suddenly drops out during the final verse of "Day Tripper," after the lyric "Tried to please her," at 1:50? (This "Day Tripper" tambourine drops out on *Past*

Masters, but gets fixed on *1*'s remix). Are some flaws less worthy than others? The roaming vocal mix on "Day in the Life" is preserved on CD: the opening verses go from right to center, the final verse comes from the left. Is the issue of consistency ever discussed at these mixing sessions? All of these are simple digital fixes, but the point is: they would have been equally simple *analog* fixes in their day. These simple flaws were more than upstaged by the band's spark and increasingly spry edits. That many missing words and missed notes were originally left in spoke to their enormous daring and focus on the larger ideas. Their blemishes were part of their appeal, just like their silliness was a key part of how seriously they took pop.

IN DECEMBER 1999, in a grisly replay of Lennon's assassination 19 years earlier, George Harrison and his wife Olivia narrowly escaped death by subduing a knife-wielding mentally ill intruder to their Friar Park British estate. Keith Richards spoke of the attack in his thoughts on Harrison in *Rolling Stone*'s tribute issue after Harrison died in 2001:

> What he didn't need, and to me what's unbelievable, is that, basically, the knifing, the attack two years ago at his house, is what did in George. Because I think he probably would have beaten the cancer if it wasn't for the blade. John was my first mate among them, because George was a bit quiet. Now I think, "Oh, one by gun, one by knife." And that's still puzzling to me in a way, although he didn't die literally from it. It's just that for such pleasant guys, who made such beautiful music and never did harm to anybody, to have to go through that kind of violence—I mean, I'm used to it, I've been stabbed several times, and the bullet wounds are healing. But with George, it was like, "Oh, I can't believe it really." You know, he was a guy who only looked out for the best in people. Of all people, it shouldn't have happened to George.

At least Harrison got to see his band's collection of 27 number-one hits, *1*, overtake the music industry in the fall of 2000, the year before he died. Selling 2.5 million units in its first month, *1* quickly became the fastest-selling CD of all time, topping the charts of 28 countries simultaneously. Alongside the *Anthology* book and the launch of the official Beatles Web site (at http://www.thebeatles.com/), it led to a euphoric Beatles revival that upstaged the songwriting of bands like Oasis and Radiohead, and guaranteed more vault releases in the years to come.

But it also raised many of the same questions posed by the *Anthology* project. Is it possible to reflect on the Beatles anymore without the influence of the *Anthology* and reunion? In the end, the *Anthology, Yellow Submarine,* and *1* titles only give the most surface-level clues about the density of creative work that took place at Abbey Road. On a commercial level, the Beatles' late career gives tacit assent to all the bootleggers who have been compiling and releasing unpublished material both before and since. Doctoring-up songs gives a false impression of what the sessions actually sounded like, and fading out tracks before the unfinished endings ("I'll Be Back") cheats you of their writing habits. And *Live at the BBC* is compelling and hilarious, but represents only about a tenth of what remains in the BBC vaults. So while it's easy to sympathize with the Beatles wanting to earn more royalties off their own work, their public image, once determinedly realistic, has now been whitewashed.

During their '60s career, they were confident and prolific enough to leave in mistakes and go public with the most uneven experiments. As elder rock statesmen, they seem obsessive about protecting their image at the expense of fidelity. And the reunion with Lennon was simply an aesthetic failure: coming after Natalie Cole's duet with her father on "Unforgettable," they can't even claim it was a technical or conceptual breakthrough. Original material of a higher standard without Lennon would have fared far better, even if it didn't measure up to their earlier work. As it is, "Free as a Bird" and "Real Love" play to the worst side of their sentimentality, and nearly every earlier track upstages these '90s numbers. Before the 1990s, the Beatles paid the highest respect to their work by leaving well enough alone;

the classic curve of their mere seven years in the studio had both eccentricity and closure. Now, much of their tidying up and repackaging has turned Beatle whimsy into artifice.

Tim Riley
February 2002

Notes

1. Member of the British Empire.
2. The New York Times Book Review, "Let Us Now Praise Famous Men," October 8, 2000, p. 10.
3. There's more where that came from: Phil Spector didn't add strings to the song "Let It Be" (p. 27), just "Across the Universe," "The Long and Winding Road," and "I Me Mine"; "How Do You Do It" (not "How Do You Do") was recorded on September 4, 1962, not in November for the second single (p. 46); the Beatles didn't play *Top Of The Pops* in 1963, they played such BBC programs as *Teenager's Turn, The Friday Spectacular, The Beat Show* and *Pop Go the Beatles* (*Top of the Pops* didn't premiere until January of 1964) (p. 61); Paul overdubbed the harmony to his own lead on "All My Loving," an early mimic of an imaginary duet with Lennon (George took this harmony on stage) (p. 74); the earliest listed performance of "I Want To Hold Your Hand" came after, not during, August 1963 (p. 85); only half of the "Long Tall Sally" EP was recorded in February of 1964, the other half was recorded in June (p. 92); Lennon takes the first guitar solo in "Long Tall Sally," not George (p. 94); the correct "Things We Said Today" lyric is "Me, I'm just the lucky kind," not "lucky guy" (p. 111).

The "three-hour jam session with Elvis" (p. 152) is irresistible, but merely myth. In the book *The Beatles Anthology* (2000), Lennon, McCartney, Harrison, Starr and roadies Neil Aspinall and Mal Evans tell of a visit to Presley's Los Angeles home with Brian Epstein for a long evening that included Charlie Rich, whose current hit, "Mohair Sam," was on Presley's stereo. For a period, apparently Elvis picked up a bass, and everyone else but Ringo picked up guitars; but a formal jam session this was not. Harrison remembers hitting up the Memphis Mafia for reefers with no success.

The guitar solo in "Nowhere Man" is a unison duet played by Harrison and Lennon on their new Fender Stratocasters. Harrison probably helped compose this section, but the final overtone's movement across the mix has long since disappeared (p. 161); In *Many Years from Now*, Paul recalls "Wait" as largely his composition with a little help from Lennon (p. 168); there's no French horn in "Here There And Everywhere," just George using his guitar's volume pedal for a sound remarkably similar to the horn on "For No One" (p. 187); *Sgt. Pepper* was recorded entirely on two four-track machines, not an eight-track (p. 213); *The Who Sell Out* was released in 1967, not 1968 (p. 213); McCartney's high-end bass figures in "With a Little Help From My Friends" answer Ringo's low end-of-first-verse tom-tom fills, not the other way around (p. 214).

There's no Mellotron on "Lucy in the Sky With Diamonds," just a Lowrey organ impersonating one (p. 215); as on "Taxman," Paul plays the guitar solo on "Good Morning, Good Morning," not George (p. 223); "A Day In The Life" was recorded live on January 19 and 20, 1967, after several days of rehearsal; the recording was built off the basic track from these sessions (p. 228); no organ on "The Fool On The Hill," just piano, flutes, recorder, harmonicas, guitar, maracas, and cymbal (p. 240); the "bassoon" on "Flying" and "Bungalow Bill" is a Mellotron on trombone setting (p. 240 and 268); there *is* harmonica since "I Should Have Known Better," on "I'm A Loser" (p. 242); George never walked out on the *White Album* sessions (p. 262); the "I'm So Tired" lyric "It's been three weeks" should be "you know it's three weeks" (p. 272); no organ on "Don't Pass Me By," just Leslie'd piano (p. 273); and phased, not electric, piano on "Birthday" (p. 276).

The *James Paul McCartney* special was taped and aired in 1973, not 1972 (p. 284); "Suzy Parker" (which some claim to be "Susie's Parlour") was pure ad-lib, not another oldie like the jams it springs from (p. 289); the scenes of London bobbies at Apple's door aren't edited in, apparently there was enough time to set up cameras from both angles once it was known the police were arriving (p. 290); Harrison's exact quote to McCartney is: "Whatever it is that'll please you, I'll do it" (p. 291); the "Across the Universe" lyric is "slither wildly as they slip away," not "slither while they pass" (p. 296); George Martin added the brass to "Let It Be," not Phil Spector (p. 297); The "I've Got a Feeling" lyric is "wandering around," not "running round the world" (p. 299); the Montreal bed-in was two months after Amsterdam, not six (p. 306); recorded in April, 1969, Harrison's "Old Brown Shoe" is not a *White Album* outtake (p. 307); James Taylor's song title is "Carolina In My Mind" (p. 309); the "synth arpeggio" on "Because" is played by a Baldwin spinet electric harpsichord (p. 326); what seems like a "synth bass" on "Mean Mr. Mustard" is just fuzz bass (p. 329); McCartney and Starr's backstage reunion was in the documentary *Wings Over America*, not *Rockshow* (p. 360); Denny Laine stayed with Wings until 1981, during the *Tug of War* sessions (p. 361); *Pipes of Peace* came out in 1983, not 1984 (p. 362); the correct title to "I Know How You Feel" is "Somebody Who Cares" (p. 363); and McCartney's "Wonderful Christmastime" single came out in 1979, not 1982 (p. 364).

4. Later, on page 143, Lewisohn describes the "Helter Skelter" session, comprised of three of the longest takes the band ever commits to tape, and which are later discarded as "rehearsals" in favor of a re-make made on September 9. Here is his description:

> Take one lasted 10'40," take two 12'35" and take three an epic 27'11," the longest ever Beatles recording. All three versions were similar: drums, bass, lead and rhythm guitars played live—positively no overdubs—with a VERY heavy drum sound, heavy guitars and a magnificent vocal delivery by Paul, with—surprisingly—all but identical lyrics to the re-made version. Each take developed into a tight and concisely played jam with long instrumental passages.

These takes are now among the most sought-after Beatle bootlegs; given everything that's been smuggled from those vaults, it's hard to believe that this session, alone, turns out to be among the rarest. It begs elucidation: did McCartney routinely improvise *new* lyrics during separate takes, as implied? Are the drums heavier than they sound on the final track? Since the Beatles rarely recorded long tracks, how did these eight-minute-plus takes "develop . . . concisely. . . ."? Does the final track capture the "essence" of these jams, or do they sound much different? Given the fact that the Beatles "jammed" so rarely in any of their sessions, this half-hour of music surely provides clues to their ensemble ticks.

SELECTED BIBLIOGRAPHY
TO THE SECOND EDITION

Secondary Sources

The Beatles' Complete Scores (Hal Leonard, 1989). Ambitious but not definitive, this first full-score treatment of Beatle songs (transcribed by Tetsuya Fujita, Yuji Hagino, Hajime Kubo, and Goro Sato) gets to the nub of what separates great songs and great playing from skeletal notational symbols. What these scores get right only underlines how far these recordings extended these compositions. The technical expertise that an ear like that of Ian McDonald brings to this material (below), with indications of "flanging" vocals (or ADT) and overdubs, is the next level this notation requires. As pure notes on a bar, the weak spots occur mainly in repeats, which were seldom unvaried. The bass part of "You Won't See Me," for instance, where McCartney begins improvising new melodies on repeats, goes unnoticed.

Revolution in the Head: The Beatles' Records and the Sixties, by Ian McDonald (Henry Holt, 1995). Essential reading for Beatleheads, despite its false premise. Where *Tell Me Why* takes the Beatles Parlophone release dates as its organizing principle, McDonald orders his narrative on the recording session dates, which misdirects the ear when it comes to larger concepts. The most dramatic example of this "intentional fallacy" comes when he notes that both "Tomorrow Never Knows" and "A Day In the Life" came quite early in the recording process for the albums they appeared on (*Revolver* and *Sgt. Pepper*, respectively). This leads McDonald to argue that neither track should be considered as a closing statement to those breakthroughs simply because they were recorded before many of the others. But interpreting the position of a song in a given sequence is surely part of what the Beatles wanted us to listen for, or they would have simply released every song in the order in which they were recorded. The larger concepts presented to us has to do with track sequencing, not the order in which songs were recorded. "A Day in the Life" may have come first, but its placement at the end of *Pepper* gives it a resonance it otherwise might not have had. Surely any interpretation of *Pepper* must take this into account. Otherwise, McDonald uses newer primary sources judiciously, has handy CD time cues, a rich understanding of studio technique, and evokes the Lennon-McCartney relationship both in and out of song with informed sensitivity.

The Beatles (20th-Century Composers), by Allan Kozinn (Phaidon Press Inc., 1995). The ultimate understated critical biography.

Get Back: The Unauthorized Chronicle of the Beatles' Let It Be Disaster, by Doug Sulpy and Ray Schweighardt (St. Martin's Press, 1997). This painstakingly detailed account of the January 1969 Twickenham and Apple basement sessions (audio and film) is a marvel of musical anthropology. At the time of its release, the general reaction to *Let It Be* was as an anticlimax to a brilliant career, a coda to brilliance. The received notion about the film is that it's the documentary of a disintegration—but there's more going on for the cameras than that. The project had actually languished on Apple's shelves for over a year, and was only completed when the cash-poor Beatles overrode McCartney and hired Allen Klein to administer their crumbling empire. Rumors of the break-up were rampant: John Lennon had already made numerous appearances billed as a solo artist with his Plastic Ono Band, McCartney released his first solo album alongside *Let It Be's* soundtrack. The project has always gotten a bum rap, both because of how oddly most of the footage screens, and for how insistent the Beatles were in what a botched job it had been. But a generation's hindsight can lose sight of what a subversive gesture this project was. In an industry notorious for rewarding non-talents, heaping Grammies and pots of money on pretty faces, the Beatles were famous both for making great music and using their fame to expand the idea of rock. Here was something new: a band on top that not only didn't take the fizz of its status all that seriously, but was actually deserving of its hype, album after album, no matter how out of control the mania seemed to get. In a very unique way, the Beatles worked to keep their aesthetics on a par with their popularity in a way very few bands have before or since.

So Let It Be can be seen from a different perspective: as a lesson on how difficult, tedious and frustrating music rehearsals can be. The magic of the movie lay in the lunchtime concert (their last public performance) the Beatles played on the roof of their Savile Row Apple building at the end of the movie (which gently echoed their lunchtime Cavern gigs six and seven years earlier). On the roof, rehearsal drudgery gave way to euphoric performance. Exposing the labor behind the accomplished playing and wonderfully original and expressive singing was a very intimate act, something only the greatest musicians risk.

At the film's climax, during the rooftop concert, the Beatles's source of confidence is made plain—not only how deeply engrained their ensemble instincts were, but also how years of dedicated toil together had enabled them to keep so much hidden from the rehearsal cameras. Nothing in the film hints at the heights of feeling they find in that farewell concert, which suggests that the drudgery wasn't so much musical as personal. If there's a guiding idea behind *Let It Be*, perhaps it's this: it's possible to excel musically in a band long after you become disenchanted with your colleagues. Or, to reverse the equation, if even close professional relationships could let you down, couldn't music be a path towards reinvigorating friendships—didn't the music finally help the Beatles transcend their own disintegration?

These authors piece together all the available footage and tape from this period to tell the story as a narrative (with paraphrases instead of quotes to dodge Apple's lawyers), and it's full of surprises: McCartney's sympathy for John and Yoko, the bands antipathy towards Michael Lindsay-Hogg (whom they snicker at as a homosexual). And finally, a list of song titles that roll from their collective unconscious, a memory bank of lyrical and melodic shadows. On Friday, January 10th, a bossa nova jam on a lyric built around "In the Middle of an Island," Lennon and McCartney veer off in different directions, first whistling a duet, then erupting into birdcalls, then "Besame Mucho," then "The Peanut Vendor," Louis Armstrong's 1931 hit, which reminds Lennon of the Young Rascals' "Groovin'," and McCartney of South American singer Yma Sumac, which then reverts to "Groovin'" and finally Elvis Presley's "I Got Stung." A compilation of this material, spilling out of them at a time when they were unguardedly fishing for ideas, would provide a pipeline to their childhood ears. If there were an analogous CD which collected all the musical references that the Beatles toss off like so many punchlines to their unfinished songs, it would diagram their roots in British big band, skiffle, and trad jazz as much as in rock 'n' roll. It shouldn't be surprising how some of the more arcane British sources feed into the Beatles' rock 'n' roll influences, but the wealth of references is dizzying.

The Beatles as Musicians: **Revolver** *Through the* **Anthology**, by Walter Everett (Oxford University Press, 1999)

The Beatles as Musicians: The Quarry Men Through **Rubber Soul**, by Walter Everett (Oxford University Press, 2001). Covered backwards in two volumes, Everett's study complements and extends Lewisohn's work, and will remain the key academic volume for some time. If you're a theory teacher looking for a great way to introduce double plagal concepts to young ears, or just want to take a dip in the brisk yet healing waters of Schenkerian analysis, start here. If you have no interest in theory, Everett still makes it worth your while: skim the technical language, and you're in for a rich narrative of detail and insight that enhances every other source.

The Beatles Gear, by Andy Babiuk (Backbeat Books, 2001). Babiuk, a guitarist in Rochester's eminent Chesterfield Kings, details each of the Beatles' instruments, a serious document for guitar hounds and drummers alike.

Web Sites
millennium pop: a journal of popular culture
http://www.geocities.com/triley60/

Beatle Links
http://www.beatlelinks.net/links/

Official Beatles Site
http://www.thebeatles.com

Internet Beatles Album
www.beatlesagain.com/

Beatleworld
http://www.beatleworld.co.uk/disc.htm

Beatle Interview database
http://www.geocities.com/~beatleboy1/index.html

The Beatles Unlimited
http://www.beatles-unlimited.com/

Beatles Gear
http://www.beatlesfabgear.com

The Beatles London News and Information Service
http://www.fabfour.addr.com/

The Beatles Bootleg Exchange
http://www.beatlegs.org

SELECTED BIBLIOGRAPHY

These are the chief sources for quotes, dates, and stories that this book is based upon; other rock books of note (Jon Landau's *It's Too Late to Stop Now*, Robert Christgau's *Any Old Way You Choose It* and *Record Guide*, Dave Marsh's numerous manifesto-biographies and *Rolling Stone Record Guide*, Simon Frith's *Sound Effects*) were reliable and influential reference works for the larger contextual picture.

Brown, Peter, and Steven Gaines. *The Love You Make: An Insider's Story of the Beatles*. McGraw-Hill, 1983. Brown, the assistant who Lennon offhandedly immortalized in "The Ballad of John and Yoko," plays down his strengths as an insider (slighting the remarkable scene of Ringo zooming around the Indy 500 in the middle of the night) and goes for the smut. In the most notorious story, Paul dances between groupies in two opposite hotel rooms, ostensibly satisfying them both. As a bestseller, it made pots of money and estranged Brown forever from the Beatles' inner circle; as a leftover tattle-tale epic, it grossly overestimates the audience's concern with the Beatles' private lives.

Campbell, Colin, and Allan Murphy. *Things We Said Today*. Pierian Press, 1980. This complete concordance of lyrics features the usual mistakes (from "Come Together": "hold you in his *arm-chair*"; from "I've Got a Feeling": "everybody put the *fool* down," overread as a coded Lennon swipe at Paul) and an arch critical essay on the Beatles' development of the idea of roman-ticism. Handy if you want to see how many times they used the word "blue."

CARR, ROY, and TONY TYLER. *The Beatles: An Illustrated Record.* Harmony, 1975. A coffee-table pictorial account of their career, mapping all the Parlophone releases and accompanied by release dates, calendars, and full-size color reproductions of album covers. The critical discussion is marginal: "Getting Better" and "Fixing a Hole" are said to be "slow and fast versions respectively of the same song," and the "White Album" essay concludes vaguely: "They were no longer invulnerable"—to what?

CASTLEMAN, HARRY, and WALTER J. PODRAZIK. *All Together Now: The First Complete Beatles Discography 1961–1975.* Ballantine, 1975. Along with its companion volume, *The Beatles Again,* the most comprehensive listing of Beatles issues, including an index of songs both by and for others, the Beatles on film, British and American charts, and notorious misconceptions (like *The Beatles in Italy,* collectors' fool's gold).

COLEMAN, RAY. *Lennon.* McGraw-Hill, 1984. Ray Coleman, a British pop-music journalist and friend of Lennon's, tells his story with enthusiasm and an obvious affection (which often spills into sentimental deification). His chief source for this largely anecdotal biography was Cynthia Lennon. More personally sympathetic than Davies or Norman, but less rigorous. Reprints some of Lennon's early love letters to Cynthia from Hamburg, a zany post-card from America, several breakup exchanges between Paul and John, and a hilarious and complimentary rebuttal to Todd Rundgren.

DAVIES, HUNTER. *The Beatles: The Authorized Biography.* McGraw-Hill, 1968; second edition, 1985. With the first Beatles biography, Davies taught the world that the Beatles were not overnight sensations. They complied with his interviews during the spring of 1967 and after *Pepper*'s release, and his encounters include a revealing sketch of Lennon and McCartney composing "With a Little Help from My Friends." But the whole reads like one long Sunday magazine article. For a journalist assembling facts and history, his account is only passable: he completely omits Lennon's introduction to Yoko at London's Indica Gallery in November 1966. In describing their musical merits, his establishment frame of reference weakens his understanding of their significance.

DAVID, EDWARD E. *The Beatles Book*. Cowles, 1968. Worth tracking down for reprints of famous statements from Nat Hentoff, Richard Goldstein (the *New York Times* reviewer who panned *Sgt. Pepper*), and Ralph J. Gleason. Also Timothy Leary's "Thank God for the Beatles," wherein he links their "beat" with the "beatitudes," and two stiff William F. Buckley, Jr. columns, the first on Lennon's "bigger than Christ" statement, the second on the overwhelming response to the first. Both shun pleasure, miscomprehending the Beatles' comic allure.

DiLELLO, RICHARD. *The Longest Cocktail Party*. Playboy Press, 1972. Tattle-tales from an office boy whose job included rolling joints and sending out for barrels of apples for press conferences. Paperback Writer becomes flesh.

EDITORS OF *ROLLING STONE*. *The Ballad of John and Yoko*. Rolling Stone/ Dolphin, 1982. A durable collection of Lennon news and interviews that appeared in the pages of *Rolling Stone*, as well as essays commissioned for the project: Robert Christgau and John Piccarella's "Portrait of the Artist as a Rock & Roll Star" is among the finest pieces on Lennon's life and art. In addition, Lennon's impassioned defense of his peace concert ("Have We All Forgotten What Vibes Are?"), Annie Leibovitz's last portraits, and a long, loving chapter of remembrances, everyone from Gerry ("How Do You Do?") Marsden to Chuck Berry.

EISEN, JONATHAN. *The Age of Rock*. Random House, 1969. Contains four Beatles essays from the intelligentisia (critic Joan Peyser, composer Ned Rorem, academics Richard Poirier and Wilfrid Mellers), whose highbrow tone makes even the better ideas sound removed from the listening—never mind dancing—experience.

———. *The Age of Rock, Volume Two*. Random House, 1970. A slim Beatles entry by J. Lawrence attempts an interpretation of *Abbey Road*, but a terrific interview by R. Meltzer (by "Andy Warhol") and a 1965 Dylan interview by Nora Ephron and Susan Edmiston. Beatles associations lace most of these commentaries.

EPSTEIN, BRIAN. *A Cellarful of Noise*. Pierian Press, 1984 (reprint). Derek Taylor wrote this book, but he recaptures Epstein's voice perfectly.

EVANS, MIKE. *The Art of the Beatles.* Contemporary, 1984. A discussion of the Beatles' ever-changing visual persona and the artists who worked on their album covers.

FAST, JULIUS. *The Beatles: The Real Story.* G. P. Putnam's Sons, 1968. A slight, forgettable journalistic treatment for parents.

FAWCETT, ANTHONY. *One Day at a Time.* Grove Press, 1976. Lennon's personal assistant recounts the years that span the breakup and the beginnings of Lennon's solo career. Well written, a notch above the usual hatchet jobs such tag-alongs normally get.

FULPEN, H. V. *The Beatles: An Illustrated Diary.* Perigee, 1982. A fan's testimonial, with an unfathomable amount of reproduced artifacts and calendar dates.

GAMBACCINI, PAUL. *Paul McCartney in His Own Words.* Flash, 1976. Pop's great cute one tap-dances his way through interviews, with the occasional dash of insight.

GARBARINI, VIC, and BRIAN CULLMAN, with BARBARA GRAUSTARK. *Strawberry Fields Forever: John Lennon Remembered.* Bantam, 1980. Considering how maudlin such tributes are (cf. the press clips in *A Tribute to John Lennon,* Proteus, 1981), this collection proves worthwhile. The introduction by Dave Marsh is an important statement; the quote from Robert Christgau's cover epiphany for the *Village Voice* is likewise insightful. But the genuine item is the reprint of Lennon's interview with *Newsweek* in the fall of his death. Although it overlaps with the ongoing *Playboy* interview from the same period, it touches on many things that that interviewer either forgot to ask or John forgot to mention. For these quotes alone, this rush-released death-profit book is worth hunting down in secondhand shops: "We did it for a big tribe, because the communication is worldwide now. But all we did is what musicians have been doing ever since the word go. Ritualized dancing, a celebration of the seasons. The Beatles were not other than society. They were part of it. The Beatles didn't lead, they were part of it."

GILLETT, CHARLIE. *The Sound of the City.* Pantheon, 1983. As indispensable to the student of rock history as Grout is to the music major, and often as boring. Detailed and thorough as this book is, it lacks spark in what some consider among the greatest stories ever told. Because of the huge scope, Gillett's treatment of the Beatles (and of all major artists) is cursory, and although he brings several crucial critical points to light, he dismisses much of their work out of hand as self-absorbed and gratuitous. "The Beatles . . . had surprisingly little stylistic influence on other innovators," Gillett claims, affronting the truth. As with his view of Elvis Presley, this is the purist's prerogative.

HARRISON, GEORGE. *I Me Mine*. Simon and Schuster, 1980. Derek Taylor wrote this one too, although George contributed original drafts of songs, blow-by-blow commentary, and (with help from Jim Horn) brass charts for "Bangla Desh."

HOWLETT, KEVIN. *The Beatles at the Beeb, 62–65*. Pierian Press, 1983, (reprint). A companion to the series, now widely available on vinyl, with transcripts of interviews (Ringo mentions his "Don't Pass Me By" in 1963), complete song index (note: John sings "Sit Right Down and Cry," not Paul), and dates of tapings and broadcasts. Producer Terry Henebery describes a typical radio session: "You had to crack the whip and get on the loudspeaker talk-back key quite a lot and say, 'Come on, chaps!' They'd be lying over the floor, giggling. And I can remember afternoons down at the BBC Paris Cinema Studio, where you were just looking at the clock, throwing your hands up in horror, thinking will they ever settle down? Stop horsing about? I mean people would go and get locked in the toilets and fool about. They treated it as a fun thing but you were, at the end of the day, getting some nice material out of them."

KESEY, KEN. *Demon Box*. Viking, 1986. "Now We Know How Many Holes It Takes to Fill the Albert Hall" begins with the 1968 Apple Christmas party, Kesey and Hell's Angels in tow, during which John and Yoko appear in matching Santa suits to pass out gifts. It ends with Lennon's assassination and the grim post-punk decay—the best written tribute.

LAING, DAVID. *The Sound of Our Time*. Quadrangle, 1969. Laing traces rock back to its folk sources and the subsequent demise of the Tin Pan Alley monopoly, and incorporates Jean-Paul Sartre's bleak theory of pop: "The Hit Parade itself is held up to the individual listener as the mirror of the authentic preferences of the People . . . and [the listener] is invited to identify with them by participating and buying a disc. In fact, however, [the listener] will only be acting like thousands of other isolated record buyers subjected to the same persuasion." "Notes on a Study of the Beatles" charts the growth of metaphysical issues in songs like "She Said She Said" and especially "Love You To."

LEIGH, SPENCER (with charts by PETE FRAME). *Let's Go Down the Cavern*. London: Vermilion, 1984. An articulate and enthusiastic account of the Liverpool beat pre- and post-Beatlemania. Leigh lets the originals have their say about their role in pop history, and the chronologies give a good understanding of the musical turf the Beatles rose up through. Several good Lennon stories to boot.

LENNON, JOHN. *The Lennon Tapes*. Jolly and Barber, 1981. Andy Peebles' fated final interview of December 6, 1980.

LEWISOHN, MARK. *The Beatles Live!* Henry Holt and Company, 1986. As Lewisohn persuasively demonstrates, it took countless live performances before the Beatles even began to dream up studio artistry. As well-researched and documented an account of their early years as seems possible, with revisionary aims (sorting out when John met Paul, and who played drums on "Love Me Do") and extensive repertoire notes.

McCABE, PETER. *Apple to the Core*. Pocket Books, 1972. A sobering account of the business and legal interests that imbue both "You Never Give Me Your Money" and "Golden Slumbers."

MARCUS, GREIL. *Mystery Train*. E.P. Dutton, 1982. Still the last word on the history of rock and the values on which it rests. Marcus circles around the Beatles rather than taking them on, but their heritage according to "Presliad," the remarkable chapter on Elvis, has never been more lovingly drawn.

MARTIN, GEORGE. *All You Need Is Ears*. St. Martin's Press, 1979. This firsthand account is strewn chronologically and contains more information about Martin's career than seems necessary, but it provides useful information regarding the use of the newfangled (now standard) Dolby noise reduction system during the *Pepper* sessions, and Martin's unconscionable treatment by EMI.

MELLERS, WILFRID. *Twilight of the Gods: The Music of the Beatles*. Schirmer, 1975. Even when Mellers admits "the Beatles cannot have known this," he insists on interpreting their music through the written classical heritage (functional harmonies, key symbolism, and primitive dance mythologies), which leads to confounding interpretations and overstated (i.e., indecipherable) logic. Unimpressive to the musically literate and seemingly out of reach to everyone else.

MELTZER, R. *The Aesthetics of Rock*. Something Else Press, 1970. Crisscrossing allusions to the fever at the Shea Stadium concert, this uproarious (mock-?) philosophical "history" of rock is riddled with Beatle insights, from the essential co-dependency of over-statement and triviality to "I Should Have Known Better" as lover's conquest. Sample: "The single-note fadeout of more than 40 seconds that follows a crescendo of equally unaccustomed non-rock harshness on . . . 'A Day in the Life' is the biggest musical reference point of them all. . . . The inclusion of this sort of thing on a record that will be distributed throughout the whole goddam world goes beyond anything Cage or any of those guys were ever in any position to do with the music-sound of the whole sound totality of the whole thing, officially decisively ending all art–non-art/music-noise distinctions forever, or until somebody forgets."

MILLER, JIM, ED. The Rolling Stone *Illustrated History of Rock 'n' Roll.* Rolling Stone Press, 1976. The bible for anyone interested in a general introduction to critics and their various styles. Greil Marcus's Beatles entry has been quoted often here and is probably the best single critical bio around.

NORMAN, PHILIP. *Shout!: The Beatles in Their Generation.* Warner Books, 1982. A better book than Davies's because it makes more of the Beatles' beginnings and doesn't mince words when it comes to Hamburg; a weak book because he's essentially against them from the start. His distaste for a lot of their music dispels interest almost immediately, and his powers of description are far from illustrative. He makes the whole story sound lucky, as though they never had any talent to begin with, and aren't excused for being human.

O'GRADY, TERENCE J. *The Beatles: A Musical Evolution.* Twayne, 1983. Expanding a doctoral thesis from the University of Wisconsin, O'Grady insists on taking the Beatles apart in academic terms, analyzing what they did even more intensively than Mellers, with all the attendant humdrum terminology. A one-dimensional approach considering their musical scope; all too often short on lyrical interpretation in favor of harmonic boasting. "While the song's meaning is not clarified," he writes of "A Day in the Life," "its uniqueness is underlined in an extraordinarily graphic way." "Happiness is a Warm Gun" gets two sentences. Beware: lots of factual errors (Capitol editions) and oversimplified musical notation.

OKUN, MILTON. *The Compleat Beatles*, Volumes I and II (with com-

mentary, discographies, filmographies). Delilah, 1981. Because
rock is an oral medium, writing it down is tricky business, especially for players of all levels. Okun has transcribed pop tunes
to song sheets for ages (*Great Songs of the Sixties* and *Seventies*),
but his piano-minded approach cheats guitarists of the goods,
especially in songs like "Across the Universe" and "And Your Bird
Can Sing." The best we've got, but still loaded with mistakes
and clumsy problem solving: "I Feel Fine" is clearly in G major
with blue notes (flat third and seventh), not "mixolydian mode,"
as Okun suggests; the omission of the opening chord to "A Hard
Day's Night" strips the song of its immediacy; the spacing nuances of the background harmonies are lost in "The Night Before" and "You're Going to Lose That Girl"; and the guitar intro
to "Drive My Car" is misplaced rhythmically. Considering the
absence of drum patterns, guitar ornaments, and studio effects,
Okun's transcriptions are even more skeletal than standard musical notation. His essay on the music betrays a lack of understanding of the Beatles' overall recording accomplishments. (All
the harmonic keys to songs are quoted from Okun even when it
gets sticky—e.g., "You Can't Do That," which the band played
in G but slowed on tape to sound in G-flat, as it did with
"Mr. Moonlight.") Anyone else out there for full-score transcriptions?

REINHART, CHARLES. *You Can't Do That: Beatles Bootlegs and Novelty
Records.* Contemporary Books, 1981. A richly detailed and inevitably incomplete listing of bootlegs, remarkable in scope and
impressive in particulars. Includes indexes of bootlegs as well as
counterfeits, novelties, and Lennon tribute issues.

SALEWICZ, CHRIS. *McCartney.* St. Martin's Press, 1986. At 250 pages the
best biographical account of the band yet and a believable view
of Paul, intelligent and fair. Everything you need to know in an
engaging style, sympathetic but probing, generous and accurate.
Top prize for correct Lennon-McCartney meeting date: July 6,
1957.

SCHAFFNER, NICHOLAS. *The Beatles Forever.* McGraw-Hill, 1977. A fan's
companion, with inside scoops on radical interpretations (wood
as a symbol for marijuana in "Norwegian Wood"?) and song
sources (the lyrics to Harrison's "The Inner Light" were "pinched
almost verbatim from a Japanese poem by Roshi, translated by
R.H. Bluth"), even though Schaffner is at his critical best on the

solo careers. Includes scads of pictures, memorabilia, record and concert dates.

SHEFF, DAVID, and G. BARRY GOLSON. *The Playboy Interviews with John Lennon and Yoko Ono.* Berkley Books, 1981. Indispensable last interview which touches on virtually all phases of Lennon's life, including a lengthy section covering songs blow-by-blow.

STOKES, GEOFFREY. *The Beatles.* Rolling Stone/Times Books, 1980. A preferably shorter version of Davies and Norman, with a more sympathetic (counterculture) frame of reference, elegantly designed by Bea Feitler.

TAYLOR, DEREK. *As Time Goes By.* Pierian Press, 1983 (reprint). Former Brian Epstein/Byrds/Apple publicist Derek Taylor, a dreamy gonzo journalist with English gentility intact, reflects on the psychedelic years with a fondness that verges on patronization.

———. *It Was Twenty Years Ago Today.* Fireside, 1987. Eyes on the calendar (and the compact disc reissue campaign), Taylor reminisces on the drugs, religion, activism, hype . . . and music of the summer of love. Reprints artifacts like the "Mr. Kite" circus poster and "A Day in the Life" newspaper article.

WEINBERG, MAX. *The Big Beat.* Contemporary, 1984. Bruce Springsteen's drummer talks to the greats, takes some ribbing, hears some tall tales (mostly from Bernard Purdy), and swaps secrets about the classics. Most of the Ringo quotes come from this book.

WENNER, JANN. *Lennon Remembers.* Popular Library, 1982. Indispensable (again) 1970 interview wherein Lennon angrily recounts his disillusion with his band's demise, reminisces about his rock 'n' roll heroes, recounts his recent work with Phil Spector, and airs probing internal questions that must have sent Paul reeling.

WIENER, JON. *Come Together: John Lennon in His Time.* Random House, 1984. Wiener's persistence in tracking down the Lennon papers won him boxes of security data tracing the FBI's surveillance of John and Yoko during the early seventies, and as a peacenik Lennon is drawn here as an unsuspecting utopian. He was really more of a self-mocking media artist, whose best ideas leave Wiener at a loss for coherent musical criticism.

WILLIAMS, ALLAN. *The Man Who Gave the Beatles Away.* Macmillan, 1974. It looks like Williams will spend his days living out his own epitaph rather than living it down. He's still available for interviews and tours, and not many would be surprised if he wrote yet another book about it all.

ACKNOWLEDGMENTS

Huzzahs and hoorahs first of all to Barbara Carlson, with bows to musicians Eloise Ristad, Doris (and her brother Eugene Pridonoff) Lehnert, Tony Lee, Duane Staggers, Ron Revier, and Cecil Effinger—Boulderite teachers with the mostest. Broad cheers to Bob Johnson (a deep, majestic bow), Father Marion Hammond (the rafters are shaking), and of course all the Moores and Evergreen's own Kamikazees (encore, encore!). Uproarious applause for supportive rockcrits Gil Asakawa and Leland Rucker; loud clamors from the gallery for Carol Hoffman, and Katie and Jake Culbertson, Joseph Schwartz, Tom Linehan, John Harvith, James Hepokoski, Dewey Ganzel and Obies all, especially upstarts Dave Periera and Debbie Zeller, and a legion of early morning television stars.

Steve Braun and Sean Kirst read early proposal drafts; they win a free drink each (guffaws and loud retorts); the steadfast Robert Freeman and Jon Engberg receive sustained ovations, while Rebecca Penneys and John Baldo summon whistles, hoots, and hollers. Cheers and exclamations for influential mentor Richard Gollin, at the University of Rochester's Film Studies Program. Standing ovation for Paul Burgett.

Enter an epic PaGodal procession: Pat Crumpley, Eric Davidson, Maria Lambros, Paul Ousley, Joe Patchen, Jeremy Pick, and Michael Rose not only debate aesthetic issues into the ground, they toot little paper horns and sport napkins atop their heads (bawdy songs, robust laughter).

In England, gratitude is due to all the Wilsons at BESGL in London, and the following Beatles people: Debbie Geller, Bob Woofinden, Simon Frith, Bill Harry, Chris Salewicz, Dave Laing, Jon Tobler, Tony Barrow, and Andy Peebles and Kevin Howlett at the BBC (who stayed late to talk through the entire discography). In Liverpool: Spenser· Leigh, Peter Trollop at the *Echo*, and beat drummer John Cochrane.

Robert Christgau's rock history course at the School for Visual Arts in January of 1986 provided a polemical slant on the business of pop over forty years. Dave Marsh talked passionately to me about "She Loves You" 's definitive rock 'n' roll greatness. Mark Lewisohn and Greil Marcus wrote encouraging letters of interest, and Don Giller, a musicological Beatlehead, spent long afternoons taping me bootlegs and talking turkey.

At Bodley Head, Chris Holifield and her staff were both patient and gracious (lengthy accolades), and Abner Stein let me use his phone and bought me lunch.

Robert Cornfield offered to handle the proposal, and Robert Gottlieb acted swiftly and encouragingly (gasps of astonishment). Adam Gopnik, an inquisitive and empowering editor, helped shape much of the large structure and edited with taste and finesse (beaming accolades). Lee Goerner saw the book through production, and deflated a lot of frustration with his easy laugh; Roane Carey carefully supervised the copyedit to completion. Patrick Dillon, a scrupulous copyeditor, gave the manuscript an extremely close reading—and the Beatles a close new listening—that sent me back to my sources and had me rethinking major points. Marysarah Quinn came up with the handsome design, Chip Kidd conceived a subtly engaging cover, Marisa Christoforou tracked down numerous copyright permissions, Max Cantor hunted down corrections for the Vintage edition, and both Mary Maguire and Jane Ziegelman were cheerfully helpful throughout (GOO GOO GOO JOOB).

Finally, effusive praise and sympathies to my family (Ann, Jenny, Laurie, Cathy, Nancy, Con, Grammy, and, of course, Julie), without whom.

Tim Riley
June 1987
Boston

INDEX

PERMISSIONS ACKNOWLEDGMENTS

views with John Lennon and Yoko Ono by David Sheff and Barry G. Golson. Copyright © 1981 by *Playboy*. Excerpts from *Paul McCartney in His Own Words* by Paul Gambaccini. Copyright © 1976 by Flash Books. Reprinted by permission of The Putnam Publishing Group. Rights in the open market to reprint from *Paul McCartney in His Own Words* by Paul Gambaccini administered by Omnibus Press, 8/9 Frith Street, London w1v 5tz. Reprinted by permission.

St. Martin's Press Inc.: Excerpts from *All You Need Is Ears* by George Martin. Copyright © 1982 by George Martin. Rights in Canada and the open market administered by Macmillan London Ltd. Reprinted by permission.

SBK Entertainment World: Excerpt from "Long Tall Sally" by Richard Penniman, Enotris Johnson and Robert Blackwell. Copyright © 1956, renewed 1984 by ATV Music Corp. All rights controlled and administered by Blackwood Music Inc. under license from ATV Music (Venice). All rights reserved. International copyright secured. Reprinted by permission. "Do You Want to Know a Secret?" by John Lennon/Paul McCartney © 1963 Northern Songs Ltd. Rights assigned to SBK Catalogue Partnership. All rights controlled and administered by SBK UNART CATALOG INC. All rights reserved. International copyright secured. Used by permission. "I Call Your Name" by John Lennon/Paul McCartney © 1963 Northern Songs Ltd. All rights for the U.S., Canada and Mexico controlled and administered by Blackwood Music Inc. under license from ATV Music (Maclen). "Things We Said Today" by John Lennon/Paul McCartney, "Tell Me Why" by John Lennon/Paul McCartney, "Any Time at All" by John Lennon/Paul McCartney, "If I Fell" by John Lennon/Paul McCartney, "A Hard Day's Night" by John Lennon/Paul McCartney, "I Don't Want to Spoil the Party" by John Lennon/Paul McCartney, "Every Little Thing" by John Lennon/Paul McCartney, "Baby's in Black" by John Lennon/Paul McCartney, "I'm a Loser" by John Lennon/Paul McCartney, "No Reply" by John Lennon/Paul McCartney, "She's a Woman" by John Lennon/Paul McCartney, "Eight Days a Week" by John Lennon/Paul McCartney, "I'll Be Back" by John Lennon/Paul McCartney © 1964 Northern Songs Ltd. All rights for the U.S., Canada and Mexico controlled and administered by Blackwood Music Inc. under license from ATV Music (Maclen). "It Won't Be Long" by John Lennon/Paul McCartney, "I'll Get You" by John Lennon/Paul McCartney © 1963, 1964 Northern Songs Ltd. All rights for the U.S., Canada and Mexico controlled and administered by Blackwood Music Inc. under license from ATV Music (Maclen). "All I've Got to Do" by John Lennon/Paul McCartney © 1961, 1964 Northern Songs Ltd. All

ABOUT THE AUTHOR

Tim Riley's commentary on pop culture and classical music has appeared in the *Washington Post*, *Boston Magazine*, the *Boston Phoenix*, *Salon*, and *Feed*. He is the author of *Hard Rain: A Dylan Commentary* and *Madonna: Illustrated*, and the publisher of *millennium pop*, an online journal about popular culture (at http://www.geocities.com/triley60). His commentary appears regularly on National Public Radio's "Here and Now."